Focus on College Success

Concise
University of Memphis
ACAD 1100

2e

Constance Staley

CENGAGE
Learning™

Australia • Brazil • Japan • Korea • Mexico • Singapore • Spain • United Kingdom • United States

CENGAGE
Learning

Focus on College Success: Concise: University of Memphis: ACAD 1100, 2e

Source:

FOCUS on College Success, Concise Edition, 2nd Edition
Dr. Constance C. Staley - University of Colorado, Colorado Springs
© 2012 Cengage Learning. All rights reserved.

Executive Editors:
 Maureen Staudt
 Michael Stranz

Senior Project Development Manager:
 Linda deStefano

Marketing Specialist:
 Courtney Sheldon

Senior Production/Manufacturing Manager:
 Donna M. Brown

PreMedia Manager:
 Joel Brennecke

Sr. Rights Acquisition Account Manager:
 Todd Osborne

Cover Image:
Getty Images*

*Unless otherwise noted, all cover images used by Custom Solutions, a part of Cengage Learning, have been supplied courtesy of Getty Images with the exception of the Earthview cover image, which has been supplied by the National Aeronautics and Space Administration (NASA).

For product information and technology assistance, contact us at
Cengage Learning Customer & Sales Support, 1-800-354-9706

For permission to use material from this text or product,
submit all requests online at **cengage.com/permissions**
Further permissions questions can be emailed to
permissionrequest@cengage.com

This book contains select works from existing Cengage Learning resources and was produced by Cengage Learning Custom Solutions for collegiate use. As such, those adopting and/or contributing to this work are responsible for editorial content accuracy, continuity and completeness.

Compilation © 2011 Cengage Learning
ISBN-13: 978-1-133-06717-7

ISBN-10: 1-133-06717-4

Cengage Learning
5191 Natorp Boulevard
Mason, Ohio 45040
USA
Cengage Learning is a leading provider of customized learning solutions with office locations around the globe, including Singapore, the United Kingdom, Australia, Mexico, Brazil, and Japan. Locate your local office at:
international.cengage.com/region.

Cengage Learning products are represented in Canada by Nelson Education, Ltd. For your lifelong learning solutions, visit **www.cengage.com/custom.**
Visit our corporate website at **www.cengage.com.**

Printed in the United States of America

BRIEF CONTENTS
ACAD 1100 – INTRO TO UNIVERSITY
UNIVERSITY OF MEMPHIS

ACAD 1100: AN OVERVIEW OF THE COURSE

Some freshman orientation courses teach only college survival skills (career counseling, academic advising, study and time management skills, etc.). Other freshman orientation courses focus exclusively on cognitive development and intellectual growth designed to engage students in a semester-long debate on the important issues of history, culture, and society.

ACAD1100 is a combination of college survival skills and cognitive development models. It is a course which offers a mix of practical college survival skills and traditional discussion of issues. The majority of the course will focus on survival skills issues and introduction to campus resources. The cognitive phase of the course will be developed by the classroom activities, supplemental reading, attending cultural events/speakers and classroom discussions.

In both the survival skills and cognitive phases of the course, students will practice the traditional skills of writing, reading, analysis, evaluation and critical thinking. The University of Memphis freshman orientation course, ACAD1100, was designed with the following goals to help prepare students to meet academic and social expectations of the University.

COURSE OBJECTIVES

In ACAD1100 Introduction to the University you will:

1. Learn about the purpose of a university education and how to realize personal goals within the existing structure;
2. Learn the purpose of the General Education core curriculum and its relationship to being an educated person and a well-rounded citizen in a democratic society;
3. Understand individuals of varying races, religions,and ethnic backgrounds, and learn to respect and value differences in others;
4. Learn how to set personal goals and to utilize other life-management techniques;
5. Learn short-term and long-range educational planning;
6. Analyze your study strategies and improve them to meet the expectations of the university;
7. Begin understanding your personal growth processes experienced during college;
8. Introduce students to career planning and career opportunities;
9. Learn academic policies and procedures at the University of Memphis;
10. Utilize technology to enhance your education process;
11. Locate and use campus and community resources and services;
12. Understand models of intellectual debate and discussion;
13. Develop university level skills in written and oral communications and in effective textbook reading;
14. Understand the value of financial literacy and learn skills to make sound financial decisions; and
15. Learn lifetime skills for academic and social success at the University and beyond University life.

FOCUS Entrance Interview

Although you may not have experienced life as a new college student for long, we're interested in how you expect to spend your time, what challenges you think you'll face, and your general views of what you think college will be like. Please answer thoughtfully.

INFORMATION ABOUT YOU

Name _____

Student Number _____ **Course/Section** _____

Instructor _____

Gender _____ **Age** _____

1. **Ethnic Identification (check all that apply):**
   - ___ American Indian or Alaska Native
   - ___ Asian
   - ___ Black or African American
   - ___ Native Hawaiian or Other Pacific Islander
   - ___ Hispanic/Latino
   - ___ White   ___ Prefer not to answer

2. **Is English your first (native) language?**
   - ___ yes   ___ no

3. **Where are you living this term?**
   - ___ in campus housing
   - ___ with my immediate family
   - ___ with a relative other than my immediate family
   - ___ on my own
   - ___ other (please explain) _____

4. **Did your parents graduate from college?**
   - ___ yes, both   ___ neither
   - ___ yes, father only   ___ not sure
   - ___ yes, mother only

5. **How many credit hours are you taking this term?**
   - ___ 6 or fewer   ___ 15–16
   - ___ 7–11   ___ 17 or more
   - ___ 12–14

6. **Did you start college elsewhere before attending this school?**
   - ___ yes   ___ no

7. **In addition to going to college, do you expect to work for pay at a job (or jobs) this term?**
   - ___ yes   ___ no

8. **If so, how many hours per week do you expect to work?**
   - ___ 1–10   ___ 31–40
   - ___ 11–20   ___ 40+
   - ___ 21–30

9. **Which of the following describes why you are working for pay this term? (Mark all that apply.)**
   - ___ to pay for college tuition
   - ___ to pay for basic expenses that I need (rent, housing, food, etc.)
   - ___ to pay for extra expenses that I want (clothes, entertainment, etc.)
   - ___ to buy a car
   - ___ to support a family
   - ___ to pay for child care
   - ___ to pay for textbooks
   - ___ to save money for the future
   - ___ to see how much I can make
   - ___ other (please explain)

   _____

10. **How will you pay for your college expenses? (Check all that apply.)**

___ my own earnings   ___ scholarships and grants

___ my parents' contributions   ___ loans

___ my spouse or partner's contributions   ___ other (please explain) _____

___ my employer's contributions

11. **If you plan to work for pay, where will you work?**

___ on campus   ___ off campus   ___ at more than one job

12. **If you are entering college soon after completing high school, on average, how many total hours per week did you spend studying outside of class in high school?**

___ 0–5   ___ 26–30

___ 6–10   ___ 31–35

___ 11–15   ___ 36–40

___ 16–20   ___ 40+

___ 21–25   ___ I am a returning student and attended high school some time ago.

13. **What was your high school grade point average?**

___ A+   ___ C+

___ A   ___ C

___ A−   ___ C−

___ B+   ___ D or lower

___ B   ___ I don't remember.

___ B−

INFORMATION ABOUT YOUR COLLEGE EXPECTATIONS

14. **How do you expect to learn best in college? (Check all that apply.)**

___ by looking at charts, maps, graphs   ___ by reading books

___ by looking at color-coded information   ___ by writing papers

___ by looking at symbols and graphics   ___ by taking notes

___ by listening to instructors' lectures   ___ by going on field trips

___ by listening to other students during in-class discussions   ___ by engaging in activities

___ by talking about course content with friends or roommates   ___ by actually doing things

15. **For each of the following pairs of descriptors, which set sounds most like you? (Please choose between the two options on each line and place a checkmark by your choice.)**

___ Extraverted and outgoing   or   ___ Introverted and quiet

___ Detail-oriented and practical   or   ___ Big-picture and future-oriented

___ Rational and truthful   or   ___ People-oriented and tactful

___ Organized and self-disciplined   or   ___ Spontaneous and flexible

16. *FOCUS* **is about 11 different aspects of college life. Which are you most interested in? Which may contain information you expect to find most challenging to apply in your own life? (Check all that apply.)**

Most interested in	Most challenging to apply to myself		Most interested in	Most challenging to apply to myself
___	___ Building dreams, setting goals		___	___ Developing your memory
___	___ Learning to learn		___	___ Reading and studying
___	___ Managing time and energy		___	___ Taking tests
___	___ Thinking critically and creatively		___	___ Building relationships, valuing diversity
___	___ Developing information literacy, writing, and speaking skills			
___	___ Engaging, listening, and note-taking in class		___	___ Choosing a major and career

17. **Which one of your current classes do you expect to find most challenging this term and why?**

Which class? (course title *or* department and course number) _____

Why? _____

Do you expect to succeed in this course? ___ yes ___ no

Perhaps (please explain): _____

18. **How many total hours per week do you expect to spend outside of class studying for your college courses this term?**

___ 0–5	___ 26–30
___ 6–10	___ 31–35
___ 11–15	___ 36–40
___ 16–20	___ 40+
___ 21–25	

19. **Which of the following on-campus resources do you plan to use once or more this term? (Please check all that apply.)**

___ library

___ campus learning centers (whatever is available on your campus, such as a Writing Center, Math Learning Center, etc.)

___ computer labs

___ the Student Success Center or New Student Center, if one is available

___ the Counseling Center, if one is available

___ professors' office hours for individual meetings/conferences/help

___ student clubs or organizations

___ none

20. **For the following sets of opposite descriptive phrases, put a checkmark on the line between the two that best represent your response.**

I expect my first term of college to:

challenge me academically	___ ___ ___ ___ ___	be easy
be very different from high school	___ ___ ___ ___ ___	be a lot like high school
be exciting	___ ___ ___ ___ ___	be dull
be interesting	___ ___ ___ ___ ___	be uninteresting
motivate me to continue	___ ___ ___ ___ ___	discourage me
be fun	___ ___ ___ ___ ___	be boring
help me feel a part of this campus	___ ___ ___ ___ ___	make me feel alienated

21. **Please mark your *top three areas of concern* relating to your first term of college by placing 1, 2, and 3 next to the items you choose.**

___ I might not fit in.

___ I might have difficulty making friends.

___ I might not be academically successful.

___ My performance might disappoint my family.

___ My personal life might interfere with my studies.

___ My studies might interfere with my personal life.

___ I might have financial difficulties.

___ My job might interfere with my studies.

___ My studies might interfere with my job.

___ My social life might interfere with my studies.

___ My studies might interfere with my social life.

___ My professors might not care about me as an individual.

___ I might not finish my degree.

___ I might miss the company of my friends.

___ I might miss the company of my family.

___ I might not manage my time well.

___ I might be bored in my classes.

___ I might feel intimidated by my professors.

___ I might feel overwhelmed by all I have to do.

___ other (please explain) _____

22. **Broadly speaking, which area do you expect to major in?**

___ Arts & Sciences	___ Nursing/Health Sciences
___ Education	___ Business
___ Engineering	___ other, please explain _____

23. **How certain are you now of a chosen major? (1 = totally sure, 5 = totally unsure)** ___

24. **How certain are you now that you will complete your degree? (1 = totally sure, 5 = totally unsure)** ___

25. **How certain are you now that you will complete your degree at this school? (1 = totally sure, 5 = totally unsure)** ___

26. **How certain are you now of your intended career choice? (1 = totally sure, 5 = totally unsure)** ___

27. **How certain are you now about whether you'll obtain an advanced degree after you finish college? (1 = totally sure, 5 = totally unsure)** ___

28. **What do you expect your grade point average to be at the end of your first term of college?**

___ A+	___ B	___ C
___ A	___ B–	___ C–
___ A–	___ C+	___ D or lower
___ B+		

29. **All college students develop expectations of what college will be like from various sources. How did you develop your expectations of what college might be like? (Mark your top three information sources with 1, 2, and 3.)**

___ TV and movies

___ friends/siblings who have already gone to college

___ discussions with teachers/counselors in high school

___ information I received from colleges in the mail

___ talks with my parents

___ talks with my friends who are also now freshmen

___ the Internet

___ other (please explain) _____

30. **How confident are you in yourself in each of the following areas? (1 = very confident, 5 = not at all confident)**

___ overall academic ability

___ mathematical skills

___ leadership ability

___ reading skills

___ public speaking skills

___ study skills

___ technology skills

___ physical well being

___ writing skills

___ social skills

___ emotional well being

___ teamwork skills

31. **Why did you take the course for which you are using this textbook? (Mark your top three reasons with 1, 2, and 3.)**

___ It was required.

___ It sounded interesting.

___ I thought it would help make my transition to college easier.

___ I thought it would help me learn about the campus.

___ I thought it would help me make friends.

___ I thought it would help me academically.

___ My parent(s) or other family member(s) thought it was a good idea.

___ My advisor recommended it.

___ A high school teacher/counselor recommended it.

___ The information I received in campus mailings convinced

___ The materials I received at freshman orientation convince

___ A friend/sibling who'd taken this course recommended it.

___ other (please explain) _____

32. **What is the most important reason you decided to attend this school? (Check one)**

___ Recommendation of friend(s) who attended here

___ Reasonable cost

___ Reputation of the school

___ Location of the school

___ Availability of academic programs I'm interested in

___ Financial aid I was offered

___ Recommendation of high school teachers/counselors

___ Campus website

___ other (please explain) _____

33. **Was this school your first choice among the colleges you considered?** ___ yes ___ no

34. **Why did you decide to go to college? (Check all that apply)**

___ because I want to build a better life for myself.

___ because I want to build a better life for my family.

___ because I want to be very well off financially in the future.

___ because I need a college education to achieve my dreams.

___ because my friends were going to college.

___ because my family encouraged me to go.

___ because it was expected of me.

___ because I was recruited for athletics.

___ because I want to continue learning.

___ because the career I am pursuing requires a degree.

___ because I was unsure of what I might do instead.

___ other (please explain) _____

35. **Looking ahead, how satisfied do you expect to be with your decision to attend this school?**

___ very satisfied

___ satisfied

___ not sure

___ somewhat dissatisfied

___ very dissatisfied

36. **What are you most looking forward to in college?** _____

_____

37. **How would you describe the best outcomes you hope for at the end of this term? Why are they important to you?** _____

_____

38. **Do you expect to achieve these outcomes? Why or why not?** _____

_____

Contents

chapter 1 — Building Dreams, Setting Goals   1

chapter 2 — Learning about Learning   27

chapter 6 — Engaging, Listening, and Note-Taking in Class — 127

chapter 7 — Developing Your Memory — 153

chapter 8 — Reading and Studying   175

chapter 9 — Taking Tests   195

Acknowledgments

It's been said that "Achievement is a we thing, not a me thing, always the product of many heads and hands." There are so many people to thank that this acknowledgements section could be as long as a chapter of *FOCUS*! However, here I'll at least mention those who have contributed the most, including all the students over the last 30-plus years who have taught me more than I've ever taught them.

Family Let me start at the center of my life. My deepest thanks go to Steve, my Sean-Connery-look-alike husband (How do I put up with it?), who almost forgot what I looked like over the last few years. As I *FOCUS*ed away in my attic office day after day and night after night, he brought me too many cups of coffee to count. I cherish his devotion. My daughters Shannon and Stephanie helped bring some much-needed balance to my life, and aside from being the most adorable children on the planet, my grandtwins Aidan and Ailie have been a living learning laboratory for me. As young children mastering one new thing after another, they truly have taught me about of the pure joy of learning. And to my beautiful 80-something Mom, who lovingly alternated between urging me to "slow down and relax" and "hurry up and finish," thanks for all your motherly love.

Reviewers The list of reviewers who have contributed their insights and expertise to *FOCUS on College Success* is long. I'd like to thank the following reviewers of the first edition, who helped to shape the second edition with their feedback. My heartfelt thanks to all of them: Peg Adams, Northern Kentucky University; Sandy Aguilar, Florida Community College at Jacksonville-Kent; Andrew J. Armijo, University of New Mexico; David Borst, Concordia University; Charles Frederick, Indiana University; Alice Godbey, Daytona State College; Wendy Grace, Holmes Community College; Dawn Green, Central Texas College ; Rhonda Hall, West Virginia University; Tuesday Hambrick, North Lake College; Cynthia S. Johnson, Palm Beach Community College; Amy Koning, Grand Rapids Community College; Harriet Napierkowski, University of Colorado; Jeanne Pettit, Northern Kentucky University; Karla Pierce, Florida Community College at Jacksonville; Mia Pierre, Valencia Community College; Terry Rafter-Carles, Valencia Community College; Alan Schlossman, Daytona State College; Cathy Seyler, Palm Beach Community College; Shane Williamson, Lindenwood University.

I'd also like to thank all the reviewers who helped to shape *FOCUS* in it's first edition: Peg Adams, Northern Kentucky University; Josie Adamo, Buffalo State College; Barbara Anderson, Midlands Technical College; Jon Aoki, University of Houston-Downtown; Mercy Azeke, Norfolk State University; Michael Becraft, Austin Peay State University; Lynda Bennett, Blue Mountain Community College; Janet Breaker, Milwaukee Area Technical College; Beverly Brucks, Illinois Central College; Toi Buchanan, Fayetteville Technical Community College; Castell Burton, Valencia Community College; David Campaigne, University of South Florida; Lea Campbell, North Harris Montgomery Community College; Barbara Chavis, Cleveland Community College; Miriam Chiza, North Hennepin

Community College; G. Jay Christensen, California State University, Northridge; Regina Vincent Clark, Tennessee State University; Karen Clay, Miami Dade College; Geoff Cohen, University of California, Riverside; Carrie Cokely, Meredith College; Della Colantone, Alderson-Broaddus College; Therese Crary, Highland Community College; Kimberly Cummings, University of Tampa; Allison Cumming-McCann, Springfield College; Janice A. Daly, Florida State University; Vrita H. Delaine, The University of Southern Mississippi; Mark Demark, Alvin Community College; Gigi Derballa, Asheville-Buncombe Technical Community College; Anne Dickens, Lee College; Michael Discello, Pittsburgh Technical Institute; Carmen Etienne, Oakland University; Sally Firmin, Baylor University; Becky Garlick, Blinn College; Sharol Gauthier, University of South Carolina Upstate; Jayne Geissler, East Carolina University; Dee Allen Goedeke, High Point University; Laura Goppold, Central Piedmont Community College; Marie Gore, University of Maryland, Baltimore County; Laurie Grimes, Lorain County Community College; Valerie Hewitt, Remington College; Joseph Jumpeter, Pennsylvania State University, Wilkes-Barre Page Keller, College of Charleston; Lois Lawson-Briddell, Gloucester County College; Kelly Lee, Orange Coast College; Janet Lindner, Midlands Technical College; Brenda Marina, The University of Akron; Marty Marty, Missouri State University; Claudia McDade, Jacksonville State University; Michelle McDaniel, Middle Tennessee State University; Bridgett McGowen, Prairie View A&M University; Aiesha Miller, The University of Akron; Brian Mitchell, Gibbs College of Boston; Karen Mitchell, Northern Essex Community College; Kelly Morales, University of Texas-Pan American; Gail Muse, Holmes Community College; Bonnie Porter Pajka, Luzerne County; Community College; Kate Pandolpho, Ocean County College; Stan Parker, Charleston Southern University; James Penven, Virginia Polytechnic Institute and State University; Joni Webb Petschauer, Appalachian State University; Amy Poland, Buena Vista University; Margaret Puckett, North Central State College; Terry Rafter-Carles, Valencia Community College; Melanie Rago, Indiana University; Margaret Rapp, Tyler Junior College; Rebecca Reed, Johnson & Wales University; Virginia Reilly, Ocean County College; Saundra Richardson, University of North Carolina at Pembroke; Chuck Rhodes, Sonoma State University; Jennifer Rockwood, The University of Toledo; Lawrence Rodriguez, Palo Alto College; Bea Rogers, Monmouth University; Keri Rogers, Sam Houston State University; Tara Ross, Keiser College; Patty Santoianni, Sinclair Community College; Sarah Shutt, J. Sargeant Reynolds Community College; Phebe Simmons, Blinn College; Brenda A. Smith, Norfolk State University; Kim Smokowski, Bergen Community College; Marilyn Starkes, Thomas Nelson Community College; Angie Walston, Barton College; Janice Waltz, Harrisburg Area Community College; Jodi Webb, Bowling Green State University; Jill Wilks, Southern Utah University.

The Wadsworth Team No book, of course, gets very far without a publisher, and FOCUS has had the best publishing team imaginable: the dynamic, highly people-skilled Annie Todd, Director of College Success; the meticulous, multi-talented Marita Sermolins, Development Editor; the energetic, industrious Kirsten Stoller, Senior Marketing Manager; true professionals who combed pages and probably did more than I'll ever know, Sara Abbott, Associate Content Project Manager; and Associate Editor, Melanie Opacki, for her work on all the outstanding supplements to *FOCUS*; the obviously talented Art Director, Pamela Galbreath; and Annie Beck, Project Manager at Lachina Publishing Services. I'd like to especially thank Larry Harwood, the master photographer who took photos of the *FOCUS* cast on the University of Colorado at Colorado Springs campus. And heartfelt thanks to Wadsworth's Annie Mitchell and Sean Wakely, who believed in this project from the very start; Sylvia Shepherd, whose creative vision shaped much of this book, and Lauren Larsen, whose wit and wisdom formed the basis for several of the early chapters.

Other Contributors   I'd also particularly like to thank the "*FOCUS* All-Stars," as I call them, my students who modeled for the photo shoots and starred in the "Inside the FOCUS Studio" videos. I'd also like to thank my colleagues at UCCS who have helped me develop many of the ideas in this book, whether they know it or not—all the Freshman Seminar faculty past and present. I also can't go without thanking the many authors who granted me permission to use their work, the career interviewees who shared their expertise and advice in each chapter, and three essential scholars who allowed me to use, apply, and extend their instruments throughout the book: Neil Fleming, Brian French, and John Bransford. And thanks to my expert student research assistants Phil Wilburn, Sarah Snyder, and Jessica Smith, and my best buddy Liz for all her encouraging words. I'd like to give a special thanks to Aren Moore who worked closely with me to create *FOCUS*Points, the interactive, multimedia PowerPoint designed for *FOCUS*. And finally, I'd like to thank Matt McClain, the comedy writer who brought his innovative humor to the learning process through podcast summaries of the chapters and television scripts for the website TV shows. He took the "big ideas" from *FOCUS* chapters and made them memorable to students by using their own best-loved media.

Above all, *FOCUS* has taught me truly to focus. Writing a book takes the same kind of endurance and determination that it takes to get a college degree. My empathy level for my students has, if anything, increased—and I am thankful for all I've learned while writing. It has been a cathartic experience to see what has filled each computer screen as I've tapped, tapped, tapped away. Ultimately, what I have chosen to put into each chapter has told me a great deal about who I am, what I know (and don't), and what I value. There's no doubt: I am a better teacher for having written this book. May all my readers grow through their *FOCUS* experience, too.

Meet the Cast

©Larry Harwood Photography. Property of Cengage Learning.

Chapter 1: Gloria Gonzales / Debbie

Hometown: Saguache, Colorado

Major: Business with a minor in Communication

Lessons Learned: Debbie learned through her first-year seminar course that it takes time and effort to establish great relationships. She got involved in intramural sports, which helped her meet new people and make friends. Although she's doing well now, she wishes she'd studied more her first term.

Toughest First-Year Class: Microeconomics because it was an entirely new subject for her.

Advice to New Students: "Get your priorities straight; college is a great place to be, so get a great start by setting good study habits, and I HIGHLY recommend a planner because you will be surprised at how fast your time can become occupied."

©Larry Harwood Photography. Property of Cengage Learning.

Chapter 2: Tammy Ko / Jessica

Hometown: Manitou Springs, Colorado

Major: Marketing

Lessons Learned: Juggling a part-time job while in school, Jessica loved living on campus her first term and meeting new people, but she regretted not talking to other students about which professors and courses to take towards her marketing major. In order to succeed, she says, you've "gotta give it all you've got!"

Toughest First-Year Class: Microeconomics because it wasn't like high school courses that just required memorizing a lot of facts.

Advice to New Students: "Talk to other students to learn about the best professors, and make sure you are studying something that you are interested in."

©Larry Harwood Photography. Property of Cengage Learning.

Chapter 3: Derek Johnson / Derrick

Hometown: Colorado Springs, Colorado

Major: Communications/Recording Arts

Lessons Learned: Even though he's not married and has no children, Derrick and his case study character have much in common—too much to do and too little time! Derrick felt his biggest mistake his first year was not asking enough questions in class. He knows now he should have asked for clarity on content or assignments he didn't understand.

Toughest First-Year Class: English because he and his instructor had differing opinions, but he communicated through the tough spots and earned an "A."

Advice to New Students: "Surround yourself with positive people. As the saying goes, 'you are the company you keep.' I've seen many of my friends drop out because the people they called friends were holding them back from their full potential. Now that I have graduated, I look back at all the people I hold close and know that I wouldn't have made it without them."

Free Time: composing music and producing films

©Larry Harwood Photography. Property of Cengage Learning.

Chapter 4: Annie Miller / Meagan

Hometown: Albuquerque, New Mexico

Major: Nursing

Lessons Learned: Megan admits that her biggest mistake her first term was not asking anyone for help with anything. But she enjoyed moving away from home and being more independent, meeting new people, and having a more laid-back academic schedule than her high school schedule had been.

Toughest First-Year Course: Calculus because she was overconfident and didn't study for exams.

Advice to New Students: "Don't give up! College is amazing! Oh, and don't spend all of your money on food."

Free Time: biking, hiking, playing Ultimate Frisbee, and giving campus tours

Chapter 5: Dario Jones / Orlando

Hometown: Fountain, Colorado

Major: MA, Communication

Lessons Learned: Start strong, work hard, and finish strong

Toughest First-Year Course: Math 099

Advice to New Students: "Get to know your instructors and fellow classmates. Ask questions in class when you're not sure about something."

Free Time: "What free time? To relax, I listen to jazz or classical music, or I'll channel surf until I find something interesting to watch."

Chapter 6: Lindsey Collier / Heather

Hometown: Her parents just moved to another state—so where is home?

Major: Nursing

Lessons Learned: Heather made the mistake of not making academics her first priority, but she learned from her first-year seminar course that she needed to be willing to sacrifice social time for study time.

Advice to New Students: "College isn't like high school—you do actually have to study three times as much for any course. No matter what course it is, study for it. You'll feel much better about receiving high marks than about partying with friends. And get involved on your campus. It's your home away from home, so why not make the most of it?"

Free Time: College Step and Dance Team

Chapter 7: Darnell Williams / Calil

Hometown: Colorado Springs, Colorado

Major: History with a secondary education emphasis

Lessons Learned: Calil noticed many similarities between himself and the FOCUS Challenge Case character he portrayed, besides playing football and watching movies. Calil, too, had problems with the transition from high school to college. He admits he was a student who "coasted" through his senior year of high school, which made his first year of college more difficult. He didn't study as hard as he should have as a first-year student.

Toughest First-Year Class: English, because he wasn't fully aware of the instructor's expectations.

Advice to New Students: "Determination is the key to success. If you are determined, there is nothing in the world that can stop you."

Chapter 8: Katie Alexander / Christina

Hometown: Colorado Springs, Colorado. Since she went to college in her hometown, Christina really enjoyed the opportunity college provided to meet new people.

Major: Nursing

Lessons Learned: Spending her free time with her friends watching movies, going bowling or dancing, and just hanging out, Christina found that like her FOCUS Challenge Case character, she, too, would make up excuses to get out of studying and doing her homework. She quickly learned the importance of reading and taking notes. "As weird as it may sound, reading cuts your end study time by more than half. Reading the material ahead of time helps you understand everything so much better."

Advice to New Students: "Stay motivated. College is going to FLY by! If you stay motivated and get good grades, it really will be over before you know it."

Chapter 9: Joe Cloud / Alvin

Hometown: Ganado, Arizona (Navajo Nation)

Major: Business

Toughest First-Year Course: Spanish because he came from a place where no other languages are ever spoken.

Lessons Learned: President of the American Indian Science and Engineering Society on campus, Alvin identifies closely with his FOCUS Challenge Case character. He, too, is one of a minority of Native Americans in higher education, so a lot of people in his hometown are carefully watching his academic success. Alvin admits his biggest mistake in his first term was not opening up to people—he came to school for class and left without trying to meet new people. But he learned from his mistakes and eventually came to value meeting all sorts of different people through activities on campus.

Advice to New Students: "Learn from my mistakes: Be open to try new things, get out of your comfort zone, and be free to be silly—everyone is at some point. You meet a lot of new people that way and it makes your first year the experience of a lifetime."

Chapter 10: Kia Washington / Charmaine

Hometown: Colorado Springs, Colorado

Major: Psychology and Sociology

Toughest First-Year Course: General psychology because there was so much to learn in such a short period of time.

Lessons Learned: In her first-year seminar, Charmaine learned how to manage her time more effectively, as well as the necessity of keeping yourself healthy in mind, body, and spirit, something she felt her FOCUS Challenge Case character could have benefited from.

Advice to New Students: "Remember to have fun in everything that you do, both academically and otherwise. Take care of yourself first and don't feel as though you have to do everything all the time; sometimes the best parts of life come during moments of down time. This is where you are able to truly reflect on what it is you're doing and remember why you're doing it in the first place!"

Chapter 11: Ethan Cole / Josh

Hometown: Fort Morgan, Colorado

Major: Sociology

Lessons Learned: Like his *FOCUS* Challenge Case character, Josh noticed that he, too, didn't always push himself to reach his potential. But he learned through his first-year seminar course that he is responsible for himself and that professors aren't like high school teachers. They will let you fail a class if you don't do what you need to. It's up to you.

Advice to New Students: "Not only did getting involved on campus help me have more fun in school, but it has also helped me academically. It has taught me how to manage my time and has made it so much easier for me to participate with confidence in class. Just make sure you get what you need to do done, and you will enjoy your college experience so much more."

Free Time: "Free time? What's that?! I'm too busy to have free time!" (But he secretly admits he snowboards, plays guitar, draws, and spends time with friends.)

MEET THE AUTHOR: Constance Staley

Hometown: Pittsburgh, Pennsylvania (although she never actually lived there. Instead, she lived all over the world and went to ten schools in twelve years.)

Background: Connie has taught at the University of Colorado at Colorado Springs for more than 30 years after getting a bachelor's degree in education, a master's degree in linguistics, and a Ph.D. in communication.

College Memories: Connie remembers loving her public speaking class as a first-year student and having tons of friends, but being extremely homesick for her family.

Advice to New Students: "Earning a college degree is hard work, takes a long time, and requires a substantial investment of your time, energy, and resources. But it's the best investment you can make in your own future—one you'll never regret."

Free Time: Spending time with her husband, her two daughters, and her boy-girl grandtwins; relaxing at her cabin in the mountains; and traveling around the country to speak to other professors who also care about their first-year students and their success.

Introduction to Students

Dear Reader,

This book is different. It won't coerce, coddle, caution, or coax you. Instead, it will give you the tools you need to coach yourself. Ultimately, this book is about you, your college career, and your career beyond college. It's about the future you will create for yourself.

FOCUS on College Success stars a cast of eleven of my own students, like a stage play. One student "actor" is featured in each chapter's opening case study. All 11 cast members reappear throughout the book, so that you'll get to know them as you read. I've been teaching for more than 30 years now and worked with thousands of students. Each case study is about a real student (with a fictitious name) that I've worked with or a composite of several students. You may find you have some things in common with them. But whether you do or not, I hope they will make this book come to life for you. You'll also be able to meet these "actors" electronically in videos called, "Inside the FOCUS Studio," on the book's premium website.

I love what I do, and I care deeply about students. I hope that comes through to you as a reader. You'll see that I've inserted some of my personality, had a bit of fun at times, and tried to create a new kind of textbook for you. In my view, learning should be engaging, personal, memorable, challenging, and fun.

Most importantly, I know that these next few years hold the key to unlock much of what you want from your life. And from all my years of experience and research, I can tell you straightforwardly that what you read in this book works. It gets results. It can turn you into a better, faster learner. Really? you ask. Really! The only thing you have to do is put all the words in this book into action. That's where the challenge comes in.

Getting a college degree takes time, energy, resources, and focus. At times, it may mean shutting down the six windows you have open on your computer, and directing all your attention to one thing in laser-like fashion. It may mean disciplining yourself to dig in and stick with something until you've nailed it. Can you do it? I'm betting you can, or I wouldn't have written this book. Invest yourself fully in what you read here, and then decide to incorporate it into your life. If there's one secret to college success, that's it.

So, you're off! You're about to begin one of the most fascinating, liberating, challenging, and adventure-filled times of your life. I may not be able to meet each one of you personally, but I can wish you well, wherever you are. I hope this book helps you on your journey.

Constance Staley

Answers to the back cover questions are 1) d; 2) d; 3) c; 4) a; 5) a.

chapter 1

Building Dreams, Setting Goals

You're about to discover....
- ✔ How this book will help you learn
- ✔ What motivates you
- ✔ How your attitude can sabotage you
- ✔ How your beliefs about your intelligence can affect your college success
- ✔ What separates performers and learners
- ✔ What your core values say about you
- ✔ Why you should distinguish between dreams and goals
- ✔ How to develop goals that work
- ✔ What it takes to succeed in college

©Larry Harwood Photography. Property of Cengage Learning.

READINESS CHECK

What do you Know?

Before beginning this chapter, take a moment to answer these questions. Your answers will help you assess how ready you are to focus.

1 = not very/not much/very little/low   10 = very/a lot/very much/high

How much do you *already* know?

Based on reading the "You're about to discover. . ." list and skimming this chapter, how much do you think you probably already know about this chapter's subject?

1 2 3 4 5 6 7 8 9 10

See if you can answer these questions about goals and dreams *before* you read.

1. **What is the difference between a learner and a performer?**

2. **What is the difference between intrinsic and extrinsic motivation?**

3. **Which four factors—all beginning with the letter "C"—are a part of intrinsic motivation—and your college success?**

How motivated are you to learn *more*?

In general, how motivated are you to learn more by reading this chapter?

1 2 3 4 5 6 7 8 9 10

How much do you think this information might affect your success in college?

1 2 3 4 5 6 7 8 9 10

How much do you think this information might affect your career success after college?

1 2 3 4 5 6 7 8 9 10

How ready are you to read *now*?

How ready are you to focus on this chapter—physically, intellectually, and emotionally? Circle a number for each aspect of your readiness to focus.

1 2 3 4 5 6 7 8 9 10

If any of your answers is below a 10, you might want to pay attention to whatever is distracting you before you start reading. For example, if you're feeling scattered, take a few moments to settle down and focus.

Finally, how long do you think it will take you to complete this chapter from start to finish?

_____ Hour(s) _____ Minutes

Gloria Gonzales

It was her first day of college. As Gloria Gonzales walked to her first class, "College Success," she had mixed feelings: excitement, anticipation, anxiety, and apprehension. She wondered if she'd meet any interesting people, if she'd like her instructor, and if she'd learn anything important in this class. After all, she'd gotten good grades in high school without even trying. If she just put in some effort, she thought, she'd be successful in college, too. How can you study something like "College Success" for a whole term? she asked herself.

Mom & Dad - last summer

To be honest, Gloria thought she probably already knew most of what there was to learn in this course, and if she didn't, so what? She knew what she had to do to get good grades—everyone does—but she didn't always choose to do it, that's all. School was part of her life, but it wasn't always her top priority. At least this course would probably be easier than her psychology course or her composition course with all that writing.

Gloria wasn't the first person in her family to go to college. Her sister had attempted it, but she'd dropped out after her first term and gotten a job. "College, who needs it?" she'd exclaimed. "I want to start earning good money right away, not years from now!" There were times when Gloria thought her sister might be right. She certainly seemed able to afford some of the things Gloria had always wanted herself. Was college really going to be worth all the time, effort, and expense? But everyone she knew was going to college; it was the right thing to do after high school, and everyone expected it of her.

Gloria's family didn't have much money. They were sacrificing to help finance her college education. She'd better perform, they'd said. They'd told her point-blank that her sister had set a bad example, and that her first-term grades had better not include anything lower than a B. Frankly, Gloria was beginning to feel a twinge of performance pressure. Of all the children in her family, her sister had always been considered the smart one, and she'd given up after only one term. If her sister couldn't do it, how could Gloria? If she were to succeed, exactly what would it take?

Despite her worries as she walked down the hallway toward the classroom, Gloria was sure of one thing: She looked good today—really good.

Her sister's skirt fit perfectly, the new red shirt was definitely her color, and thankfully it was a good hair day. Gloria had always been able to make heads turn.

Beneath it all, Gloria knew what she wanted, anyway. She was going into the fashion industry. She'd dreamed of that since she was ten years old. She wasn't sure exactly what she'd need to do to make it, but she'd worked in a clothing store at the mall all through high school, and she was good at it. In fact, the store kept trying to give her more hours because she had such exceptional customer service skills. She thought she'd probably just work her college courses around her thirty-five hours a week there.

Gloria's parents wanted her to major in engineering because they thought it would be a lucrative and stable profession. They were always clipping articles about engineering jobs from the newspaper and giving them to her, but she kept telling them she had no interest. "There'll always be good jobs for engineers," they said. She'd heard it so many times that her usual response

now was "Yeah, whatever. . . ." Gloria knew her parents meant well, but they had never gone to college, and frankly, sometimes they interfered a little too much. Did they want to live her life *for* her? While they talked engineering, she dreamed of becoming a famous fashion designer with her own line of clothing. She was going to call it "Gloria." Her parents had named her after their favorite rock-and-roll song of all time, "G-L-O-R-I-A." Imagine— her own clothing label with her name on it!

As she reached for the classroom doorknob, Gloria couldn't help wondering about the two questions at the forefront of her mind: "What will college really be like?" and "Will I be successful?" She took a deep breath as she opened the classroom door. *This is it*, she thought. Somehow, she felt as if she were outside herself, watching on the big screen— replete with Panavision and DTS sound. *This is real; this is me, starring in my own movie*, she said to herself. And even though it felt good, Gloria had to wonder about the ending. All she could do was hope for the best.

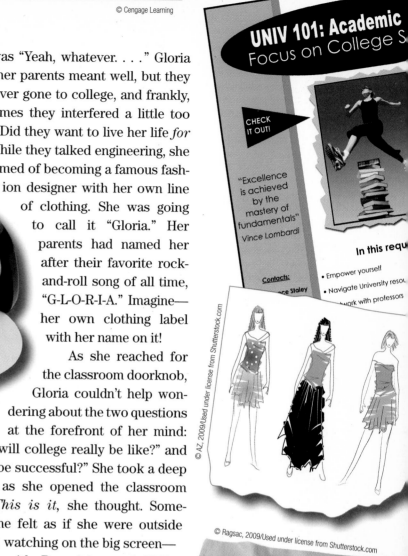

UNIV 101: Academic
Focus on College S

CHECK IT OUT!

"Excellence is achieved by the mastery of fundamentals"
Vince Lombardi

In this requ

Contacts:
ce Staley

• Empower yourself
• Navigate University resou
• work with professors

Classified Ads

ENGINEERING PROFESSIONALS NEEDED

ACME ENGINEERING SOLUTIONS is a growing engineering and consulting company in North America. We design, develop and manufacture a wide range of instruments and tools for mechanical industries.

JOB TITLE: ENGINEERING ASSOCIATE

RESPONSIBILITIES:
• Develop and design service products and solutions, including retrofits for existing designs, solutions for field repairs, solutions which broaden our service scope.
• Provide inventive engineering support for our on site operations.
• Contribute to reverse engineering efforts to satisfy customer demand for needed field, shop service repairs.
• Serve as the technical advisor to our engineers stationed in field locations, corporate headquarters and elsewhere around the country;
• Draft detailed blueprints and specifications for our products and sub-contracted components.

We are looking for a "team player" who has a relevant four-year BS degree in Engineering.

HOW TO APPLY:
Julie.Anderton@AcmeEngineeringSolutions.com

A distributor of office and computer products is in "URGENT" need of individuals to fill-up the following positions.

Chique Street South M

Course Schedule
Main Campus

FALL SEMESTER

ent: Gonzales,Gloria

e ID	Course Title	Hrs	Days	Meeting Times	Bldg	Room	Meeting Dates	Stat
n 100	INTRO TO PSYCH				BLDG	210	8/18/08-12/17/09	ENRO
130	ENGLISH COMP						/08-12/17/09	ENRO
101	COLLEGE SUCCE							
	Credit Load							

Work Schedule Week # 46

	Sunday	Monday	Tuesday	Wedensday	Thursday	Friday	Saturda
Abel, Nora	8-5	2-CL			8-5	9-6	8-5
Collins, Becky	2-CL					2-CL	9-6
Gonzales, Gloria		8-5	9-6	2-CL			
Harper, Alex			2-CL		9-6	8-5	10-7
Monahan, Zoe		10-7	9-6	8-5	10-7	2-CL	
Parker, Patricia				2-CL			

What Do You Think?

1. Describe Gloria's motivation to succeed in college. Is she sufficiently motivated to succeed?
2. Describe Gloria's beliefs about her intelligence. Does she think college is mostly about effort or about ability? Is Gloria a *learner* or a *performer*?
3. Is Gloria's vision of a famous fashion designer a goal or a dream? Why?
4. Identify three things that show focus and might help Gloria make good life management choices.
5. What elements of Gloria's situation are similar to your own college experience thus far?

Who Are You? And What Do You Want?

Imagine this voicemail greeting: "Hi. At the tone, please answer two of life's most important questions. Who are you? And what do you want?" Beep. Can you answer these questions right now? How much do you really know about yourself and what you want from this life of yours?

Don't worry. These aren't trick questions and there are no wrong answers. But there are some answers that are more right for you than others. College is a great time to think about who you are and what you want. In addition to learning about biology or history or business—whatever you choose for a major—college will be a time to learn about yourself: your motivation, values, dreams, and goals. College is a time when you'll make some of the most important choices of your life. Which major will you choose? Which career will you aim for? How many lifelong friends will you make? From this point on, it's up to you. Have you ever heard this phrase with ten two-letter words: "If it is to be, it is up to me"? It's true.

Think about it: a college education is one of the best investments you can make. Once you've earned a college degree, it's yours forever. Someone can steal your car or walk away with your cell phone, but once you've earned a college degree, no one can ever take it from you. Your choice to be a college graduate will pay off in many ways. So even if you aren't sure exactly how you want to spend the rest of your life right now, you can't go wrong by investing in your future.

This book starts with the big picture: your life. It's about managing your life, being fully invested in what you're doing, and using your abilities to their utmost. Notice the phrase "managing your life"—not *controlling* your life. Let's face it: many things in life are beyond our control. But you can manage your life by making smart choices, setting realistic goals, monitoring your time and energy, motivating yourself, and ultimately creating your own future. As the title of this book states boldly, it's about focus.

For many of us, focusing is a challenge. We work too many hours, crowd our lives with obligations, and rush from one thing to the next. We're good at multitasking—or so we think. We can surf the Internet, listen to a new CD, text our friends, and read this chapter—all at the same time! While we've become skilled at multitasking, we may have sacrificed some of the self-discipline required for in-depth study. Multitasking may be common practice today, but learning to focus is

I wonder how far my sister will go without a degree.

" Furious activity is no substitute for understanding."

H. H. Williams, British poet and playwright

> **"** What is important is to keep learning, to enjoy challenge, and to tolerate ambiguity. In the end there are no certain answers."

Martina Horner, former President of Radcliffe College

what most college students need. In fact, recent research indicates that multitasking hurts your brain's ability to learn, and that what you do manage to learn while you're distracted by other things is harder to use and recall.[1]

Of course, some people achieve success without a college degree, but by and large, they're the exception. Even Steven Spielberg, self-made billionaire in the film industry and winner of Academy Awards for *Schindler's List* and *Saving Private Ryan*, felt the need to finish the college degree he had started more than thirty years before. "I wanted to accomplish this for many years as a 'thank you' to my parents for giving me the opportunity for an education and a career, and as a personal note for my own family—and young people everywhere—about the importance of achieving their college education goals," he said. "But I hope they get there quicker than I did. Completing the requirements for my degree 33 years after finishing my principal education marks my longest post-production schedule."[2]

If you read this book carefully and follow its advice, it will help you become the best student you can possibly be. It will give you practical tools to help you manage your life. It will take you beyond college into your career. And most of all, it will encourage you to become a true scholar. That is this book's challenge to you as you begin your college career.

EXERCISE 1.1

We'd Like to Get to Know You…

Take a few minutes to finish the following statements. Think about what each sentence says about you. Use your responses to introduce yourself to the class or form pairs, talk over your responses together, and use your partner's answers to introduce him or her to the class.

1. I'm happiest when _____.
2. I'm disappointed when _____.
3. If I had an extra $100, I'd _____.
4. The thing I'm most proud of is _____.
5. Once people get to know me, they're probably surprised to find I'm _____ _____.
6. My family wants me to _____.
7. I'd really like to become _____.
8. My friends enjoy me because _____.
9. I've been known to consume large quantities of _____.
10. I'd rather be _____ than _____.
11. When I'm under pressure, _____.
12. My best quality is _____.
13. My worst quality is _____.
14. The academic skill I'd most like to develop is _____.
15. One thing I'd like to figure out about myself is _____.

Spending Time "in the System"

? challenge **❝** reaction **✳** insight **!** action

Challenge: How do people learn?

Reaction: _____

Spending time "in the system"? No, being in college isn't like being in jail—far from it. Many people reflect back on their college days as one of the most enjoyable, active, and interesting times of their lives. Get involved on campus, make life-long friends, and gain as much as you can from your college experience.

"The system" is the approach used in this book to structure productive learning: the Challenge → Reaction → Insight → Action system. It is based on the work of Dr. John Bransford and his colleagues, who together wrote an influential book called *How People Learn*.

Figure 1.1 summarizes how learning requires focus, and focus involves the four steps in this system. This book asks you to write and discuss things along the way: your reactions, your insights, and the actions you plan to take. You'll come to realize things about yourself. This book's goal for you is *transformative learning*: "a process of examining, questioning, validating, and revising [your] perceptions."[3] What you'll learn by reading it has the potential to *transform*, or *change* you, so that you're ready to meet the many challenges that await you in college and in life. Here's a step-by-step explanation of the learning system used in this book.

STEP 1: Accept the *FOCUS* challenge. Every time you study a new subject or take a new course, you are challenged, right? Within each chapter of this book, you'll be presented with challenges, beginning with a case study about a college student—perhaps someone like you or a friend—who is experiencing something new and difficult. Research shows that people can learn more from examples of things going wrong than they can from examples of things going

FIGURE 1.1

How People Learn

Source: Based on J. Bransford, et al. (2000). *How People Learn: Brain, Mind, Experience, and School.* Washington, DC: National Academy Press.

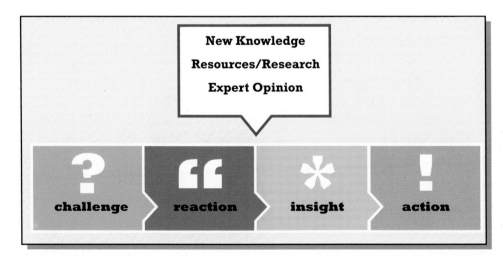

perfectly smoothly. You'll be presented with additional challenges related to the chapter's content to pique your curiosity, motivate you to keep reading, and start a learning chain reaction. Don't skip over this step; it's an important part of the learning process. Challenge yourself!

STEP 2: React to the challenge. Whenever you're learning something new, the best place to start is by figuring out what you think you already know—let's call it your gut reaction. You're a novice to any new field you're studying, not an expert, but you bring with you to the learning process a set of preconceptions, assumptions, sometimes biases or misperceptions, and of course, all your previous experiences. Your reaction to each challenge will tell you what you think you already know. By the end of the chapter, you'll know more about all the challenges you've encountered throughout your reading. The goal of this book is to help you become a deep learner, as opposed to skimming the surface and simply rushing on to the next assignment and the next course—as many college students do. It will ask you to pause, take stock, focus, and think.

STEP 3: Use new knowledge to gain insights. After your initial reaction, you must pay attention to your inner voice—insights you've gained from new knowledge. An "Insight → Action" activity at the end of every chapter will help you keep track of them. Let's say, for example, that you read later in this chapter about goal setting. When you first thought about it, the whole idea of setting goals seemed simple, but after reading about it, you decide you really hadn't ever thought about it very deeply and hadn't thought much at all about setting your own goals. The difference between step 2 (whatever reaction you provided to the challenge) and step 3 (the insights you've gained) demonstrates that learning is taking place.

STEP 4: Use your insights to propel you toward action. Insights have no impact unless they lead to change. Decide how an insight affects your existing beliefs, how it changes them, and, therefore, what you've learned. Your insights may lead you to change your behavior, develop an informed opinion, or

> " Surround yourself with people who take their work seriously, but not themselves, those who work hard and play hard."
>
> **Colin Powell, former U.S. Secretary of State**

make choices about your education, your job, your family, or your life. The bottom line is: You must use your insights to take action. To become real, new knowledge must lead to personal insights that result in action.

Each step in this four-part system is important. For example, if you skip step 2, *react to the challenge*, by identifying what you *think* you know, you may assume you already know all the new information you're reading or hearing. You may think, "Sure, of course, that makes sense. I already knew that," when you really didn't. Realizing there's a gap between steps 2 and 3—what you thought you knew and the insights you've gained from new knowledge—is important. And actually putting the insights you gain into real, live, honest-to-goodness action is vital.

As you work through this book, the Challenge → Reaction → Insight → Action system will continue cycling back to step 1, presenting you with new challenges. If you follow the system built into this book and integrate it into your other academic pursuits, you can become a lifelong learner. Thinking in terms of the learning cycle will become ingrained.

How Motivated *Are* You and *How* Are You Motivated?

? challenge	❝ reaction	＊ insight	! action

Challenge: How intrinsically motivated do you think you are on a scale of 1 to 10 with 10 meaning EXTREMELY ACADEMICALLY MOTIVATED and 1 meaning NOT VERY MOTIVATED AT ALL? Why does this number seem right to you?

Reaction: _____

EXERCISE 1.2

Academic Intrinsic Motivation Self-Assessment

Read each of the following statements and circle the number beside each statement that most accurately represents your views about yourself.

	Completely Not True	Somewhat Not True	Neutral	Somewhat True	Completely True
1. I have academic goals.	1	2	3	4	5
2. I am confident I can complete my degree.	1	2	3	4	5
3. I determine my career goals.	1	2	3	4	5
4. I enjoy solving challenging, difficult problems.	1	2	3	4	5
5. I work on an assignment until I understand it.	1	2	3	4	5
6. I am confident I will graduate from college.	1	2	3	4	5
7. I determine the quality of my academic work.	1	2	3	4	5

	Completely Not True	Somewhat Not True	Neutral	Somewhat True	Completely True
8. I am pursuing a college degree because I value education.	1	2	3	4	5
9. I feel good knowing that I determine how my academic career develops.	1	2	3	4	5
10. I have high standards for academic work.	1	2	3	4	5
11. Staying in college is my decision.	1	2	3	4	5
12. I study because I like to learn new things.	1	2	3	4	5
13. I enjoy doing outside readings in connection to my future coursework.	1	2	3	4	5
14. I am intrigued by the different topics introduced in my courses.	1	2	3	4	5
15. I study because I am curious.	1	2	3	4	5
16. I look forward to going to class.	1	2	3	4	5
17. I am excited to take more courses within my major.	1	2	3	4	5
18. I enjoy learning more within my field of study.	1	2	3	4	5
19. I like to find answers to questions about material I am learning.	1	2	3	4	5
20. I enjoy studying.	1	2	3	4	5
21. I have pictured myself in a profession after college.	1	2	3	4	5
22. I am excited about the job opportunities I will have when I graduate.	1	2	3	4	5
23. I have pictured myself being successful in my chosen profession.	1	2	3	4	5
24. I believe I will make a substantial contribution to my chosen profession.	1	2	3	4	5
25. I feel good knowing I will be a member of the professional community in my area of study.	1	2	3	4	5

Total each column, then add your scores across. _____ + _____ + _____ + _____ + _____ =

_____ OVERALL SCORE

Continue reading to find out what your overall score means.

Source: French, F.B., & Oakes, W. (2003). Measuring academic intrinsic motivation in the first year of college: Reliability and validity evidence for a new instrument. *Journal of the First Year Experience* 15(1), 83–102.

When it comes to getting a college education, where does motivation come into the picture? In general, motivation is your desire to engage and put forth effort, even when the going gets rough. The word *motivation* comes from Medieval Latin, *motivus*, meaning moving or impelling. What moves you to learn? There are many ways to define motivation, and different people are motivated by different things.

How motivated would you be to learn something difficult, such as a new language, one you'd never studied before? Let's say that you were offered a chance to learn Finnish, a challenging language that is not related to English. For example, in Finnish *Kiitoksia oikein paljon* means "thank you very much." Finnish would be a challenge to learn. To determine your level of motivation, it would help to know your attitude toward Finland and Finnish people, whether you needed to learn Finnish for some reason, how you felt about learning it, if you thought you could learn it successfully, if you were reinforced in some way for learning it, and just how stimulating you found the learning process to be.[4] In other words, your motivation level depends on many factors, right?

You'd probably be more motivated to learn Finnish if these sorts of things were part of the picture: (a) you were going to visit relatives in Finland and were excited about it, (b) you'd always excelled at learning foreign languages and you expected to learn this one easily, (c) your boss was planning to transfer you to Helsinki as part of a big promotion, or (d) you enjoyed your Finnish language class, thought the instructor was a gifted teacher, and found the other students to be as motivated as you were. So, whose job is it to motivate you? Your instructor's? Your parents'? This book's? Yours? *Can* anyone else besides you motivate you? This book will ask you: how motivated *are* you to succeed in college? And *how* are you motivated?

To assess your own motivation, it's important to understand the difference between extrinsic and intrinsic motivation. Figure 1.2 has some good examples. People who are *extrinsically*, or externally, motivated learn in order to get a grade, earn credits, or complete a requirement, for example. They are motivated by things outside themselves. People who are *intrinsically*, or internally, motivated learn because they're curious, fascinated, or challenged, or because they truly want to master a subject. They are motivated from within. Let's be realistic, however. Extrinsic motivation is real and important. You need a particular number of credit hours to graduate. You'd rather get A's than F's. But how intrinsically motivated you are in college will have a great deal to do with just how successful you are. The motivation to become truly educated must come from within you.

You completed the Academic Intrinsic Motivation Scale (AIMS) in the previous exercise, which is designed to measure your intrinsic, or internal, motivation to succeed in college in terms of these four C-Factors:

Good point. Is it my motivation or my parents'?

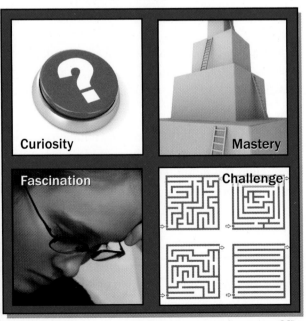

Extrinsic Motivation

Grades

Credits

Pay

Parents

Intrinsic Motivation

Curiosity

Mastery

Fascination

Challenge

CURIOSITY Do you want to learn new things? Are you truly interested in what you're learning? Do you ask questions? Do you allow your curiosity to propel your learning? Each chapter includes a short article on what is required for college success. You'll read cutting-edge information that may pique your curiosity and lead you to consider exploring the original source or related material on your own.

> "You are never given a wish without the power to make it come true. You may have to work for it, however."
>
> **Richard Bach, from *Illusions***

CONTROL Do you think the academic investment you make will lead to successful outcomes? Do you believe you can control how successful you'll be? You are encouraged throughout this book to apply what you are reading about to your most challenging class this term and to take charge of your own learning, which is vital to college success.

CAREER OUTLOOK Are you goal oriented? Are you future oriented? Can you imagine yourself graduating and getting a job you want? Each chapter includes an interview with a professional. As you read these interviews, think about the interviewees' stories and their successes, and ask yourself whether you have the interest and motivation required to get where they are. Following the interview, you'll read some quick facts to see how this career might fit you.

I'm goal oriented, but I'm just not sure what it will take . . .

CHALLENGE Does your college coursework challenge you appropriately? Too much challenge can cause you to become frustrated and give up. Not enough challenge can cause you to lose interest.[5] In general, if a course is too challenging, get help from a tutor or Learning Center on campus. If it's too easy, bump up the challenge yourself. Adjusting the level of challenge to one that's right for you is key to keeping yourself motivated to learn. Online quizzes for each chapter will challenge you so that you can work at your best. For more practice online, access the CourseMate via www.cengage brain.com/shop/ISBN/0495906425 to take the Challenge Yourself Online Quiz.

If your overall score on the AIMS in Exercise 1.2 was 100–125, you're intrinsically motivated at a high level. If you scored between 75 and 99, you're intrinsically motivated at a moderate level, but increasing your intrinsic motivation may help you achieve more. If you scored below 75, a lack of intrinsic motivation could interfere with your college success. If you're intrinsically motivated, you'll accept challenges, react to them by identifying what you already know, seek insights from new knowledge, and take action based on what you've learned.

EXERCISE 1.3

The Ideal Student

Create your own personal top-ten list of the characteristics of an ideal student. Bring your completed list to your next class session where everyone can read their lists, and begin to add, delete, merge, and create a master list to which everyone can subscribe. Put your initials next to each of the ten items on the master list that you promise to do throughout the term. Your personal top-ten list, which your instructor may discuss with you individually at a later time, will become your learning contract for the course.

Give Yourself an Attitude Adjustment

There's a difference of opinion on the subject of attitude. Some people say attitude is not all that important. Attitude-schmattitude, they say. Others say that *attitude* is more important than *aptitude*. What do you think?

In research studies conducted by Rick Snyder at the University of Kansas, students who scored high on a measure of hope got higher grades. Snyder explained that students with high hopes set themselves higher goals and know how to work hard to attain them.

Quick quiz. How many times in the past week did you catch yourself saying "Whatever . . . ," and rolling your eyes? Whatever-ness—an attitude of cynicism, apathy, disdain, or impatience—takes a lot less effort than optimism, respect, kindness, or any other positive response. Whether you realize it or not, whatevers chip away at your motivation, and they can contribute to self-sabotaging your opportunities to succeed in life. When it comes to your college education, one good thing you can do for yourself is to purge the word *whatever* from your vocabulary. Your education is much too important for whatevers—and so are you.

Oops! Whatever is one of my favorite words!

Six Ways to Adjust Your Attitude

The good thing about attitude is that you can change it yourself. As you think about benefits of fine-tuning your attitude, keep these eight recommendations in mind:

1. **Know that you always have choices.** Regardless of circumstances—your income, your background, or your prior academic record—you always have a choice, even if it's limited to how you choose to perceive your current situation.

2. **Take responsibility for your own outcomes.** Coach Vince Lombardi used to have his players look in a mirror before every game and ask themselves, "Am I looking at the person who is helping me win or the one who is holding me back?" Blaming others simply reduces your own power to work toward constructive responses to challenges.

3. **Choose your words carefully.** "Can't" and "won't" are two of the biggest inhibitors to a healthy attitude. Also pay attention to how you describe things. Is the cup half empty or half full? State things in the positive rather than the negative (for example, "stay healthy" rather than "don't get sick"). Language is a reflection of attitude.

> ❝ A positive attitude is your most priceless possession, one of your most valuable assets. To a great extent, it determines the overall quality of your life."
>
> **Keith Harrell, from *Attitude Is Everything***

4. **Fill your mind with messages about the attitude you want to have.** The old saying, "garbage in, garbage out," applies to attitudes as well. There are countless books, CDs, and films that offer positive, motivating messages. Paying attention to role models whose traits you admire is also a great way to bolster your outlook.

5. **Convert turning points into learning points.** Instead of beating yourself up when things don't go well, figure out why. See what you can learn from the experience and then move on. As Henry Ford once said, "Failure is the opportunity to begin again, more intelligently."

6. **Acknowledge your blessings.** Taking time at the end of each day to recognize and feel gratitude for the blessings in your life—no matter how large or small—is a great way to amplify a positive attitude.

Courtesy of Eric Sween.

CAREER OUTLOOK: *Eric Sween, Psychologist*

Q1: How does your work relate to dreams and goals?

As a psychologist, I help people make meaning of the events in their lives. In my private practice I see both individuals and couples. People come into therapy when they feel stuck with something in their lives—unemployment, relationships, or divorce, for example. Others come to therapy because they feel too anxious, or because someone close to them has died. My responsibilities include listening, understanding people's perspectives, and helping them set and reach their goals.

Q2: What are the three most important skills you need to do well in this career?

First, a therapist needs to be able to listen really well and appreciate another person's perspective. Second, a therapist must be genuinely curious about people and try to understand what is most meaningful to them. And

finally, it's important to be flexible and tailor what you do with each person you are working with. Some people need problem solving and concrete steps, and some really just need to be heard by someone who cares.

Q3: What advice would you give college students who are interested in exploring a career in psychology or psychotherapy?

Earn that degree, and beyond that, continue your schooling. If you are interested in any career that involves psychology, spend time with people. People are endlessly interesting. Talk to people who are different from you and see if you can understand another person's worldview. If you enjoy doing these things, then you might enjoy a career similar to the one I've chosen.

HOW WOULD *YOU* LIKE IT?

Have you ever considered a career as a psychologist or counselor?

Facts to Consider[6]

Academic preparation required: a master's or doctoral degree

Future workforce demand: growth projected at a faster rate than the average job category through 2016, particularly for highly trained specialists

Work environment: about 34 percent of psychologists are self-employed; the rest work in clinics, hospitals, schools, nonprofit agencies, or industrial settings

Essential skills: listening, communicating, analyzing, rapport building (for clinical psychologists), and research and statistical skills (for experimental psychologists)

Questions to Ponder

1. Do you have (or could you acquire) the skills this career requires?

2. Are you interested in a career like this? Why or why not?

For more career activities online, access the CourseMate via www.cengagebrain.com/shop/ISBN/0495906425 to do the Team Career exercises.

BOX 1.1

Statements That Ought to Be Outlawed in College . . . and Why

Since words reflect attitudes (and help shape them), listen for statements like these escaping from your mouth. They can negatively affect your attitude and therefore your learning:

- **"I thought college classes would be more interesting than they are."** *Interesting* is in the mind of the beholder.

- **"I didn't learn a thing in that class."** Actively search for what you can take away from a class, even if it didn't quite meet your expectations.

- **"The textbook is really dull. Why bother reading it?"** Reading may not be your favorite pastime, but you may learn more from a textbook than you can predict.

- **"The professor is soooo-o-o boring."** In life, we all interact with all types of personalities, so begin to appreciate differences in communication styles now.

- **"Why do I have to take this required course? What's the point?"** The point is to broaden your horizons, expand your skills as a critical thinker, and become a lifelong scholar.[7]

Why can't I just jump into my major? Those classes will be fun!

EXERCISE 1.4

Your Academic Autobiography

Write a three-page academic autobiography describing your preparation for college. Describe the quality of your primary, middle, and high school learning experiences. Did they prepare you for what you're experiencing now in college? What do you think will be your strengths and weaknesses as a college student? Look back at your academic self throughout your schooling and look ahead to the kind of student you're planning to be in college, then write your academic autobiography. Or as an alternative, create a presentation answering these questions for your classmates.

Ability versus Effort: What's More Important?

Successful people have several things in common: they love learning, seek challenges, value effort, and persevere even when things become difficult.[8] They demonstrate both ability and effort. These two things are the basic requirements for success.

Many people think ability is more important than effort. Either you have it or you don't. But here's a new way of thinking about the question. Take the notion of genius, for example. Experts used to think that a genius was someone born with extraordinary talent, like Mozart. From an early age, geniuses demonstrate exceptional natural abilities, they thought. But experts have changed their thinking: "What Mozart had, we now believe, was . . . the ability to focus for long periods of time. The key factor separating geniuses from the merely accomplished is not a divine spark. . . . It's deliberate practice. Top performers spend more hours (many more hours) rigorously practicing their craft." Effort counts much more than you might think.[9]

Challenge: What is intelligence? Where does it come from? How do your views of intelligence affect you and your learning?

Reaction: _____

Theories of Intelligence Scale

Using the following scale, indicate the extent to which you agree or disagree with each of the following statements by writing the number that corresponds to your opinion in the space next to each statement. There are no right or wrong answers.

1	2	3	4	5	6
Strongly Agree	Mostly Agree	Agree	Disagree	Mostly Disagree	Strongly Disagree

_____ 1. You have a certain amount of intelligence, and you can't really do much to change it.

_____ 2. You can learn new things, but you can't really change your basic intelligence.

_____ 3. You can always substantially change how intelligent you are.

_____ 4. No matter how much intelligence you have, you can always change it quite a bit.

Research shows that what you *believe* about your own intelligence—your *mindset*—can make a difference in how successful you'll be in college. At first glance this statement seems absurd. What does what you believe about intelligence have to do with how smart you really are?

The scaled questions demonstrate that there are two basic ways to define intelligence. Some of us are *performers*, who agree with statements 1 and 2, while others of us are *learners*, who agree more with statements 3 and 4. *Performers* believe that intelligence is a fixed trait that cannot be changed. From the moment you're born, you have a certain amount of intelligence that's been allotted to you, and that's that. *Learners*, on the other hand, believe you can grow your intelligence if you capitalize on opportunities to learn. Whenever you tackle a tough challenge, you learn from it. The more you learn, the more intelligent you can become. Understanding which view of intelligence you endorse will make a difference in how you approach your college classes, as well as the outcomes—both positive and negative—that you'll achieve.

" Only the curious will learn and only the resolute overcome the obstacles to learning. The quest quotient has always excited me more than the intelligence quotient."

Eugene S. Wilson, former Dean of Admissions, Amherst College

Think about all the courses you're enrolled in this term. Use the following matrix to analyze your C-Factors for these courses. Describe each course in terms of its *challenge* level, your *curiosity* about the subject, how much *control* you believe you have to succeed, and the way each class impacts your *career outlook*. Once you've determined the levels of challenge, curiosity, control, and career outlook you perceive in your courses, remember that it's *your* responsibility to adjust them.

- Which classes will be your most challenging this term?
- What is the relationship between the four C-Factors and your intrinsic motivation to learn in each course?
- What can you do to increase your intrinsic motivation and become more successful?

Course Title	Challenge	Curiosity	Control	Career Outlook	Adjustments Required
Composition	Very High: never been good at writing	Very Low: had a discouraging teacher in H.S.	Moderate: probably higher than it feels to me	Will need to know how to write in any job	Need to spend more time pre-writing and going to the campus Writing Center for help

Students who are taught the value of a learning mindset over a performance mindset can actually achieve more than students who don't.[10] In one study, college students' view of intelligence predicted the goals students valued in college. *Performers* were more likely to want to give up in challenging situations; *learners* wanted to try harder. Over their years at the university, *performers*, who had originally entered with higher SAT scores, did not perform better than *learners*, and they had lower self-esteem.[11] In one study that measured the electrical activity in college students' brains as they performed a difficult task, brain activity showed that *performers* cared most about whether their answers were right or wrong, while *learners* were interested in follow-up information they could learn from.[12] Yet another study showed that *learners* are more likely to buckle down academically, even when they feel depressed.[13] It's clear: believing you're a *learner* provides advantages in motivation, achievement, enjoyment, and commitment.

Regardless of what you believe about your precise intelligence level, the fact is this: *intelligence can be cultivated through learning.* And people's theories about their intelligence levels can be shifted.

> " It's always smart to learn from your mistakes. It's smarter to learn from the mistakes of others." **Hillel Segal and Jesse Berst, computer experts**

What Drives You? Values, Dreams, and Goals

? challenge	" reaction	* insight	! action

Challenge: What are your core values? Can you list five?

Reaction: _____ _____ _____ _____ _____

Before tackling the big questions about what you want to create with your life, it's important to first take a close look in the mirror. Who are you? What makes you tick? What do you value? What are your goals? Where will your dreams take you?

EXERCISE 1.6

Core Values Self-Assessment

Review the following list and check off the items that you value. Don't spend too much time thinking about each one; just go with your initial gut reaction. For each item, ask yourself "Is this something that's important to me?"

For me, it's about fame, success, happiness, creativity, and wealth!

_____ Health	_____ Fame	_____ Financial wealth
_____ Fitness/Physical strength	_____ Independence	_____ Commitment
_____ Loyalty	_____ Honesty	_____ Compassion
_____ Academic achievement	_____ Children	_____ Leisure time
_____ Success	_____ Leadership	_____ Balance
_____ Happiness	_____ Family	_____ Friendship
_____ Social life	_____ Marriage/Partnership	_____ Recognition
_____ Athletics	_____ Spirituality	_____ Status
_____ Creativity	_____ Variety	_____ Wisdom
_____ Meaningful work	_____ Challenge	_____ Time spent alone
_____ Adventure	_____ Personal growth	_____ Other (list here)

Now review all of the items you checked off and circle the five that are most important to you at this point in your life. Then rank them by putting a number next to each of the five circled values with number one as your top priority. Finally, take stock. Is this the person you want to be? Is there anything about your values that you would like to change? If so, why not go ahead and do it?

Values at the Core

What do you value in life? By taking time to examine your personal values, managing your life will become easier and make more sense. Values can be intangible concepts such as love or respect, or tangible things such as family or money, and understanding how they motivate you isn't as simple as it might seem. Values can change as you go through life. For example, if you're single now, you may value the freedom to meet a variety of potential romantic partners. Just get to know people and have fun, that's all. Later, however, you may want a committed relationship because you value companionship and stability more than you used to. For this reason, it's important to reassess your values from time to time and reprioritize them.

> " Knowing others is intelligence; knowing yourself is true wisdom. Mastering others is strength; mastering yourself is true power."
>
> **Lao Tzu, Taoist philosopher**

> "Self-knowledge is far more important than self-confidence."
>
> **Simon Cowell,** *American Idol* **judge, from** *I Don't Mean to Be Rude, But . . .*

Another complicating factor is that values can conflict with one another. Suppose that you value honesty and kindness, and you are at a party and a friend asks you what you think of her new hair color. You honestly think it's hideous, but telling her so would hurt her feelings, thus violating your value of being kind. How do you respond? That would depend on which value is a higher priority for you. You have to make an on-the-spot decision about which value to tap. Once you define your values, however, they can serve as guideposts in helping you make choices every day—everything from the insignificant day-to-day choices to more significant ones such as which major to pursue in college.

In the Challenge → Reaction → Insight → Action system, knowing your values in life is key to understanding your reaction. Once you've defined your values, you can use them in your daily life to guide your actions. For example, if academic achievement is one of your top values, the next time you have the urge to cut class, consider the impact that choice would have on your value system. There is a great inner satisfaction that comes from living a life tied to core values.

Dreams versus Goals

> "The best way to predict the future is to create it."
>
> **Peter Drucker, management expert (1909–2005)**

Do you agree or disagree with this statement: "I can be anything I want to be"? If you are like most students, people have probably told you this all your life. Your parents and teachers all want you to have positive self-esteem, and certainly there are many career options available today. But is it true? Can you be *anything* you want to be? What's the difference between a dream and a goal?

As a college student, you may dream of being a famous doctor or a famous athlete or just plain famous. That's the beauty of dreams—you can imagine yourself in any career, any circumstances. When you're dreaming, you don't even have to play by the rules of reality. Dreams are fantasy-based—*you* in a perfect world. But when it's time to come back to reality, you discover that there are, in fact, rules. You may have dreamed of becoming a top-earning NBA player or a top fashion model when you were a child, but you have grown up to be the same height as Uncle Al or Aunt Sue—and that's not tall enough.

Dreams alone are not enough when it comes to "creating the future." As professional life coach Diana Robinson says, "A dream is a goal without legs." And without legs, that goal is going nowhere. Dreaming is the first step to creating the future you want, but making dreams come true requires planning and hard work. Suppose you want to become a fashion designer because you like

Hey! I do!

clothes and people always tell you you look good. As you continue through college, however, you will come to understand the nuts and bolts of the fashion design business. The fashion industry might be challenging to break into, but that doesn't mean you should abandon your dream. You must find a reality-based path to help you turn your dreams into goals. Just dreaming isn't enough.

I wonder how I can start doing that . . .

Dreams are exciting; you can let your imagination run wild. Goals are real; you must work out how to actually achieve your dreams. Goal setting is an important part of the life management skills this book will help you develop. Your goals may not seem at all clear to you right now, but the important thing is to learn that there's a right way and a wrong way to go about goal setting. The best way to ensure that the goals you set will serve you well is to make sure you *FOCUS*. Here's a brief overview of what that means.

F **Fit.** Your goal must fit your values, your character, and who you are as a person. Goals that conflict with any of these things will not only be difficult to accomplish, but they just won't work. If your goal is to become a writer for a travel magazine because you love adventure, but you have a fear of flying, you're in trouble.

O **Ownership.** You must own your goal: see it, taste it, want it! It must be your goal, not someone else's goal for you. Ask yourself: Does the thought of achieving this goal get me fired up? Do I genuinely own this goal or do I feel I ought to have this goal because it sounds good or pleases someone else?

C **Concreteness.** For any goal to be effective, it must be real. In other words, you must be able to describe your goal—and it's ultimate outcome—in complete and specific detail, including your deadline for accomplishing it. "To run a mile in less than six minutes by March 4th" is much more concrete than "to eventually run faster." The more concrete, the better.

U **Usefulness.** Goals must have utility, or usefulness. They must serve a purpose, and that purpose should be tied to your long-term vision of the person you want to become. For example, if you want to work for an international corporation some day, it would be useful to begin studying a foreign language now.

Maybe I should sign up for that sketch design class I've heard about.

S **Stretch.** In the business world, people talk about stretch goals. These are goals that require employees to stretch beyond their usual limits to achieve something more challenging. The key to stretching is to find a good balance between being realistic and being challenged. Goals must be based in reality, but also offer you a chance to grow beyond the person you currently are.

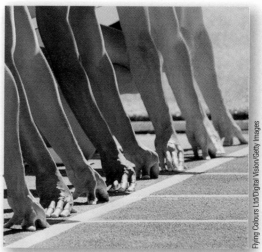

> ❝ What you get by achieving your goals is not as important as what you become by achieving your goals."
>
> **Zig Ziglar, Motivational speaker, writer, and trainer**

Flying Colours Ltd/Digital Vision/Getty Images

Goals should be set for different time frames in your life to include both short- and long-term goals. Once your long-term goals are set (though they may shift over time as *you* shift over time), you will then want to set some short-term goals, which act as intermediate steps to achieving your long-term goals.

Long-Term Goals What do I want to accomplish…	Short-Term Goals What do I want to accomplish…
In my lifetime?	This year?
In the next twenty years?	This month?
In the next ten years?	This week?
In the next three to five years?	Today?

College Success: You Make the Call

What does it mean to succeed? Actually, success is difficult to define, and different people define success differently. Right now in college, you may think of success in terms of your future income. But is success simply about material wealth? Is it about fame? Status?

???

CURIOSITY: *HOW RAPT ARE YOU?*

Stop Tweeting. Close your Facebook. Turn off your smartphone. Crank down the iTunes, and listen up. Attention is a hot new topic that neuroscientists are focusing on.

According to attention expert Winifred Gallagher in her book *Rapt: Attention and the Focused Life*, today we live in a distraction-rich world. "People don't understand that attention is a finite resource, like money. Do you want to invest your cognitive cash on endless Twittering or Net surfing or couch potatoing? You're constantly making choices, and your choices determine your experience." "Multitasking is a myth. You cannot do two things at once. It's either this or that," Gallagher claims.

Our brains can switch between tasks at astonishing speed, and switching makes us feel efficient. But try this experiment: read this section out loud while you type something else. Just how efficient are you?

© Stephen Coburn, 2009. Used under license from Shutterstock.com

Here's a fascinating notion of Gallagher's. If you look back at your life, you'll see that who you are is based largely on what you've chosen to pay attention to. In what ways might that be true for you? Your life, Gallagher says, is the sum of what you focus on.

In the "Age of Distraction," is it possible to lead a focused life? Learning how to focus—really focus—like any other skill takes discipline and effort. It takes tremendous brain power to ignore all the "incomings" that hit us every day. We must learn to deliberately create our own "distraction-proof personal pods" to do it. Her recommendation? Spend the first 90 minutes of every day concentrating on your most important task. During that time, don't answer e-mails, don't Google, don't text, don't make phone calls—just focus. Paying attention to how you pay attention leads to a fuller, richer, more successful life.[14]

According to motivational author Robert Collier, "Success is the sum of small efforts, repeated day in and day out." Perhaps to you, success is somewhere off in the distant future, and it happens more or less suddenly, like winning the lottery. Actually, success begins right now. You should be the one to define what success will look like in your life, but generally, success is *setting out to do something that's personally meaningful, and then being fully engaged while doing it.* It's that simple.

In order to understand your own definition of success in college, first you need to ask yourself why you're here. Why *did* you come—or return—to college, anyway? Do you want to develop into a more interesting, well-rounded, educated human being? Are you working toward a degree that leads to a specific career? Do you have children and want an education in order give them a better life? Did your mom or dad tell you that college wasn't optional?

We will assume that part of your definition of succeeding in college includes *graduating* from college. This book will provide you with an honest look at what that takes, including many opportunities to assess yourself in these areas. It will also offer an array of tools you can use throughout your college career and in your life beyond college.

Graduating from College: What It Takes

| ? challenge | 66 reaction | * insight | ! action |

Challenge: What does it take to succeed in college? List five things you see as essential traits or characteristics.

Reaction: _____ _____ _____ _____ _____

EXERCISE 1.7

College Success Factors

Many factors (besides past grades and entrance test scores) impact your success in college. Read down this list and ask yourself how you measure up in each of these areas. Mark an honest response from 1 to 7. If you're just beginning college and you're unsure about how you'll do, use your habits in the past to gauge your responses.

1	2	3	4	5	6	7
NO!	NO	No	Maybe/Sometimes	Yes	YES	YES!

_____ **Ability to adapt.** Are you the type of person who thrives in new environments? Do you enjoy meeting new classmates, new professors, and new counselors? In general, do you like—and do well—with change?

_____ **Attitude.** Do you have a positive attitude toward your education? Do you want to be here? Are you motivated to learn and grow? Are you willing to do the hard work involved in earning a college degree? Are you respectful of your instructors, your fellow students, and yourself?

_____ **Maturity.** Are you emotionally mature? Are you willing to display the level of maturity required to manage your college education over time and earn a degree?

(continued)

Maybe I should work on my score on this one.

_____ Class attendance. Do you have a good track record of attending class in the past? Are you willing to commit to attending each of your college classes regularly, regardless of whether or not you actually *feel* like attending on a particular day? Did you know that class attendance is a major predictor of college success?

_____ Study habits. Do you spend enough time studying? Do you study until you understand the material or do you simply study until you're out of time or need to move on to the next thing? Are you willing to make the necessary commitment to time spent studying?

_____ Note-taking skills. Note-taking is not an ability we're born with. It's a skill that must be learned and can be taught to just about anyone. How complete and comprehensive are your notes? Do you work with them after class (color-coding, retyping, and so on)? Do you work with your notes so that they're useful aids at exam time?

_____ Academic support services. Do you know what resources are available on campus to help you with academic issues? Have you visited any offices that provide support services on your campus to familiarize yourself with them? Are you willing to use a tutor to help with a particular course that overwhelms you?

_____ Personal support system. How strong is your personal support system? Who cares about your success in college? Do you have parents, siblings, and friends who support you, encourage you, and ask how you're doing? How willing are you to make friends on campus who also value academic success?

_____ Faculty connections. Do you plan to interact with your instructors? Are you interested in knowing more about your professors, their backgrounds, and their academic interests beyond the particular class you're taking with them? Are you willing to visit your instructors during their office hours if you are having difficulty with a class? Would you consider finding a mentor among your instructors?

_____ Campus connection. Are you connected to people and events on your campus? Are you involved in any co-curricular activities in which you interact with others? Do you plan to participate in or attend on-campus events? Sometimes students unknowingly fall prey to the PCP (parking lot, class, parking lot) syndrome. They're only on campus for their classes, and as soon as class is over, they're outta there. Believe it or not, connecting to your campus, other students, and your instructors is critical to your success.

_____ Time management skills. Are you capable of managing your time effectively so that the important things—not necessarily just the urgent or exciting, fun things—get completed? Do you use a specific system for time management? Are you willing to learn these skills? Do you understand that time management is really about energy management?

_____ Money management skills. How good are you at managing your money? Are you currently debt-free aside from any student loans required to attend college? Some students fall into the trap of using their school loans or grants to pay off credit card debt. Or they work far too many hours, which takes time away from their studies and makes academic success difficult to achieve. While managing your money isn't an academic skill, per se, not knowing how to do it can substantially impact your college career.

Now add up your scores on each item for a final tally. While this list isn't exhaustive, these factors are vital to college success. If your score was 60 or higher, you're in good shape. If not, take a close look at the areas that could affect your college success, read more about them in this book, and develop insights that lead to more effective action.

Some students think a college degree is a simple financial transaction. Not so. There's much more to it than that. A college education requires more than a financial commitment. It requires you to invest your ability, your intellect, your drive, your effort—and yourself.

Did you notice that most of the things listed in Exercise 1.7 are not talents you're simply born with? That's the good news. These factors that support your goal of graduating from college are things you can become better at if you are committed to doing so. And in making commitments to improving these factors *now*, you are making a commitment to graduate from college *later*.

The Bad News: Obstacles along the Way

Getting accepted to college is a good thing! You should feel proud. But realistically, the distance between getting accepted to college and graduating from college is considerable, and the journey can be both exhilarating and discouraging at times. Of all the college students who began as first-year students in 1992, only two-thirds had graduated eight years later.[15]

Risk factors include working more than thirty hours per week, going to school part-time, being a single parent or having children at home, and being a first-generation college student.[16] The important thing to keep in mind as you think about risk factors is that they alone cannot determine your ultimate level of success. Don't throw in the towel now if you had a child at age sixteen or are working thirty-five hours per week off campus. These factors are presented merely as information to assist you on your journey. They are simply *predictors*—not *determiners*. Only you can determine your outcomes in life, and that includes college.

It's worth taking a close look at these success inhibitors now, rather than becoming a statistic yourself later. Your effort, attitude, and willingness to get any help you need to succeed are all vital. Henry Ford was right: "Whether you think you can or you can't, you're right."

The Good News: Benefits at the End of the Road

Regardless of how you choose to define success as it pertains to your college experience, it's a fact that there are plenty of benefits to graduating from a college or university. Here's a quick look at some of them:

1. **Higher earning potential.** On average, college graduates earn twice as much income as their peers with only a high school diploma (see Figure 1.3).[17]

2. **Lower unemployment rates.** College graduates are more employable than their non-degreed peers. This is especially helpful during cyclic downturns in the economy, when many people—even talented and committed employees—find themselves out of work.

> " Students' expectations must match reality, they must be challenged, and they must make connections with their teachers and their peers."
>
> **Dr. Vincent Tinto, expert on higher education**

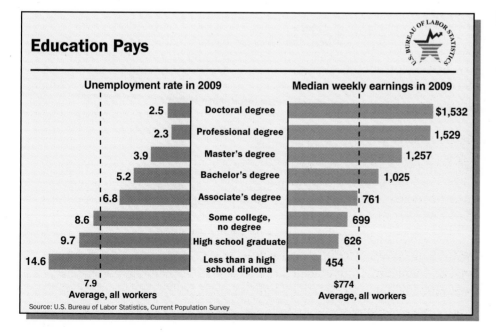

Education Pays

U.S. BUREAU OF LABOR STATISTICS

Unemployment rate in 2009		Median weekly earnings in 2009
2.5	Doctoral degree	$1,532
2.3	Professional degree	1,529
3.9	Master's degree	1,257
5.2	Bachelor's degree	1,025
6.8	Associate's degree	761
8.6	Some college, no degree	699
9.7	High school graduate	626
14.6	Less than a high school diploma	454
7.9 Average, all workers		$774 Average, all workers

Source: U.S. Bureau of Labor Statistics, Current Population Survey

FIGURE 1.3

Education, Earnings, and Employment: The Quantifiable Value of a College Degree

BOX 1.2 | Campus Resources: HELP Is Not a Four-Letter Word

It's not uncommon for new college students to feel isolated, even at a small school. Everything about your college experience is new, and you're adjusting gradually. As you adjust, remember that everyone needs a little help sometimes. Whatever the problem, your campus has all kinds of resources available for the taking, but you must take them. They won't come to you.

Social Connections

How can I meet other students? Does your campus have a Student Center, Student Union, or University Center? Take advantage of favorite gathering spots on campus. Not only can you meet people, but you can also scan the bulletin boards for information. If you're finding it hard to meet people, could it be because you're not around? To meet people, it helps to be where they are.

Academic Resources

How can I learn more about how I learn? Check to see if your campus has a Learning Center, an office that helps with learning disabilities, or a place you can go to fill out a learning style instrument. If writing is a struggle, look for your campus's Writing Center. If your calculus class is giving you fits, find the Math Learning Center. Or particular courses may offer what's called Supplemental Instruction, extra help beyond class sessions with basic principles or homework assignments. And get to know your academic advisor as if she or he were your best friend. That person can save you time and money and steer you toward classes in which you're most likely to be successful.

Adjustment

What if I need a counselor? College is a time of accelerated personal development and wonderful discoveries. But it may also be a time when you face challenging issues, such as leaving the comfort zone of your family; breaking up or beginning a new romance; or dealing with feelings of anxiety, isolation, or depression. The Counseling Center on your campus can help you work through a variety of issues. Many students—more than ever, many colleges report—are taking advantage of what Counseling Centers have to offer. And if you find yourself in the middle of a real crisis, call the campus hotline for immediate help.

Finances

Where can I find information about financial aid or get help with money problems? Your campus Financial Aid Office can help with loans, scholarships, and grants to pay for college. If you have a financial emergency—you lost the lease on an apartment, the residence halls are full, and you'll be living out of your car—help is available from the Red Cross or Salvation Army. If it's a matter of just blowing your budget, you can find advice, often free, from consumer credit agencies. Your campus may also offer free workshops on managing your money through a Learning Center or Student Success Center.

Logistics

How can I find my way around? Some universities are like small cities. Often you can download a campus map from the college's website that will help. Even though you will look like a tourist, carry it around to lower your stress level when you need to find something for the first time.

Technology

What if I have a technology meltdown? The new version of the old "my dog ate my homework" story relates to numerous variations on a theme: technology crashing. Your campus may not have round-the-clock advice from techies, but the Computer Help Desk can often solve what sounds like a complicated problem with simple advice. Also, use the campus computer labs. You can make good use of short blocks of time—or long ones—between classes.

Health

Are health services available to students? Many campuses have a Student Health Center where you can find a range of free or inexpensive services—everything from flu shots to strep throat tests to birth control advice if you're sexually active. Join the recreation center, if your campus has one, or an intramural team, coach a children's soccer team, or devote some time to exercise each day to stay healthy.

Majors and Careers

What do I want to be when I grow up? Thinking ahead to a career is sometimes difficult when so much is going on. Sometimes a career is nothing like you imagined—or preparing for one entails much more than you'd predict. Become an intern to try out a career or visit your campus's Career Center. Experts there can give you diagnostic tests to help you discover a major and career for which you are well-suited.

Et cetera

Where can I buy my books? Textbooks are a significant investment these days, and it's important to buy the right editions for your classes. Buying books online may save you money, although you'll have to wait for shipment. The bookstore is a much quicker option, and it's a good idea to find out where it is, no matter where you buy your books. You'll most likely need it for other school supplies.

What if I'm in need of Campus Security? If you feel unsafe walking to your car late at night or you need information about parking permits on campus, check with the Campus Security or Public Safety Office. They're there for your protection.

What's the bottom line? Get to know your campus and its full range of offerings—and take advantage of everything that's in place to help you be as academically successful as possible.

3. **Wisdom.** College students have the opportunity to gain understanding about a broad range of topics—politics, sociology, and history, to name a few. A well-educated person knows Sigmund Freud's contribution to psychological theory, Charles Darwin's contribution to evolutionary theory, and Adam Smith's contribution to economic theory. But beyond theories, facts, and dates, a well-educated person knows how to think critically, contribute to society, and manage his or her life.

4. **Insight.** College students have the opportunity to understand themselves better as they participate in the academic, social, and co-curricular opportunities of higher education.

5. **True scholarship.** College students have the opportunity to become lifelong learners. True scholarship is not about making the grade. It's about becoming the best student-learner you can be—inside or outside of the classroom.

6. **Lifelong friendships.** Many college graduates report that some of their strongest lifelong relationships were formed during their time at college. Choosing to attend college and choosing a specific major puts you in touch with a network of people who share your specific interests.

This Course Has a Proven Track Record

If you're reading this book, there's a good chance you're enrolled in a first-year seminar course. It may be called "Freshman Seminar," "First-Year Forum," "University 101," "First-Year Experience," "College Success," "A Learning Community," or any of a host of other names. These courses are designed to introduce you to college life, familiarize you with your own campus, and help you refine your academic skills. Do they work? According to experts, "In short, the weight of evidence indicates that FYS [first-year seminar] participation has statistically significant and substantial, positive effects on a student's successful transition to college. . . . And on a considerable array of other college experiences known to be related directly and indirectly to bachelor's degree completion."[18] In general, students who participate in first-year seminars complete more credit hours, adjust to college more quickly, become more involved in campus life, view themselves and their skills more accurately, enjoy and appreciate their college experience, and ultimately, graduate. That's what this course is about. Now it's up to you!

> " Ability is what you're capable of doing. Motivation determines what you do. Attitude determines how well you do it."
>
> **Lou Holtz, former college football coach and ESPN sports analyst**

? **challenge**　" **reaction**　* **insight**　! **action**

Now What Do You Think?

1. At the beginning of this chapter, Gloria Gonzales, an excited but anxious student, was about to begin her college career. Now after reading this chapter, would you respond differently to any of the questions you answered about the "FOCUS Challenge Case"? Knowing what you know now, how would you advise her? Write a paragraph ending to the story, incorporating your best advice.

(continued)

2. What do you think about the Challenge → Reaction → Insight → Action system? Does it make sense? Do you understand how it works? Write a few paragraphs describing it in your own words.

3. What types of things fascinate you and fire up your intrinsic motivation? Why are they intrinsic motivators for you?

4. What actions can you take to become more of a *learner* and less of a *performer,* particularly in your most challenging class this term?

5. Think about one of your goals for the future. Run it through a quick check to ensure that it's a *FOCUS* goal. Circle the appropriate answer:
   - Does this goal fit me?   Yes   No
   - Do I really want this goal? Do I own it?   Yes   No
   - Does my goal have concrete details and deadlines?   Yes   No
   - Is this goal useful to me? Does it serve a purpose?   Yes   No
   - Does this goal stretch me? Is it challenging, yet achievable?   Yes   No

   If you answered "no" to any of the previous questions, your goal needs to be more *FOCUS*ed. What must you do to make that happen?

6. Why did you choose to attend college? Be as specific as you can in listing the reason(s). Review your list and put an asterisk next to the most positive, goal-oriented reasons. After reading this chapter, can you identify your greatest challenges and what you'll do to overcome them?

What did you Learn?

On a scale of 1 to 10, answer the following questions now that you've completed this chapter.

1 = not very/not much/very little/low   10 = very/a lot/very much/high

In hindsight, how much did you already know about this subject before reading the chapter?

1   2   3   4   5   6   7   8   9   10

Can you answer these questions about goals and dreams more fully now that you've read the chapter?

1. **What is the difference between a learner and a performer?**

2. **What is the difference between intrinsic and extrinsic motivation?**

3. **Which four factors—all beginning with the letter "C"—are a part of intrinsic motivation—and your college success?**

How useful might the information in this chapter be to you? How much do you think this information might affect your success in college?

1   2   3   4   5   6   7   8   9   10

How much do you think this information might affect your career success after college?

1   2   3   4   5   6   7   8   9   10

How long did it actually take you to complete this chapter (both the reading and writing tasks)? _____ Hour(s) _____ Minutes

 Challenge Yourself Online Quiz. To find out how much you've learned, access the CourseMate via www.cengagebrain.com/shop/ISBN/0495906425 to take the Challenge Yourself Online Quiz.

Take a minute to compare these answers to your answers from the "Readiness Check" at the beginning of this chapter. What gaps exist between the similar questions? How might these gaps between what you thought before starting the chapter and what you now think after completing the chapter affect how you approach the next chapter in this book?

I listened to the mp3 chapter summary and watched the "Inside the FOCUS Studio" TV show available on the CourseMate via www.cengagebrain.com/shop/ISBN/0495906425. Great way to review before taking the online quiz!

2 Learning about Learning

You're about to discover . . .
- ✔ How learning changes your brain
- ✔ How people are intelligent in different ways
- ✔ How you learn through your senses
- ✔ How to become a more efficient and effective learner

©Larry Harwood Photography. Property of Cengage Learning.

READINESS CHECK | What do you **Know?**

Before beginning this chapter, take a moment to answer these questions. Your answers will help you assess how ready you are to focus.

1 = not very/not much/very little/low   10 = very/a lot/very much/high

How much do you already know?

Based on reading the "You're about to discover. . ." list and skimming this chapter, how much do you think you probably already know about this chapter's subject?

1 2 3 4 5 6 7 8 9 10

See if you can answer these questions about learning to learn before you read.

1. **What does the term "multiple intelligences" mean? Can you name three different types of intelligences?**

2. **What does VARK stand for? Can you identify the letters as they relate to students' preferences for taking in information?**

How motivated are you to learn more?

In general, how motivated are you to learn more by reading this chapter?

1 2 3 4 5 6 7 8 9 10

How much do you think this information might affect your success in college?

1 2 3 4 5 6 7 8 9 10

How much do you think this information might affect your career success after college?

1 2 3 4 5 6 7 8 9 10

How ready are you to read now?

How ready are you to focus on this chapter—physically, intellectually, and emotionally? Circle a number for each aspect of your readiness to focus.

1 2 3 4 5 6 7 8 9 10

If any of your answers is below a 10, you might want to pay attention to whatever is distracting you before you start reading. For example, if you're feeling scattered, take a few moments to settle down and focus.

Finally, how long do you think it will take you to complete this chapter from start to finish?

_____ Hour(s) _____ Minutes

Tammy Ko

Pleasantville H
Yearbook

How depressing!" Tammy Ko whispered under her breath as she walked out of her "Introduction to Criminology" class on a dark, rainy Thursday afternoon. *What's with him, anyway?* she asked herself pointedly about the professor.

University Program Description:

FORENSIC CHEMISTRY

purpose of law is forensic science. Forensic Scientists use empirical methods to gain objective data for use in chemistry focuses specifically on the composition, structure, and properties of matter, as well as the study of field of the Forensic discipline includes studies of DNA and other complex chemical compounds.

rapidly growing field of study, and has many possible career options, including: Crime Scene Investigator, Technologist/Technicians, Forensic Science Technician, Analyst, Medical Examiner, Toxicologist Forensic, Anthropologist, Fingerprint Examiner, Laboratory Director, and Professor.

Course Work

an Year
103 - General Chemistry I
106 - General Chemistry II
108 - Introduction to Chemistry Lab Research
1 - Introduction to Criminology
H 135 - Calculus I
H 136 - Calculus II
L 121 - General Biology
ctive - 3 credits

Sophomore Year
CHEM 331 - Organic C
CHEM 332 - Organic C
CHEM 337 - Practical
CHEM 338 - Practical
CJ 215 - Statistics fo
CJ 225 - Violence in
MATH 235 - Calculu
Electives - 6 credits

Junior Year
CHEM 417 - Ana
CHEM 418 - Ana
CHEM 420 - Pra
CHEM 451 - Ph
CHEM 452 - P
CHEM 455 - E
CHEM 483 -
PES 213 - G
Electives - 6

Senior Year
CHEM 401 - Inorganic Chemistry I
CHEM 402 - Inorganic Chemistry Laboratory
CHEM 495 - Chemistry Seminar I
CHEM 496 - Chemistry Seminar II
Chemistry electives (upper division) - 9 credits
Electives - 12 credits

ECTIVES
CSI: Fact or Fantasy?
Interview and Interrogation Techniques
Professionalism and Ethics
Investigation of Injury and Death
Crime Scene & Crime Lab
Psychosocial of Forensic Science
Legal Aspects of Forensic Science

-166-

Tammy was a first-semester student at a large state campus several hours from her tiny hometown, where she'd been a popular student. If you leafed through her high school yearbook, you'd see Tammy's picture on nearly every page. There Tammy had been a big fish in a small pond, but now it was the other way around.

Even though she found college life at the large state university overwhelming, Tammy was excited about her major, forensic chemistry. The crime shows on TV were her favorites. She watched them all each week. She rationalized how much time it took by thinking of it as career development. The fun was picturing herself as

an investigator solving headline cases: "Man Slain, Found in City Park" or "Modern Day 'Jack the Ripper' Terrorizes Las Vegas." She could envision herself hunched over laboratory equipment, testing intently for fibers or DNA, and actually breaking the case.

When she registered for classes, her academic advisor had told her that taking an "Introduction to Criminology" course from the sociology department would be a good idea. "It'll teach you how to think," he'd said, "and it'll give you the background you need to understand the criminal mind. At the end of this class," he said, "you'll know if you really want to pursue a career in forensics." *Maybe it would teach me how to think,* Tammy thought to herself now that the term was underway, *if only I could understand the professor. Forget understanding the criminal mind—I'd just like a glimpse into his!*

Professor Caldwell was quiet and reserved, and he seemed a bit out of touch. He dressed as if he hadn't bought a new piece of clothing in as many years as he'd been at the university. In class, he was very articulate, knowledgeable, and organized with his handouts neatly piled on the desk, and he covered each day's material methodically point by

Dr. Caldwell

point. Tammy wished he'd leave his notes occasionally to explore fascinating, related tangents. Tammy had always preferred teachers who created exciting things to do in class over teachers who went completely by the book.

Tammy's biggest complaint about Professor Caldwell was that he only talked about *theories* of criminology. When was he ever going to get to the hands-on part of the course? She couldn't help thinking, *When will we stop talking about theories and start working on real cases—like the ones on all those TV shows?*

To make matters worse, learning from lectures was not Tammy's strong suit. She hadn't done well on the first exam because she'd had to resort to memorizing things that didn't make much sense to her, and her D grade showed it. The exam consisted of one question: "Compare and contrast two theories of criminology discussed in class thus far." Tammy hated essay tests. She was at her best on tests with right or wrong answers, like true-false or multiple-choice questions. Making sense out of spoken words that go by very quickly during a lecture and trying to psych out professors' preferred answers on essay tests were challenges to her.

But her "Introduction to Criminology" class was far from hands-on. In fact, Tammy had noticed that many of her teachers preferred talking about things to doing things. They seemed to take more interest in theories than in the real world. *Too bad, she thought, the real world is where exciting things happen.* Although she hated to admit it, sometimes Tammy couldn't wait for her college career to be over so that she could begin her real career.

A few of Tammy's friends had taken Professor Caldwell's classes. "Just try and memorize the stuff; that's all you can do," they'd advised her. Regardless of what they happened to be talking about, somehow the conversation always came around to Professor Caldwell and how impossible it was to learn in his classes.

GREETINGS FROM PLEASANTVILLE

Shot To Death

Name: TAMMY KO

ESSAY TEST
INTRO TO CRIMINOLOGY
DR. CALDWELL

65% D

QUESTION: COMPARE AND CONTRAST TWO THEORIES OF CRIMINOLOGY DISCUSSED IN CLASS THUS FAR

Classical Theory was first developed by Cesar Beccarhia in the century. Classical theory says that people engage in a social ideal. They must balance between freedom and happiness. Classical theory also describes special and general deterrence. General deterrence is punishing a person for a crime. Special deterrence is making examples of people so that others don't do the same thing. Neoclassical theory was developed in the century and includes the concepts of free will and penitentiaries. These systems are the basis for the US Government system of justice. The positivist approach includes the ideas of free will and determinism. It says that there is a fundamental difference between criminals and non-criminals. It also says that there are many factors that contribute to The positivist approach also suggests that there is subjectivism in social In other words, social science is based on the viewpoint of each individual not specific facts or data. Finally the biological theories suggest that criminals biologically superior to non-criminals

What Do You Think?

1. Why is Tammy having difficulty learning in her "Introduction to Criminology" class?

2. Is Tammy smart? If so, in what ways? What sensory modality does Tammy prefer for taking in information? Does she learn best by watching, listening, reading and writing, or doing?

3. How would you describe Professor Caldwell's teaching style?

4. What should Tammy do to become a better learner in Professor Caldwell's class?

Go to the HEAD of the Class: Learning and the Brain

? challenge 〉 " reaction * insight 〉 ! action

Challenge: What is learning? Can you define the process?

Reaction: _____

EXERCISE 2.1

Assessing Your Views on Learning

The following statements represent common student views on learning. Think about each statement, and mark it true or false based on your honest opinion.

I'd say number 3 is definitely true—at least for me!

_____ 1. Learning is often hard work and really not all that enjoyable.

_____ 2. Memorization and learning are basically the same thing.

_____ 3. The learning done in school is often gone in a few weeks or months.

_____ 4. In college, most learning takes place in class.

_____ 5. Learning is usually the result of listening to an instructor lecture or reading a textbook.

_____ 6. The best way to learn is by working alone.

_____ 7. Most students know intuitively how they learn best.

_____ 8. Teachers control what students learn.

_____ 9. Learning only deals with subjects taught in school.

_____10. The learning pace is controlled by the slowest learner in the class.

You probably noticed that many of these statements attempt to put learning in a negative light. How many did you mark true? This chapter will help you understand more about learning as a process and about yourself as a learner. As you read, your goal should be to use the insights you gain to become a better learner.

L et's start our exploration of the learning process close to home—in our own heads. What's going on up there, anyway? While your hands are busy manipulating test tubes in chemistry lab, or your eyes are watching your psychology professor's PowerPoint presentation, or your ears are taking in a lecture on American politics, what's your brain up to? The answer? Plenty.

Use It or Lose It

The human brain consists of a complex web of connections between neurons. This web grows in complexity as it incorporates new knowledge. But if the connections are not reinforced frequently, they degenerate. As you learn new things, you work to hardwire these connections, making them less susceptible to degeneration. When your professors repeat portions of the previous week's lecture or assign follow-up homework to practice material covered in class, they're helping you to form connections between neurons through repeated use—or, in other words, to learn. Repetition is vital to learning. You must use and reuse information in order to hardwire it.

Giving your brain the exercise it needs—now and in your years after college—will help you form connections between neurons that, if you keep using them, will last a lifetime. From a biological point of view, that's what being a lifelong learner means. The age-old advice "use it or lose it" is true when it comes to learning.

Ask Questions and Hardwire Your Connections

Your professors have been studying their disciplines for years, perhaps decades. They have developed extensive hardwired connections between their brain neurons. They are *experts*.

By contrast, you are a *novice* to whatever discipline you're studying. You've not yet developed the brain circuitry that your professors have developed. This realization points to a potential problem. Sometimes professors are so familiar with what they already know from years of traveling the same neuron paths that what you're learning for the first time seems obvious to them. Without even realizing it, they can expect what is familiar to them to be obvious to you. Think of how challenging it is when you try to teach something that you understand thoroughly to another person who doesn't, like teaching someone who has never used a computer before how to upload an assignment.

Since you're a novice, you may not understand everything your professors say. Ask questions, check, clarify, probe, and persist until you do understand. Sometimes your confusion is not due to a lack of knowledge, but a lack of the *correct* knowledge. For example, you may study for a test by doing only one thing—reading and re-reading the textbook. Actually, it's important to be familiar with an array of study tools and choose the ones that work best for you.

Think of it this way. Some of the neural connections you brought with you to college are positive and useful, and some are counterproductive. When you learn, you not only add new connections, but you rewire some old connections. While you're in college, you're under construction![1]

Don't look now, but you're a very busy person! If you were watching a movie of your life at this moment, what would the scene look like? A cell phone in your hand, a website open on your computer screen, your iPod plugged in, and this book propped in your lap? So much to do, so little time! All we can hope for is that some scientist somewhere will invent a way to get a bigger, better brain! But let's face it: brain enhancement surgery won't be available any time soon.

Even so, scientists have been busy recently learning more about this heady organ of ours. Now in new and fascinating ways, the sciences of biology and psychology are joining hands to study the human brain.[2]

What's the secret to a healthy brain? When we think of fitness, most of us think from the neck down—strong abs, bulging pecs, and tight glutes. But brain health tops them all. New evidence shows that physical exercise helps our brains shrug off damage, reinforce old neural networks, forge new ones, and ultimately result in a better brain!

Current research focuses on a protein called BDNF (for brain-derived neurotrophic factor). BDNF, which helps nerve cells in our brains grow and connect, is important for development in the womb, but it's also important in adult brains. Simply put: it helps us learn. According to researchers, rats that eat a high-calorie, fast-food diet and have a couch-potato lifestyle have less BDNF in their brains. Omega-3 fatty acids found in fish normalize BDNF levels and counteract learning disabilities in rats with brain injuries. Scientists are working to see if the same thing may be true for humans.[3]

"Exercise your brain. Nourish it well. And the earlier you start the better," scientists tell us.[4] New research indicates that education is a great way to nourish our brains. People who are less educated have twice the risk of getting Alzheimer's disease in later life, and less educated people who have ho-hum, nonchallenging jobs have three to four times the risk. According to researchers, "College seems to pay off well into retirement."[5] It can help you build a better brain!

Take Charge and Create the Best Conditions for Learning

© Collin Anderson/Blend Images/Corbis

" When we come to know something, we have performed an act that is as biological as when we digest something."

Henry Plotkin, *Darwin Machines and the Nature of Knowledge* (1994)

Throughout this discussion, we've been talking about internal processes in your brain. *Your* brain, not anyone else's. The bottom line is this: Learning must be *internally initiated*—by you. It can only be *externally encouraged*—by someone else. You're in charge of your own learning. Learning changes your brain.

Let's look at food as an analogy: If learning is a process that is as biological as digestion, then no one can learn for you, in the same way that no one can eat for you. The food in the refrigerator doesn't do you a bit of good unless you walk over, open the door, remove the object of your desire, and devour it. It's there for the taking, but you must make that happen. To carry the analogy further, you eat on a daily basis, right? "No thanks, I ate last week" is a senseless statement. Learning does for your brain what food does for your body. Nourish yourself!

Brain researchers tell us the best state for learning has ten conditions.

1. **You're intrinsically motivated (from within yourself) to learn material that is appropriately challenging.**

> **Examine where your motivation to learn comes from.** Are you *internally* motivated because you're curious about the subject and want to learn about it or externally motivated to get an A or avoid an F? Can you generate your own internal motivation, rather than relying on external motivators? This book has built-in reminders to boost your intrinsic motivation. Use them to your advantage as a learner.

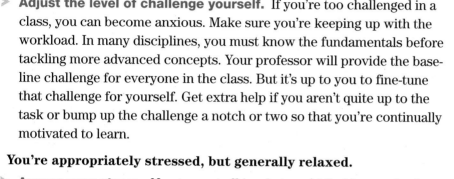
> **Adjust the level of challenge yourself.** If you're too challenged in a class, you can become anxious. Make sure you're keeping up with the workload. In many disciplines, you must know the fundamentals before tackling more advanced concepts. Your professor will provide the baseline challenge for everyone in the class. But it's up to you to fine-tune that challenge for yourself. Get extra help if you aren't quite up to the task or bump up the challenge a notch or two so that you're continually motivated to learn.

2. **You're appropriately stressed, but generally relaxed.**

> **Assess your stress.** No stress at all is what you'd find in a no-brainer course. Some stress is useful; it helps engage you in learning. How stressed are you—and why—when you get to class? Are you over-stressed because you haven't done the reading and hope you won't be called on? Prepare for class so that you're ready to jump in. Or are you understressed because you don't value the course material? Consider how the information can be useful to you—perhaps in ways you've never even thought of.

©Larry Harwood Photography. Property of Cengage Learning.

> **Attend to your overall physical state.** Are you taking care of your physical needs so that you can stay alert, keep up with the lecture, and participate in the discussion?

3. **You enter into a state researchers call "flow" when you're so totally absorbed in what you're doing that you lose track of everything else.**[6]

> **Identify the kinds of learning situations that help you "flow."** Do you get fully engaged by hands-on activities? Do you find that certain courses naturally capture your attention so that you're surprised when it's time for class to end? Understanding your own preferences as a learner are key here.

> **Think about what you can do as a learner to get yourself there.** Not all classes or subjects will naturally induce a flow state in you, so ask yourself what *you* can do to focus on learning and exclude distractions.

4. **You're curious about what you're learning, and you look forward to learning it.**

> **Get ready to learn by looking back and by looking ahead.** When you're about to cross the street, you must look both ways, right? Keep

Take Charge and Create the Best Conditions for Learning 33

that image in mind because that's what you should do before each class. What did class consist of last time? Can you predict what it will consist of next time?

Right! But Caldwell needs a major makeover!

> **Focus on substance, not style.** Despite society's obsession with attractiveness, grooming, and fashion, a student's job is to ask: What can I learn from this person? Passing judgment on physical appearance just encourages you to play the blame game and derails your learning.

5. **You're slightly confused, but only for a short time.**[7]

> **Use confusion as a motivator.** You may not be getting the lecture's main points because you don't understand new terms used along the way. Look them up early on in the learning process. Ask yourself what background information would help things click—and find out the answers to those questions.

> **Ask questions!** To your professor, questions indicate *interest*, not *idiocy*. Don't be afraid to probe more deeply into the material.

6. **You search for personal meaning and patterns.**

If I do become a CSI, I guess I might have to know some things about the criminal mind..

> **Ask yourself: What's in it for me?** Why is knowing this important? How can I use this information in the future? Instead of dismissing material that appears unrelated to your life, try figuring out how it *could* relate. You may be surprised!

> **Think about how courses relate to one another.** How does this new knowledge align with other things you're learning in other courses? Does sociology have anything to do with history? Psychology with economics?

7. **Your emotions are involved, not just your mind.**

> **Evaluate your attitudes and feelings.** Do you like the subject matter? Do you admire the teacher? Remember that high school teacher, the one whose class you just couldn't stand? Not every class will be your favorite. That's natural. But if a class turns you off as a learner, instead of allowing your emotions to take over, ask why and whether your feelings are in your best interest.

> **Make a deliberate decision to change negative feelings.** Fortunately, feelings can be changed. Hating a course or disliking a professor can only build resentment and threaten your success. It's possible to do a one-eighty and transform your negative emotions into positive energy.

" Personal participation is the universal principle of knowing."

Michael Polanyi, Hungarian-British scholar (1891–1976)

8. **You realize that as a learner you use what you already know in constructing new knowledge.**[8]

> **Remember that passive learning is an oxymoron.** When it comes to learning, you are the construction foreman, building on what you already know to construct new knowledge. You're not just memorizing facts someone else wants you to learn. You're a full partner in the learning process!

> **Remind yourself that constructing knowledge takes work.** No one ever built a house by simply sitting back or just hanging out. In your college courses, you must identify what you already know and blend new knowledge into the framework you've built in your mind. By constructing new knowledge, you are building yourself into a more sophisticated, more polished, and most certainly, more educated person.

9. **You understand that learning is both conscious and unconscious.**

> **Watch where your mind goes when it's off duty.** Does learning take place when you're not deliberately trying to learn? Some of what you learn will be immediately obvious to you, and some will dawn on you after class is over. Pay attention to your indirect learning and move it into your line of vision.

> **Remember that both kinds of learning are important.** Both conscious learning and unconscious learning count. There are no rules about when and where learning can occur.

10. **You're given a degree of choice in terms of what you learn, how you do it, and feedback on how you're doing.**

> **Make the most of the choices you're given.** College isn't a free-for-all in which you can take any classes you like toward earning a degree. However, which electives you choose will be up to you. Or if your instructor allows you to write a paper or shoot a video, choose the option that will be more motivating for you. When you receive an assignment, select a topic that fires you up. It's easier to generate energy to put toward choices you've made yourself.

" It is what we think we know already that often prevents us from learning."

Claude Bernard, French physiologist (1813–1878)

Reflect on yourself as a learner in your toughest class this term. How optimal are the conditions for learning? Put a checkmark in the box if any of the following conditions are present. If not, beside each item, write in a suggestion to help create the condition yourself and improve your own learning.

Ten Conditions for Optimal Learning   **Course Title:** _____

1. You're intrinsically motivated to learn material that is appropriately challenging.

2. You're appropriately stressed, but generally relaxed.

3. You enter into a state researchers call flow.

4. You're curious about what you're learning, and you look forward to learning it.

5. You're slightly confused, but only for a short time.

6. You search for personal meaning and patterns.

7. Your emotions are involved, not just your mind.   *Hating this class won't help me. I need to adjust my attitude.*

8. You realize that as a learner you use what you already know in constructing new knowledge.

9. You understand that learning is both conscious and unconscious.

10. You're given a degree of choice in terms of what you learn, how you do it, and feedback on how you're doing.

> **Use feedback to improve, and if feedback is not given, ask for it.** It's possible to get really good at doing something the wrong way. Take a golf swing or a swimming stroke, for example. Without someone intervening to give you feedback, it may be difficult to know how to improve. Your instructors will most likely write comments on your assignments to explain their grades. Assessing your work is their job; it's what they must do to help you improve. Take their suggestions to heart and try them out.

Multiple Intelligences: *How Are You Smart?*

? challenge > **" reaction**   *** insight** > **! action**

Challenge: Are people smart in different ways? How so?

Reaction: _____

Multiple Intelligences Self-Assessment

On each line, put checkmarks next to all the statements that best describe you.

Linguistic Intelligence: The capacity to use language to express what's on your mind and understand others ("word smart")

_____ I'm a good storyteller.

_____ I enjoy word games, puns, and tongue twisters.

_____ I'd rather listen to the radio than watch TV.

_____ I've recently written something I'm proud of.

_____ I can hear words in my head before I say or write them.

_____ When riding in the car, I sometimes pay more attention to words on billboards than I do to the scenery.

_____ In high school, I did better in English, history, or social studies than I did in math and science.

_____ I enjoy reading.

Logical-Mathematical Intelligence: The capacity to understand cause/effect relationships and to manipulate numbers ("number/reasoning smart")

_____ I can easily do math in my head.

_____ I enjoy brainteasers or puzzles.

_____ I like it when things can be counted or analyzed.

_____ I can easily find logical flaws in what others do or say.

_____ I think most things have rational explanations.

_____ Math and science were my favorite subjects in high school.

_____ I like to put things into categories.

_____ I'm interested in new scientific advances.

Spatial Intelligence: The capacity to represent the world visually or graphically ("picture smart")

_____ I like to take pictures of what I see around me.

_____ I'm sensitive to colors.

_____ My dreams at night are vivid.

_____ I like to doodle or draw.

_____ I'm good at navigating with a map.

_____ I can picture what something will look like before it's finished.

_____ In school, I preferred geometry to algebra.

_____ I often make my point by drawing a picture or diagram.

Bodily-Kinesthetic Intelligence: The capacity to use your whole body or parts of it to solve a problem, make something, or put on a production ("body smart")

_____ I regularly engage in sports or physical activities.

_____ I get fidgety when asked to sit for long periods of time.

_____ I get some of my best ideas while I'm engaged in a physical activity.

_____ I need to practice a skill in order to learn it, rather than just reading or watching a video about it.

_____ I enjoy being a daredevil.

_____ I'm a well-coordinated person.

_____ I like to think through things while I'm doing something else like running or walking.

_____ I like to spend my free time outdoors.

(continued)

Musical Intelligence: **The capacity to think in music, hear patterns and recognize, remember, and perhaps manipulate them ("music smart")**

_____ I can tell when a musical note is flat or sharp.

_____ I play a musical instrument.

_____ I often hear music playing in my head.

_____ I can listen to a piece of music once or twice, and then sing it back accurately.

_____ I often sing or hum while working.

_____ I like music playing while I'm doing things.

_____ I'm good at keeping time to a piece of music.

_____ I consider music an important part of my life.

Interpersonal Intelligence: **The capacity to understand other people ("people smart")**

_____ I prefer group activities to solo activities.

_____ Others think of me as a leader.

_____ I enjoy the challenge of teaching others something I like to do.

_____ I like to get involved in social activities at school, church, or work.

_____ If I have a problem, I'm more likely to get help than tough it out alone.

_____ I feel comfortable in a crowd of people.

_____ I have several close friends.

_____ I'm the sort of person others come to for advice about their problems.

> *My highest intelligence is in the Interpersonal category. That sounds about right.*

Intrapersonal Intelligence: **The capacity to understand yourself, who you are, and what you can do ("self-smart")**

_____ I like to spend time alone thinking about important questions in life.

_____ I have invested time in learning more about myself.

_____ I consider myself to be independent minded.

_____ I keep a journal of my inner thoughts.

_____ I'd rather spend a weekend alone than at a place with a lot of other people around.

_____ I've thought seriously about starting a business of my own.

_____ I'm realistic about my own strengths and weaknesses.

_____ I have goals for my life that I'm working on.

Naturalistic Intelligence: **The capacity to discriminate between living things and show sensitivity toward the natural world ("nature smart")**

_____ Environmental problems bother me.

_____ In school, I always enjoyed field trips to places in nature or away from class.

_____ I enjoy studying nature, plants, or animals.

_____ I've always done well on projects involving living systems.

_____ I enjoy pets.

_____ I notice signs of wildlife when I'm on a walk or hike.

_____ I can recognize types of plants, trees, rocks, birds, and so on.

_____ I enjoy learning about environmental issues.

Which intelligences have the most check marks? Write in the three intelligences in which you had the most number of check marks.

_____   _____   _____

Although this is an informal instrument, it can help you think about the concept of multiple intelligences, or MI. *How* are you smart?

Based on Armstrong, T. (1994). *Multiple intelligences in the classroom.* Alexandria, VA: Association for Supervision and Curriculum Development, pp. 18–20.

Have you ever noticed that people are smart in different ways? Consider the musical genius of Mozart, who published his first piano pieces at the age of five. Or think about Olympic Gold Medalist Lindsey Vonn, who learned to ski when she was two. Not many of us are as musically gifted as Mozart or as physically gifted as Lindsey Vonn, but we all have strengths. You may earn top grades in math, and not-so-top grades in English, and your best friend's grades may be just the opposite.

According to Harvard psychologist Howard Gardner, people can be smart in at least eight different ways. Most schools focus on particular types of intelligence, linguistic and logical-mathematical intelligence, reflecting the three R's: reading, writing, and 'rithmetic. But Gardner claims intelligence is actually multifaceted. It can't be measured by traditional one-dimensional standardized IQ tests and represented by a three-digit number: 100 (average), 130+ (gifted), or 150+ (genius). Gardner defines intelligence as "the ability to find and solve problems and create products of value in one or more cultural setting."[9] Figure 2.1 gives you an image for each of the eight Multiple Intelligence catetories to help you remember them.

So instead of asking the traditional question "How smart are you?" a better question is "How are you smart?" The idea is to find out *how*, and then apply this understanding of yourself to your academic work in order to achieve your best results.

Translate Content into Your Own Intelligences

Do you sometimes wonder why you can't remember things for exams? Some learning experts believe that memory is intelligence-specific. You may have a good memory for people's faces but a bad memory for their names. You may be able to remember the words of a country-western hit but not the dance steps that go with it. The Theory of Multiple Intelligences may explain why.[10]

(clockwise from top left): © Alan Merrigan, 2009. Used under license from Shutterstock.com; © Denisenko, 2009. Used under license from Shutterstock.com; © Mopic, 2009. Used under license from Shutterstock.com; © Morgan Lane Photography, 2009. Used under license from Shutterstock.com; © william casey, 2009. Used under license from Shutterstock.com; © Sean Nel, 2009. Used under license from Shutterstock.com; © Yuri Arcurs, 2009. Used under license from Shutterstock.com; © YAKOBCHUK VASYL, 2009. Used under license from Shutterstock.com.

FIGURE 2.1

Multiple Intelligences

How are you smart?

Since my highest intelligence is interpersonal, I should probably study for Professor Caldwell's class with someone else. Talking about things would help.

Examine your own behaviors in class. If your instructors use their linguistic intelligence to teach, as many do, and your intelligences lie elsewhere, can you observe telltale signs of your frustration? Instead of zeroing in on the lecture, do you fidget (bodily-kinesthetic), doodle (spatial), or socialize (interpersonal)? You may need to translate the information into your own personal intelligences, just as you would if your professor speaks French and you speak English. If you're having learning problems in one of your classes, it may be partially due to a case of mismatched intelligences between yours and your instructor's.

Let's say one of your courses this term is "Introduction to Economics," and the current course topic is the Law of Supply and Demand. Basically, "the theory

FIGURE 2.2

Study Techniques for Different Intelligences

Linguistic --→	1. Rewrite your class notes. 2. Record yourself reading through your class notes and play it as you study. 3. Read the textbook chapter aloud.
Logical Mathematical --→	1. Create hypothetical conceptual problems to solve. 2. Organize chapter or lecture notes into logical flow. 3. Analyze how the textbook chapter is organized and why.
Spatial --→	1. Draw a map that demonstrates your thinking on course material. 2. Illustrate your notes by drawing diagrams and charts. 3. Mark up your textbook to show relationships between concepts.
Bodily–Kinesthetic --→	1. Study course material while engaged in physical activity. 2. Practice skills introduced in class or in the text. 3. Act out a scene based on chapter content.
Musical --→	1. Create musical memory devices by putting words into well-known melodies. 2. Listen to music while you're studying. 3. Sing or hum as you work.
Interpersonal --→	1. Discuss course material with your classmates in class. 2. Organize a study group that meets regularly. 3. Meet a classmate before or after class for coffee and course conversation.
Intrapersonal --→	1. Keep a journal to track your personal reactions to course material. 2. Study alone and engage in internal dialogue about course content. 3. Coach yourself on how to best study for a challenging class.
Naturalistic --→	1. Search for applications of course content in the natural world. 2. Study outside (if weather permits and you can resist distractions). 3. Go to a physical location that exemplifies course material (for example, a park for your geology course).

of supply and demand describes how prices vary as a result of a balance between product availability at each price (supply) and the desires of those with purchasing power at each price (demand)."[11] To understand this law, you could read the textbook (linguistic); study mathematical formulas (logical-mathematical); examine charts and graphs (spatial); observe the Law of Supply and Demand in the natural world, through the fluctuating price of gasoline, for example (naturalist); look at the way the Law of Supply and Demand is expressed in your own body, using food as a metaphor (bodily-kinesthetic); reflect on how and when you might be able to afford something you desperately want, like a certain model of car (intrapersonal); or write (or find) a song that helps you understand the law (musical). You needn't try all eight ways, but it's intriguing to speculate about various ways to learn that may work for you, rather than assuming you're doomed because your intelligences don't match your instructor's.

Use Intelligence-Oriented Study Techniques

What if your strongest intelligence is different from the one through which course material is presented? What can you do about it? Take a look at Figure 2.2 for techniques for studying using different intelligences. Tweaking the way you study may make a world of difference.

Develop Your Weaker Intelligences

It's important to cultivate your weaker intelligences. Why? Because life isn't geared to one kind of intelligence. It's complex. A photo journalist for *National Geographic*, for example, might need linguistic intelligence, spatial intelligence, interpersonal intelligence, and naturalist intelligence. Being well-rounded, as the expression goes, is truly a good thing. Artist Pablo Picasso once said, "I am always doing that which I cannot do, in order that I may learn how to do it." Remember that no one is naturally intelligent in all eight areas. Each individual is a unique blend of intelligences, and most people are strong in only two or three. But the Theory of Multiple Intelligences claims that we all have the capacity to develop all of our eight intelligences further. That's good news!

How Do You Perceive and Process Information?

? challenge **❝ reaction** **✳ insight** **! action**

Challenge: You've lived with yourself for many years now, but how well do you know yourself as a learner?

Reaction: List as many descriptive phrases about your learning preferences as you can. For example, you might write, "I learn best when I listen to an instructor lecture" or "I learn best when I make color-coded binders for each class." Use this activity to discover some specifics about your learning style.

I learn best when I'm actively involved, working with other students—and when I can understand the professor!

Style—we all have it, right? What's yours? Baggy jeans and a T-shirt? Flip-flops, even in the middle of winter? A stocking cap that translates into I-just-rolled-out-of-bed-before-class? When it comes to appearance, you have your own style.

Think about how your mind works. For example, how do you decide what to wear in the morning? Do you turn on the radio or TV for the weather forecast? Jump on the Internet? Stick your head out the front door? Throw on whatever happens to be clean? We all have different styles, don't we?

So what's a learning style? A learning style is defined as your "characteristic and preferred way of gathering, interpreting, organizing, recalling, and thinking about information."[12] The way you perceive information and the way you process it—your perceiving/processing preferences—are based in part on your senses. Which sensory modalities do you prefer to use to take in information—your eyes (visual-graphic or visual-words), your ears (aural), or all your senses using your whole body (kinesthetic)? Which type of information sinks in best? Which type of information do you most trust to be accurate?

To further understand your preferred sensory channel, let's take this example. You decide to buy a new car and you must first answer many questions: What kind of car do you want to buy—an SUV, a sedan, a sports car, a van, or a truck? What are the differences between various makes and models? How do prices, comfort, gas mileage, and safety compare? Who provides the best warranty? Which car do consumers rate highest? How would you go about learning the answers to all these questions?

Marcela Barsse/MarsBars/
iStockphoto.com

Visual: Some of us would **look.** We'd study charts, graphs, and photographs comparing cars, mileage, fuel tank capacity, maintenance costs, and customer satisfaction. We learn from pre-organized, visual representations.

Johanna Goodyear/Dreamstime
.com

Aural: Some of us would **listen.** We'd ask all our friends what kind of cars they drive and what they've heard about cars from other people. We'd pay attention as showroom salespeople describe the features of various cars. We learn through sounds by listening.

Nadezda Firsova/iStockphoto
.com

Read/Write: Some of us would **read** or **write.** We'd buy a copy of *Consumer Reports'* annual edition on automobiles, or copies of magazines like *Car and Driver*, and write lists of each car's pros and cons. We learn through words by reading and writing.

Pascal Genest/iStockphoto.com

Kinesthetic: Some of us would want to **do it.** We'd go to the showroom and test drive a few cars to physically try them out. We learn through experience when all our sensory modalities are activated.

What would you do? Eventually, as you're deciding which vehicle to buy, you might do all these things, and do them more than once. But learning style theory says we all have preferences in terms of how we perceive and process information.

VARK Learning Styles Assessment

Choose the answer that best explains your preference and circle the letter. Please select <u>more than one response</u> if a single answer does not match your perception. Leave blank any question that does not apply.

1. You are helping someone who wants to go downtown, find your airport or locate the bus station. You would:
   a) draw or give her a map.
   b) tell her the directions.
   c) write down the directions (without a map).
   d) go with her.

2. You are not sure whether a word should be spelled "dependent" or "dependant." You would:
   a) see the word in your mind and choose by the way different versions look.
   b) think about how each word sounds and choose one.
   c) find it in a dictionary.
   d) write both words on paper and choose one.

3. You are planning a group vacation. You want some feedback from your friends about your plans. You would:
   a) use a map or website to show them the places.
   b) phone, text or email them.
   c) give them a copy of the printed itinerary.
   d) describe some of the highlights.

4. You are going to cook something as a special treat for your family. You would:
   a) look through the cookbook for ideas from the pictures.
   b) ask friends for suggestions.
   c) use a cookbook where you know there is a good recipe.
   d) cook something you know without the need for instructions.

5. A group of tourists wants to learn about the parks or wildlife reserves in your area. You would:
   a) show them Internet pictures, photographs or picture books.
   b) talk about, or arrange a talk for them on, parks or wildlife reserves.
   c) give them a book or pamphlets about the parks or wildlife reserves.
   d) take them to a park or wildlife reserve and walk with them.

6. You are about to purchase a digital camera or cell phone. Other than price, what would most influence your decision?
   a) Its attractive design that looks good.
   b) The salesperson telling me about its features.
   c) Reading the details about its features.
   d) Trying or testing it.

7. Remember a time when you learned how to do something new. Try to avoid choosing a physical skill, like riding a bike. You learned best by:
   a) diagrams and charts—visual clues.
   b) listening to somebody explaining it and asking questions.
   c) written instructions—e.g., a manual or textbook.
   d) watching a demonstration.

8. You have a problem with your knee. You would prefer that the doctor:
   a) show you a diagram of what was wrong.
   b) describe what was wrong.
   c) give you a pamphlet to read about it.
   d) use a plastic model of a knee to show what was wrong.

9. You want to learn a new software program, skill or game on a computer. You would:
   a) follow the diagrams in the book that came with it.
   b) talk with people who know about the program.
   c) read the written instructions that came with the program.
   d) use the controls or keyboard and try things out.

(continued)

10. I like websites that have:
    a) interesting design and visual features.
    b) audio channels where I can hear music, radio programs or interviews.
    c) interesting written descriptions, lists and explanations.
    d) things I can click on or try out.

11. Other than price, what would most influence your decision to buy a new non-fiction book?
    a) The cover looks appealing.
    b) A friend talks about it and recommends it.
    c) You'd quickly read parts of it.
    d) It contains real-life stories, experiences and examples.

12. You are using a book, CD or website to learn how to take photos with your new digital camera. You would like to have:
    a) diagrams showing the camera and what each part does.
    b) a chance to ask questions and talk about the camera and its features.
    c) clear written instructions with lists and bullet points about what to do.
    d) many examples of good and poor photos and how to improve them.

13. Do you prefer a teacher or a presenter who uses:
    a) diagrams, charts or graphs?
    b) question and answer, talk, group discussion or guest speakers?
    c) handouts, books or readings?
    d) demonstrations, models, field trips, role plays or practical exercises?

14. You have finished a competition or test and would like some feedback. You would like to have feedback:
    a) using graphs showing what you had achieved.
    b) from somebody who talks it through with you.
    c) in a written format, describing your results.
    d) using examples from what you have done.

15. You are going to choose food at a restaurant or cafe. You would:
    a) look at what others are eating or look at pictures of each dish.
    b) ask the server or friends to recommend choices.
    c) choose from the written descriptions in the menu.
    d) choose something that you have had there before.

16. You have to give an important speech at a conference or special occasion. You would:
    a) make diagrams or create graphs to help explain things.
    b) write a few key words and practice your speech over and over.
    c) write out your speech and learn from reading it over several times.
    d) gather many examples and stories to make the talk real and practical.

Source: N. Fleming. (2001–2007). VARK, *a Guide to Learning Styles*. Version 7.0. Available at http://www .vark-learn.com/english/page.asp?p=questionnaire. Adapted and used with permission from Neil Fleming.

Scoring the VARK

Let's tabulate your results.

Count your choices in each of the four VARK categories.	(a)	(b)	(c)	(d)
	Visual	Aural	Read/Write	Kinesthetic

My VARK scores are K = 14, A = 6, V = 5, R = 4 Since I prefer my chem lab over lecture classes, I'm not surprised that I'm kinesthetic!

Now that you've calculated your scores, do they match your perceptions of yourself as a learner? Could you have predicted them? The VARK's creators believe that *you* are best qualified to verify and interpret your own results.[13]

Using Your VARK Preferences

Knowing your preferences can help you in your academic coursework. If your highest score (by 4 or 5 points) is in one of the four VARK modalities, that particular learning modality is your preferred one.[14] If your scores are more or less even between several or all four modalities, these scores mean that you don't have a strong preference for any single modality and are instead multimodal. A lower score in a preference simply means that you are more comfortable using other styles. If your VARK results contain a zero in a particular learning modality, you may realize that you do indeed dislike this mode or find it unhelpful. It may be helpful to reflect on why you omit this learning modality. To learn more about your results and suggestions for applying them, see Figure 2.3 for your preferred modality.

FIGURE 2.3

Visual, Aural, Read/Write, and Kinesthetic Learning Strategies

	Everyday Study Strategies	Exam Preparation Strategies
VISUAL	• Convert your lecture notes to a visual format. • Study the placement of items, colors, and shapes in your textbook. • Put complex concepts into flowcharts or graphs. • Redraw ideas you create from memory.	• Practice turning your visuals back into words. • Practice writing out exam answers. • Recall the pictures you made of the pages you studied. • Use diagrams to answer exam questions, if your instructor will allow it.
AURAL	• Read your notes aloud. • Explain your notes to another auditory learner. • Ask others to "hear" your understanding of the material. • Record your notes or listen to your instructors' podcasts. • Realize that your lecture notes may be incomplete. You may have become so involved in listening that you stopped writing. Fill your notes in later by talking with other students or getting material from the textbook.	• Practice by speaking your answers aloud. • Listen to your own voice as you answer questions. • Opt for an oral exam if allowed. • Imagine you are talking with the teacher as you answer questions.
READ/WRITE	• Write out your lecture notes again and again. • Read your notes (silently) again and again. • Put ideas and principles into different words. • Translate diagrams, graphs, etc., into text. • Rearrange words and "play" with wording. • Turn diagrams and charts into words.	• Write out potential exam answers. • Practice creating and taking exams. • Type out your answers to potential test questions. • Organize your notes into lists or bullets. • Write practice paragraphs, particularly beginnings and endings.
KINESTHETIC	• Recall experiments, field trips, etc. Remember the real things that happened. • Talk over your notes with another "K" person. • Use photos and pictures that make ideas come to life. • Go back to the lab, your manual, or your notes that include real examples. • Remember that your lecture notes will have gaps if topics weren't concrete or relevant for you. • Use case studies to help you learn abstract principles.	• Role-play the exam situation in your room (or the actual classroom). • Put plenty of examples into your answers. • Write practice answers and sample paragraphs. • Give yourself practice tests.

Most college classes emphasize reading and writing; however, if your lowest score is in the read/write modality, don't assume you're academically doomed. VARK can help you discover alternative, more productive ways to learn the same course material. You may learn to adapt naturally to a particular instructor or discipline's preferences, using a visual modality in your economics class to interpret graphs and a kinesthetic modality in your chemistry lab to conduct experiments.

However, you may also find that you need to deliberately and strategically re-route your learning methods in some of your classes, and knowing your

That's right. I can't change the way Professor Caldwell teaches. I'll guess I'll just have to change the way I study.

Courtesy of Neil Fleming.

CAREER OUTLOOK: *Neil Fleming, University Professor, Creator of the VARK*

Q1: What's it like to be a college teacher? What are the pros and cons?

Although I write and speak widely, teaching is my favorite job because you get to talk with so many interesting people (students) and you sometimes make a difference in their lives. There are those great moments when you see that a student has "gotten it." Those "Aha!" moments are priceless. You also get to learn new things with your students so you stay a learner for life and never "mature"! The bad days are those when you realize that you have "missed" some students or that they have somehow lost interest in you and what you teach.

Q2: Do most students understand how they learn? What is your understanding of how learning happens?

Unfortunately, some students have to experience failure before they learn about their own learning, and that is a tragic waste. Many students know in some detail how

they learn, but they are seldom asked by teachers. We all learn in particular ways. Sometimes those ways serve us well. We need to understand what those ways are and cultivate them. But other times our learning preferences don't serve us well because of the particular material we're trying to learn. It's sort of like trying to build a house without the right tools. It's just not going to work, or at the very least,

it's going to be a struggle. In those cases, we need to adjust our learning to fit the content and the situation.

In general, I know students have learned something well when they can teach it to someone else.

Q3: In your opinion, are most students today visual, aural, read/write, or kinesthetic learners?

The VARK data I've collected indicate that the most

common preference for students is kinesthetic, that is, they want to experience the learning or have the teacher relate the learning to things that they know, have seen, or can do. The plain truth is that the teacher who can provide links to the reality of students is going to reach more students.

HOW WOULD *YOU* LIKE IT?

Have you ever considered a career as a college professor?

Facts to Consider[15]

Academic preparation required: A master's degree, or more often, a doctoral degree is required, although in some fields highly cultivated expertise or practical experience is all you need.

Future workforce demand: Prospects for new jobs are expected to grow much faster than average, although many openings will be for part-time teachers.

Work environment: College professors have flexible schedules, teach a wide variety of

subjects (usually in one field), and conduct research.

Essential skills: reading, writing, communicating with individual students, to a classroom of students, or in work-related committees, collecting and analyzing data, and using technology to teach, communicate, and present information.

Questions to Ponder

1. Do you have (or could you acquire) the skills this career requires?

2. Are you interested in a career like this? Why or why not?

For more career activities online, access the CourseMate via www.cengagebrain.com/shop/ISBN/0495906425 to do the Team Career exercises.

VARK preferences can help you do that. Learning to capitalize on your preferences and translate challenging course material into your preferred modality may serve you well. Remember these suggestions about the VARK, and try them out to see if they improve your academic results.

1. VARK preferences are not necessarily strengths. However VARK is an excellent vehicle to help you reflect on how you learn and begin to reinforce the productive strategies you're already using or select ones that might work better.

2. If you have a strong preference for a particular modality, practice multiple suggestions listed in Figure 2.2 for that particular modality. Reinforce your learning through redundancy.

3. An estimated 60 percent of people are multimodal. In a typical classroom of 30 students (based on VARK data):

   > 17 students would be multimodal,

   > 1 student would be visual,

   > 1 student would be aural,

   > 5 students would be read/write,

   > 6 students would be kinesthetic,

   and the teacher would most likely have a strong read/write preference![16]

4. If you are multimodal, as most of us are, it may be necessary to use all your modalities to boost your confidence in your learning. Practice the suggestions for all of your preferred modalities.

" Each person is an exception to the rule."

Carl Jung, Swiss psychiatrist (1875–1961)

©Larry Harwood Photography. Property of Cengage Learning.

5. While in an ideal world, it would be good to try to strengthen lesser preferences, you may wish to save that goal for later in life. Fleming's students eventually convinced him that college isn't the place to experiment. Academic results are important, and often scholarships and graduate school acceptance hang in the balance. You, too, may decide it's better to try to strengthen existing preferences now and work on expanding your repertoire later. This book will give you an opportunity to practice your VARK learning preferences—whatever they are—in each chapter.

Ultimately, learning at your best is up to you. Early on, this chapter discussed Multiple Intelligences. Like most people, you are probably strongest in two or three. Within your multiple intelligences, you have preferences as a visual, aural, read/write, kinesthetic, or multimodal learner. You know much more about yourself than you did at the beginning of this chapter, or perhaps you've validated what you've suspected all along. Each chapter of this book will remind you of your VARK preferences with special activities to reinforce your preferred sensory modalities.

Gaining the insights provided in this chapter and acting on them have the potential to greatly affect your college success. Understand yourself, capitalize on your preferences, build on them, focus, and learn!

Learning how to learn is life's most important skill."

Tony Buzan, memory expert

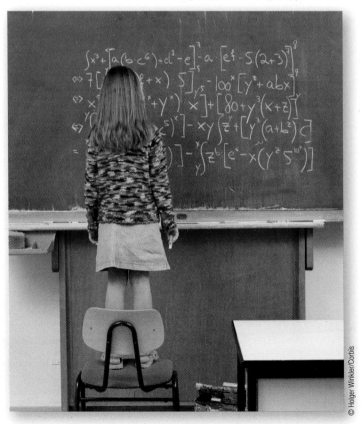

© Holger Winkler/Corbis

Complete the recommended activity for your preferred VARK learning modality. If you are multimodal, select more than one activity. Your instructor may ask you to (a) give an oral report on your results in class, (b) send your results to him or her via e-mail, (c) post them online, or (d) contribute to a class chat.

Visual: Put together a collage of photos that represents how you learn. Post it on the course blog or web-site, assemble it on a posterboard, or make a PowerPoint slide show.

Aural: Discuss your 1) multiple intelligences or 2) VARK preferences with your friends or family. See if they can predict their own scores (generally). Access the CourseMate via www.cengagebrain .com/shop/ISBN/ 0495906425 to listen to the iAudio summary for this chapter.

Read/Write: Write a one-page summary of what you have learned about yourself as a result of reading this chapter.

Kinesthetic: Use a variety of kinesthetic learning techniques to prepare for an upcoming quiz or exam in this class or another one. Did the techniques help you master the material? Report your results.

(from left to right) Marcela Barsse/MarsBars/iStockphoto.com; Johanna Goodyear/Dreamstime.com; Nadezda Firsova/iStockphoto.com; Pascal Genest/iStockphoto.com

? **challenge**   66 **reaction**   * **insight**   ! **action**

Now What Do You Think?

1. At the beginning of this chapter, Tammy Ko, a frustrated and disgruntled student, faced a challenge. Now after reading this chapter, would you respond differently to any of the questions you answered about the "FOCUS Challenge Case"? Knowing what you know now, how would you advise her? Write a paragraph ending to the story, incorporating your best advice.

2. What are your most developed intelligences? Describe a situation in which you excelled as a learner and how the Theory of Multiple Intelligences helps explain your success.

3. What is or are your VARK preferences? Are they what you predicted? How will you capitalize on them to learn at your best?

4. This chapter asked you to assess your learning in two different ways by thinking about your multiple intelligences and sensory modalities. We learned from Tammy's notes that she has high Interpersonal Intelligence and is a kinesthetic learner according to the VARK. How do these assessments fit together for her? How do your assessments fit together for you? How is the new picture of yourself as a learner similar to or different from what you used to think about yourself? How will it change the way you approach learning in the future?

On a scale of 1 to 10, answer the following questions now that you've completed this chapter.

1 = not very/not much/very little/low   10 = very/a lot/very much/high

In hindsight, how much did you already know about this subject before reading the chapter?

1 2 3 4 5 6 7 8 9 10

Can you answer these questions about learning about learning more fully now that you've read the chapter?

1. **What does the term "multiple intelligences" mean? Can you name three different types of intelligences?**

2. **What does VARK stand for? Can you identify the letters as they relate to students' preferences for taking in information?**

How useful might the information in this chapter be to you? How much do you think this information might affect your success in college?

1 2 3 4 5 6 7 8 9 10

How much do you think this information might affect your career success after college?

1 2 3 4 5 6 7 8 9 10

How long did it actually take you to complete this chapter (both the reading and writing tasks)? _____ Hour(s) _____ Minutes

Aced all three levels of the online quiz!

 Challenge Yourself Online Quiz. To find out how much you've learned, access the CourseMate via www.cengagebrain.com/shop/ISBN/0495906425 to take the Challenge Yourself Online Quiz.

Take a minute to compare these answers to your answers from the "Readiness Check" at the beginning of this chapter. What gaps exist between the similar questions? How might these gaps between what you thought before starting the chapter and what you now think after completing the chapter affect how you approach the next chapter in this book?

chapter 3

Managing Your Time and Energy

You're about to discover...

✔ Why time management alone doesn't work

✔ How time management differs from energy management

✔ How to calculate your study hours

✔ How to schedule your way to success

✔ How common time-wasters creep in, and how to bust them

✔ How the P word can derail you

✔ How to realistically balance work, school, and personal life

---

READINESS CHECK | What do you **Know?**

Before beginning this chapter, take a moment to answer these questions. Your answers will help you assess how ready you are to focus.

1 = not very/not much/very little/low   10 = very/a lot/very much/high

How much do you *already* know?

Based on reading the "You're about to discover. . ." list and skimming this chapter, how much do you think you probably already know about this chapter's subject?

1 2 3 4 5 6 7 8 9 10

See if you can answer these questions about managing time and energy *before* you read.

1. **What's the difference between time management, attention management, and energy management? How are they different, and what do they have in common?**

2. **What percentage of college students admit to procrastinating on assignments? What's the major reason they procrastinate according to research?**

3. **Identify three specific techniques for balancing your life.**

How motivated are you to learn *more?*

In general, how motivated are you to learn more by reading this chapter?

1 2 3 4 5 6 7 8 9 10

How much do you think this information might affect your success in college?

1 2 3 4 5 6 7 8 9 10

How much do you think this information might affect your career success after college?

1 2 3 4 5 6 7 8 9 10

How ready are you to read *now?*

How ready are you to focus on this chapter—physically, intellectually, and emotionally? Circle a number for each aspect of your readiness to focus.

1 2 3 4 5 6 7 8 9 10

If any of your answers is below a 10, you might want to pay attention to whatever is distracting you before you start reading. For example, if you're feeling scattered, take a few moments to settle down and focus.

Finally, how long do you think it will take you to complete this chapter from start to finish?

_____ Hour(s) _____ Minutes

DEREK JOHNSON

A s Derek Johnson walked out of his World History class on Wednesday evening, he felt panicked. The professor had just assigned a twelve-page paper, due one month from today. *How could she?* Derek thought. *Doesn't she realize how busy I am?* The syllabus had mentioned a paper, but twelve pages seemed downright excessive. He sent a tweet complaining about it from his phone on his way to his next class. Twitter was quickly becoming Derek's favorite way to communicate.

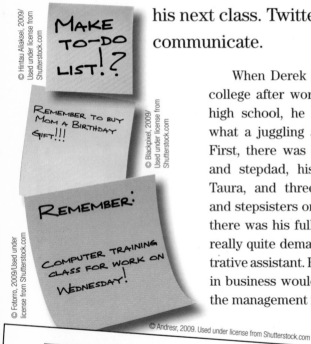

When Derek had decided to go to college after working for a year after high school, he hadn't quite realized what a juggling act it would require. First, there was his family—his Mom and stepdad, his five-year-old sister, Taura, and three other stepbrothers and stepsisters on his Dad's side. Then there was his full-time job, which was really quite demanding for an administrative assistant. He hoped that a degree in business would help him move into the management ranks, where the salaries were higher.

Add to that singing in his church choir, coaching the youth soccer league, competing in cycling races, and working out every morning at the gym. Derek had been a high school athlete, and physical fitness was a priority for him.

His head began to swim as he thought about all his upcoming obligations: his mother's birthday next week, the dog's vet appointment, his stepbrother who was coming to town for a visit, the training class he was required to attend for work. Something had to go, but he couldn't think of anything he was willing to sacrifice to make time for a twelve-page paper. Maybe he'd have to break down and buy one of those planners, but weren't most people who use those slightly, well . . . compulsive?

Still, the paper was to count as 25 percent of his final grade in the course. He decided he'd try and think of a topic for the paper on his way home. But then he remembered that his mom had asked him to stop at the store to pick up groceries. Somewhere on aisle 12, between the frozen pizza and the frozen yogurt, Derek's thoughts about his research paper vanished.

What are you doing?

Heading to world history class. I have a 12 page paper due in a few weeks! This isn't fair!!

update

me Profile Find People Settings

HISTORY PAPER OUTLINE

INTRO...

6:30

The following week, the professor asked the students in the class how their papers were coming along. Some students gave long accounts of their research progress, the wealth of sources they'd found, and the detailed outlines they'd put together. Derek didn't raise his hand.

A whole week has gone by, Derek thought on his way back to his car after class. *I have to get going!* Writing had never exactly been Derek's strong suit. In fact, it was something he generally disliked doing. Through a great deal of hard work, he had managed to earn a 3.8 GPA in high school—a record he planned to continue. A course in World History—not even in his intended major—was *not* going to ruin things! The week had absolutely flown by, and there were plenty of good reasons why his paper was getting off to such a slow start.

It was true that Derek rarely wasted time, except for occasionally watching his favorite TV shows. But then again, with such a jam-packed schedule, he really felt the need to unwind once in a while. Regardless, he rarely missed his nightly study time from 11:00 p.m. to 1:00 a.m. Those two hours were reserved for homework, no matter what.

At the end of class two weeks later, Derek noticed that several students lined up to show the profes- sor the first drafts of their papers. *That's it!* Derek thought to him- self. *The paper is due next Wednesday. I'll spend Monday night, my only free night of the week, in the library. I can get there right after work and stay until 11:00 or so. That'll be five hours of concentrated time. I should be able to write it then.*

Despite his good intentions, Derek didn't arrive at the library until nearly 8:00 p.m., and his work session wasn't all that pro- ductive. As he sat in his library stall, he found himself obsessing about things that were bothering him at work. His boss was being difficult, and his team of coworkers couldn't agree on some important issues about their current project. Finally, when he glanced at his watch, he was shocked to see that it was already midnight! The library was closing, and he'd only written three pages. Where had the time gone?

On his way out to the car, his cell phone rang. It was his Mom, wonder- ing if he could watch Taura tomorrow night. She was running a fever. Oh, and his boss had called about an emergency meeting at 7:00 a.m. *If one more thing goes wrong . . .* , Derek thought to himself. His twelve-page paper was due in two days.

Clock: © CROM 2009. Used under license from Shutterstock .com Child: © Studio 1One, 2009/Used under license from Shutterstock.com

© Cengage Learning

WORLD HISTORY
Fall Semester Syllabus

Instructor: Julia Alexander
Office: Main Hall 320
Email: Julia.Alexander@campusmail.edu
Phone: 555-3424
Office Hours: 12:30-3pm daily

Required Textbook:
World History, 6th Edition. By William J. Duiker and Jackson J. Spielvogel ISBN: 049...

Grading:

Quizzes:	10 @ 10 points each	
Midterm Exam:		100pts
Cultural Analysis:		100pts
Course Essay:		50pts
Final Exam:		150pts
TOTAL:		100pts
		500pts

Part I: Pre-Civilization and the Fertile Crescent
  Week One: Agriculture and Mesopotamia
  Week Two: The Nile Valley and the Near East

Part II: Ancient Civilizations
  Week Three: The World of Homer
  Week Four: Classical Greece and the Golden Age
  Week Five: Rome: The Rise of the Republic
  Week Six: Imperial Rome
  Week Seven: Rome: The Fall of the Empire
  Week Eight: China and the Far East
  Week Nine: The Indian Subcontinent

Part III: Growth and Expansion
  Week Ten: Muslim Culture
  Week Eleven: Yuan and Ming Dynasties
  Week Twelve: Byzantium
  Week Thirteen: The Middle Ages
  Week Fourteen: The Middle Ages continued
  Week Fifteen: The Renaissance
  Week Sixteen: The N...

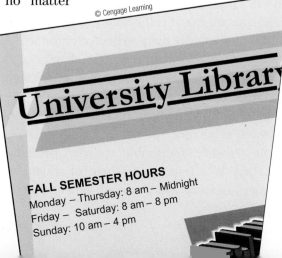

© Cengage Learning

University Library

FALL SEMESTER HOURS

Monday – Thursday: 8 am – Midnight
Friday – Saturday: 8 am – 8 pm
Sunday: 10 am – 4 pm

What Do You Think?

1. Describe Derek's time management strategies. Are they working? Is time management Derek's only problem?

2. Describe the time-wasters that are a part of Derek's schedule. Do you think procrastination is an issue for Derek? What's behind his failure to make progress on his paper?

3. Suggest three realistic ways for Derek to balance work, school, and his personal life.

4. What aspects of Derek's situation can you relate to personally? What other time management issues are you experiencing in your life right now?

Time Management Isn't Enough

Challenge: What is time management and how does it work?

Reaction: _____

_____

No KIDDING! →

> In truth, people can generally make time for what they choose to do; it is not really the time but the will that is lacking."
>
> **Sir John Lubbock, British banker, politician, and archaeologist (1834–1913)**

Before delving into the details of time management skills, let's clarify one important point. There's a sense in which the phrase *time management* is misleading. Let's say you decide to spend an hour reading the assigned short story for your literature class. You may sit in the library with your book propped open in front of you from 3:00 to 4:00 o'clock on the dot. But you may not digest a single word you're reading. You may be going through the motions, reading on autopilot. Have you managed your time? Technically, yes. Your planner says, "Library, short story for Lit 101, 3:00–4:00 p.m." But did you get results? Time management expert Jeffrey Mayer asks provactively in the title of his book: *If You Haven't Got the Time to Do It Right, When Will You Find The Time to Do It Over?*. Now that's a good question!

It's not just about managing your time, it's about managing your attention. Attention management is the ability to focus your attention, not just your time, toward a designated activity so that you produce a desired result. Time management may get you through reading a chapter of your chemistry textbook, but attention management will ensure that you understand what you're reading. It's about *focus*. Without attention management, time management is pointless.

Succeeding in school, at work, and in life is not just about what you do. It's about what gets done. You can argue about the effort you put into an assignment all you want, but it's doubtful your professor will say, "You know what? You're right. You deserve an A just for staying up late last night working on this paper." Activity and accomplishment aren't the same thing. Neither are

Dr. Constance Staley, University of Colorado at Colorado Springs

quantity and quality. Results count. So don't confuse being busy with being successful. Staying busy isn't much of a challenge; being successful is.

Here's a list of preliminary academic time-saving tips. However, remember that these suggestions won't give you a surefire recipe for academic success. To manage your time, you must also manage yourself: your energy, your behavior, your attention, your attitudes, *you.* Once you know how to manage all that, managing your time begins to work. Here are some suggestions worth trying:

> **Have a plan for your study sessions; include time allotments for each topic or task.** Build predictions of how much time you think each assignment will need into your plan, but make adjustments if you get hung up.

> **Keep track of what derails you.** If you come to understand your patterns, you may be better able to control them.

> **Turn off your phone or tell other people you live with that you don't want to be disturbed if a call comes in for you.** Let them know what time they can tell callers to call you back.

> **If you're working on your computer, work offline whenever possible.** If you must be online to check sources frequently, don't give in to the temptation to check your social networking account or e-mail every ten minutes.

> **Take two minutes to organize your workspace before beginning.** Having the resources you need at your fingertips makes the session go much more smoothly, and you won't waste time searching for things you need.

> **If you are in a study group, make sure everyone is clear about assigned tasks for the next session.** Lack of clear communication about expectations is a big time-waster for study groups.

> **Learn to say no.** Saying no to someone, especially someone you care about, can feel awkward at first, but people close to you will understand that you can't do everything.

I NEED TO WORK ON THIS!

> **Focus.** You can't do anything if you try to do everything. Multitasking may work for simple matters, such as scheduling a doctor's appointment while heating up a snack in the microwave. But when it comes to tasks that require brainpower, such as studying or writing, you need a single-minded focus.

> **Slow down.** As they say, "haste makes waste." Working at something a million miles a minute will most likely result in mistakes, superficial

thinking, and poor decisions. Ironically, if you rush, you may run out of time and end up settling for less than your best.

> **Don't make a habit of putting other people's priorities above your own.** In other words, don't let their *lack* of planning affect your attempts to plan. Those who truly care for you will understand you need to stay focused on your priorities.

This, too. ⟶

Energy, Our Most Precious Resource

| **?** challenge | **❝** reaction | **✳** insight | **❗** action |

Challenge: What's the difference between *time* management and *energy* management?

Reaction: _____
_____

"We live in a digital time. Our rhythms are rushed, rapid-fire and relentless, our days carved up into bits and bytes. . . . We're wired up but we're melting down." So begins a bestselling book, *The Power of Full Engagement: Managing Energy, Not Time, Is the Key to High Performance and Personal Renewal.* The authors, Jim Loehr and Tony Schwartz, have replaced the term *time management* with the term *energy management*. Their shift makes sense. Since most of us are operating in overdrive most of the time, energy is our most precious resource.

Energy management experts say you can't control time—everyone has a fixed amount—but you can manage your energy. And in fact, it's your responsibility to do so. Once a day is gone, it's gone. But your energy can be renewed.

It's clear that some things are energy *drains*, zapping your drive: bad news, illness, interpersonal conflict, bureaucratic hassles, a heavy meal, rainy days. Likewise, some things are energy *gains*, giving you a surge of fresh vitality: a new job, good friends, music, laughter, fruit, coffee. It's a good idea to recognize your own personal energy drains and gains so that you know how and when to replenish your supply.[1] Energy management experts say it's not just about *spending time*, it's about *expending energy*:

Energy gains:
- *Working out*
- *Music*
- *Taura!!*

> *physical* energy

> *emotional* energy

> *mental* energy

> *spiritual* energy

Of the four dimensions of energy, let's take a closer look at the first two. To do your very best academically, it helps to be *physically* energized and *emotionally* connected. Physical energy is measured in terms of *quantity*. How much energy do you have—a lot or a little? Emotional energy, on the other hand, is measured by *quality*. What kind of energy do you have—positive or negative? If you put them together into a two-dimensional chart with *quantity* as the

❝ Today is the tomorrow we worried about yesterday."
Anonymous

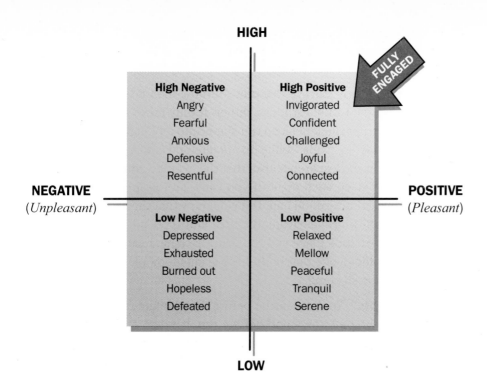

HIGH

High Negative	High Positive
Angry	Invigorated
Fearful	Confident
Anxious	Challenged
Defensive	Joyful
Resentful	Connected

NEGATIVE *(Unpleasant)* — **POSITIVE** *(Pleasant)*

Low Negative	Low Positive
Depressed	Relaxed
Exhausted	Mellow
Burned out	Peaceful
Hopeless	Tranquil
Defeated	Serene

LOW

FULLY ENGAGED

FIGURE 3.1

The Dynamics of Energy[2]

vertical axis and *quality* as the horizontal axis, you get something like Figure 3.1.

When you're operating in the upper right quadrant with high, positive energy, you're most productive, which makes sense. The question is: How do you get there? How do you make certain you're physically energized and emotionally connected so that you can do your best, academically?

Get Physically Energized

To make sure you're physically energized, try these suggestions.

1. **Go with the flow.** Have you noticed times of the day when it's easier to concentrate than others? Perhaps you regularly crash in the middle of the afternoon, for example. This is partly due to the patterns of electrical impulses in your brain, alpha rhythms that are unique to each individual. In other words, everyone has a biological clock. Paying attention to your body's natural rhythms is important. Plan to do activities that require you to be alert during your natural productivity peaks. That's better than plodding through a tough assignment when the energy just isn't there. Use low energy times to take care of mindless chores that require little to no brainpower.[3]

2. **Up and at 'em.** What about 8:00 a.m. classes? Don't use your body's natural rhythms as an excuse to sleep through class! ("I'm just not a morning person....") If you're truly not a morning person, don't sign up for early morning classes. Some students get into the *social* habit of staying up late into the wee, small hours, and then they just can't get up in the morning.

> " Performance, health and happiness are grounded in the skillful management of energy."
>
> **Jim Loehr and Tony Schwartz, from** *The Power of Full Engagement*

Sleeping through your obligations won't do much for your success—and you'll be playing a continual game of catch-up, which takes even more time.

3. **Sleep at night, study during the day.** Burning the midnight oil and pulling all-nighters aren't the best ideas, either. It only takes one all-nighter to help you realize that a lack of sleep translates into a plunge in performance. Without proper sleep, your ability to understand and remember course material is impaired. Research shows that the average adult requires seven to eight hours of sleep each night. If you can't get that much for whatever reason, take a short afternoon nap. Did you know that the Three Mile Island nuclear meltdown in Pennsylvania in 1979 and the Chernobyl disaster in the Ukraine in 1986 took place at 4 a.m. and 1:23 a.m., respectively? Experts believe it's no coincidence that both these events took place when workers would normally be sleeping.[4]

4. **"Prime the pump."** You've heard it before: Food is the fuel that makes us run. The better the fuel, the smoother we run. It's that simple. A solid diet of carbs—pizza, chips, and cookies—jammed into the fuel tank of your car would certainly gum up the works! When the demands on your energy are high, such as exam week, use premium fuel. If you don't believe it, take a look at how many of your classmates get sick during midterms and finals. Watch what they're eating and note how much sleep they're getting, and you'll get some clues about why they're hacking and coughing their way through exams—or in bed missing them altogether.

Get Emotionally Connected

Physical needs count, to be sure, but emotional connections are part of the picture, too. See if you agree with these suggestions.

1. **Communicate like it matters.** Sometimes we save our best communicating for people we think we have to impress: teachers, bosses, or clients, for example. But what about the people we care about most in our lives? Sometimes these people get the leftovers after all the "important" communicating has been done for the day. Sometimes we're so comfortable with these people that we think we can let it all hang out, even when doing so is *not* a pretty sight. Communicate as if everything you said would actually come true—"Just drop dead," for instance—and watch the difference! Communicating with people we care about is one of our primary vehicles for personal renewal.

2. **Choose how you renew.** Finish this analogy: junk food is to physical energy as _____ is to emotional energy. If you answered "TV," you're absolutely right. Most people use television as their primary form of emotional renewal, but, like junk food, it's not that nutritious and it's easy to consume too much. Try more engaging activities that affirm you: singing or reading or playing a sport.[5]

Guess I could cut back.

3. **Let others renew you.** Remember that people don't just make demands on your time, they can provide emotional renewal. There's pure joy in a child's laugh, a friend's smile, a father's pat on the back. These small pleasures in life are priceless—prize them!

"I'll Study in My Free Time" ... and When Is That?

| ? challenge | " reaction | * insight | ! action |

Challenge: List all the activities you engage in during an average school day.

Reaction: _____

_____

EXERCISE 3.1

Self Assessment—Where Did the Time Go?

Fill in the number of hours you spend doing each of the following, then multiply your answer by the number given (7 or 5 to figure weekly amounts) where appropriate.

Number of hours per day

Sleeping: _____ × 7 = _____

Personal grooming (for example, showering, shaving, putting on makeup): _____ × 7 = _____

Eating (meals and snacks; include preparation or driving time): _____ × 7 = _____

Commuting during the week (to school and work): _____ × 5 = _____

Doing errands and chores: _____ × 7 = _____

Spending time with family (parents, children, or spouse): _____ × 7 = _____

Spending time with boyfriend or girlfriend: _____ × 7 = _____

Number of hours per week

At work: _____

In classes: _____

At regularly scheduled functions (church, clubs, etc.): _____

Socializing, hanging out, watching TV, talking on the phone, etc.: _____

Now add up all the numbers in the far right column, and subtract your total from 168, the number of hours in a week. This is the number of hours you have remaining in your week for that ever-important task of studying.

Is the number you arrived at too low? Are you already below zero? Start over on this chart, and write in studying first (above the first item—sleeping), before anything else. Then make adjustments elsewhere. How many hours per day should you study, based on how many courses you are taking and how challenging they are? Achieving real success in college takes time!

Ask ten students when they study, and chances are at least eight will reply, "in my free time." The irony in this statement is that if you actually waited until you had free time to study, you probably never would. Truthfully, some students are amazed at how easily a day can race by without ever thinking about cracking a book. This is why you should actually *schedule* your study time, but to do that, you should first be aware of how you're currently spending those twenty-four hours of each day.

Notice that the Exercise you just completed places studying at the bottom of the list, even though it's vital to your success in college. It reflects a common attitude among college students, namely that studying is what takes place after everything else gets done. Where does schoolwork rank on *your* list of priorities?

If succeeding in college is a top priority for you, then make sure that you're devoting enough time to schoolwork outside the classroom. Most instructors expect you to study two to three hours outside of class for every hour spent in class. If it's a particularly challenging class, you may need even more study time. You can use the following chart to calculate the total number of hours you ought to expect to study—effectively—each week:

Credit hours for less demanding classes: _____ × 2 hours = _____ hours

Credit hours for typical/average classes: _____ × 3 hours = _____ hours

Credit hours for more challenging classes: _____ × 4 hours = _____ hours

Expected total study time per week = _____ hours

Remember, just putting in the time won't guarantee that you'll truly *understand* what you're studying. You need to ensure that your study time is productive by focusing your attention and strategically selecting study techniques that work best for you.

WORLD HISTORY IS MY HARDEST CLASS. DOES THIS MEAN I SHOULD BE STUDYING HISTORY AT LEAST 12 HOURS PER WEEK? MAN!

BOX 3.1   Lame Excuses for Blowing Off Class

Do you find yourself skipping class at times in order to do something else: getting an oil change for your car, soaking up the sun's rays, or socializing with some friends you ran into on the way to class? If so, ask yourself this: Would you walk into a gas station, put a couple of $20 bills down on the counter to prepay for a tank of gas, and then put in a dollar's worth and drive off? Absolutely not, you say?

Would you buy a $10 movie ticket and then just toss it in the trash because you decided there was something else you'd rather do on the spur of the moment? No way!

Why, then, would you purchase much more expensive "tickets" to class—the average cost of an hour in class is roughly upwards of $200 per hour—and then toss them in the trash by not attending? Don't you value your money more than that? More importantly, don't you value *yourself* more than that?

The next time you're tempted to opt out of your scheduled classes, ask yourself if you really want to throw away money, in addition to the opportunity. Check your priorities, then put one foot in front of the other and walk into that classroom. In the long run, it's the best investment in your own future.

Schedule Your Way to Success

EXERCISE 3.2

Time Monitor

Can you remember how you spent all your time yesterday? Create a Time Monitor that lists a day's worth of time in fifteen-minute segments. Fill in as much as you can remember about how you spent your time yesterday from 7:00 a.m. to midnight. Be as detailed as possible, filling in each fifteen-minute segment. For example, your first 30 minutes could look like this:

7:00 a.m.: Woke up, drank coffee

7:15 a.m.: Continued drinking coffee

Now monitor how you use your time today (or tomorrow if you're reading this at night) on a Time Monitor. Again, be very specific. You will refer back to this exercise later in this chapter.

CURIOSITY: *CHOOSE TO CHOOSE!*

Have you ever thought about how many dozens, if not hundreds, of choices you make each day? From the second you wake up, you're making decisions, even about the simplest things, like whether to order a cappuccino or a latté; decaf, half-caf, or high-octane; nonfat, two-percent, or the real deal.

Psychologist and professor Barry Schwartz, in his book, *The Paradox of Choice: Why More Is Less*, believes that making nonstop choices can actually cause us to "invest time, energy, and no small amount of self-doubt, and dread." Choosing a new cell phone plan can take some people weeks while they research models of cell phones, minutes available, quotas of text messages, and Internet access, not to mention the fine print. Simply put: Being flooded with choices, while it feels luxurious, can be stressful and even unrewarding. Paralysis, anxiety, and stress rather than happiness, satisfaction, and perfection can be the result of too much "more."

Some of us, Schwartz says, are "maximizers"; we don't rest until we find the best. Others of us are "satisficers"; we're satisfied with what's good enough, based on our most important criteria. Of course, we all do some "maximizing" and some "satisficing," but generally, which are you?

Here are Schwartz's recommendations to lower our stress levels in a society where more can actually give us less, especially in terms of quality of life:

1. **Choose to choose.** Some decisions are worth lengthy deliberation; others aren't. Be conscious of the choices you make and whether they're worth the return on your investment. If you need a pair of new jeans, don't spend the better part of the afternoon launching a citywide search. "Satisfice": it's just a pair of jeans. On the other hand, if it's a truly important task, like a paper that's worth 25 percent of your grade, make a conscious choice to "maximize." "Maximize" when it counts and "satisfice" when it doesn't.

2. **Remember that there's always greener grass somewhere.** Someone will always have a better job than you do, a nicer apartment, or a more attractive romantic partner. Regret or envy can eat away at you, and second-guessing can bring unsettling dissatisfaction.

3. **Regret less and appreciate more.** While green grass does abound, so do sandpits and bumpy roads. That's an important realization, too! Value the good things you already have going for you.

4. **Build bridges, not walls.** Think about the ways in which the dozens of choices you've already made as a new college student give you your own unique profile or "choice-print": where you live, which classes you take, clubs you join, campus events you attend, your small circle of friends, and on and on. Remember that, and make conscious choices that will best help you succeed.[6]

There is no one right way to schedule your time, but if you experiment with the system presented in this book, you'll be on the right path. Eventually, you can tweak the system to make it uniquely your own. Try these eight steps, and schedule your way to success!

STEP 1: Fill out a "Term on a Page" calendar. Right up front, create a "Term on a Page" calendar that shows the entire school term on one page. (See Exercise 3.3.) You will need to have the syllabus from each of your classes and your school's course schedule to do this step properly. The following items should be transferred onto your "Term on a Page" calendar:

> Holidays when your school is closed

> Exam and quiz dates from your syllabi

> Project or paper deadlines from your syllabi

> Relevant administrative deadlines (e.g., registration for the next term, drop dates)

> Birthdays and anniversaries to remember

> Important out-of-town travel

> Dates that pertain to other family members, such as days that a relative will be visiting—anything that will impact your ability to attend classes or study

STEP 2: Invest in a planner. While it's good to have the big picture, you must also develop an ongoing scheduling system that works for you. Using the "It's all right up here in my head" method is a surefire way to miss an important appointment, fly past the deadline for your term paper without a clue, or lose track of the time you have left to complete multiple projects.

Although your instructor will typically provide you with a class syllabus that lists test dates and assignment deadlines, trying to juggle multiple syllabi—not to mention your personal and work commitments—is enough to drive you crazy. You need *one* central clearinghouse for all of your important deadlines,

" Take care of your minutes, and the hours will take care of themselves."

Lord Chesterfield, British statesman and diplomat (1694–1773)

Term on a Page

Take a few minutes right now to create your own Term on a Page using the charts in Figure 3.2.

FIGURE 3.2

Term on a Page

Term _____ Year _____

Month:	Sunday	Monday	Tuesday	Wednesday	Thursday	Friday	Saturday

Month:	Sunday	Monday	Tuesday	Wednesday	Thursday	Friday	Saturday

Month:	Sunday	Monday	Tuesday	Wednesday	Thursday	Friday	Saturday

Month:	Sunday	Monday	Tuesday	Wednesday	Thursday	Friday	Saturday

Month:	Sunday	Monday	Tuesday	Wednesday	Thursday	Friday	Saturday

appointments, and commitments. This central clearinghouse could be a hard copy planner, your cell phone's calendar, an online calendar, a web-based tool you sign up for, or something else. What's more important than what you choose is whether or not you use it faithfully! And even though it's good to have everything in one central place, redundancy can help, too. If you lose your cell phone, you don't want your entire life to fall apart! Have a scheduling back-up. Many new college students find that an ordinary paper-and-pencil daily calendar from an office supply store works best. Having a full page for each day means you

CAREER OUTLOOK: *Judith Cara, Public Relations Manager, Intel Corporation*

Q1: How important is time management in the field of public relations?

Public relations is just what it sounds like—the internal office that connects a company and the public at large. We handle good news and bad and work closely with community organizations and the media. Much of my job consists of keeping all of the balls up in the air at the same time. This job is not for somebody who feels compelled to finish one task before moving on to the next one.

Q2: What is the most challenging time management issue in your job? How do you deal with it?

Public relations is definitely not a job for someone who wants to work 9 a.m. to 5 p.m. A school board meeting may require my presence until 11 p.m., or a telephone conference call with my counterparts in Asia can take place at 6 a.m. Of course, a 6 a.m. telephone call can be handled from my home and I still get a kick out of sitting at home in my pajamas, talking to my colleagues around the world, while my two dogs are sprawled across my feet!

The field of public relations is all about relationships, so an outgoing personality, an ability to talk to strangers, and excellent networking skills are important.

Q3: How important is scheduling in your job?

Scheduling is an important component of my position, and Intel uses online meeting planning for calendar scheduling. At any given moment, my online calendar is up-to-date so that anyone can see times when I'm available

for a meeting. Despite this, I sometimes get double or even triple booked, and then I need to prioritize which meeting is most important.

Q4: What advice would you give college students who are interested in exploring a career in public relations?

If you are interested in pursuing a public relations career, find a public relations professional in your community and ask that person to spend a little time with you. Job

shadowing is a very effective way to see first-hand what is involved. Most of us are extraverts so we're happy to mentor others who have an interest in our field.

HOW WOULD *YOU* LIKE IT?

Have you ever considered a career in public relations?

Facts to Consider[7]

Academic preparation required: a college degree in public relations, communication, journalism, or some related field, along with an internship in public relations or similar work experience

Future workforce demand: Employment in this field is expected to grow at greater than average rates, but competition for entry-level jobs will be high.

Work environment: Public relations or communication specialists focus on building and maintaining an organization's relationship

with the public. They work with the media, community members, interest groups, government, and investors, for example. Public relations specialists often work forty-hour weeks, but they may occasionally need to work overtime or even around the clock during times of crisis.

Essential skills: creativity, initiative, communication, problem solving, and team working

Questions to Ponder

1. Do you have (or could you acquire) the skills this career requires?

2. Are you interested in a career like this? Why or why not?

For more career activities online, access the CourseMate via www.cengagebrain.com/shop/ISBN/0495906425 to do the Team Career exercises.

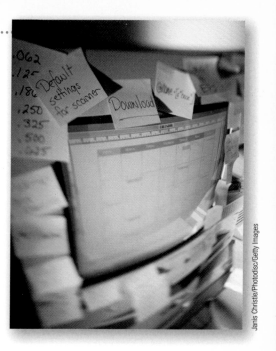

Janis Christie/Photodisc/Getty Images

> "Nothing is so fatiguing as the eternal hanging on of an uncompleted task."
>
> **William James, American psychologist and philosopher (1842–1910)**

can write your daily to-do list right in your planner (more on to-do lists later), and that can be a huge help.

STEP 3: Transfer important dates. The next step is to transfer important dates for the whole term from your "Term on a Page" overview to the appropriate days in your planner. This may seem repetitious, but there's a method to the madness. While it's important to be able to view all of your due dates together to create a big picture, it's equally important to have these dates recorded in your actual planner because you will use it more regularly—as the final authority on your schedule.

STEP 4: Set intermediate deadlines. After recording the important dates for the entire academic term, look at the individual due dates for major projects or papers that are assigned. Then set intermediate stepping-stone goals that will ultimately help you accomplish your final goals. Working backward from the due date, choose and record deadlines for completing certain chunks of the work. For example, if you have a research paper due, you could set an intermediate deadline for completing all of your initial research or writing a first draft.

STEP 5: Schedule fixed activities for the entire term. Next you'll want to schedule in all fixed activities throughout the entire term: class meeting times and reading assignments, religious services you regularly attend, club meetings, and regular co-curricular activities such as athletics or choir.

STEP 6: Check for schedule conflicts. Now, take a final look at your planner. Do you notice any major scheduling conflicts, such as a planned trip to your sister's wedding smack dab in the middle of midterm exam week? Look for these conflicts now, when there's plenty of time to adjust your plans and talk with your instructor to see what you can work out.

STEP 7: Schedule flextime. Although scheduling flextime seems like a contradiction of terms, it's important! You do need personal time for eating, sleeping, exercising, and other regular activities that don't have a set time frame. Despite your planner, life will happen. Several times each week, you can count on something coming up that will offer you a chance (or force you) to revise your schedule. The decision of how high the item ranks on your priority list rests with you, but the point is to leave some wiggle room in your schedule.

STEP 8: Monitor your schedule every day. At this point, you've developed a working time management system. Now it's important to monitor your use of that system on a daily basis. Each morning, take time to preview what your planner has planned for you. Each night, take three minutes to review the day's activities. How well did you stick to your schedule? Did you accomplish the tasks you set out to do? Do you need to revise your schedule for the rest of the week based on something that happened—or didn't happen—today? Don't skip this step. Mentally playing out the day in advance and reviewing afterwards will help you internalize what must be accomplished and help you create a pace for each day. Unless you're willing to take this last step, everything else you do in steps one through seven won't matter!

To Do or Not to Do? There *Is* No Question

Part of your personal time management system should be keeping an ongoing to-do list. While the concept of a to-do list sounds relatively simple, there are a few tricks of the trade.

Before the beginning of each school week, brainstorm all the things that you want or need to get done in the upcoming week. Using this random list of to-do items, assign a priority level next to each one. The A-B-C method is simple and easy to use:

A = must get this done; highest priority

B = very important to get done at some point

C = must do it right away, but it's not an extremely high priority

The two factors to consider when assigning a priority level to a to-do item are *importance* and *urgency*, creating four time zones. Use Figure 3.3 as a guide.[8]

After you've assigned a time zone to each item, review your list of A and B priorities and ask yourself:

1. **Do any of the items fit best with a particular day of the week?** For example, donating blood may be a high priority task for you, yet you don't want to do it on a day when you have co-curricular sports planned. That might leave you with two available days in the upcoming week that you can donate blood.

2. **Can any items be grouped together for easier execution?** For example, you may have three errands to run downtown on your to-do list, so grouping them together will save you from making three separate trips.

3. **Do any A and B priorities qualify as floating tasks that can be completed anytime, anywhere?** For example, perhaps you were assigned an extra long reading assignment for one of your classes. It's both important and urgent, an A priority item. Bring your book to read while waiting at the dentist's office for your semi-annual teeth cleaning appointment, a B priority. Planning ahead can really help save time.

Handwritten margin note:
A = 7:30 AM MEETING AT WORK

B = VET APPOINTMENT, COULD DELAY

C = CYCLING RACE DEADLINE

Handwritten margin note:
WHAT CAN I AFFORD TO GIVE UP? MAYBE NOT WORK OUT EVERY DAY?

FIGURE 3.3

Time Zones

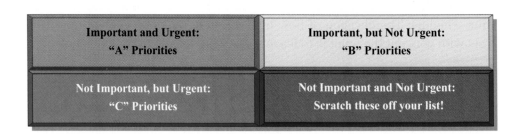

Important and Urgent: "A" Priorities	Important, but Not Urgent: "B" Priorities
Not Important, but Urgent: "C" Priorities	Not Important and Not Urgent: Scratch these off your list!

4. **Do any priorities need to be shifted?** As the days pass, some of your B priorities will become A priorities due to the urgency factor increasing. Or maybe an A priority will become a C priority because something changed about the task. This is normal.

As for those not-urgent, not-important to-do items, scratch them off the list right now. Life is too short to waste time on unimportant tasks. Give yourself permission to focus on what's important. Since time is a limited resource, one of the best ways to guarantee a successful college experience is to use it wisely. If you don't already use these tools on a regular basis, give them a shot. What do you have to lose except time?

EXERCISE 3.4

So Much to Do—So Little Time

Assume this is your to-do list for today (Monday). Assign each item one of the four time zones described earlier: A, B, C (and strike through any items that are not urgent and not important). Finally, renumber the items to indicate which you would do first, which second, and so forth.

Start time: 9:00 a.m., Monday morning, during the second week of the fall term.

1. _____ Return Professor Jordan's call before class tomorrow. He left a message saying he wants to talk to you about some problems with your LIT 101 paper.

2. _____ Pick up your paycheck at McDonald's and get to the bank before it closes at 5:00 p.m. this afternoon.

3. _____ Call the new love interest in your life and ask about going to the party together this weekend before someone else does.

4. _____ Visit the Speech Center to get critiqued on your first speech due Friday. It's closed evenings.

5. _____ Call your favorite aunt. She lives overseas in a time zone seven hours ahead of yours. Today is her fortieth birthday.

6. _____ Stop by the Health Center to take advantage of free meningitis vaccinations today only.

7. _____ Listen to the new music you downloaded yesterday.

8. _____ Leave a note asking your roommate or family member to please stop leaving messes everywhere. It's really aggravating.

9. _____ Read the two chapters in your history textbook for the in-class quiz on Wednesday.

10. _____ Watch the first episode of the new reality TV show you've been waiting for at 9 p.m. tonight.

11. _____ Write a rough draft of the essay due in your composition class on Thursday.

12. _____ Check with your RA about inviting a high school friend to spend the weekend.

13. _____ Return the three library books that are a week overdue.

14. _____ Call your math Teaching Assistant and leave a message asking for an appointment during her office hours to get help with the homework due on Wednesday. Nearly everyone is confused about the assignment.

15. _____ Go to the campus Athletic Banquet tonight at 6 p.m. to receive your award.

Identify the criteria you used in making your decisions.

How Time Flies!

? **challenge** " **reaction** * insight ! action

Challenge: What are the most common ways you waste time? What can be done about them?

Reaction: _____

_____

According to efficiency expert Michael Fortino, in a lifetime, the average American will spend:

> Seven years in the bathroom

> Five years waiting in line

> Two years playing telephone tag

> And six months waiting at red lights[9]

> Six years eating

> Three years in meetings

> Eight months opening junk mail

What a waste of time! We can't do much about some of these items, but what *can* we do about other time-wasters? Plan—schedule—organize! Think about the issue of control in time management, and write in examples for the following:

1. Things you think you can't control, and you can't: _____

2. Things you think you can't control, but you can: _____

3. Things you think you can control, but you can't: _____

4. Things you think you can control, but you don't: _____

5. Things you think you can control, and you can: _____

Perhaps you wrote in something like *medical emergencies* for (1). You could have written in *family or friends barging into your room* for (2). For (4), maybe you could control your *addiction to social networking*, but you don't. And for (5), perhaps you wrote in *your attention*. You're absolutely right. But what about (3)? Did anything fit there? Are there things you think you can control, but you can't? Try and think of something that would fit into (3), and then think of creative ways you really could control this situation if you tried.[10]

The P Word. Read This Section Now! . . . or Maybe Tomorrow . . . or the Next Day . . . or . . .

? **challenge** " **reaction** * insight ! action

Challenge: What are the most common reasons you procrastinate?

Reaction: _____

_____

Picture this: You sit down to work on a challenging homework assignment. After a few minutes, you think, *Man, I'm thirsty*, so you get up and get a soda. Then you sit back down to continue your work. A few minutes later, you decide that some chips would go nicely with your soda and off you go again. Again, you sit down to face the task before you, as you concentrate more on eating than on working. Ten minutes go by and a nagging thought starts taking over: *Must do laundry*. Up you go again and throw a load of clothes in the washer. Before long you're wondering where all the time went. Since you only have an hour left before your next class, you think, *Why bother getting started now? Doing this project will take much more time than that, so I'll just start it tomorrow*. Despite good intentions at the beginning of your work session, you've just succeeded in accomplishing zip, nadda, nothing.

Congratulations! You—like thousands of other college students—have just successfully procrastinated! Researchers define procrastination as "needlessly delaying tasks to the point of experiencing subjective discomfort."[11] And according to researchers, 70 percent of college students admit to procrastinating on their assignments.[12]

You may be in the majority, but alas, in this case, there's no safety in numbers! Academic procrastination is a major threat to your ability to succeed in college. And procrastination in the working world can actually bring your job, and ultimately your career, to a screeching halt. Plenty of people try to rationalize their procrastination by claiming that they work better under pressure. However, the challenge in college is that during some weeks of the term, every single class will have an assignment or test due, all at once, and if you procrastinate, you'll not only generate tremendous anxiety for yourself, but you'll lower your chances of succeeding on any of them.

Before you can control the procrastination monster in your life, it's important to understand *why* you procrastinate. Think about all the instances in which you don't procrastinate: meeting your friends for dinner, returning a phone call from a classmate, going to the store. Why are those things easy to do, but getting started on an assignment is difficult until you feel the jaws of a deadline closing down on you?[13] Procrastinators don't tend to be less smart or have a definitive psychological type. They do, however, tend to have lower self-confidence and get lost in their own thoughts.[14] In fact, according to one recent study, procrastination's root cause is a lack of confidence.[15] The reasons for procrastinating vary from person to person, but once you know your own reasons for putting things off, you'll be in a better position to address the problem from its root cause.

The next time you find yourself procrastinating, ask yourself why. Procrastination is self-handicapping: "It's like running a full race with a knapsack full of bricks on your back. When you don't win, you can say it's not that you're not a good runner, it's just that you had this sack of bricks on your back."[16] In addition to understanding why you procrastinate, try these ten procrastination busters to help you kick the habit.

1. **Keep track (of your excuses).** Write them down consistently, and soon you'll be able to recognize them for what they are. Hold yourself accountable. Own your responsibilities—in school and in the rest of your life.

2. **Break down.** No, not psychologically, though sometimes it can feel like you're headed that way. Break your project into its smaller components. A

[handwritten note in margin:] GOOD VIDEO ON PROCRASTINATION AVAILABLE ON THE CourseMate VIA WWW.CENGAGEBRAIN.COM/SHOP/ISBN/0495906425. GLAD TO KNOW I'M NOT THE ONLY ONE WHO PROCRASTINATES, BUT I DO HAVE TO WORK ON IT!

term paper, for example, can be broken down into the following smaller parts: prospectus, thesis, research, outline, small chunks of writing, and bibliography. Completing smaller tasks along the way is much easier than facing a daunting monster of a project.

3. **Trick yourself.** When you feel like procrastinating, pick some aspect of the project that's easy and that you would have to do anyway. If the thought of an entire paper is overwhelming you, for example, work on the bibliography to start. Starting with something—*anything*—will get you into the rhythm of the work.

Good idea for my history paper!

4. **Resolve issues.** If something's gnawing at you, making it difficult to concentrate, take care of it. Sometimes you must deal with a noisy roommate, your friends vying for your attention, or something equally intrusive. Then get down to work.

5. **Get real.** Set realistic goals for yourself. If you declare that you're going to finish a twelve-page paper in two hours, you're already doomed. Procrastinators are characteristically optimistic. They underestimate how much time something will take. Make it a habit to keep track of how long assignments take you in all your courses so that you can be increasingly realistic over time.

6. **Think positively.** Our imaginations can work for or against us. Don't let yours go haywire with thoughts that you're not up to the task or that your professor will hate your paper, so why bother. It has been said that the average person has 65,000 to 75,000 thoughts a day, and that many of these are negative. Don't imagine what can go wrong with your project. Imagine what can go right by getting it done on time and doing it well. Assume the best and you'll find it easier to get started.

7. **Make a deal with yourself.** Even if it's only spending fifteen minutes on a task that day, do it so that you can see progress.

8. **Overcome fear.** Many of the reasons for procrastinating have to do with our personal fears. We may fear not doing something perfectly, or failing completely—or even the responsibility that comes with success to keep succeeding. But as Susan Jeffers, author and lecturer states, "Feel the fear, and do it anyway!"

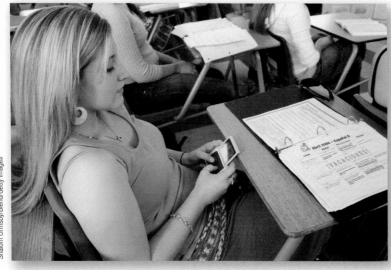

Shalom Ormsby/Blend/Getty Images

9. **Get tough.** Sometimes projects simply require discipline. The best way to complete a daunting task is to simply dig in. Become your own taskmaster, crack the proverbial whip, and force yourself to focus on those things that are high priorities, but perhaps not your idea of fun.

> " Things which matter most should never be at the mercy of things which matter least."
>
> **Johann Wolfgang von Goethe, German writer and scholar (1749–1832)**

Does procrastination enter into the picture when it comes to your most challenging course this term? What impact does procrastination have on your potential success in this course? On your life as a student?

Examine this list of common reasons people procrastinate. Which ones apply to you in your most challenging course? Put a checkmark next to all the reasons that help explain your tendency to procrastinate. For each item with a checkmark, list one thing you can do to control your learning in this course.

- ☐ Avoiding something you see as unpleasant
- ☐ Wanting to do something perfectly
- ☐ Feeling overwhelmed by all you have to do
- ☐ Being intimidated by the task itself
- ☐ Hoping to avoid responsibility
- ☐ Fearing failure
- ☐ Fearing success

- ☐ Fearing new or added responsibilities
- ☐ Not realizing how important the task is
- ☐ Reacting to your own internal conflict
- ☐ Protecting your self-esteem
- ☐ Waiting for a last-minute adrenaline rush
- ☐ Just plain not wanting to

10. **Acknowledge accomplishment.** We're not talking major shopping sprees at Neiman Marcus here. We're talking reasonable, meaningful rewards commensurate with the action completed. Go buy yourself a small treat, call your best friend in another state, take a relaxing soak in the bathtub, or do something to celebrate your accomplishments—big and small—along the way. Acknowledgment, from yourself or others, is a great motivator for tackling future projects.

Beyond Juggling: *Realistically* Manage Work, School, and Personal Life

? **challenge** ⟩ 66 **reaction** ⟩ * **insight** ⟩ ! **action**

Challenge: How do successful people juggle work, school, and personal life?

Reaction: _____

_____

Your personal time management needs depend on who you are and how many obligations you have. Today's college students are more diverse than ever. Increasing numbers of college students are also parents, full- or part-time employees, husbands or wives, community volunteers, soccer coaches, or Sunday school teachers. How on earth can you possibly juggle it all?

Tetra Images/Tetra Images/Corbis

" The trouble with the rat race is that even if you win, you're still a rat."

Lily Tomlin, comedian

The answer? You can't. According to work-life balance expert Dawn Carlson, juggling is a knee-jerk coping mechanism—the default setting when time gets tight and it seems that nothing can be put on the back burner. If you, like millions of others, feel overworked, overcommitted, and exhausted at every turn, you may have already learned that you can't juggle your way to a balanced life. It's impossible.[17]

Now for the good news. Balance among work, school, and personal life is possible. All of us have three primary areas of our lives that should be in balance, ideally—meaningful work (including school), satisfying relationships, and a healthy lifestyle. In addition to work and relationships, we all need to take care of ourselves. See what you think of these five rebalancing strategies. The idea is you can't have it all, but you can have it better than you do now.

1. **Alternating.** If you use this strategy, your work-life balance comes in separate, concentrated doses. You may throw yourself into your career with abandon, and then cut back or quit work altogether and focus intensely on your family. You may give your job 110 percent during the week, but devote Saturdays to physical fitness or to your family or running all the errands you've saved up during the week. Or you save Tuesdays and Thursdays for homework, and go to classes Mondays, Wednesdays, and Fridays. People who use this strategy alternate between important things, and it works for them. An alternator's motto is "I want to have it all, but just not all at once."

2. **Outsourcing.** An outsourcer's motto might be "I want to have it all, not do it all." This strategy helps you achieve work-life balance by giving someone else some of your responsibilities—usually in your personal life—to free up time for the tasks you care about most. If you have enough money, hire someone to clean the house or mow the lawn. If you don't, trade these jobs among family, friends, or neighbors who band together to help each other. Of course, there are ways this strategy could be misused by college students, like downloading your paper from the Internet with a charge card! Warning: This practice will definitely be hazardous to your academic health! In fact, your college career may be over!

3. **Bundling.** This strategy helps you rebalance your life by killing two birds with one stone. Examine your busy life and look for areas in which you can double dip, such as combining exercising with socializing. If your social life is suffering because of time constraints, take walks with a friend so that you can talk along the way. Do your laundry with your roommate so that you can chat about your classes. A bundler's motto is "I want to get more mileage out of the things I do by combining activities." Bundling is efficient because it allows you to do two things at once.

4. **Techflexing.** Technology allows us to work from almost anywhere, anytime, using technology. If you telecommute from home several days a week for your job, you might get up early, spend some time on e-mail, go out for a run, have breakfast with your family, and then get back on your computer. In the office, you use texting to stay connected to family members or a cell phone to call home while driving to work. Chances are you can telecommute to your campus library and do research online, check in with your professor during online office hours, register for classes online, and pay all your bills

TAKE TAURA WITH ME TO THE GYM? :)

online, including tuition. Use technology, and the flexibility it gives you, to your advantage to merge important aspects of your life.

5. **Simplifying.** People who use this strategy are ready to cry uncle. They've decided they don't want it all. They've reached a point where they make a permanent commitment to stop the craziness in their lives. The benefit of simplifying is greater freedom from details, stress, and the rat race. But there are trade-offs, of course. They may have to take a significant cut in pay in order to work fewer hours or at a less demanding job. But for them, it's worth it.[18]

These five strategies, used separately or in combination, have helped many people who are dealing with work, school, and family commitments at the same time. They all require certain trade-offs. None of these strategies is a magic solution.

But the alternative to rebalancing is more stress, more physical and emotional exhaustion, more frustration, and much less personal satisfaction. If you focus on rebalancing your life—making conscious choices and course corrections as you go—small changes can have a big impact. Work-life balance isn't an all-or-nothing proposition. It's an ever-changing journey. So take it one step at a time.

? challenge   **" reaction**   *** insight**   **! action**

Now What Do You Think?

1. At the beginning of this chapter, Derek Johnson, a frustrated and disgruntled student, faced a challenge. Now after reading this chapter, would you respond differently to any of the questions you answered about the "FOCUS Challenge Case"? Knowing what you know now, how would you advise him? Write a paragraph ending to the story, incorporating your best advice.

2. How would you evaluate your time management skills right now? Would you give yourself an A, B, C, or below? Why? What specific strategies from this chapter would help you manage your time better?

3. Do you feel that your energy fluctuates throughout an average day? Describe your biological clock. What actions can you take to regulate your physical and emotional energy for the sake of your own productivity?

4. If you feel the need to rebalance your life due to the pressures of managing work, school, family, and friends at the same time, take some time to work through the following Rebalancing Plan worksheet.[19]

Why do I need to rebalance? _____

What rebalancing strategies will I use? _____

How will I do it? _____

How will I let go of _____ ? _____

Tasks that I should completely eliminate: _____

Tasks that I can outsource or give to others: _____

Expectations of others that affect me: _____

Time-consuming possessions or relationships that bring little value to me: _____

_____

Adapted from K. Sandholtz, B. Derr, F. Buckner, D. Carlson (2002). *Beyond Juggling: Rebalancing your busy life.* San Francisco: Berrett-Koehler Publishing.

Complete the recommended activity for your preferred VARK learning modality. If you are multimodal, select more than one activity. Your instructor may ask you to (a) give an oral report on your results in class, (b) send your results to him or her via e-mail, (c) post them online, or (d) contribute to a class chat.

Visual: Buy a set of adhesive colored dots from a local office supply store. Go through this chapter putting red dots by things you'll try right away, yellow dots by things that sound like a good idea, and green dots by things you're already doing well now.

Aural: Access the CourseMate via www.cengagebrain .com/shop/ISBN/ 0495906425 to listen to the iAudio summary for this chapter. As soon as you've finished, write down three ideas that stuck in your head.

Read/Write: Write a case study about yourself and time management.

Kinesthetic: Find a YouTube or other online resource on time management that adds to this chapter. Show your YouTube or "compete" with other "K" students to show the best one in class.

(from left to right) Marcela Barsse/MarsBars/iStockphoto.com; Johanna Goodyear/Dreamstime.com; Nadezda Firsova/iStockphoto.com; Pascal Genest/iStockphoto.com

REALITY CHECK | What did you Learn?

On a scale of 1 to 10, answer the following questions now that you've completed this chapter.

1 = not very/not much/very little/low   10 = very/a lot/very much/high

In hindsight, how much did you already know about this subject before reading the chapter?

1   2   3   4   5   6   7   8   9   10

Can you answer these questions about managing time and energy more fully now that you've read the chapter?

1. **What's the difference between time management, attention management, and energy management? How are they different, and what do they have in common?**

2. **What percentage of college students admit to procrastinating on assignments? What's the major reason they procrastinate according to research?**

3. **Identify three specific techniques for balancing your life.**

How useful might the information in this chapter be to you? How much do you think this information might affect your success in college?

1   2   3   4   5   6   7   8   9   10

How much do you think this information might affect your career success after college?

1   2   3   4   5   6   7   8   9   10

How long did it actually take you to complete this chapter (both the reading and writing tasks)? _____ Hour(s) _____ Minutes

 Challenge Yourself Online Quiz. To find out how much you've learned, access the CourseMate via www.cengagebrain.com/shop/ ISBN/0495906425 to take the Challenge Yourself Online Quiz.

Take a minute to compare these answers to your answers from the "Readiness Check" at the beginning of this chapter. What gaps exist between the similar questions? How might these gaps between what you thought before starting the chapter and what you now think after completing the chapter affect how you approach the next chapter in this book?

chapter 4

Thinking Critically and Creatively

©Larry Harwood Photography. Property of Cengage Learning.

You're About to Discover . . .
- ✔ What focused thinking is
- ✔ Why critical thinking is important
- ✔ How a four-part model of critical thinking works
- ✔ How to analyze arguments, assess assumptions, and consider claims
- ✔ How to avoid mistakes in reasoning
- ✔ What metacognition is and why it's important
- ✔ How you solve problems and make decisions
- ✔ How to become a more creative thinker

READINESS CHECK What do you **Know?**

Before beginning this chapter, take a moment to answer these questions. Your answers will help you assess how ready you are to focus.

1 = not very/not much/very little/low   10 = very/a lot/very much/high

How much do you *already* know?

Based on reading the "You're about to discover. . ." list and skimming this chapter, how much do you think you probably already know about this chapter's subject?

1 2 3 4 5 6 7 8 9 10

See if you can answer these questions about critical and creating thinking *before* you read.

1. **What's the difference between thinking and critical thinking?**

2. **Identify three specific types of faulty reasoning.**

3. **What's the difference between critical thinking and creative thinking?**

How motivated are you to learn *more*?

In general, how motivated are you to learn more by reading this chapter?

1 2 3 4 5 6 7 8 9 10

How much do you think this information might affect your success in college?

1 2 3 4 5 6 7 8 9 10

How much do you think this information might affect your career success after college?

1 2 3 4 5 6 7 8 9 10

How ready are you to read *now*?

How ready are you to focus on this chapter—physically, intellectually, and emotionally? Circle a number for each aspect of your readiness to focus.

1 2 3 4 5 6 7 8 9 10

If any of your answers is below a 10, you might want to pay attention to whatever is distracting you before you start reading. For example, if you're feeling scattered, take a few moments to settle down and focus.

Finally, how long do you think it will take you to complete this chapter from start to finish?

_____ Hour(s) _____ Minutes

Annie Miller

Growing up in a big city was definitely a good thing. So Annie Miller thought, anyway. Every day that went by, she missed L.A. more and more. She missed the fast pace, the diversity, the lifestyle. Why had she decided to go to such a small college after growing up in such a large city? She knew that it was because she wanted every aspect of her life at college to be different. She wanted to live on a different coast, have new friends, and study something exciting. Her huge high school had been amazing in its own way, but now she wanted a more personal education at a place where everyone knew everyone, like at the small liberal arts college she had chosen on the East Coast.

Philosophy 100 Syllabus

Dr. Samuel Courtney
dress: S.Courtney@univmail.edu
urs: MWF 8am-10am
cation: University Hall 1020
e Big Questions" (7th edition), by Robert C. Solomon and Kathleen M. Higgins

ntent: As our text suggests, this course will seek to answer some of the "big questions".
explore ideas about the nature of knowing, free will, logic, and critical and reflective
During this course I encourage you to ask questions and think critically. There is no
ng as a stupid question.

ethod: Since this is a philosophy class, for our class method we will turn to one of the
g fathers of critical and philosophical thinking: Socrates. Consequently, we will be
e 'Socratic method' when approaching course material. This means that instead of
a lecture, I will ask you, the students, questions in order to create a lively discussion.

ng: This course will include 3 exams, each worth 20% of your overall grade. There will
5 quizzes during the semester, all of which contribute to another 20% of your grade.
, class participation will count for the final 20% of your grade. It is imperative that you
every class session, and that you are actively participating in class discussions.

se Outline:
ad of giving a week-by-week overview of the class, here is a list of the topics we'll be
ssing. This way, we can move at our own pace; talking in-depth about topics in which we
more interest, and quickly moving past those in which we don't.

- What Philosophy Is
- Greek Philosophy
- Chinese Philosophy
- Ethics
- Enlightenment
- Knowledge
- Skepticism
- Rationalism
- Empiricism

Her first semester of classes consisted of a college success course, an English composition class, Introduction to Poetry, and Philosophy 100. She was excited by the idea of learning in small classes with wise and learned professors. But Philosophy 100 had turned out to be a very challenging course. Professor Courtney had announced on the first day of class that he believed in the Socratic method of teaching. He taught by asking questions of students instead of lecturing. "Socrates, perhaps the greatest philosopher of all time," he announced the first day, "is the father of critical thinking. In this class, you'll learn to think critically. *That* is what college is all about."

Professor Courtney began every class session with a hypothetical situation and always randomly chose a student to respond. His opening went something like this:

Assume it's Valentine's Day. A young man makes a trip to the biggest jewelry store in the mall to buy his fiancée a gift. He's saved up for a long time to afford 24 karat gold earrings and he's ready to choose the best money can buy. He finds the perfect pair and hands over his credit card. But when the salesclerk brings the receipt for him to sign, he notices that instead of $300, she has missed a digit, and the receipt reads $30. He now faces a dilemma: Does he sign and say nothing, or point out the error and pay the full amount? What should he do?

One student responded with, "He should sign his name and then take off quickly. This mistake was the clerk's, not his. If someone catches the mistake later, he can just claim he didn't notice. Maybe no one will ever figure it out, and he'll be $270 richer!" Professor Courtney continued, "On what ethical principle do you base your response?" The student faltered, and the professor moved on to someone else, raising other points that hadn't been considered.

"But what if his fiancée decides to exchange the earrings for another pair? What if the clerk is fired for making a $270 mistake? What if the clerk were your sister or your best friend? What if the hero of a movie did what you're proposing? What if the clerk were you?" he continued. "What would Socrates say about what you should do? According to Socrates, no one errs intentionally. This means that whenever we do something wrong—including something *morally* wrong—it is out of ignorance rather than evil motives. If the young man decides to capitalize on the clerk's error, what are his motives—and are they evil? What would be the *right* thing to do?"

Professor Courtney continued putting students on the spot and raising questions posed by other philosophers they were studying. The questions seemed endless. Annie found herself listening more carefully than in her other classes so that she would be ready to jump in if called upon. And she silently thought through others' answers, too. Even though she had to admit that the learning environment was stimulating, speaking in front of other students made Annie nervous.

"There aren't always right answers," Professor Courtney told them. "What's important is thinking through the problem. The process of learning to think can be more important than the answer itself."

Frankly, that explanation didn't sit well with Annie. *If there aren't right answers, what am I doing in college? Things should be black and white, true or false, right or wrong. I'm paying tuition to hear what the professor thinks, not all the other students in class. He knows the right answers. Why doesn't he just tell us?*

Without fail, Annie always left Professor Courtney's class with a headache from thinking so hard. Her best friend Hannah suggested that she look up his online ratings to find out what other students had said about him. "If his ratings are bad," she said, "just drop the course. At the very least you'll find out if there are secrets to getting an A in his class." But when Annie did that, she found mostly glowing praise: "I thought he was an impossible teacher at the time," wrote one student, "but he really taught me to think. Now I'm grateful!"

Compared to Philosophy 100, all her other classes seemed effortless. She had to admit that she much preferred classes in which she could express herself creatively, like Introduction to Poetry.

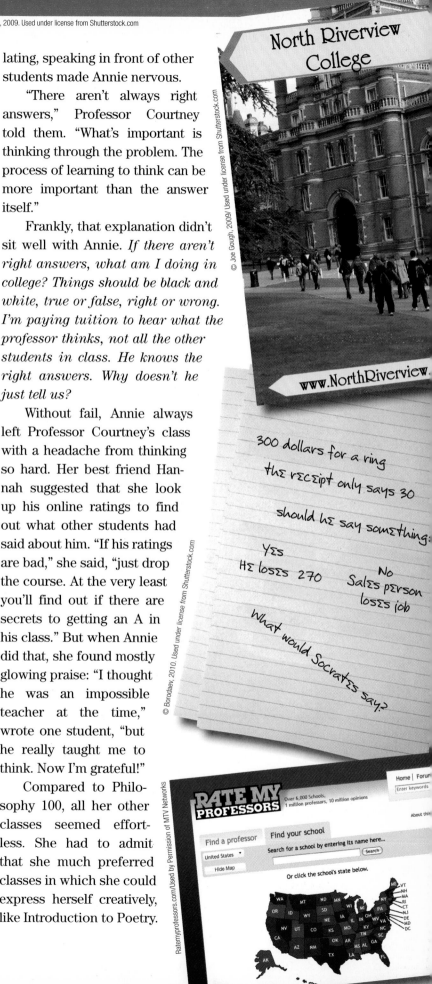

North Riverview College

www.NorthRiverview.

300 dollars for a ring
the rεcεipt only says 30

should hε say somεthing?

Yεs
Hε losεs 270

No
Salεs pεrson losεs job

What would Socratεs say?

What Do You Think?

1. Do you agree with Professor Courtney's statement that "there aren't always right answers"? If that's true, why is getting a college education so important?

2. Even though Professor Courtney's teaching methods made her nervous, why did Annie find the learning environment in his class to be stimulating?

3. Annie says she prefers creative thinking to critical thinking. Why might that be true for Annie or any student, potentially?

4. Identify three things Annie should do to get the most from Professor Courtney's class.

Rethinking Thinking

? **challenge** " **reaction** * **insight** ! **action**

Challenge: What's the difference between thinking and critical thinking?

Reaction: _____

Thinking is a natural, ongoing, everyday process we all engage in. In fact, we can't really turn it off, even if we try. We're always on. Everyone thinks all the time, right? It happens any time you talk to yourself, doesn't it? However, some experts say school teaches us how to regurgitate, not how to think.

In many ways, thinking is like speaking. But if you take a public speaking course, you're bound to be a better speaker by the end of it by knowing more about how to consciously direct your voice, gestures, and delivery. In a similar way, you can become a better thinker by learning how to direct your brain. *Focused thinking*—thinking critically and creatively—is what this chapter is about.

Picture this: You're in the library. It's late, and you're tired. You're supposed to be studying for your political science test, but instead of thinking about foreign policy, your mind begins drifting toward the foreign vacation you took last summer, how tan you were when you returned, and how much fun it was to be with your friends.

Would the mental process you're engaging in while sitting in the library be called *thinking*? For our purposes in this chapter, the answer is no. Here thinking is defined as a focused cognitive activity you engage in for a reason. You direct your thoughts toward a particular topic. You're the *active* thinker, not the *passive* daydreamer who is the victim of a wandering mind. Focused thinking is deliberate and intentional, not haphazard or accidental. You choose to do it for a reason.

> ‘Knowledge is power.’ Rather, knowledge is happiness. To have knowledge, deep broad knowledge, is to know truth from false and lofty things from low.”
>
> **Helen Keller, American author, activist, and lecturer**
> **(1880–1968)**

Focused thinking is like a two-sided coin. Sometimes when you think, you *produce* ideas. That's what this chapter calls *creative thinking*, and that's something we'll deal with later. The other side of thinking requires you to *evaluate* ideas—your own or someone else's. That's *critical thinking*. The word critical comes from the Greek word for *critic (kritikos)*, meaning "to question or analyze." You focus on something, sort through the information, and decide which ideas are most sensible, logical, or useful. When you're thinking critically, you're asking questions, analyzing arguments, assessing assumptions, considering claims, avoiding mistakes in reasoning, problem solving, decision making, and all the while, thinking about your thinking.

Why Think Critically?

? challenge	66 reaction	* insight	! action

Challenge: Why improve your critical thinking skills? In what specific ways will improved skills benefit you?

Reaction: _____

_____

Critical thinking is a particular kind of focused thinking. It is purposeful, reasoned, and goal-directed. It's thinking that aims to solve problems, calculate likelihood, weigh evidence, and make decisions.[1] Critical thinkers develop standards they can use to judge advertisements, political speeches, sales pitches, movies—you name it.[2] Critical thinking is not jumping to conclusions, buying arguments lock, stock, and barrel, accepting controversial ideas at face value, ignoring the facts, or disregarding the evidence.

Unfortunately, some people are noncritical thinkers. They may be biased or prejudiced or closed-minded. Other people are *selective* critical thinkers. When it comes to one particular subject, they shut down their minds. They

©Larry Harwood Photography. Property of Cengage Learning.

can't explain their views, they're emotional about them, and they refuse to acknowledge any other position. Their particular positions may be right or wrong in your view, but the important issue is whether they are thinking critically about them. Why do they believe these things? Only if they understand the *why*, can they explain their views to someone else or defend them under fire. The importance of *why* can't be overstated. Some people, of course, have already thought through their beliefs, and they understand their positions and the reasons for them very well. Arriving at that point is the goal of aspiring critical thinkers.

EXERCISE 4.1

And Just Why Is Critical Thinking Important?

Here is a list of reasons why it's important to improve your critical thinking skills. Beside each entry, mark the degree to which you'd like to concentrate your efforts as a college student, soon ready to enter a new career path. On a scale from 1 to 10 with 10 representing the highest degree, would you like to:

1. _____ **Become a more successful college student?** Most college courses require you to think critically (in answering essay questions, for example). In one study of over 1,100 college students, higher scores on critical thinking skills tests correlated highly with better grades.[3] Critical thinkers, for example, can ask better questions in class. There's even evidence that interaction with other students in co-curricular activities can help you develop as a critical thinker.[4]

2. _____ **Become a better citizen?** Critical thinking is the foundation of a strong democracy. Voters must think critically about candidates' messages and their likelihood of keeping campaign promises. It's easy to talk about balancing the budget, or improving education, but the truth is these highly complex tasks are very challenging to carry out. The American public must sift through information and examine the soundness of politicians' arguments in order to keep our democracy strong.

3. _____ **Become a better employee?** A workforce of critical—and creative—thinkers helps the American economy thrive and individuals become more successful. The U.S. Department of Labor reports that today's jobs require employees who can deal with complexity, learn and perform multiple tasks, analyze and deal with a wide variety of options, identify problems, perceive alternative approaches, and select the best approach.[5] Employers are "practically begging" for employees who can "think, collaborate, communicate, coordinate, and create."[6]

4. _____ **Become a more savvy consumer?** In today's marketplace, everyone wants your dollars. If you acted on every ad you read in magazines or watch on television, you'd run out of money very quickly. Critical thinking will help you evaluate offers, avoid slick come-ons, and buy responsibly.

5. _____ **Build stronger relationships?** Critical thinking helps us understand our own and others' actions and become more responsible communicators. Whether with friends or romantic partners, relationships take work. Sometimes you have to figure out what your partner really means or listen between the lines for important clues. Actually, critical thinking is at the heart of every relationship you care about.

6. _____ **Become a lifelong learner?** Your education doesn't end when you get your diploma. In many ways the real exams begin afterward when you put your classroom learning to the test. And in today's world you must continue to learn as you transition through jobs to give your life more meaning—personally and professionally. You'll need to keep expanding your skills, no matter what your career is.

A Four-Part Model of Critical Thinking

Challenge: Reasoning, problem solving, and decision making are all part of critical thinking. How are these three things related?

Reaction: _____

Like your writing or speaking skills, well-cultivated critical thinking skills can serve as the infrastructure for taking on all of your academic challenges. But let's ask an important question: How do you do it? We'll look at the four primary components of critical thinking, and at the end of this chapter, we'll use a realistic news story, one that is relevant to many college campuses, to allow you to apply what you've learned and provide a memorable example. Take a look at Figure 4.1 to preview the four-part model of critical thinking.

I. Reasoning: The Foundation of Critical Thinking

Reasoning, the foundation of critical thinking, is the ability to come to a conclusion based on one or more arguments. A strong argument is convincing because it backs up its claim with evidence. If no one would disagree with what you're saying, it's not an argument. It's self-evident. "Grass is green" is not an argument. But "Cows that are grass-fed make the best meat" (if supporting evidence is provided) is. Do you see the difference?

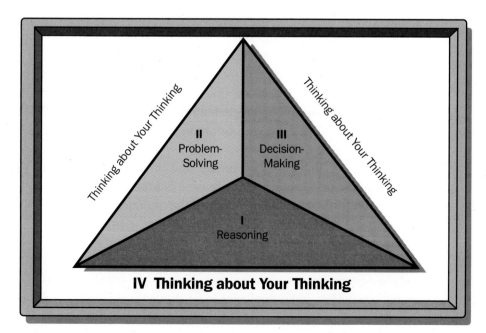

FIGURE 4.1

Critical Thinking Is Focused

Here's a four-part model of critical thinking. Your reasoning skills underlie everything. They are the foundation upon which your problem-solving and decision-making skills rest, and your metacognitive skills, or thinking about your thinking, surround all the focused thinking you do.

© John Lund/CORBIS

How good are you at creating a sound argument? Let's say that you're trying to convince your roommate to stop inviting people into your room while you're studying for major exams. What evidence would you use to convince her? How good are you at evaluating someone else's argument? For example, you're trying to decide whether an online discount is really a good deal. Would you take the advertiser's word for it or do some research to compare prices on your own? Throughout the rest of this chapter, ask yourself: Are there ways I can improve my reasoning skills?

Analyzing Arguments

? challenge **""** reaction * insight ! action

Challenge: What does the term *argument* have to do with critical thinking? How do you recognize a *sound* argument?

Reaction: _____

_____

I love this YouTube vid!

Have you ever seen the *Monty Python Flying Circus* "Argument Clinic Sketch"? In this bizarre skit a man comes to an "argument clinic" to buy an argument. The two arguers—"professional" and customer—engage in an interminably long, "yes, it is" "no, it isn't" squabble.

Critical thinking is about arguments. But when most of us think of an argument, that's the kind of bickering we think of. In the middle of the "Argument Clinic" sketch, however, the customer actually makes an important point. He protests that they're not really arguing; they're just contradicting each other. He continues, "An argument is a connected series of statements intended to establish a proposition." That's the kind of argument that's related to critical thinking.

Critical thinking is about an argument that *one* person puts forth. Attorneys—for both the prosecution and defense—put forth their closing arguments at the end of a trial. A politician puts forth an argument about where he stands on the issues. A professor puts forth an argument to persuade her class to learn important content in her discipline.

Arguments are said to be inductive or deductive. *Inductive* arguments go from specific observations to general conclusions. In criminal trials, the prosecution puts together individual pieces of evidence to prove that the defendant is guilty: eyewitnesses put him at the scene, the gun store salesman remembers selling him a pistol, and his fingerprints are on the weapon.

Therefore, the prosecutor argues that the defendant is guilty. Other arguments are said to be *deductive*, meaning they go from broad generalizations to specific conclusions. All serial killers have a particular psychological profile. The defendant has this psychological profile. Therefore the defendant is the killer.

What do arguments do? They try to persuade. Arguments contain clear reasons to believe someone or something. Once you understand what an argument is, you must also understand that arguments can be sound or unsound. If I tell you that two plus two equals four, chances are good that you'll believe me. If, on the other hand, I tell you two plus two equals five, you'll flatly deny it. If I say "Cats have fur." "Dogs have fur." "Therefore dogs are cats," you'll tell me I'm crazy—because it's an unsound argument.

The standard we use to test the soundness of arguments is logic, which is a fairly extensive topic. Let's just say for our purposes here that arguments are sound when the evidence to support them is reasonable, more reasonable than the evidence supporting other opinions. The important point is that a sound argument provides at least one good reason to believe. Let's look at an example:

> *I don't see why all first-year students have to take Freshman Composition. It's a free country. Students shouldn't have to take courses they don't want to take.*

Based on our definition, is this example an argument? Why or why not? Is the statement "It's a free country" relevant? What does living in a free country have to do with the curricula in colleges and universities? Nothing. *Relevancy* is a condition needed for a sound argument.

Now look at this example:

> *I don't see why all first-year students have to take Freshman Composition. Many students developed good writing skills in high school, and their Verbal SAT scores are 600 or higher.*

Is this second example an argument? Why or why not? The first example doesn't give you a good reason to believe the argument; the second example does. A true argument must contain at least one reason for you to believe it.

Here's another warning. Not everything that sounds like an argument is one. Look at this example:

> *Everyone taking Calculus 100 failed the test last Friday. I took the test last Friday. Therefore, I will probably get an F in the course.*

Is that a sound argument—or is something missing? Even though all three sentences may be true, they don't constitute a sound argument. What grade has this student earned on earlier calculus tests? How many tests are left in the course? The information present may not be adequate or enough to predict an F in the course. *Adequacy* is another condition needed for a sound argument. This alternative, on the other hand, is a sound argument:

> *Everyone taking Calculus 100 failed the test last Friday. I took the test last Friday. Therefore, I earned an F on the test.*

When you're deciding on the soundness of an argument, you must look for two things: *relevance* and *adequacy*.[7]

Not all arguments are sound. Have you ever heard this tale? A scientist decided to begin a new study to find out what makes people drunk. He planned an orderly, methodical experiment. On Monday night, he drank three tall glasses filled half and half with scotch and water. The next morning, he recorded his results: intoxication. On Tuesday night, he drank three tall glasses of whiskey and water. On Wednesday night, he drank three tall glasses of rum and water. On Thursday night, he drank three tall glasses of vodka and water. Each morning, the results he recorded were identical. He had become highly intoxicated. His faulty conclusion? Water makes people drunk.

Funny example of an unsound argument!

Not only is it important to be able to construct sound arguments, but it's also important to be able to recognize them. As a consumer in today's information society, you must know when to buy into an argument, and when not to.

Assessing Assumptions

When you're thinking critically, one of the most important kinds of questions you can ask is about the *assumptions* you or someone else are making, perhaps without even realizing it. Assumptions can limit our thinking. Consider this well-known puzzle, and afterward, examine how your assumptions may have interfered with solving it.

??? Got me on this one . . .

> *One day Kerry celebrated her birthday. Two days later her older twin brother, Harry, celebrated his birthday. How could that be?*

You may have solved this puzzle if you were willing to question the underlying assumptions that were holding you back. (Answer is upside down at the bottom of this page.)

People reveal their underlying assumptions in what they say. If you listen carefully, you can uncover them. "Go on for a graduate degree after I finish college? No way! I'm out of here in four years, no matter what!" This student's underlying assumption is that college itself isn't as important as what comes afterward (like making money). This student may just tolerate her classes without getting engaged in the subject matter, and she checks off requirements as quickly as she can. Too bad.

> " Great minds discuss ideas. Average minds discuss events. Small minds discuss people."
>
> **Eleanor Roosevelt, First Lady of the United States (1884–1962)**

Considering Claims

Evaluating claims is one of the most basic aspects of reasoning. A claim is a statement that can be true or false, but not both. This is different from a fact, which cannot be disputed. What's the difference between a *fact* and a *claim*? Facts can't be disputed; claims can be true or false, but they must be one or the other, not both.

> *FACT: Ronald Reagan, George H. Bush, and Bill Clinton have been presidents of the United States during the last thirty years.*
>
> *CLAIM: Bill Clinton was the most popular American president in the last thirty years.*

The fact is obvious. The claim requires evidence to support it. As a critical thinker, it's important to use your reasoning skills to evaluate evidence. Generally speaking, be wary of claims that

> are supported by unidentified sources ("Experts claim . . .").

> are made by interested parties who stand to gain ("Brought to you by the makers of . . .").

Kerry and Harry are not twins. Harry and his brother are twins, and they are older than Kerry.

FIGURE 4.2

The Question Pyramid

Source: Adapted from Hellyer, R., Robinson, C., & Sherwood, P. (1998). *Study skills for learning power.* New York: Houghton Mifflin, 18.

LEVEL 4: What if ?

CREATIVE THINKING

Why? ← Level 3: Why and how questions → How?

Complex Reasoning:
Critical thinking
Problem solving
Decision making

BASIC REASONING

Who? ← Level 2: Who and what questions → What?

Level 1:
Basic yes/no questions
Is someone trying to convince me of something? If yes...

SIMPLE REASONING

> are put forth by a lone individual claiming his experience as the norm ("I tried it and it worked for me!").

> use a bandwagon appeal ("Everybody's doing it.").

> lie with statistics ("over half" when it's really only 50.5 percent).

On the other hand, we must also keep an open mind and be flexible in our thinking. If you get good evidence to support a view that contradicts yours, be willing to modify your ideas. One way to evaluate the validity of claims is to use the Question Pyramid above. Consider claims by asking these four key questions: "who?" "what?" "why?" and "how?" Figure 4.2 shows how the questions progress from level 1 to 3.

Avoiding Faulty Reasoning

? **challenge** " **reaction** ＊ insight ! action

Challenge: List as many reasoning mistakes as you can. Can you provide an example of one or two of them?

Reaction: _____

_____

Fact: Half the class failed the first test in Phil 100.
Opinion: Phil 100 is the hardest class I'll ever take!

Although we can certainly improve our critical-thinking skills, it's impossible to be a perfect critical thinker 100 percent of the time. As thinkers, we make mistakes, and sometimes others try to trick us with false arguments. It's important to cultivate both types of critical thinking skills: your *productive* skills, which you use as a speaker and writer, and your *receptive* skills, which you use as a reader and listener. As responsible communicators, we must understand what a sound argument is and know how to construct one ourselves. We must also understand what a defective argument is in order to avoid getting sucked in when we shouldn't.

Here is a top-ten list of logical fallacies, or false logic strategies, we can slip into—or others can use against us—if we're not careful. For each of the ten types, read through the example and then see if you can come up with one of your own.

1. **False cause and effect** (assuming one cause for something when other causes are possible, too)

   I moved into my new dorm room last month. I've failed every exam I've taken since. Living in the residence hall is blowing my GPA!

2. **Personal attack** (reacting to a challenge by attacking the challenger)

   How could anyone believe our professor's views on ethics? We all know he's a very poor teacher.

3. **Unwarranted assumption** (taking too much for granted without evidence)

   You say universities give women equal opportunities. I say they don't. Reply: It's true. I read it on a website.

4. **Emotional appeal** (appealing to someone's feelings in order to gain acceptance of an argument)

   If you care about the institution that made you what you are today, you'll dig deep into your pockets and send a financial contribution now.

5. **False authority** (attributing your argument to someone else in a supposed position of power to get you off the hook)

   I'd really like to be able to change your grade, but my Department Chair frowns upon that.

6. **Hasty conclusion** (jumping to a conclusion when other conclusions are possible)

   I'm sure my roommate stole my textbook. He's too cheap to buy his own.

Jac Depczyk/Getty Images

7. **Straw man** (attempting to "prove" an argument by overstating, exaggerating, or oversimplifying the arguments of the opposing side)

   We should relax the entrance requirements to help attract more students. Reply: You actually want the quality of students here to take a nose dive? Oh, right, why don't we all just teach high school instead?

8. **Shifting the burden of proof** (shifting the responsibility of proving an assertion to someone else because you have no evidence for what you assert)

The zero-tolerance policy on alcohol in the residence halls is working. Reply: No, it's not. Reply back: Oh yeah? Prove it.

9. **Oversimplification/overgeneralization** (reducing a complex issue to something very simple or stereotyping)

    College professors have it made. They teach a couple classes a week for a few hours, and then they have free time the rest of the week. That's the kind of job I want!

10. **Either/or thinking** (taking only an extreme position on an issue when other positions are possible)

    Either we ban alcohol on campus or we'll go bankrupt from lawsuits.

EXERCISE 4.2

Rocky Mountain State University Case Study and Simulation

Great Bluffs Herald

Saturday, September 18, 2010

Cheap Beer + Fraternities = Recipe for Death

Great Bluffs, Colorado It's that time of year again. The fall semester began last month at Rocky Mountain State University, and again this year, a student died of alcohol poisoning within the first three weeks of classes. Clark Cameron of Valdosta, Georgia, a Gamma Beta Gamma pledge, was found dead yesterday morning in the GBG fraternity house on campus. The body of the collapsed student was found in a third-floor bedroom. An anonymous call to 9-1-1 came in at 6:15 a.m.: "We've got a guy here. We can't wake him, and we know he drank way too much last night." Cameron was pronounced dead on arrival at Great Bluffs General Hospital.

The incident represented RMSU's third death from alcohol poisoning in as many years. Roland Bishop, the University's new president, is said to deeply mourn the loss of another RMSU freshman. "No student should die during his first few weeks of college—what should be one of the most exciting times of his life. It's insane and very, very sad."

The national Gamma Beta Gamma office has suspended the RMSU chapter until further notice and banned its 83 members from participating in any Greek events.

Bishop will convene a cross-university panel of faculty, staff, and students to investigate the Greek system on campus and drinking privileges at all campus social functions, including athletic events. Professor Juan Cordova, Theology Department Chairperson, will head the new committee. A report with specific recommendations to President Bishop is expected by the end of the term.

Alcohol is to blame for the deaths of 1,825 college students per year, according to figures from the National Institute on Alcohol Abuse and Alcoholism. About 599,000 students between the ages of 18 and 24 are injured annually while under the influence of alcohol, more than 696,000 are assaulted by another student who has been drinking, and more than 97,000 students are victims of alcohol-related sexual assault or date rape.

Voted the number two party school in the nation, Rocky Mountain State University is known for its "party-hardy" social life. Away from home for the first time, many freshmen get swept up by the party scene. President Bishop's office indicates that moving "rush" further into the semester is one option under consideration. The president believes that students need more time to adjust to the transition from high school and get their academic careers underway. Being driven to drink, sometimes excessively, is often a "rite of passage" in sororities and fraternities, a spokesman for the President said in a telephone interview. The University will also explore creating several alcohol-free residence halls where students who want to buckle down academically can do so without fearing social pressure to party.

(continued)

After this article appeared in the *Great Bluffs Herald,* many readers sent letters to the editor on September 20 and 21. Examine the following excerpts.

Trevor Ryan, RMSU Student, Denver, Colorado: "My first few weeks as a freshman at RMSU have been awesome. I knew I wanted to pledge GBG before I ever got here, and I have to say the "rush of rush" was totally cool—one of the highlights of my life so far. I'd do it all over again tomorrow. But I didn't want to join GBG just for the parties. It's an excellent organization with high academic standards. All the members say so." ← *unwarranted assumption!*

Mitch Edgars, Father, Englewood, Colorado: "For me, college was a time of awakening. I had plenty of 'good times' and I want my son to do the same. You can't stop college kids from drinking. It's that simple. Sure, all college kids make mistakes. But if they're smart, they'll learn from them. I know my son pretty well, and he makes good decisions most of the time. I don't care what anybody says, experience is still the best teacher."

Carlos Cordova, RMSU Student, Brooklyn, New York: "This whole incident has been very hard on me. Clark was my roommate, and we were getting along great. I still can't believe this happened to him. Yeah, I was at the football game with him where he started drinking and then later at the frat party where he got totally wasted. But I lost him in the crowd, and I went back to the dorm around midnight. I wonder if I could have done something."

Evan Riley, RMSU Senior, Aspen, Colorado: "As president of the Interfraternity Council on campus, I feel fraternities and sororities across the country are being demonized by the press. We're not like that. We are service organizations and we participate in lots of community activities, like the Holiday Fundraiser in Great Bluffs. Last year GBG raised more money for the homeless than any other organization on campus. At a time like this, though, everybody forgets that. We become the bad guys. The University just wants someone to take the fall, and I know it's going to be us. It's unfortunate that a few irresponsible students ruin it for everyone. Ask anyone who's a member: overall, sororities and fraternities do much more good than bad. It's really not fair!" ← *oversimplification*

Professor Ruby Pinnell, Biology Department, RMSU: "As a biologist, I see all the physiological damage today's college students are doing to themselves. The national study I spearheaded last year found that 31 percent of college students meet the clinical criteria for alcohol abuse, and 6 percent could be diagnosed as being alcohol-dependent. Young people don't realize that binge drinking could be risking serious damage to their brains now and actually cause increased memory loss later in adulthood. Many college males consume as many as 24 drinks in a row. These are very sad statistics."

Rufus Unser, Great Bluffs, Colorado, Citizen, Neighbor, and Voter: "I'm sick of my tax dollars going to fund institutions made up of immature college students who make bad decisions. A *Great Bluffs Herald* article published last year reported that neighbors living within one mile of college campuses are 135 percent more likely to suffer from public disturbances—also called "secondhand effects." My house is down the block from the GBG fraternity house, and sometimes the noise is so loud that I have to call the cops! Worse than that, I'm getting ready to sell my house and move into a retirement home next year. I'll bet my property values have dropped because of all the bad press! Higher education? That's a misnomer. 'Lower education' is more like it these days!" ← *Either-or thinking*

Jim McArthur, Director, RMSU Residence Life: September is National Alcohol and Drug Addiction Recovery Month, and we're doing everything we can to help educate students about the risks of alcohol poisoning. The binge drinking problem at RMSU isn't unique, and it's not going to go away by itself. We offer weekly classes on drinking responsibly, but no one signs up for them. We put up posters about the dangers of alcohol all over campus, and we also train all of our RAs on alcohol abuse as part of their preparation for the job. They try to keep tabs on their freshmen, but to tell you the truth, I think some of the RAs drink a bit too much, too. This is society's problem, not just RMSU's."

Sergeant Rick Fuller, Great Bluffs Police Department: "I've worked in the Great Bluffs Police Department for 15 years now, and I've seen a dramatic rise in the number of arrests for alcohol possession by minors, arrests for selling alcohol to minors, and alcohol-related admissions to Great Bluffs General Hospital's ER. It's an epidemic, I'm afraid. I also know from my police work that alcohol abuse is a factor in 40 percent of violent crimes committed in the U.S."[8]

Now that you've read the story from the *Great Bluffs Herald* and the excerpts from letters to the editor, answer the following questions:

1. What are the facts relating to the alcohol problem at RMSU? How do you know they're *facts* and not *claims?*

2. Do you see logical fallacies in any of the eight letters to the editor of the *Great Bluffs Herald?* If so, which can you identify? What assumptions do the letter writers hold?

3. Identify an issue that has been generating debate on your campus, in your residence hall, or in a class. Make a list of the claims made on each side of the debate and consider each claim. Then, make a list of the arguments and evaluate each argument, looking at *relevancy* and *adequacy*. Next, list the assumptions that the arguments are based on. Finally, be creative and come up with a new approach to the issue. Is there another way to frame the debate? How can you look at the issue in an entirely different way?

VARK It!

Complete the recommended activity for your preferred VARK learning modality. If you are multimodal, select more than one activity. Your instructor may ask you to (a) give an oral report on your results in class, (b) send your results to him or her via e-mail, (c) post them online, or (d) contribute to a class chat.

Visual: Create a collage that depicts each letter writer's point of view. Be certain to find a way to highlight the faulty reasoning.

Aural: As a group, talk through the case. Focus on questions like these: Does the incident sound realistic? If you ran the university, how would you handle the situation?

Read/Write: Write a press release sent from the university to local media outlets. How would you present this difficult situation to readers in the general public?

Kinesthetic: Assume you are a member of President Bishop's new task force on alcohol policy. Role play members of the task force at their first meeting.

(from left to right) Marcela Barsse/MarsBars/iStockphoto.com; Johanna Goodyear/Dreamstime.com; Nadezda Firsova/iStockphoto.com; Pascal Genest/iStockphoto.com

II. Problem Solving: The Basic How-To's

When you have to solve a problem, your critical thinking skills should move front and center. Perhaps you need to find a way to earn more money. You run short each month, and the last few days before payday are nerve-racking. What should you do? Use a shotgun approach and try many different strategies at once or devise a more precise way to get the best results? See if the following steps make sense to you and seem like something you might actually do.

STEP 1: Define the problem. What is the exact nature of the problem you face? You must define the problem if you hope to solve it. For example:

> Is it that you don't monitor your spending and run out of money long before the next paycheck?

> Is it that you've never created a budget and you spend money randomly?

I. DEFINE:
My philosophy class is killing me!

Left column (handwritten notes)

2. BRAINSTORM:
-Drop the class
-Study harder
-Get advice from my advisor
-Form a study group
-Go see Prof Courtney

3. SET CRITERIA:
a) time
b) effectiveness
c) convenience

4. EVALUATE:
-Drop the class (but losing my financial aid would be VERY inconvenient!)
-Study harder (I already am!)
-Get advice from my advisor (could take some time to get in to see her)
-Form a study group (when could we all meet?)
-Go see Prof (could work, but he might be hard to talk to)

5. CHOOSE: Going to see Prof Courtney would be best.

6. PLAN: E-mail him tonight to make an appointment. Enter the day and time on Google Calendar.

STEP 2: Brainstorm possible options. List all of the possible solutions you can come up with. For example:

> Eat all your meals in the residence hall instead of hitting the fast-food joints so often.

> Stop ordering in pizza four nights a week when you get the munchies at midnight.

> Ask your parents for more money. They told you to let them know when you need more.

> Look for a job that pays more. Tips at the Pancake House where you work don't really amount to much.

> Capitalize on your particular skills to earn extra money. If you're a whiz at math, you could sign on as a tutor at the Math Learning Center on campus.

STEP 3: Set criteria to evaluate each option. For example:

> *Distance* is important. Your car isn't very reliable, so it would be good to find a job you can walk or ride your bike to.

> *Good pay* is important. In the past, you've always had low-paying jobs. You need whatever solution you arrive at to be worth your while.

> *Time* is important. You're taking a challenging load of classes, and you need to keep up your grades to keep your scholarship.

STEP 4: Evaluate each option you've proposed. For example:

> Eat all your meals in the residence hall. (This is a good idea because you've already paid for those meals, regardless of which solution you choose.)

> Stop ordering in pizza four nights a week. (This is also a good option because impromptu expenses like this can mount exponentially.)

> Ask your parents for more money. (You'd really like to avoid this option. You know they're already making sacrifices to help you through school.)

> Get a job that pays more. (Unfortunately, your campus is half an hour from the center of town where all the posh restaurants are.)

> Capitalize on your particular skills to earn extra money. (Tutors are paid more than minimum wage, and the Math Learning Center is across from your residence hall.)

STEP 5: Choose the best solution. In this case, it looks like the Math Learning Center fits the bill!

STEP 6: Plan how to achieve the best solution. When you call the Math Learning Center to find out how to apply, you discover that you need a letter of recommendation from a math professor. You e-mail your calculus professor and set up a meeting for later in the week. When the letter is ready, you call the Math Learning Center again to make an appointment to schedule an interview, and so forth.

STEP 7: Implement the solution and evaluate the results. A month or two after you take on the tutoring job, you evaluate if this solution is really the best one. You may need to request more hours or different days. Or you may find that this job leads to a better one as a Teaching Assistant for the math department. At any rate, you've used your critical thinking skills to solve a problem, systematically, logically, and effectively.

7. IMPLEMENT: Wε'll sεε, but at lεast I havε a plan.

III. Decision Making: What's Your Style?

Arguments lead to decisions, and it's important to make good ones! After you've evaluated the arguments put forth, you must often do something about them. Before you know it, you'll be deciding on a major if you haven't already, a career field, a place to live, a romantic partner—you name it.

When you have an important decision to make, your critical thinking skills should kick into action. The more important the decision, chances are the more thoughtful the process of deciding should be. But people make decisions in their own way. To some extent, decision making is individualistic.

Alan J. Rowe and Richard O. Mason wrote a book about four basic decision-making styles used by managers. Although you may not be a manager now, think about what your style may be when you do have a position of responsibility. Here are the four styles they describe. See which one sounds as if it might describe you.

© Hemera Technologies/
Photos.com/Jupiter Images

> **Directive.** This decision-making style emphasizes the here and now. Directives prefer structure and using practical data to make decisions. They look for speed, efficiency, and results, and focus on short-term fixes. Directive decision makers base their decisions on experience, facts, procedures, and rules, and they have energy and drive to get things done. On the down side, because they work quickly, they are sometimes satisfied with simplistic solutions.

© Ian Scott, 2009. Used under
license from Shutterstock.com

> **Analytical.** This decision-making style emphasizes a logical approach. Analyticals search carefully for the best decision, and they sometimes get hung up with overanalyzing things and take too long to finally make a decision. They are sometimes considered to be impersonal because they may be more interested in the problem than in the people who have it. But they are good at working with data and doing careful analysis.

© Hemera Technologies/
Jupiter Images

> **Conceptual.** This decision-making style emphasizes the big picture. Conceptuals are adaptable, insightful, and flexible, and they look for innovative solutions. They are sometimes too idealistic, but they take risks and are very creative.

> **Behavioral.** This decision-making style emphasizes people. Behaviorals enjoy people and the social aspects of work. They use their feelings to assess situations, communicate well, and are supportive of others. On the other hand, they are sometimes seen as wishy-washy or are criticized because they can't make hard decisions or can't say no.

Whether you're in college to prepare for a career field or retool for a new one, eventually, you will have to make important decisions on a daily basis. It's useful to begin thinking about your decision-making style now.

IV. Thinking about Your Thinking

One of the most important aspects of critical thinking is that it evaluates itself. As you're solving problems, for example, you're thinking about how you're thinking. You're assessing your progress as you go, analyzing the strengths and weaknesses in your thinking, and perhaps even coming up with better ways to do it. We call that metacognition, and that's one reason this book contains "Insight → Action" exercises—to give you opportunities to think about how you're thinking and make note of those thoughts. Whenever you're faced with learning something new, metacognition involves three elements. Ultimately, these elements should become the foundation of all your learning experiences so that you improve your metacognitive skills as you go.

> **Develop a plan of action.** Ask yourself what you already know that can help you learn something new. What direction do you want to go in your thinking? What should be your first task? How much time should you give yourself? Talk through your plan with someone else.

> **Monitor your plan.** While you're working, ask yourself how you're doing. Are you staying on track? Are you moving in the right direction? Should you slow down or speed up? What should you do if you don't understand what you're doing? Keep track of what works for you and what doesn't.

©Larry Harwood Photography. Property of Cengage Learning.

" Education is nothing more, nor less, than learning to think!"

Peter Facione, professor, administrator, author, consultant, and critical thinking expert

> **Evaluate the plan.** How well did you do? Did you do better than expected or not as well as you expected? What could you have done differently? Can you apply what you just did here to future tasks? Give yourself some feedback.[9]

Courtesy of Edward Sherwin.

CAREER OUTLOOK: *Edward Sherwin, Lawyer*

Q1: What do lawyers do on a day-to-day basis?

Different kinds of lawyers do very different kinds of work. Lawyers may prosecute or defend alleged criminals. They may represent people and businesses in lawsuits ranging from car accidents and divorces to giant securities and consumer fraud actions. Some lawyers write wills, contracts, and real estate documents, or advise businesses on how to acquire other companies or raise money from investors. Or lawyers may work within government to write new laws and regulations. One way or another, most lawyers talk with their clients, research past legal decisions, develop strategies to help their clients, and negotiate with attorneys representing other parties.

Q2: What are three important skills a person needs in order to be a lawyer?

- Being a good listener: You need to understand your client's problem in order to come up with a good solution.
- Judgment: You may have to make critical decisions on your client's behalf, often with little time to think.

- Discretion: You will learn your clients' most sensitive personal and business information.

Q3: In the legal profession, how important is the art of asking questions?

Asking the right question at the right time—like during the cross-examination of a key opposing witness—can make or break a case. For most lawyers, though, the most important questions you ask will be of your clients so that you can help them navigate their particular problems.

Q4: How important is a lawyer's ability to analyze arguments, assess assumptions, and consider claims?

These are probably the most important skills a lawyer can bring to the table. Lawyers look at past legal decisions that can help them analyze new situations. The right answer will rarely, if ever, leap directly from the pages, so the key is to find evidence to support your position and to distinguish or discredit the position of your opponent.

Q5: Do law schools use the term critical thinking?

Many law professors and students use the phrase "thinking like a lawyer" to describe the particular critical thinking skills used in the profession. Specifically, this means using logical arguments, discarding arguments that are faulty, using logic, and being able to make fine distinctions between cases.

HOW WOULD *YOU* LIKE IT?

Have you ever considered a career as a lawyer?

Facts to Consider[10]

Academic preparation required: A bachelor's degree, three years of law school, and passing the bar exam in the state in which you'd like to practice law are required.

Future workforce demand: Prospects for new jobs will increase at an average rate in the future, although competition to get into law school is intense and competition for new jobs can be keen.

Work environment: About 27 percent of lawyers are self-employed, working in their own practices or as partners in other law practices. Lawyers work in criminal or civil law,

researching, interviewing, and arguing cases in courtrooms. They work in many different areas of the law: environmental, bankruptcy, intellectual property, probate, and international law, for example. Lawyers who are not in private practice may work for government agencies or for non-profit organizations. Many lawyers work long hours, often more than 50 hours per week.

Questions to Ponder

1. Do you have (or could you acquire) the skills this career requires?
2. Are you interested in a career like this? Why or why not?

For more career activities online, access the CourseMate via www.cengagebrain.com/shop/ISBN/0495906425 to do the Team Career exercises.

Becoming a Better Critical Thinker

Sharpening your critical thinking skills is vital because these skills underlie all the others in your academic repertoire. If you think well, you will be a better writer, a better presenter, a better listener, and a better reader. You will be more likely to engage more fully in your academic tasks because you will question, probe, analyze, and monitor yourself as you learn. Here are some suggestions for improving your skills. As you read them, think about how they pertain to you.

> " And how is education supposed to make me feel smarter?"
>
> **Homer Simpson, television cartoon character, *The Simpsons***

1. **Admit when you don't know.** If you don't know enough to think critically about something, admit it, and then find out more. With the volume of information available in today's world, we can't possibly know everything about anything. But the good news is that information is readily available. All you need to do is read, listen, point, and click to be well informed on many issues.

2. **Realize you have buttons that can be pushed.** We all have issues we're emotional about. That's normal. It's natural to feel strongly about some things, but it's also important to understand the reasons why so that you can explain your views to someone else. And of course, realize that you're not the only one with buttons. Your teacher, roommate, significant other, boss, everyone else has them, too.

3. **Learn more about the opposition.** Many times, it's more comfortable to avoid what we don't agree with and selectively validate what we already believe. But part of being a well-educated person means learning about the history, backgrounds, values, and techniques of people you disagree with so that you can anticipate and deal with their arguments more effectively.

4. **Trust and verify.** During the cold war, President Ronald Reagan liked to quote an old Russian saying to his Soviet counterpart, Mikhail Gorbachev: "Doveryay, no proveryay," or "Trust, but verify." Being a good critical thinker means achieving a balance between blind faith and healthy skepticism.

5. **Remember that critical thinking is the cornerstone of all academic achievement.** There's nothing more important than learning to think critically. In college and in life, the skills discussed in this chapter will make you a better college student, a better citizen, a better employee, a savvier consumer, a better relational partner, and a better lifelong learner.

I watched the video on critical thinking available on the CourseMate via www.cengagebrain.com/shop/ISBN/0495906425. Really helped me get it!

Unleash Your Creativity!

Whether you're eighteen or eighty-one, it's safe to say that your life has been changed by an unending stream of new inventions. Which of the following have come into existence during your lifetime? iPods? GPS systems in cars? The

Xbox? DVDs? Microwavable mac and cheese? IMAX movies? Side-impact air bags? Singer Bob Dylan crooned memorable words in 1964: "The times, they are a-changin'." He was right then, and it's still true now.

Creativity affects us all. It's true that some of these items haven't made a big impact. But other inventions affect you every single day. In his bestselling book, *The Rise of the Creative Class*, Richard Florida notes that in 1900, less than 10 percent of American workers were doing creative work. Farms and factories were most people's work sites. Eighty years later, the figure had only risen to 20 percent. But today, a full third of our working population engages in employment that gets their creative juices flowing, whether they're artists, designers, writers, analysts, musicians, or entrepreneurs. The creative sector of our economy accounts for nearly half of all wage and salary income—$1.7 trillion per year. Today's "no collar" workplace is fueled by creativity. And Florida says, we've barely scratched the surface. Human creativity is virtually limitless.[11]

Diversity in our surroundings is one thing that increases the potential for creativity. Creativity comes in all sizes, ethnicities, preferences, and genders. If you're around other open-minded, flexible, tolerant, forward-looking, innovative people, you're more likely to live up to your own creative potential. And in case you're wondering, you don't have to be an artist to be creative. Creativity simply means finding new and better ways to do things. In many ways, it's a choice you make; you *decide* to be creative.[12]

What does all this have to do with you as an entering college student? Florida says that the rise of the creative sector has also changed the way people work and their expectations. No longer

I just don't know if I see myself as creative . . .

> " I can't understand why people are frightened by new ideas. I'm frightened by the old ones."

John Cage, American composer (1912–1992)

CURIOSITY: *ARE YOU TALENTED?*

Who me? Creative? Talented? Gifted? Nah! Some people say: "I'm not creative. I have no talent. I'm just an ordinary guy." Other people settle for good instead of reaching for great. What does it take to become a truly great thinker, a great creator, a great athlete, a great musician, a great anything?

According to Daniel Coyle, best-selling author of the acclaimed new book, *The Talent Code,* talent is something you grow into, not something you're born with. Coyle traveled the world to visit "talent hotbeds," little places that produce great talent: a tennis camp in Russia, a music academy in upstate New York, and an inner city school in California, for example. As he examined these origins of greatness, he discovered that talent is grown by a combination of three principles:

Deep Practice: Deep practice isn't just practicing regularly or even practicing a great deal, it's practicing a certain way: very slowly and deliberately. That's how your brain gains mastery. Deep practice is also based on stops and starts, on mistakes, on analyzing what went wrong, and trying over and over again until you can do it perfectly.

Ignition: Any kind of practice, let alone deep practice, would be torture unless you really cared. Something or somebody must light a spark in you and ignite the fire that fuels your learning. You must be motivated from within to be great.

Master Coaching: To become truly great, it takes an older, wiser, and more experienced teacher, someone who can show you things you don't see in yourself and help you reach your potential. Olympic athletes need coaches, just as great minds need teachers.

Talent, according to Daniel Coyle, is something that can be grown depending on how much you want it and hard you're willing to work to get it.

are many Americans' aspirations to make a million dollars and buy the house of their dreams. It's about having enough money to be comfortable while doing enjoyable, interesting, and creative work. The best people in any field aren't motivated solely by money. They are motivated by passion for what they do.

Creativity: "Thinking Outside the . . . Book"

? **challenge** ▶ ❝ **reaction** * **insight** ▶ ! **action**

Challenge: What's the difference between *critical* thinking and *creative* thinking?

Reaction: _____

Do you believe this statement? *Everyone has creative potential.* It's true. Most of us deny it, however. "Me, creative? Nah!" We're often unaware of the untapped ability we have to think creatively. Try this experiment. Look at the following list of words, and divide the list into two (and only two) different categories, using any criteria you devise. Take a few moments and see what you come up with.

> *dog, salad, book, grasshopper, kettle, paper, garbage, candle*

Whenever this experiment is tried, people always come up with very creative categories. They may divide the words into things that you buy at a store (dog, salad, kettle, paper, candle), things that move on their own (dog, grasshopper), things that have a distinct smell (dog, candle, garbage), words that have two consonants, and so forth. People never say it can't be done; they always *invent* categories. Interesting, isn't it? Our minds are hungry for the stimulation of a creative challenge.

The fact is that intelligence has more to do with coming up with the right answer, and creative thinking has more to do with coming up with many right answers. Often we get so focused on the *right* answer that we rush to find it instead of exploring all the possibilities. Creative thinking is thinking outside the box, or in terms of getting an education, perhaps we should call it thinking outside the book. Going beyond the obvious and exploring possibilities are important parts of becoming an educated person. Employers report that many college graduates today have specific skills, but that what they rarely see "is the ability to use the right-hand side of the brain—creativity, working in a team."[13]

❝ A mind that is stretched to a new idea never returns to its original dimensions."

Oliver Wendell Holmes, American poet (1809–1894)

In Figure 4.2 we looked at the Question Pyramid. Creative thinking is at the top of the pyramid. It goes beyond critical thinking, is predictive, and multidimensional. It asks "What if ...?" questions. Here are some interesting ones: "What if everyone was allowed to tell one lie per day?" "What if no one could perceive colors?" "What if universities didn't exist?" "If you looked up a word like *squallizmotex* in the dictionary, what might it mean?"[14]

According to creativity expert Alan Rowe, our creative intelligence demonstrates itself in four major styles. Each of us has aspects of all four styles of creativity.

66 If you have an apple and I have an apple and we exchange these apples, then you and I will still each have one apple. But if you have an idea and I have an idea and we exchange these ideas, then each of us will have two ideas."

George Bernard Shaw, Irish literary critic, playwright, and essayist, 1925 Nobel Prize for Literature (1856–1950)

> **Intuitive** This creative style is best described as *resourceful*. If you are an Intuitive, you achieve goals, use common sense, and work to solve problems. You focus on results and rely on past experience to guide your actions. Managers, actors, and politicians are commonly Intuitives.

> **Innovative** This creative style is best described as *curious*. Innovatives concentrate on problem solving, are systematic, and rely on data. They use original approaches, are willing to experiment, and focus on systematic inquiry. Scientists, engineers, and inventors typically demonstrate the Innovative creative style.

> (**Imaginative**) This creative style is best described as *insightful*. Imaginatives are willing to take risks, have leaps of imagination, and are independent thinkers. They are able to visualize opportunities, are artistic, enjoy writing, and think outside the box. Artists, musicians, writers, and charismatic leaders are often Imaginatives.

This is so me!

> **Inspirational** This creative style is best described as *visionary*. Inspirationals respond to societal needs, willingly give of themselves, and have the courage of their convictions. They focus on social change and the giving of themselves toward achieving it. They are often educators, motivational leaders, and writers.[15]

Which is most likely your predominant creative style? Think about how you can make the best use of your natural style. How will your creativity affect the major or career you choose? Most people have more than one creative style. Remember that motivation, not general intelligence, is the key to creativity. You must be willing to tap your creative potential and challenge yourself to show it.[16]

Ten Ways to Become a More Creative Thinker

Becoming a more creative thinker may mean you need to accept your creativity and cultivate it. Consider these suggestions on how to think more creatively.

1

mu

4   **2**

3

FIGURE 4.3

The Pillow Method

Position 1—I'm right and you're wrong.
Position 2—You're right and I'm wrong.
Position 3—We're both right.
Position 4—We're both wrong.

1. I'm a student paying tuition for PHIL 100.
2. Professor is an expert in philosophy.
3. 1 and 2 are true.
4. 1 and 2 are false. Just because I pay doesn't mean I can buy knowledge. Being an expert doesn't always make the professor a great teacher.

mu = It really doesn't matter. He's here to teach, and I'm here to learn.

1. **Find new eyes.** Find a new perspective on old issues. Here's an interesting example. Years ago, a group of Japanese schoolchildren devised a new way to solve conflicts and build empathy for others' positions, called the Pillow Method. Figure 4.3 is an adaptation of it, based on the fact that a pillow has four sides and a middle, just like most problems.

   The middle or *mu* is the Zen expression for "it doesn't really matter." There is truth in all four positions. Try it: take a conflict you're having difficulty with at the moment, and write down all four sides and a middle.[17]

2. **Accept your creativity.** Many mindsets block creative thinking: "It can't be done!" "I'm just not the creative type." "I might look stupid!" Many people don't see themselves as creative. This perception can become a major stumbling block. If creativity isn't part of your self-image, you may need to revamp your image. Everyone has creative potential. You may just have to learn how to tap into yours.

3. **Make your thoughts visible.** For many of us, things become clear when we can see them, either in our mind's eye or displayed for us. Even Einstein, a scientist and mathematician, had a very visual mind. Sometimes if we write something down or sketch something out, we generate a new approach without really trying.

4. **Generate lots of ideas.** Thomas Edison held 1,093 patents, still the record. He gave himself idea quotients. The rule he set for himself was that he had to come up with a major invention every six months and a minor invention every ten days. Bach wrote a cantata every week, even if he was ill.

5. **Don't overcomplexify.** In hindsight, many of the most ingenious discoveries are embarrassingly simple. Biologist Thomas Huxley said, after reading Darwin's explanation of evolution: "How extremely stupid not to have thought of that!" But sometimes the most simple solution is the best one.[18]

6. **Capitalize on your mistakes.** Remember that Thomas Edison tried anything he could think of for a filament for the incandescent lamp, including a whisker from his best friend's beard. All in all, he tried about 1,800 things before finding the right one. Afterwards he said, "I've gained a lot of knowledge—I now know a thousand things that won't work."[19]

7. **Let it flow.** Mihaly Csikszentmihalyi, the author of *Flow: The Psychology of Optimal Experience* and many other books on creativity, discovered something interesting. For his doctoral thesis, he studied artists by taking pictures of them painting every three minutes. He was struck by how engaged they were in their work, so engaged that they seemed to forget everything around them. He began studying other "experts": rock climbers, chess players, dancers, musicians,

❝ A hunch is creativity trying to tell you something."

Frank Capra, Italian American film director (1897–1991)

surgeons. Regardless of the activity, these people forgot the time, themselves, and their problems. What did the activities have in common? Clear, high goals and immediate feedback. Athletes call it being in the zone. Csikszentmihalyi's suggestions for achieving flow are these: Pick an enjoyable activity that is at or slightly above your ability level, screen out distractions, focus all your senses and emotions, and look for regular feedback on how you're doing.[20]

8. **Bounce ideas off others.** One good way to become more creative is to use your family or friends as sounding boards. Sometimes just verbalizing something helps you understand more about it. Each person who provides a critique will give you a new perspective, possibly worth considering.

9. **Stop searching for the "right" answer.** This advice doesn't pertain to your upcoming math exam. But it does to apply to situations in which there are many ways to solve a problem. There may be more than one acceptable solution. Fear of mistakes can be debilitating.

10. **Detach your self-concept.** For most of us, creativity is often linked to self-concept. An idea is your brainchild, and you want it to win approval. You've invested part of yourself in giving birth to it. But there's nothing like self-imposed judgment to shut down your creative juices. Your idea may not succeed on its own, but it may feed into someone else's idea and improve it. Or an idea you have about this problem may inform the next problem that challenges you. In the end, in addition to finding a workable solution, what's important is engaging in the creative process with others.

These are all great ideas!

? challenge "reaction * insight ! action

Now What Do You Think?

1. At the beginning of this chapter, Annie Miller, a frustrated student, faced a challenge. Now after reading this chapter, would you respond differently to any of the questions you answered about the "FOCUS Challenge Case"? Knowing what you know now, how would you advise her? Write a paragraph ending to the story, incorporating your best advice.

2. Identify a time, subject, or event in which you used your critical thinking skills for your own benefit. Perhaps you investigated the salary range for a new job or read blogs on a particular subject to gain new perspectives. Explain what you did, how you went about it, and why. What did you learn about yourself?

3. Provide real examples of critical thinking from any of your current classes. Are you being asked on exams to compare and contrast? To sort through evidence and make decisions? In class discussions are you encouraged to disagree with your instructor or classmates for the sake of a healthy, vigorous debate? How do you handle these situations? Do you think they help you learn? If so, how?

4. Do you see yourself as a creative person? Instead of thinking about whether you're creative or not, ask yourself this question, *"How* am I creative?" Describe the ways.

5. Think of a problem you're facing right now. Use the Pillow Method described in Figure 4.3 to analyze the problem. Do you find this approach helpful?

REALITY CHECK | What did you Learn?

On a scale of 1 to 10, answer the following questions now that you've completed this chapter.

1 = not very/not much/very little/low   10 = very/a lot/very much/high

In hindsight, how much did you already know about this subject before reading the chapter?

1 2 3 4 5 6 7 8 9 10

Can you answer these questions about critical and creative thinking more fully now that you've read the chapter?

1. **What's the difference between thinking and critical thinking?**

2. **Identify three specific types of faulty reasoning.**

3. **What's the difference between critical thinking and creative thinking?**

How useful might the information in this chapter be to you? How much do you think this information might affect your success in college?

1 2 3 4 5 6 7 8 9 10

How much do you think this information might affect your career success after college?

1 2 3 4 5 6 7 8 9 10

How long did it actually take you to complete this chapter (both the reading and writing tasks)? _____ Hour(s) _____ Minutes

 Challenge Yourself Online Quiz. To find out how much you've learned, access the CourseMate via www.cengagebrain.com/shop/ISBN/0495906425 to take the Challenge Yourself Online Quiz.

Take a minute to compare these answers to your answers from the "Readiness Check" at the beginning of this chapter. What gaps exist between the similar questions? How might these gaps between what you thought before starting the chapter and what you now think after completing the chapter affect how you approach the next chapter in this book?

chapter 5

Developing Information Literacy, Writing, and Speaking Skills

©Larry Harwood Photography. Property of Cengage Learning.

YOU'RE ABOUT TO DISCOVER . . .

✓ HOW TECHNOLOGY IMPACTS OUR LIVES

✓ HOW TO USE TECHNOLOGY TO DO ACADEMIC RESEARCH

✓ HOW TO CULTIVATE YOUR RESEARCH SKILLS

✓ WHAT INFORMATION LITERACY SKILLS ARE AND WHY THEY'RE IMPORTANT

✓ HOW TO BEST PRESENT RESEARCH THROUGH WRITING AND SPEAKING

✓ WHAT PLAGIARISM IS AND HOW TO AVOID IT

READINESS CHECK | What do you **Know?**

Before beginning this chapter, take a moment to answer these questions. Your answers will help you assess how ready you are to focus.

1 = not very/not much/very little/low   10 = very/a lot/very much/high

How much do you *already* know?

Based on reading the "You're about to discover. . ." list and skimming this chapter, how much do you think you probably already know about this chapter's subject?

1 2 3 4 5 6 7 8 9 10

See if you can answer these questions about information literacy, writing, and speaking skills *before* you read.

1. **How would you define research? What steps are involved?**

2. **What is information literacy?**

3. **Identify the three stages involved in the writing process.**

How motivated are you to learn *more*?

In general, how motivated are you to learn more by reading this chapter?

1 2 3 4 5 6 7 8 9 10

How much do you think this information might affect your success in college?

1 2 3 4 5 6 7 8 9 10

How much do you think this information might affect your career success after college?

1 2 3 4 5 6 7 8 9 10

How ready are you to read *now*?

How ready are you to focus on this chapter—physically, intellectually, and

emotionally? Circle a number for each aspect of your readiness to focus.

1 2 3 4 5 6 7 8 9 10

If any of your answers is below a 10, you might want to pay attention to whatever is distracting you before you start reading. For example, if you're feeling scattered, take a few moments to settle down and focus.

Finally, how long do you think it will take you to complete this chapter from start to finish?

_____ Hour(s) _____ Minutes

DARIO JONES

Ever since grade school, Dario Jones had been called a geek. It was a label he hated, but, honestly, most people probably thought of him that way. As a kid, Dario lived for computer games. He played them nearly every waking hour. In the morning, he'd shower in record time, throw on whatever clean clothes he could find, and use any spare minutes for computer games. When he got home, he'd log right back on again. His Dad tried threatening him: "You'll lose your eyesight and flunk out of school." Once he faked a sore throat and played

World of Warcraft at home for a week, while his parents were at work. As he got older, his Dad warned: "You'll never get a date." But Dario wasn't worried. Second Life relationships were enough. Real-life relationships were too much trouble. His cyber life was much more exciting than his real life. Dario spent more time—even sacrificing precious hours of sleep—surfing the Internet, envisioning how he could improve websites, and grooming his MySpace page than he spent talking to any living being. So Dario graduated from a technical high school and got a job immediately as a tech support specialist. "No degree required," the ad had said.

But a few months down the road the obvious truth dawned on him. Why was he wasting his time in a dead-end job? The world of computer glitches didn't really interest him. The world of web design did. But somehow after high school, he hadn't thought about it much and went to work for the first company that offered him a job.

Eventually, Dario made a decision. He needed to change his life. He drove to the college campus across town and parked in the parking lot. He sat in his car for a while, and then

Siren Tech Support

Dario Jones
Tech Support Specialist

www.SirenTech.com
Dario.Jones@SirenTech.com
(o) 888-555-8383
c 555-123-8385

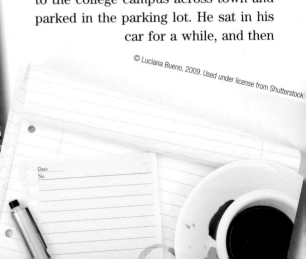

Date
No

bit the bullet, walked through the door, and talked with someone. As it turned out, that was the last official day to enroll for the semester. So with the help of a friendly advisor, who took him to the Financial Aid office and helped him fill out the application, Dario was in college. He'd have to increase his hours at work to afford tuition, but he thought it would be worth it.

But Dario quickly discovered that *talking* on the phone with customers about computers and *studying* computers were two very different things. Right off the bat, he discovered that Introduction to Computer Science required a research paper with an accompanying oral presentation, which, he had to admit, freaked him out. The assigned topic was Globalization and Internet Commerce. Even though he had always considered himself to be a technology expert, frankly, he didn't know where to start. *Step one*, Dario thought to himself, *is to Google*. He always Googled everything: the directions to a new Mexican restaurant—his favorite food—or some little-known fact that he wondered about, like how many Chihuahuas were sold in the United States last year. (He had just bought one.) But when he Googled "Internet Commerce," he got 24 million hits. *Better regroup*, he advised himself.

But how? Should he go to the library on campus, or try to do his research online in the comfort of his own apartment? Physically going to the library seemed unnecessary when so much information was available online.

Then he had a flash of inspiration: Wikipedia. He found a page on "Electronic Commerce." At least that was a start—that is, until he looked at his instructor's handout on the assignment. Students were discouraged from using Wikipedia as a primary research source. The handout said "Information literacy is required." He got another idea: He'd close Wikipedia and go back to Googling. This time he'd try "Electronic Commerce." *Ah, only 11 million hits this time.* He was on a roll. He plugged in "E-Commerce," "E-Business," and "Globalization." He tried "Global Issues," but before he knew it, he found himself knee-deep in articles about global warming. He was so far afield now that he couldn't find his way back to his topic. Should he shut everything down and start over or just give up?

Dario's paper was due the following day. At the last minute, he panicked. He found a few useful things online, and in the interest of time, he cut and pasted from the Internet until he'd filled ten pages. At least he had something to turn in. He wondered if this was the way to do research and whether he'd broken any rules. *Well, at least there will always be computer glitches*, he thought pessimistically. But to be honest, a career solving other people's technical problems wasn't at all what he wanted to do with his life.

Web Design Works

Learn How to Website Wiz

Call 555-4842

Introduction to C
CS
Research Pap

TOPIC: Globalization and Internet Comme

For this assignment you will write a 10 page relationship between globalization and Intern focus on how globalization has affected Intern relationship may be a two-way street. In othe commerce has changed the pace of globalizatio

POTENTIAL AREAS OF RESEARCH FOC

alization?

Corporations

ccess
ng
on of Cultures
rce in the 21ˢᵗ Century
actors
n Factors
a Global Village

CES: The sole use of research
ouraged. You may use

kipedia.

W http://en.wikipedia.org/wiki/Electronic_commerce

Edit View Favorites Tools Help

W Electronic commerce - Wikipedia, the free encyclopedia

Help us provide free content to the world by donating today!

article | discussion | edit this page | history

Electronic commerce

From Wikipedia, the free encyclopedia

Electronic Commerce, commonly known as (electronic marketing) **e-commerce** or **eCommerce** consists of the buying and selling of products or services over electronic systems such as the Inte other computer networks. The amount of trade conducted electronically has grown extraordinarily widespread Internet usage. The use of commerce is conducted in this way, spurring and drawing innovations in electronic funds transfer, supply chain management, Internet marketing, online tran processing, electronic data interchange (EDI), inventory management systems, and automated collection systems. Modern electronic commerce typically uses the World Wide Web at least a point in the transaction's lifecycle, although it can encompass a wider range of technologies su as well.

WIKIPEDIA
The Free Encyclopedia

Main page
Contents
Featured content
Current events
Random article

earch

Introduction to Computer Science
CS 112

Instructor: Dr. Greg Otis
Office: Hansford Hall 230
Office Hours: T, W 2:00-4:00 PM

Description:
The Internet has fundamentally changed the landscape of the business world. Today, commerce conducted on the Internet plays a major role in the world's economy. In this class you will learn about how Internet business differs from traditional business models, how to analyze Internet business ventures, and how to become an Internet entrepreneur.

Course Objectives:
1. To

What Do You Think?

1. The instructor's assignment required "information literacy." What is information literacy? Dario is tech-savvy, but does he have the right skills? Why or why not?

2. What mistakes does Dario make in researching his paper?

3. Did Dario plagiarize his paper—or did he simply find the sources he needed and use them? Give the reasons behind your answer.

4. Dario is not only having trouble researching his paper, but he's also worried about his upcoming presentation. What can be done to overcome speaking anxiety?

Technology Skills: Wireless, Windowed, Webbed, and Wikied

Challenge: In what ways does technology improve our lives, and in what ways does it complicate it? See if you can identify three of each.

Reaction: _____

_____

_____

Many of us have a love-hate relationship with technology: We love the convenience but hate the dependence. But in college, information literacy and technology skills will be other keys to your academic success. You'll need to know things like how to use Microsoft Word with agility to produce a polished essay, how to design an information-rich and visually compelling PowerPoint presentation, and how to use one or more of the many course management systems available like Blackboard. You don't have to be a technology guru, but you will need to call upon your technology skills to conduct research for your college classes. Many college students are tech savvy, but their skills are more about entertainment than education.

HMM . . . ARE MINE???

Use Technology to Your Academic Advantage

Challenge: How will technology help you in your college coursework? List three ways that you've already experienced or expect to experience.

Reaction: _____ _____ _____

When you first arrive on campus or even before, you'll see evidence of technology everywhere. You may be asked to respond to an on-screen quiz in class by using your cell phone. You'll get an e-mail account and be sent official college documents, like your tuition bill and weather alerts. You will take entire courses or parts of courses online so that you can learn on your own time at your own pace. Many of your instructors will use course management systems, streaming video, and websites in the classroom to increase your learning. And the good news is that 60.9 percent of college students say it helps.[1]

What academic benefits does technology provide?[2] Technology will help you:

> **Manage your courses.** Many of your college classes will be conducted partially or wholly online, using technology shells, like Blackboard, Moodle, Desire2Learn, or eCompanion. Course management systems help you:

- Track grades, assignments, and tests
- Take sample tests and quizzes (or real ones)
- Get the course syllabus
- Turn in assignments online
- Access readings and other course materials
- Post to an online discussion[3]

> **Interact with course content, classmates, and your instructor.** You may have heard the term "Web 2.0." It's not a new version of the Internet. It refers to creative uses of it, like Facebook, Wikis, and blogs, where instead of just reading passively, users help create the content. For example, your instructor may post a question or comment and ask you to post your responses online and to respond to those of your classmates. Everyone can get to know you by your online personality, and some students say they become better writers by reading other students' responses to their blogs (Web logs). In addition to these Web 2.0 possibilities, you will undoubtedly use e-mail, Facebook your classmates, and listen to podcasts, if your professor posts an audio version of her lecture.

WEB 2.0 IS MY LIFE!

> **Complete assignments.** Your college classes will ask you to use at least three types of software in your academic work:

- Microsoft Word allows you to type, edit, alphabetize, index, footnote, and do many other things to prepare papers for your classes.
- Microsoft PowerPoint, used as an electronic visual aid for oral presentations, allows you to create an on-screen guide for your listeners (and you, if you glance periodically and subtly for clues).
- Microsoft Excel spreadsheets are good for tabulating, record keeping, and organizing.

The industry standard for these applications is generally the Microsoft products listed here, although other possibilities exist. If you need help learning any of these applications, your campus techies, instructors, or online tutorials (which can easily be found by Googling) can help.

> **Increase your learning.** You may also find yourself using textbook websites, like the one you're using for *FOCUS on College Success.* Often these websites are tied closely to the textbook you're using in class, and

they contain information and activities to enrich your learning experience, like videos, quizzes, and iAudio chapter summaries. Use these resources to help you master course material.

How Tech Savvy Are You?

What kinds of computer skills will help you excel in college and what kind of skills are employers looking for? Look at the lists below. Which of the following tasks can you perform *right now* (without clicking on "help" or Googling)? These software applications are considered to be the "industry standard" used in most organizations.

	Basic	Moderate	Advanced
MS Word	__ open a document __ bold text __ cut and paste __ undo and redo __ change the page orientation	__ count words __ highlight text __ insert page numbers __ justify a paragraph __ add bullets	__ alphabetize lists __ create footnotes __ use Autocorrect __ record/run macros __ merge documents
MS PowerPoint	__ create slides __ delete slides __ insert clip art __ choose a design template __ add new slides	__ animate slides __ change background colors __ add transitions between slides __ create and run a slide show __ print slides, handouts, and outlines	__ merge slides from another slideshow __ insert hyperlinks __ edit hyperlinks __ change animation timing __ change animation order
MS Excel	__ create spreadsheets __ move data around __ make calculations __ create a chart __ copy/merge cells	__ use the SUM function to create formulas __ use the fill handle to copy a cell __ use a VBA macro __ freeze panes __ format cells, rows, and columns	__ create formulas using the IF function __ use absolute references __ use Excel as a database __ use VLOOKUP __ use PivotTables

If you're surprised by how few checkmarks you were able to make above, now is the right time to gear up! Take an online tutorial, sign up for a workshop on campus, or enroll in a computer literacy class. Not only will you be able to apply your skills to all your classes, but you'll be ramping up for the job waiting for you in the world of work.[4]

I THOUGHT I'D HAVE MORE CHECKMARKS ON THIS. I'M GOING TO ACTUALLY TRY DOING SOME OF THESE.

The Internet: The Good, the Bad, and the Ugly

The Good

For many of us, the Internet is how we get our news, our research, our entertainment, and our communication. When it comes to all the potential benefits of the Internet, think about advantages like these:

> **Currency.** While some of the information posted on the Internet is outdated, much of it is up-to-the-minute. Reports, articles, and studies that might take months to publish in books or articles are available on the Web as soon as they're written.

> **Availability.** The Internet never sleeps. If you can't sleep at 2:00 a.m., the Internet can keep you company. Unlike your real instructor who teaches other classes besides yours and attends marathon meetings, Professor Google is always in. For the most part, you can check your e-mail or log onto the Internet from anywhere, any time.

> **Scope.** You can find out virtually anything you want to know on the Internet from the recipe for the world's best chocolate chip cookie to medical advice on everything from **A**thlete's Foot to **Z**its.

> **Interactivity.** Unlike other media, the Internet lets you talk back—instantly and constantly. You can add to your Facebook page daily or edit a Wikipedia entry whenever you like.

> **Affordability.** As of June 2010, there were 1,966,514,816 online Internet users worldwide; more than 239 million Americans are online today.[5] For most, when it comes to the Internet, the price is right. After you buy a computer, and pay a monthly access fee, you get a great deal for your money.

HADN'T THOUGHT ABOUT THESE SPECIFIC FEATURES.

Teo Lannie/PhotoAlto Agency RF Collections/Getty Images

The Bad

Too much of a good thing can be bad. When anything becomes that central to our lives, it carries risks like the following:

> **Inaccuracy.** Often we take information presented to us at face value, without questioning it. But on many Internet sites, the responsibility for checking the accuracy of the information presented there is yours. Not everything published online is true or right.

> **Laziness.** It's easy to allow the convenience of the Internet to make us lazy. Why bother doing hours of library research on the topic for your paper when others have already been there, done that, and published it on the Internet? For one thing, if you don't give the rightful author credit, that's plagiarism, which can give you a zero on an assignment, or even

> " For a list of all the ways technology has failed to improve the quality of life, please press three."
>
> **Alice Kahn, technology author**

BOX 5.1 Netiquette: Online Manners Matter

Professionalism is important in college, and it doesn't just apply to how you act in class, like getting to class on time or turning in your assignments when they're due. Online communication like e-mail has netiquette (or network etiquette) rules like these:

1. **Don't send a message you don't want to risk being forwarded to someone else.**

2. **Don't hit the "send" key until you've given yourself time to cool off, if you're upset.**

3. **Don't forward chain e-mails.**

4. **Don't do business over your school e-mail account.**

5. **Don't spread hoaxes about viruses or false threats.**

6. **Don't type in all CAPS.** That's called SHOUTING, and it makes you look angry.

7. **Don't be too casual—use good grammar and correct spelling.**

8. **Don't forget important details.**

9. **Don't hit the "Reply to All" key, when you mean to hit the "Reply" key.**

10. **Don't forget to fill in the subject line.** That gives readers a chance to preview your message and decide how soon they need to get to it.

How *Not* to Win Friends and Influence People Online

All four of these e-mail messages from students violate the rules of netiquette. See if you can identify the rule number from Box 5.1 that's been violated in each case.

UGH—MY EMAILS ARE JUST LIKE HERS!

From Matt   Rule: _____

Professor X,

I just looked at the online syllabus for Academic Success 101. Why didn't you tell us that our first paper is due on Monday? I will be very busy moving into a new apartment this weekend. Writing an essay for your class is the last thing I want to have to think about.

From Tiffany   Rule: _____

Prof X,

i didn't know u were makin us write a paper over the weekend. i won't be able to do it. i hop you don't mind.

From Xavier   Rule: _____

PROFESSOR X,

I CAN'T GET MY PAPER DONE BY MONDAY. LET ME KNOW WHAT I SHOULD DO.

From Dameon   Rule: _____

Hey, Section 3

Can you believe our instructor? She assigns a big writing assignment after only one day of class! Who in their right mind would be remotely interested in sitting in their crummy little room writing a bunch of meaningless junk, when we haven't even learned anything yet? What kind of teacher are we stuck with here? Somebody out there respond to me, OK? I'm totally hacked off!

As a class, discuss your responses and see if you all agree on which rules were broken in the four examples provided.

cause you to fail a course. But another thing worth considering is that the *how* of learning is as important as the *what*. If all you ever did was cut, paste, and download, you wouldn't learn how to do research yourself.

> **Overdependence.** A related problem with anything that's easy and convenient is that we can start depending on it too much. National studies report that many of us lack basic knowledge. Using the Internet as your sole source of information can lure you into surface, rather than deep learning.

The Ugly

The Internet can be used in foul ways. Take a look at one student's social networking page in Figure 5.1 and see if you can guess where things are headed.

Like the hypothetical Victoria Tymmyns (or her online name, VicTym) featured in this figure, some students publish inappropriate, confidential, and potentially dangerous information on their Facebook and MySpace accounts. Victoria has posted her address, phone numbers, and moment-by-moment location. You can see that she's now being stalked. And other kinds of danger can result from bad judgment, too. What some students post just for fun can later cost them a job opportunity.

It's important to remember that the Internet itself is neutral. It can be used constructively or destructively, based on the choices you make. It can be an exciting, invigorating, essential part of your college experience. Use it wisely!

ISpy.com

[View More Photos of Me](#)

Basic Info [edit]
Name: Victoria Tymmyns
Looking For: A Good Time
Residence: 456 Pine Valley
Birthday: June 12, 1990

Contact Info [edit]
Email: VicTym@rmsu.edu
AIM Screenname: VicTym
Mobile: 719.111.1112
Current Address: 123 Fake St.
Great Bluffs, CO 80900

Personal Info [edit]
Activities: Drinkin' at "Annie Oakley's" every Fri. night.
Karaoke at "All That Jazz" every Sat. night.

Favorite Music: Black Flag, NIN, DK, the Clash
Favorite Movies Shrek, Dracula

Work Info [edit]
Company: Common Grounds Coffee Shop
Schedule: Work M – F 7AM –2PM

Status   edit

Doin' shots at Annie Oakley's!

RMSU Friends

425   friends at RMSU   See All

Seymore Bonz   **N.O. Body**

Friends in Other Networks

Cal (51)
UF (40)
CMU (63)
KSCC (7)
RMSU (425)

The Wall [edit]

 N.O. Body wrote: at 11:00am August 1, 2010
Saw u dancing at Annie Oakley's!! Whatta hottie! We should meet.

 N.O. Body wrote: at 1:00pm August 1, 2010
Aw come on! U know u want to meet me!

 N.O. Body wrote: at 3:02pm August 1, 2010
Still no response? What 's up? Do u wanna play or not?

 Seymore Bonz wrote: at 4:27pm August 1, 2010
R we still hookin up w/the gang at Annie Oakley's tonight?
Meet you guys at the front door at 10.

 N.O. Body wrote: at 5:20pm August 1, 2010
Sounds fun. Maybe i'll see u there.

 Bay-Bee Face wrote: at 10:17pm August 2, 2010
Can you believe how we much we rocked last night? What was the deal with that guy
who kept staring at us? He gave me the creeps!! You switched shifts w/Mary right?
Working at 4?

 N.O. Body wrote: at 12:39pm August 2, 2010
Gee, BTW u were dressed, I just assumed u liked being stared at… U looked really
cute at work.

 N.O. Body wrote: at 2:21pm August 3, 2010
What's the matter sweetheart? U looked unhappy to see me at work today. Why
didn't u talk to me? BTW, nice house u got. Who knew you lived in such a nice neighborhood.

 N.O. Body wrote: at 12:57pm August 5, 2010
Nice dog u have. Ur parents must be outta town—no one's been home all night.

 N.O. Body wrote: at 7:26pm August 5, 2010
U never showed up for ur shift today. I waited all day for u. Saw your friends. They said
somebody poisoned your dog. That's a shame—such a yappy little thing. I hate stuck-up
women. Guess I'll just have to find u in person…

WHOA! MAYBE I SHOULDN'T POST WHAT I'M DOING ALL THE TIME.

FIGURE 5.1

Fictional Ispy.com page

Companion, M. (2006). Victoria Tymmyns
Ispy.com. Used with permission.

It's noon. You decide to check your online life while you chow down a giant burrito. Three pokes and five new requests from potential Facebook friends. After a bit of browsing, you decide to update your photo albums by uploading several shots from your weekend adventures. The clock ticks away. It's already 4:30. Four and a half hours have just gone by, and your chem class has already started!

Does this scenario sound uncomfortably familiar? You hate to admit it, but you're caught in the Net, spending so much time on the Internet that you're neglecting other areas of your life.

Are *you* addicted? Ask yourself these questions: Do you obsess about your online life and get nervous if you haven't checked your e-mail or MySpace account for a while? Do you spend more time with your online friends than your real friends? Do you interrupt yourself constantly to check your e-mail or update your online profile while doing internet research for your class projects? If the answers to the questions in this paragraph are yes, are *you* ready to consider that you may be overly dependent on the Internet?[6]

Don't get caught in the Net. Think about the impact it could have on your college success. Try these suggestions:

1. **Monitor your time online.** Estimate right now how much time you spend online per week. Then actually time yourself. Is your estimate accurate? Or are you way off base?

2. **Set limits.** Give yourself a hard-and-fast time limit, and stick to it.

3. **Shorten your online sessions.** Set an old-fashioned timer, and when it goes off, get up and do something else.

4. **Separate work and play online.** When work and play are combined, it's easy to lose track of what's what. You end up wasting time because it feels as if you're doing something productive when you really aren't.

5. **Take a tech vacation.** Turn off your computer for a day, and then extend the time to a week or more. Use a computer lab on campus to do your assignments, rather than tempting yourself to spend hours online at home. Train yourself to withdraw, little by little.

6. **Get a life.** Take up yoga, chess, or swimming. Make some new friends, start a relationship, or join a club on campus.

7. **Talk to people who care about you—a family member or a counselor on campus.** Recognizing the problem and admitting it are the first steps. Being one-sided isn't healthy. There are experts and support groups available to help you deal with your problem and make your real life more fulfilling.[7]

THIS COULD TOTALLY BE ME!

Research Skills and Your College Success

Research isn't necessarily a mysterious thing that scientists in white coats do in laboratories. Research is simply finding answers to questions, either real questions you encounter every day or questions that are assigned to you in your classes. Doing research on your own can be a powerful way to learn, sometimes even more so than hearing answers from someone else, even if those people are your instructors. While going off to a research expedition in the actual, physical library on campus may sound like exhausting busywork, the skills you stand to gain are well worth the effort. And knowing how to do research online in today's world of electronic resources is vital!

Conducting research teaches you some important things about how to formulate a question and then find answers. And it's not just finding answers so that you can scratch a particular assignment off your to-do list. It's about learning an important process. When you get into the world of work, your instructors won't be there to supply answers, so knowing how to figure things out on your own will be key to your success. So, exactly what is college-level research?

What Research Is *Not*	What Research Is
Research isn't just going on a "search and employ" mission. It's not just seeing what all you can find and then using it to check off an assignment on your to-do list.	**Research starts with a question.** If an assignment is broad, you must come up with a specific question to research yourself. More about that later.
Research isn't just moving things from Point A (the library) to Point B (your paper).	**Research is a process with a plan.** A plan is something many students lack. They jump in without a question—or a plan.
Research isn't random rummaging through real or virtual files to find out something.	**Research is goal-oriented.** You've formulated a question, developed a plan, and now you begin to find answers by using both online sources and ones that sit on your library's shelves.
Research isn't doing a quick Internet search. The cutting and pasting some students do to fill a paper's page requirements is actually plagiarism!	**Research often involves breaking a big question into several smaller ones.**[8]

NEVER THOUGHT ABOUT THIS . . .

Navigating the Library

Beyond navigating the web to find research for your assignments, it's important to learn your way around the actual, physical space of the library on your campus. The library has many useful resources, including real, very knowledgeable librarians who are there to help you. Asking a reference librarian for help can save you hours of unproductive digging on your own.

Let's say, for example, that you are assigned a research paper for your English Composition class. The field is wide open; you may select any topic you wish. We'll assume you're a marketing major and that you decide to do your research paper on something related to your major. You're also a social media fan, and you've been doing some thinking about how these two things—marketing and social media—connect. How should you proceed? Here are some of the resources your library offers and how you should use them when you're assigned a research project like this one:

I SHOULD GET TO KNOW A LIBRARIAN ON CAMPUS SO I CAN GET HELP WITH MY PAPER!

> **Card catalog.** Explore your library's catalog that lists all of the books available to you. Card catalogs used to be actual cards in file cabinet drawers, but now most libraries put all the information about their holdings online. Go to your college's website, and from there, you can find your way to your college library's home page. Click on the library's catalog button.

> **Databases.** If you go to your library's home page, you can link to the list of online databases it subscribes to. Databases identify articles from academic journals and sometimes contain entire articles online. Generally, different databases exist for different disciplines, for example:

Education	ERIC (Educational Resources Information Center)
Psychology	**PsycInfo**
Business	**Business Source Premier**

But more general databases also exist. You might want to search through: Academic Search Premier, WilsonWeb OmniFile Full Text Mega, and Academic OneFile.

The key to making the most of databases is to find the right search words to plug into the database's search engine. That's where a short coaching session with a real reference librarian can be enormously helpful.

> **Stacks.** Physically walk through the stacks or collections of books and periodicals (journals, magazines, newspapers, and audiovisual resources, for example). Get to know the stacks in your library, and figure out how to find what you need. Look for the Library of Congress numbers posted on signs at the end of each row of books. When you find the book you're looking for, you're likely to find other books in that section that would also be useful to you. That's why even though doing online research is convenient, there's no substitute for "being there."

©Larry Harwood Photography. Property of Cengage Learning.

VARK It!

Complete the recommended activity for your preferred VARK learning modality. If you are multimodal, select more than one activity. Your instructor may ask you to (a) give an oral report on your results in class, (b) send your results to him or her via e-mail, (c) post them online, or (d) contribute to a class chat.

  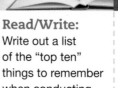

Visual: Draw an actual floor map of your library so that you know how to find sources easily.

Aural: Interview a reference librarian on campus to find out specific ways she or he helps students do research.

Read/Write: Write out a list of the "top ten" things to remember when conducting research and read it to the class.

Kinesthetic: Find three books on Internet marketing and present their bibligraphic information in class.

(from left to right) Marcela Barsse/MarsBars/iStockphoto.com; Johanna Goodyear/Dreamstime.com; Nadezda Firsova/iStockphoto.com; Pascal Genest/iStockphoto.com

Information Literacy and Your College Success

Much of the research you do for your college assignments will take place online. Information literacy is defined as knowing *when* you need information, *where* to find it, *what* it means, *whether* it's accurate, and *how* to use it. Simply put, it's "the ability to use technology to solve information problems." Information

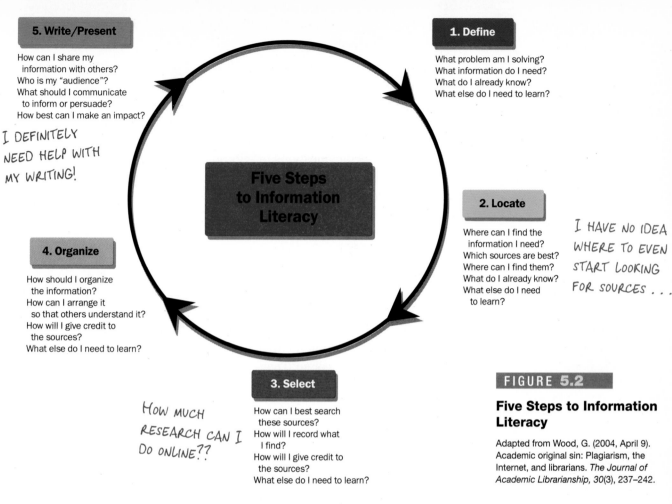

FIGURE 5.2

Five Steps to Information Literacy

Adapted from Wood, G. (2004, April 9). Academic original sin: Plagiarism, the Internet, and librarians. *The Journal of Academic Librarianship, 30*(3), 237–242.

5. Write/Present
How can I share my information with others?
Who is my "audience"?
What should I communicate to inform or persuade?
How best can I make an impact?

I DEFINITELY NEED HELP WITH MY WRITING!

1. Define
What problem am I solving?
What information do I need?
What do I already know?
What else do I need to learn?

Five Steps to Information Literacy

2. Locate
Where can I find the information I need?
Which sources are best?
Where can I find them?
What do I already know?
What else do I need to learn?

I HAVE NO IDEA WHERE TO EVEN START LOOKING FOR SOURCES . . .

4. Organize
How should I organize the information?
How can I arrange it so that others understand it?
How will I give credit to the sources?
What else do I need to learn?

3. Select
How can I best search these sources?
How will I record what I find?
How will I give credit to the sources?
What else do I need to learn?

HOW MUCH RESEARCH CAN I DO ONLINE??

literacy includes five components, as seen in Figure 5.2. Think about them as a step-by-step process as we work through an assignment.[9]

Step 1. Define

Define what the assignment requires of you. Imagine you were assigned a *research* paper. You aren't being asked to summarize or *evaluate* a topic. You are being asked to *find out about it*. But marketing and social media is a huge topic. You must narrow it down and decide which specific research question (or questions) you want to focus on.

If you knew very little about marketing and social media, you might start, by Googling your topic to help you define it. But the Internet is huge and unstructured. There's really no way to organize that much information into simple, neat categories.[10] And how do you whittle down millions of hits?

If you don't know anything about the topic you need to research, the Internet is a great place to start. You can type in "marketing social media" using a search engine and information appears instantly. The problem is that you now have too much information, and the challenge is knowing what to do next. Instead of being overwhelmed by the number of hits, use your Google search to help you see your topic from different angles and narrow it to specific research questions, like these:

1. **Avoiding Social Media Marketing Mistakes** (What are the pitfalls?)

2. **Why Business as Usual No Longer Works** (Why are the old "tried and true" methods sometimes less effective than new online tools?)

3. **Three Advantages of Social Media Marketing: Visibility, Speed, and Cost** (What are the reasons why it works?)

Let's take that last focused topic and run with it. Suppose you have a new business that you're trying to get off the ground. It's a good idea, but you have to build your customer base fast in a cost-effective way before your start-up money runs out. So the three keys to your success are visibility, speed, and cost. Now we've taken a big, broad topic (marketing and social media) and broken it down into three specific questions or subtopics to research. Your preliminary Google and Wikipedia searches can help you identify what the smaller chunks of your topic could be. But they can't do *all* the work for you, and you can't stop there. You have to know what to do next.

Step 2. Locate

If you've identified electronic sources, bookmark them in a file labeled with the name of your project. If they're print resources, physically find them in the library. If they're not available in your own campus library, see if it participates in an interlibrary loan agreement among libraries. Your own library may be able to borrow the resource from another library. (But be aware that this process may take up to two weeks or so. That's why it's important to start your research projects early!)

Step 3. Select

With so much information available, how do we know what to believe? Whether or not it's true, we tend to think that if something is on television or in a book or online, it must be important. Exercise your critical thinking skills and turn them into critical searching skills. Just because information is published doesn't automatically make it right or true. You must read, interpret, and evaluate research to decide whether to use it. Use these five criteria to evaluate any website you come across:

1. **Currency.** How up to date is the information? Some websites don't list a date at the bottom of the screen (where copyright information is often found). If you don't see one, try using other hints on the site to get at how old the information is ("According to a study published in 1995 . . ."). You may find that you need to search for something more up to date.

2. **Accuracy.** How accurate is the information presented? If a website makes an unbelievable claim ("Lose up to 10 pounds a week and still eat everything you want!") or presents shaky statistics to make a case, it's important to be skeptical. Take responsibility to validate the information elsewhere.

3. **Authority.** Does the sponsor of the website have the credentials to post the information you see? Chances are "Steve's Picks" is a collection of one person's opinions. Compare that to a film reviewer's site with information compiled by a professional film critic for a major newspaper. Which one would you trust more? You may not agree with Steve or the professional film critic, but one has credentials, and the other doesn't. Note that domains are often a good indicator for all five of these criteria. For example, if you're looking for accurate statistics, go to a .gov site (government, like the Bureau of Labor Statistics at www.bls.gov). If you're looking for an objective website about a particular cause, go to a .org site, like www.cancer.org (organization, like the American Cancer Society). If you're

©Larry Harwood Photography. Property of Cengage Learning.

" Plans are only good intentions unless they immediately degenerate into hard work."

Peter Drucker, management expert (1909–2005)

looking for information about buying and selling, go to a .com site (commercial, like www.marketing.com).

4. **Objectivity.** Does the website sponsor have a reason to convince you of something, or is it presenting unbiased information? If the site wants you to order something online because it claims to have better products than those you can buy at a store, for example, you should be suspicious.

5. **Coverage.** If a website just presents one side of an issue or a very small piece of a larger picture, check to make sure you're getting all the information you need. If you're left wondering, *but what about . . . ?* you're probably having the right reaction.

Step 4. Organize

Now that you have located the information you need, using a variety of sources, and selected those that will be most useful to you in your research project, it's time to organize. Your paper will be easier to write now that you have created three subtopics: visibility, speed, and cost. Now is the time to begin taking notes on index cards or highlighting pieces of information you want to quote word-for-word (giving credit to the author) or paraphrase (putting information into your own words). You can literally put the index cards, printed articles, and photocopied pages from books you find during your research into three piles and work from those. Organization is the key to an excellent research paper. To help you keep track of the sources you find, consider these suggestions:

> **Pay attention to details.** Write the name of the book or article, author, place of publication, publisher, date, or URL at the top of an index card with your notes or on a photocopied page of information you plan to use. This hint is important. Forgetting to write down the name of a book, title of an article, or page number of a reference has resulted in many a late-night trip to the library or frantic searching through an online database. Here's an example of what two index cards (of the same paragraph) would look like:

> *Work is either fun or drudgery. It depends on your attitude. I like fun.*
>
> **Colleen C. Barrett, President and Corporate Secretary, Southwest Airlines**

[Weber. L. (2009). *Marketing to the Social Web: How Digital Customer Communities Build Your Business.* New York: Wiley.]

Direct Quote

Social networks are places where people with a common interest or concern come together to meet people with similar interests, express themselves, and vent. . . . Some sites are devoted specifically to image-sharing, open to the wide world or restricted to a select few through password protection. YouTube (now owned by Google) serves up 10 billion videos a month to U.S. Viewers alone: photos and videos posted on Flickr (now owned by Yahoo!) attract more than 40 million visitors monthly. Marketing to the Social Web, p. 5.

[Weber. L. (2009). *Marketing to the Social Web: How Digital Customer Communities Build Your Business.* New York: Wiley.]

Paraphrase

Social networks are online places where people come together to communicate about things they care about. Some sites are especially for image-sharing. YouTube videos are watched by 10 billion Americans per month and Flickr is visited by 40 million visitors per month. Marketing to the Social Web, p. 5.

If you have ideas of your own that don't come from any book, write them on cards or pages, too, and label them, "My Own Ideas."

> **Decide on an organizational format.** Once you have your note cards in stacks, decide on the organizational format that would be most effective. Your research focuses on three different things—visibility, speed, and cost—which lends itself to what's called a *topical* format. Your research will fall into one of those three topics. If you were comparing social media effects in Europe, Asia, and North America, you might use a *compare and contrast* format. If you were going to present *solutions* to the three opportunities (or challenges) you're exploring (visibility, speed, and cost), you'd use a *problem-solution* format. Decide how best to present your information, and then follow the format you choose.

Step 5. Write and Present

Although all five steps of the Information Literacy model are important, Step 5 is especially so. Think about how far you've come. The research is done. It's time to do something with it.

Writing and critical thinking are inextricably linked. When you write, you're thinking on paper. Doing it well will help you become a better critical thinker and learner in all your courses.[11]

How should the writing process work, ideally? It should involve three basic stages: prewriting, writing, and rewriting.

Prewriting

Just as you prethink what you're going to say, you must prewrite what you're going to put down on paper. Actually, Steps 1 through 4 are part of the prewriting process. But you must also ask yourself questions like these:

"I do not like to write—I like to have written."

Gloria Steinem, journalist and political activist (1934–)

1. **What is the assignment asking me to do?** Zero in on the verbs in the assignment. The specifics of the assignment must be crystal clear to you, and if you're given a choice of topic, pick something that really interests you.

2. **Who is my audience, and what do I want them to know or do?** Once you know who you're writing to or for, then you can ask: What do I want them to know? Am I trying to inform, persuade, or entertain them? You'll use your research differently, depending on your specific purpose.

3. **Have I done enough research?** If you've followed the guidelines provided so far in this chapter about research, it's now time to ask: Do I have enough support for my thesis? Have I gathered sufficient statistics, expert testimony, and examples to persuade my reader?

4. **Can I compose a strong thesis statement?** Your paper's thesis statement should be the specific argument you're making, summarized into one sentence, ideally. For example, for the scenario we've been using, your thesis may be something like: "In today's world, social media marketing works better than conventional methods for three reasons: visibility, speed, and cost." Formulating a strong thesis is half the battle.

5. **Set in-between target dates for the three stages of writing, even if your instructor doesn't.** Some instructors will ask to see your work at each stage of the writing project. To beat the odds, schedule in-between deadlines for yourself for prewriting, writing, and rewriting to keep the project moving along.

Writing

Have you ever experienced writer's block, or nowadays, the "tyranny of the blank screen"? You sit down to write and suddenly go blank? Whatever you call it, you'll be relieved to know there are ways around it.

Just write freely about whatever comes into your head, whether it's on target or not. But, how do you start? Take a look at these techniques for starting the writing process.

1. **Begin by writing what's on your mind.**

   I'm having trouble starting this paper because there's so much to talk about in terms of social media and marketing. All businesses want to grow, but there are different ways to do it. Why not just go with tried true marketing methods like making cold calls, sending flyers through bulk mail, or creating radio and TV ads? Today, thanks to social media, there are better ways. When visibility, speed, and cost are factors—and they usually are—you need to update your marketing strategies.

   Now stop and look at what you've written. Based on your "stream of consciousness," you now have the beginnings of a paper. You can talk about how new social media marketing techniques can work better for the three reasons you've identified, and you're on your way.

2. **Begin with the words, "The purpose of this paper is . . . ."** and finish the sentence. You may be surprised by what comes out of your fingertips.

3. **Work with a tutor in your campus Writing Center.** Sometimes talking through the assignment with someone else can help, particularly if that person is a writing expert. Or talk it through with your roommate or a family member.

4. **Change the audience.** If it helps, assume you're writing your paper to someone who sharply disagrees with you or to a middle school student who just asked you a question. Sometimes thinking about your audience—instead of the topic in isolation—helps you zero in on the writing task.

5. **Play a role.** Imagine yourself as a nationally known tech guru or a network newscaster deciding what to include on the evening news. Separate yourself from the task, and see it from another perspective.

Rewriting is often called "revision," and that's a powerful term. It means not merely changing, but literally re-seeing, re-en*vision*ing your work. Sometimes students think they're revising when they're actually just editing: tinkering with words and phrases, checking spelling, changing punctuation. But the word revision actually means more than that. It means making major organizational overhauls, if necessary. Try these suggestions for rewriting to see if they work for you:

1. **Leave it alone.** To help you see your paper as others will see it, set it aside for a while. If you can wait an hour, a day, or a weekend before revising, you'll have distanced yourself long enough to see your writing for what it is, and then improve it. Of course, this suggestion isn't meant to serve as an excuse for a late paper. But coming back later is usually illuminating.

" I must write it all out, at any cost. Writing is thinking. It is more than living, for it is being conscious of living."

Anne Morrow Lindbergh, American writer and aviation pioneer (1906–2001)

I WISH I'D READ THIS SOONER!

> " A C essay is an A essay turned in too soon."
>
> **John C. Bean, Professor of English, Seattle University**

2. **Ask for feedback.** One way of discovering how your writing will affect others is simply to ask them. Share your writing before it becomes final.

3. **Edit ruthlessly!** Cutting a favorite phrase or section may feel like lopping off an arm or a leg. But sometimes it must be done. The goal here is to produce the best paper possible, even if it's painful!

4. **Proofread, proofread, proofread!** You may think you have just written an unbelievable essay, but if it's littered with errors, your instructor may pay more attention to those than to your paper's brilliant ideas. Sometimes it also helps to proofread out loud. Somehow hearing the words, especially if you're an aural learner, makes errors more apparent. And remember that Spell check, for all its convenience, can let you down. If the word you use is an actual one, but not the right on, it will give its approval, regardless. (Did you catch the spelling error in that last sentence? Spell check didn't.)

One more tip. Throughout these three stages be prepared to move fluidly from one to the other at the slightest provocation. If you're rewriting and you come across some <u>prewriting</u> information (as in *new research*), copy it down and fit it in. If in the <u>prewriting</u> stage you think of <u>writing</u> that strikes you as powerful—a good argument or a well-constructed phrase—write it down.[12]

Build a Better Paper: The Seven C's

? challenge	〞 reaction	✳ insight	! action

Challenge: Without looking ahead, can you identify seven traits of good writing (all beginning with the letter C) that college students should aim for? Finish this sentence with seven adjectives beginning with C: Good writing should be 1) <u>c</u>lear, etc.

Reaction:

1. _____

2. _____

3. _____

4. _____

5. _____

6. _____

7. _____

In many ways, writing is like building. But instead of using nails, planks, and sheetrock to construct our communication, we use words, sentences, and paragraphs. Here are seven suggestions—all of which begin with C to help you remember them.[13]

1. **Be C̲lear.** Unfortunately, the English language gives you endless opportunities to write something quite different from what you mean. You can flip through your thesaurus and use a word that sounds good, but isn't recognizable (as in profundity, below), or you can write a convoluted sentence that can't be understood. Compare the problems in these two sentences, both of which are unclear:

   > ➤ *The profundity of the quotation overtook its author's intended meaning.*

   > ➤ *The writing was profound, but on closer examination, not only was it devoid of content, but it was also characterized by a preponderance of flatulent words.*

   Yes, many of us will be able to figure out what these sentences mean, though perhaps we'll need to check the dictionary. Sometimes beginning college students decide they must write to *impress* rather than to *express*. They assume instructors like this kind of convoluted writing. They think it sounds more academic. Instructors see through that guise.

2. **Be C̲omplete.** Ask yourself what your reader needs to know. Sometimes we're so close to what we're writing that we leave out important information, or we fail to provide the background the reader needs to get our meaning. Put yourself in your reader's shoes.

3. **Be C̲orrect.** If your writing is littered with grammatical, spelling, and punctuation errors, readers may generalize that you also don't know what you're writing about either. If grammar, punctuation, and usage aren't your strong points, ask someone you know who's a crackerjack writer to look over your first draft.

4. **Be C̲oncise.** In the past, you may have used tricks like enlarging the font or increasing the margins to fill an assigned number of pages. But college students sometimes face the opposite problem: they find that writing less is more challenging than writing more. Think of this formula: A given idea expressed in many words has relatively little impact. But that same idea expressed in few well-chosen and well-combined words can be penetrating.

5. **Be C̲ompelling.** Your writing should be interesting, active, and vivid, so that people want to read what you have to say.

7 "C's"—INTERESTING WAY OF REMEMBERING HOW TO WRITE WELL!

Don't agonize. Organize."

Florynce Kennedy, American lawyer and African American activist

6. **Be <u>C</u>ourteous.** Courtesy is important in any kind of writing. E-mail is often one place where people are discourteous to one another in writing—perhaps because distance gives them courage or they're so out of sorts. Having a meltdown on paper or your computer screen is rarely the right choice.

7. **Be <u>C</u>onvincing.** You'll be a more successful writer if you support your views with solid evidence and credible testimonials. Give specific examples to illustrate your point—anecdotes, testimonials from experts, experiences, analogies, facts, statistics—and your writing will be more credible.

Keep these seven C's in mind. The secret to learning to think in college is to become a better writer. And as you're learning critical thinking skills, you'll also become a more clear, complete, correct, concise, compelling, courteous, and convincing writer.

Research: In a Manner of Speaking . . .

Instead of using your research for a paper, your assignment may ask you to use it for a presentation. Your public speaking skills will be on the line.

Most people think of public speaking as an episode, a one-time event. You stand up to give a speech, and when you're finished, you sit down. But actually, there's a sense in which all the speaking we do is public. On the job, you'll communicate with others every day.

Craft a Winning Presentation: The Seven P's

? challenge ⟩ **❝ reaction** ⟩ **✳ insight** ⟩ **❗ action**

Challenge: Without looking further in this section, can you identify seven useful key points, all beginning with P, that relate to presentations? When preparing a presentation, it's important to think about 1) purpose, etc.

Reaction:

1. _____
2. _____
3. _____
4. _____

5. _____
6. _____
7. _____

Many of the suggestions about using your research in this chapter apply to both writing and speaking. As both a writer and a speaker, you should be clear, complete, correct, concise, compelling, courteous, and convincing. You should choose an organizational pattern and use it to help your audience understand what you're saying. (Unlike reading a written paper, they only have one chance to hear your words go by.) You must have a strong thesis in a speech, just as you must in a paper. But let's examine some other advice that relates primarily to speaking. Use these suggestions to create winning presentations that set you apart in all your courses.[14]

1. **<u>P</u>urpose.** What is the purpose of your presentation? Often the purpose is given to you directly by your instructor: Prepare a five-minute speech *to*

inform. . . . But other assignments will allow you to select your own purpose: "The Trials and Tribulations of a Commuting Student" (to inform), "Sustainability in an Age of Materialism" (to persuade), "Five Sure-Fire Ways to Flunk Out of College . . . Not!" (to entertain), "How Being President of the Student Body Can Change Your Life" (to inspire). Knowing exactly what you're trying to accomplish helps!

2. **People.** Who will be your listeners? Generally, you'll be speaking to an audience of students in your classes, right? But what are their specific characteristics as they relate to your purpose? For example, if you're addressing

NOW THE 7 "P's" OF PRESENTATIONS—I LIKE IT!

Courtesy of Ward Larsen.

CAREER OUTLOOK: *Lauren Ward Larsen, Speaker, Johnson & Johnson*

Q1: What's it like to be a professional speaker? Who are your audience members and what is your message?

Being a professional speaker is the most rewarding career I've had so far because it allows me to combine the things I enjoy most from the professional positions I've held in the past. Eight years ago, after having my life saved by more than 200 pints of donated blood, I was able to combine my efforts and create a career in public speaking. Johnson & Johnson was willing to support me as a professional speaker. Because my topic impacts people of all ages, I have spoken to many different types of audiences. One of the greatest challenges and joys of being a speaker is to know my audience and figure out how best to motivate them to action.

Q2: In some ways, speaking requires marketing skills. What kind of research do you do that helps you market your ideas? How important are

research skills to both speakers and marketers?

The ability to research not only your topic, but also your audience, is a critical skill for anyone who wants a career in marketing. Researching my audience in advance is key to giving a talk that is meaningful to each group. I use several tools to do this: the Internet, any existing publications from the host organization, and simply asking the group that invited me

to tell me about the people who will be in the audience. I try to personalize my talks to the audience as much as possible, such as including a reference to a local story about my topic.

Q3: This chapter identifies seven P's to keep in mind in order to craft a winning presentation. Which of these do you emphasize, personally, and why?

The most important P in my work is People. In essence,

I am motivating people to feel compassion for the life-threatening challenges faced by others, and then turning that compassion into action by donating blood. In the marketing of "good causes" I must connect with the people in my audiences because they are the people I am trying to inspire toward a specific action.

HOW WOULD *YOU* LIKE IT?

Have you ever considered a career in marketing? Here are some facts about this career to consider and some questions about yourself to ponder.

Facts to Consider[15]

Academic preparation required: a college degree in marketing, public relations, communication, journalism, or some related field, along with an internship or similar work experience

Future workforce demand: competition for entry-level jobs will be high

Work environment: Marketing firms can be large or small, and the pace within them is

typically high-energy and brisk. Earnings are high, travel is often frequent, and the hours can be long and include weekends and evenings.

Essential skills: creativity, initiative, technology, and communication skills

Questions to Ponder

1. Do you have (or could you acquire) the skills this career requires?

2. Are you interested in a career like this? Why or why not?

For more career activities online, access the CourseMate via www.cengagebrain.com/shop/ISBN/0495906425 to do the Team Career exercises.

PREPARATION WILL HELP LOWER MY ANXIETY!

parents and friends at commencement, you might create a different speech than the one you'd present to your co-members of a student club on campus.

3. **Place.** Where will you deliver your presentation? The location of your presentation may affect its tone and style. A presentation you might give to a group of tourists at a national park would allow for informality, and your visual aid would be the scenery around you. But if you gave the same presentation as a geography major to high school seniors, you'd be more formal and scholarly, using a PowerPoint presentation or maps in the classroom.

4. **Preparation.** How should you prepare your speech? Developing the content of a speech is often similar to writing a paper. You'll need to develop a thesis statement and find support for each point by researching examples, statistics, and expert testimonies. Depending on the assignment, you might write out your speech or create a set of PowerPoint slides with talking points. Then, after you know what you're going to say, you'll need to write an attention-grabbing introduction and a memorable conclusion.

5. **Planning.** What planning should you do? For example, are visual aids available, or do you need to bring your own? Is there a plug in the room, if you need one? Should you bring a backup of your presentation on a flash drive? Many a speaker has been unnerved at the last minute by some overlooked detail.

I'M AN INTROVERT. THIS MIGHT BE A CHALLENGE!

6. **Personality.** How can you connect with the audience? How can you demonstrate your competence, charisma, and character to your listeners? Eye contact is important. Look at each person individually, if possible. Inspire trust by telling a story or relating your topic to some aspect of your own experience. Rather than playing a role, act natural and be yourself.

GOOD ADVICE. THAT'S WHAT I HAD PLANNED TO DO . . .

7. **Performance.** This last P relates to delivering your presentation. Rehearsal is important (although too much rehearsal can make your presentation sound singsongy and memorized). Beware of bringing a full written draft to the podium. If you do, you may be tempted to read it, which is the last thing you want to do. Aim for a dynamic delivery, both verbally and nonverbally, that helps keep your listeners listening.

CONTROL: *YOUR TOUGHEST CLASS*

Identify your most challenging assignment this term that will require you to use your information literacy skills. What is the specific assignment? Now go through the five steps to information literacy as they relate to your assignment. What will you do to complete each step in order to do your best on your paper or presentation? Be as detailed as possible, answering the questions for each step.

1. DEFINE:
2. LOCATE:
   (a) Find three books on your topic, and list their titles, authors, publication dates, and publishers.
   (b) Find three articles from scholarly journals, and list their bibliographic information.
   (c) Work with one or more reference librarians, and list the librarian's name, and the day and time of your work session.
   (d) Find three relevant websites and list their URLs.
3. SELECT:
4. ORGANIZE:
5. WRITE/PRESENT:

BOX 5.2

PowerPoint or PowerPointless? Five Ways to Make Your Presentations Stand Out

Instead of (or in addition to) writing a research paper, your instructor may require you to present your findings in an oral presentation using PowerPoint. While PowerPoint has the potential to be a powerful visual aid, it can also be PowerPointless if some simple rules are ignored. Keep these five suggestions in mind to turn presentations you create for class assignments into powerful ones:

1. **DO use your whole brain.** When it comes to designing PowerPoint presentations, the challenge is to combine useful information with attractive design. Think of it as using both sides of your brain—your logical left hemisphere and your creative right hemisphere. For example, which of the following presentations would you rather listen to—Presentation 1 or Presentation 2?

Presentation 1   Presentation 2

2. **DO use color to your advantage.** Choose an attractive color scheme and stick to it. That doesn't mean that every background on every slide must be the same. In fact, if you do that, your listeners may die of boredom. But if your title slide is blue, orange, and white, then use one, two, or all three of these colors in some hue or shade on every slide.

3. **DON'T crowd your slides with text.** Your listeners won't pay attention to you if they're spending all of their time reading. Be kind, and spare them the trouble by limiting the text on your slides. Some of the most deadly PowerPoint presentations are those in which the speaker turns around, faces the screen, and flies through slide after slide.

4. **DON'T let your slides steal the show.** Always remember that YOU are the speaker. Your slides shouldn't be so fascinating that your audience ignores you. Any special effects should be used sparingly to make a point, rather than to shock your listeners.

5. **DO include a bibliography slide, both for words and images.** Some students assume that plagiarism only pertains to writing papers. Not so! Always give credit where credit is due. List your references, either on individual slides (if you use a direct quote, cite it) or on one slide at the end. GREAT INFO!

One final thing: After you've finished a major research project that leads to a paper or presentation, you're not finished. It's time to sit back and think about what you've accomplished. Are you pleased with your work? What have you learned? What will you do differently next time? If you do this every time you finish a research project, you'll build your skills over time and take them with you to your other college classes, graduate school, or the world of work.

Downloading Your Workload: The Easy Way Out?

? challenge **ᶦᶦ reaction** **✱ insight** **! action**

In your opinion, is the following passage plagiarized? Compare these two examples:

Original passage: The emotional importance of a spoken message is conveyed by its semantic content ("what" is said) and by the affective prosody used by the speaker ("how" it is said). The listener has to pay attention to both types of information in order to comprehend the emotional message as a whole.

Source: Vingerhoets, G., Berckmoes, C., & Stroobant, N. (2003). Cerebral hemodynamics during discrimination of prosodic and semantic emotion in speech studied by transcranial doppler ultrasonography. *Neuropsychology*, 17(1), 93–99.

Student paper: The emotional importance of a spoken message is transmitted by its meaning ("what" is said) and by the emotional overtones used by the speaker ("how" it is said). The listener has to pay attention to both types of content in order to understand the emotional message as a whole.

Has this student committed plagiarism? Why or why not?

One of the trickiest aspects of writing papers for your college courses can be expressed in these three words: *What is plagiarism?* First, you should understand the difference between *intentional* and *unintentional* plagiarism. Intentional plagiarism is deliberately downloading a paper from an online source or cutting and pasting text from a website or book, for example. However, you run the risk of committing unintentional plagiarism if you don't understand what plagiarism is or you forget which book you used so you don't cite the words you've borrowed from someone else. Technology today makes plagiarism all too convenient and easy, but by the same token, finding plagiarism in students' papers has become easy for instructors, too. The bottom line? Follow the guidelines you get from your instructors, or ask your instructor questions if you're not sure. Both intentional and unintentional plagiarism can hurt you academically. These FAQs will help.

Q1: If I just list all the sources I used in writing a paper in the bibliography, won't that cover everything? List all your sources in the bibliography at the end of your paper, but also mention that they are others' ideas as you present them. Generally, it's a good idea to cite the original author soon after you present that idea in your paper or speech. In a research paper, it's also useful to name the author(s) ("According to Staley, college success skills are critical in the first year of college."). Each discipline uses a particular format to cite references. These are called *style sheets*, such as

> *MLA* (Modern Language Association) is often used in the humanities (English, art, and philosophy, for example).

> *APA* (American Psychological Association) is often used in the social sciences (psychology, communication, and sociology).

> *Chicago Manual of Style* is used in history.

Check with your instructor if you're not certain which one to use, and Google these terms to find the specifics of formatting.

TORSTEN SILZ/AFP/DDP/Getty Images

Q2: Must I cite all my sources if I just put ideas into my own words? Yes, you must cite all your sources, even though you may think that your paper looks cluttered. In academic writing, you must cite all the information you use, whether you paraphrase it, quote it, or summarize it.

Q3: But I didn't know anything at all about this subject before I started this assignment. Does that mean I should cite everything? Some ideas are common knowledge that need not be cited. For example, it's a well-known fact that the Civil War lasted from 1861 to 1865. If you cited this piece of common knowledge, who would you cite? Generally, however, your motto should be, "Better safe than sorry." As a rule, you must cite quotations, paraphrases, or summaries. If you use the exact words of someone else, put quotation marks around them, or if they're longer than four lines, indent them in a block. (And generally, only use long quotes if something has been said in a remarkable way.) Also cite specific facts you're using as support and distinctive ideas belonging to others, even if you don't agree with them.

Q4: I've been doing a lot of reading for this paper. Now I'm not really sure which ideas came from others and which are my own. How do I avoid plagiarism? The best solution here is to take careful notes as you do your research and document where you found each piece of information. Avoid cutting and pasting text. That practice can backfire later when you can't remember what you've extracted and what represents your own thoughts and wording. And remember this: Plagiarism applies to speaking as well as writing!

Now look back at your answers to the Challenge → Reaction at the beginning of this section and see if you would change any of them.

> " Borrowed thoughts, like borrowed money, only show the poverty of the borrower."
>
> **Lady Marguerite Blessington, English socialite and writer (1789–1849)**

? challenge **" reaction** *** insight** **! action**

Now What Do You Think?

1. At the beginning of this chapter, Dario Jones, a confused college student, faced a challenge. Now after reading this chapter, would you respond differently to any of the questions you answered about the "FOCUS Challenge Case"? Knowing what you know now, how would you advise him? Write a paragraph ending to the story, incorporating your best advice.

2. Which of the Five Steps to Information Literacy is the most difficult for you? Which ones do you resist and which ones to you delve into with eagerness? Explain why.

(continued)

3. Which of the three stages of the writing process is most challenging for you? Explain why. Are you eager to get going, so you skip prewriting? Do you have trouble getting your thoughts on paper as you write? Is time management an issue for you, so that there's no time left for rewriting?

4. Of the seven P's, which will you most need to work on? Do you tend to give one factor less attention than you should? List three specific ways that you can improve your speaking skills in college.

5. List three specific actions you will take to avoid plagiarism at all costs. For example, you may decide to begin taking notes on index cards and list a reference at the top of every card when you do research.

REALITY CHECK | What did you Learn?

On a scale of 1 to 10, answer the following questions now that you've completed this chapter.

1 = not very/not much/very little/low   10 = very/a lot/very much/high

In hindsight, how much did you already know about this subject before reading the chapter?

1 2 3 4 5 6 7 8 9 10

Can you answer these questions about information literacy, writing, and speaking skills more fully now that you've read the chapter?

1. **How would you define research? What steps are involved?**

2. **What is information literacy?**

3. **Identify the three stages involved in the writing process.**

How useful might the information in this chapter be to you? How much do you think this information might affect your success in college?

1 2 3 4 5 6 7 8 9 10

How much do you think this information might affect your career success after college?

1 2 3 4 5 6 7 8 9 10

How long did it actually take you to complete this chapter (both the reading and writing tasks)? _____ Hour(s) _____ Minutes

 Challenge Yourself Online Quiz. To find out how much you've learned, access the CourseMate via www.cengagebrain.com/shop/ISBN/0495906425 to take the Challenge Yourself Online Quiz.

Take a minute to compare these answers to your answers from the "Readiness Check" at the beginning of this chapter. What gaps exist between the similar questions? How might these gaps between what you thought before starting the chapter and what you now think after completing the chapter affect how you approach the next chapter in this book?

chapter 6

Engaging, Listening, and Note-Taking in Class

You're about to discover . . .
- ✔ How to get engaged in class
- ✔ How to listen with focus
- ✔ How to vary your listening styles according to lecture styles
- ✔ How to ask questions in class
- ✔ How to take good notes
- ✔ How to use your notes to achieve the best results

Photodisc/Getty Images

©Larry Harwood Photography. Property of Cengage Learning.

READINESS CHECK — What do you **Know?**

Before beginning this chapter, take a moment to answer these questions. Your answers will help you assess how ready you are to focus.

1 = not very/not much/very little/low   10 = very/a lot/very much/high

How much do you *already* know?

Based on reading the "You're about to discover. . ." list and skimming this chapter, how much do you think you probably already know about this chapter's subject?

1 2 3 4 5 6 7 8 9 10

See if you can answer these questions about engaging, listening, and note-taking in class *before* you read.

1. **What does in mean to sit in the "T zone" in class and why is it important?**

2. **This chapter discusses "hard" and "soft" listening skills. What's the difference between the two and which one is the right one to use in class?**

3. **Identify three possible formats for taking notes in class.**

How motivated are you to learn *more*?

In general, how motivated are you to learn more by reading this chapter?

1 2 3 4 5 6 7 8 9 10

How much do you think this information might affect your success in college?

1 2 3 4 5 6 7 8 9 10

How much do you think this information might affect your career success after college?

1 2 3 4 5 6 7 8 9 10

How ready are you to read *now*?

How ready are you to focus on this chapter—physically, intellectually, and emotionally? Circle a number for each aspect of your readiness to focus.

1 2 3 4 5 6 7 8 9 10

If any of your answers is below a 10, you might want to pay attention to whatever is distracting you before you start reading. For example, if you're feeling scattered, take a few moments to settle down and focus.

Finally, how long do you think it will take you to complete this chapter from start to finish?

_____ Hour(s) _____ Minutes

Lindsey Collier

It was Lindsey Collier's first trip home since classes started. Thanksgiving! In addition to the family's traditional feast, she was eager to see her eight-year-old sister, her brother who was a sophomore in high school, and her parents. After she left home, she began to appreciate her family more than ever. What great people they are, she kept thinking. Still, she wondered: Will they be glad to see me? Will I fit back into the family? Will Mom have converted my bedroom into a guest room? Will Dad still want to watch our favorite TV shows together? A million questions were running through her mind. Even though they talked on the phone and sent e-mails and text messages nearly every day, actually seeing her family for the first time in three months was going to seem strange. She imagined that Max, the family's golden retriever, would be the first one to greet her. She expected to miss him, but not this much!

Text Message:

From: Mom

Hi Lindsey, we miss you! I can't wait to have you home for Thanksgiving. I hope you're doing well in school.

Love you.

Nov 7th, 5:34 pm

She knew one thing for sure: Her parents would ask questions about how her classes were going. *Pretty well*, she thought. She'd gotten a B on her English paper, a B on her first math exam, an A on her College Success "Academic Autobiography," and an A– on her philosophy paper. But then there was Information Systems 102, her computer literacy course. That was a different story.

Her computer literacy instructor was a graduate teaching assistant. This was his first experience teaching a college course, he had announced on the first day of class, and English was his second language. His lectures were jam-packed with information that went right over Lindsey's head. Take last Wednesday's lecture, for example:

The real beginning of modern computers goes back to the seventeenth century and intellectual giants such as Descartes, Pascal, Leibnitz, and Napier. In mathematics, particularly, tremendous progress was made in revolutionizing how people saw the world, and their calculations became so laborious that they needed a more sophisticated computing machine.

The development of logarithms by the Scottish mathematician John Napier in 1614 stimulated the invention of the various devices that substituted the addition of logarithms for multiplication. Napier published his great work of logarithms in the book called *Rabdologia*. This was a remarkable invention since it enabled people to transform multiplication and division into simple addition and subtraction. His logarithm tables soon came into widespread use. Napier is often remembered more by another invention of his, nicknamed "Napier's Bones." This was a small instrument constructed of 10 rods, on which were engraved the multiplication tables. They are referred to as bones because the first set was made from ivory and resembled a set of bones. This simple device enabled people to carry out multiplication quickly if one of the numbers was only one digit (i.e., 6 × 6,742).[1]

Lindsey tried to pay attention to his words and copy down the writing scribbled all over the board, but no matter how hard she tried, her mind seemed to drift to the new guy she'd just met. Frankly, she just wasn't interested in all this stuff. Information seemed to fly out of her instructor's mouth at mach speed, and she used her instructor's accent as an excuse. Taking notes that quickly was just plain impossible. She tried giving him quizzical looks to communicate "Slow down, please," but he probably couldn't see her face in the back row.

Since nothing the professor said caught her interest, she knew that asking questions in class would only prove that she wasn't paying attention. Trying to read and take notes from the textbook chapters *before*

class took more discipline than she could muster. Once she even tried bringing her laptop to class to take notes, but she couldn't type fast enough, and none of it made much sense. So she drifted to her Facebook page and passed the time in class that way, even though she knew that wasn't a good idea.

Lindsey had thought about trying to stop in during the instructor's office hours some morning, but she worked off-campus as a breakfast server at a local restaurant. She could try making an appointment with him, she thought, but was he really willing to meet with every single student who had a scheduling conflict? *That's why he has office hours*, she told herself. And after all, he was working hard at the same time to earn an advanced degree himself. Besides, did she really want to discuss how poorly she was doing? It was too late in the term to drop the class, and she needed the credits for financial aid. Still, she had to figure something out or computer literacy was going to blow her GPA and her parents' impression that she was doing great in college.

NOVEMBER

Mom, Make this for Thanksgiving!

Thanksgiving Cranberry Salad

Serves: 8   Ready In: 30 minutes

Ingredients:

3 cups chopped cranberries
2 cups miniature marshmallows
1 cup sugar
2 cups chopped unpeeled apples
1/2 cup seedless grapes
1/2 cup chopped walnuts
1/4 teaspoon salt
1 cup whipped cream

© Cengage Learning

© Cengage Learning

Information Systems 102: Computer Literacy

Syllabus

Instructor: R. Singh, TA
Office: University Hall 3424
Office Hours: Mon, Wed, Thurs, 10 am-1 pm

Grading:
    Homework Assignments   25%
        -Lab Assignments
        -Internet Activities   25%

What Do You Think?

1. List five mistakes Lindsey is making.

2. Now list five things that Lindsey should do immediately to improve her computer literacy classroom experience.

Get Engaged in Class

? challenge " reaction * insight ! action

Challenge: What is *engagement?* Exactly what does it take to become engaged in class?

Reaction: _____

No, this chapter isn't about buying a ring and getting down on one knee. It's about your willingness to focus, listen, discuss, ask questions, take notes, and generally dive into your classes. It's about being a full participant in what you're learning, not just a spectator sitting on the sidelines. It's about not just memorizing information for exams and then forgetting it. You see, the secret to college success hinges on this one word: *engagement.*

Think about this analogy. How did you learn to swim? Did you read books about swimming? Did you get advice from your friends about swimming? Did you sit on the edge of the pool and watch other people swim? No, you probably jumped in and got wet, right? The same thing is true with your college classes. The more willing you are to jump in and get wet, the more engaged you'll be in the learning process.

Dare to Prepare

If you want to get a head start on developing good academic habits in class, then start before you get there. Preparation separates students into two categories: those who excel at learning and those who don't. Although not all students see the value of preparation, do more than your classmates do—dare to prepare! Follow these suggestions and you'll find that it's easier to get engaged in class because you're ready.

1. **Look ahead.** By checking your course syllabus before class, you'll be prepared for the upcoming topic. You'll also avoid the "oops" factor of sitting down, looking around, and noticing that everyone else knows something you don't about what's supposed to happen today.

Read chapter 6 for IS 102 tonight!!!!

2. **Do the assigned reading.** If you have a reading assignment due for class, do it, and take notes as you read. Write in the margins of your textbook or on sticky notes. Question what you're reading and enter into a mental dialogue with the author. Having some background on the topic will allow you to listen

more actively and participate more intelligently during any discussion. Instead of hearing it for the first time, you'll *reinforce* what you've already read. According to one study, as few as one-third of your classmates will have done the assigned reading prior to class. That factoid isn't a reason to excuse yourself from reading; instead it gives you insider information on how *you* can shine in class by comparison.[2]

3. **Show up physically.** Not only is attending class important for your overall understanding of the material, but it may move your grade up a few notches. Even if attendance isn't required by your instructor, require it of yourself. Research says that missing classes is definitely related to your academic performance.[3] And once you give yourself permission to skip one single, solitary class, it becomes easier to do it the next time, and the time after that. Studies indicate that on any given day, approximately one-third of your classmates will miss class and that most students think that several absences during a term is "the standard."[4] Exercise good judgment, even if your classmates don't!

4. **Show up mentally.** Showing up means more than just occupying a seat in the classroom. It means assessing what you bring to the class as a learner on any particular day. Do a mental "Readiness Check" when you arrive in class. If you're not ready, what can you do to rally for the cause?

5. **Choose your seat strategically.** Imagine paying $150 for a concert ticket, just like everyone else, and then electing to sit in the nosebleed section as high up and far away from the action as you could get. Sitting in the back means you're more likely to let your mind wander and less likely to hear clearly. Sitting in the front means you'll keep yourself accountable by being in full view of the instructor and the rest of the class. What's the best spot for great concentration? Front and center, literally—the "T zone"! In one study, students who sat at the back of a large auditorium were six times more likely to fail the course, even though the instructor had assigned seats randomly![5]

6. **Bring your tools.** Bring a writing utensil and notebook with you to every class. Your instructor may also ask you to bring your textbook, calculator, a blue book for an exam, or other necessary items. If so, do it. Question: how seriously would you take a carpenter who showed up to work without a hammer, nails, and screwdriver? Get the point?

7. **Don't sit by your best friend.** Resist the temptation to sit next to your best buddy in order to catch up on all the latest campus news during class. Of course, it's important to have friends, but class is hardly the best time to devote yourself to helping your friendship blossom.

8. **Posture counts!** Your parents may have told you more than once as a kid: "Sit up straight!" Sitting up straight in class will help you develop a healthy mind. It's hard to focus when you're slouched into a position that screams, "I could really use a power nap about now!" When your body says, "I'm ready to learn," your mind follows suit.

9. **Maintain your health.** Being sick can wreak havoc on your ability to concentrate, listen well, and participate. Take the preventative approach

> " What actually correlates with success are not grades, but 'engagement'—genuine involvement in courses and campus activities. Engagement leads to 'deep learning,' or learning for understanding. That's very different from just memorizing stuff for an exam, then forgetting it."
>
> **John Merrow, reporter, *USA Today***

I've cut IS 102 three times already!!! Ugh!

No more Facebook in class either!

I'll sit in the "T zone" next class and see if it helps.

Not my issue. I'm good here.

©Larry Harwood Photography. Property of Cengage Learning.

by getting enough sleep, eating well, and exercising. Remember, *energy management* is key to your ability to focus.

10. **Focus.** After sitting down in class each day, take a moment to clear your head of all daydreams, to-do's, and worries. Take a deep breath and remind yourself of the opportunity to learn that lies ahead. Think of yourself as a reporter at a press conference, listening intently because you'll be writing a story about what's going on. You *will* be writing a "story"—often in response to an essay question on an exam!

Follow the Rules of Engagement

Just as is the case with most places you can think of, college classrooms have rules about how to behave. You don't find people yelling in church or staring at other people in elevators or telling jokes at funerals. There are rules about how to behave in a variety of contexts, and college classrooms are no exception.

1. **Be aware that gab is not a gift.** In class, gabbing while others are speaking is inappropriate. And it's certainly not a gift—especially to your instructor. In fact, side conversations while your professor is lecturing or your classmates are contributing to the discussion are downright rude. If you're seated next to a gabber, don't get sucked in. Use body language to communicate that you're there to learn, not to gab. If that's not enough to set the gabber straight, politely say something like, "I really need to pay attention right now. Let's talk more later, okay?" If that doesn't work, move to a different seat next time. Don't let other students cheat you out of learning.

2. **Control your hunger pangs.** If your class meets through a meal hour, get in the habit of eating before or after class. Crunching and munching in the classroom may get in the way of others' learning, not to mention the distraction caused by enticing smells. Instructors differ on their preferences here. It's a good idea to find out what your instructors' preferences are, and then abide by them.

3. **Turn off your cell phone, please!** There's a reason why people are asked to turn off their cell phones before concerts, athletic events, or movies. Imagine being in a jam-packed theater trying to follow the film's plot with cell phones going off every few seconds. You've paid good money to see a film. The same thing goes for your college classes.

4. **Better late than never?** Students arriving late and leaving early are annoying, not only to your instructor, but to your classmates. To them, it looks like you don't value the other students or the class content. How would you like dinner guests to arrive an hour late, after you'd slaved over a hot stove all day? Your instructors have prepared for class, and they feel the same way. Build in time to find a parking place, hike to the building where class is held, or stop for a coffee. Do everything you can to avoid coming late and leaving early.

5. **Actively choose to engage, not disengage.** Engagement isn't something that just happens to you while you're not looking. It's a choice you make, and

> " Every person in this life has something to teach me—and as soon as I accept that, I open myself to truly listening."
>
> **John Lahr, drama critic**

©Larry Harwood Photography. Property of Cengage Learning.

> " Politeness is the art of choosing among one's real thoughts."
>
> **Adlai Stevenson II,**
> **U.S. Presidential candidate**
> **(1900–1965)**

sometimes it's a difficult choice because the material isn't naturally appealing to you, or the course is a required one you didn't choose, or you're just plain out of sorts. Choose to engage, anyway. Instead of actively choosing to *dis*-engage in class by sleeping through lectures, surfing the Internet, or texting friends, choose to engage by leaning forward, processing information, finding your own ways to connect to the material, and formulating questions to ask.

Listening with Focus

? challenge   " reaction   * insight   ! action

Challenge: What is *focused listening*? How can you achieve it?

Reaction: _____

Listening with focus is more than just physically hearing words as they stream by. It's actually a complicated process that's hard work.

"Easy Listening" Is for Elevators— Focused Listening Is for Classrooms

Stores, restaurants, and elevators are known for their programmed, background easy listening music. Chances are you hardly notice it's there. Listening in class, however, requires actual skill, and you'll be doing a great deal of it as a college student. Experts estimate that the average student spends 80 percent of class time listening to lectures.[6]

Many of us naively believe that listening is easy to do. If you happen to be around when there's something to listen to, you can't help but listen. Not so! Did you know that when you're listening at your best, your respiration rate, heartbeat, and body temperature all increase? Just as with aerobic exercise, your body works harder when you're engaging in focused listening. When all is said and done, listening is really about energy management. You can't listen well when your energy is zapped, when you've pulled the mother of all all-nighters, or when your stomach is growling with a vengeance. Focused listening means that you've cleared the deck for class, and you're focusing on engagement.

I did not know that!

Here are some techniques for improving your listening skills in the classroom. Read through the list, then go back and check off the ones you're willing to try harder to do in class this week.

☐ **Calm yourself.** Take a few deep breaths with your eyes closed to help you put all those nagging distractions on the back burner during class time.

☐ **Be open.** Keep an open mind and view your class as yet another opportunity to strengthen your intellect and learn something new. Wisdom comes from a broad understanding of many things, rather than from a consistently limited focus on practical information.

Listening with Focus   133

☐ **Don't make snap judgments.** Remember, you don't have to like your instructor's wardrobe to respect his knowledge. Focus on the content he's offering you. You may not even agree with what he's saying, but he may be leading up to a point you can't predict and turn the argument around. Don't jump to conclusions about content or style.

✓ ☐ **Assume responsibility.** Speak up! Ask questions! Even if you have a professor with an accent who's difficult to understand, the burden of clarification rests with you. You will interact with people with all sorts of accents, voices, and speech patterns throughout your life. It's up to you to improve the situation.

☐ **Watch for gestures that communicate "Here comes something important!"** Some typical examples include raising an index finger, turning to face the class, leaning forward from behind the podium, walking up the aisle, or using specific facial expressions or gestures.

☐ **Listen for speech patterns that subtly communicate "Make sure you include this in your notes!"** For example, listen for changes in the rate, volume, or tone of speech, longer than usual pauses, or repeated information.

☐ **Uncover general themes or roadmaps for each lecture.** See if you can figure out where your instructor is taking you *while* he's taking you there. Always ask yourself, "Where's he going with this? What's he getting at? How does this relate to what was already said?"

☐ **Appreciate your instructor's prep time.** For every hour of lecture time, your teacher has worked for hours to prepare. Although she may make it look easy, her lecture has involved researching, organizing, creating a PowerPoint presentation, overheads, or a podcast, and preparing notes and handouts.

☐ **Trick yourself into focused listening.** If you find it hard to get interested in the material, trick yourself by paying attention to the person delivering the message. While tricking yourself isn't always a good idea, it can work if you know what you're doing and why.

Listening Is More Than Hearing

Perhaps you've never thought about it, but, actually, listening and hearing aren't the same thing. Hearing—the physiological part—is only the first stage of a four-stage process. Listening is a much more complex process—especially *focused listening*, or listening at your best. The four stages of focused listening are shown in Figure 6.1.

1. **Sensing:** receiving the sounds through your auditory system. As you sit in class, sound waves enter your ears and register in your brain.

2. **Interpreting:** understanding the message. Sounds themselves don't mean anything until you assign meaning to them. Instead of just random noise, the instructor's message must mean something to you.

3. **Evaluating:** weighing evidence. You decide if something is true or important by sorting fact from opinion. Both interpretation and evaluation in class may involve asking questions to clarify things.

4. **Responding:** providing feedback or taking action. You respond by participating in the discussion, asking significant questions, and taking down clear, meaningful notes to study later.[7]

Not sure I ever get to stage 2 in IS 102!

1. sensing **2. interpreting**

4. responding **3. evaluating**

(clockwise from top left): © ArchMan, 2009/Used under license from Shutterstock.com; © Michael D Brown, 2009/Used under license from Shutterstock.com; © WilleeCole, 2009/Used under license from Shutterstock.com; © Petr Vaclavek, 2009/Used under license from Shutterstock.com

FIGURE 6.1

Four Stages of Focused Learning

As you're listening in class, you must cycle through all four of these stages. You must *sense* the sound waves coming from your instructor, a classmate, or a guest speaker, *interpret* them, *evaluate* them, and *respond* by jumping into the discussion yourself, asking questions, and taking the best notes you can. If you're not focused, it's possible to skip a step or "listen out of order." You may take notes without really *interpreting* what you're hearing. You're operating on autopilot—you skip the interpretation step completely, and write down things you don't really understand. (And consequently, you can't interpret your notes later.) Or you may try and write down every word you hear without *evaluating* its importance, getting bogged down in insignificant detail.

Listen Hard!

It's estimated that college students spend ten hours per week listening to lectures.[8] Professors can speak 2,500–5,000 words during a fifty-minute lecture. That's a lot of words flying by at breakneck speed, so it's important to listen correctly. But what does *that* mean?

Think about the various situations in which you find yourself listening. You often listen to empty chit-chat on your way to class. "Hey, how's it going?" when you spot your best friend in the hallway is an example, right? Listening in this type of situation doesn't require a lot of brainpower. Although you wouldn't want to spend too much time on chit-chat, if you refused to engage in any at all, you'd probably be seen by others as odd, withdrawn, shy, or arrogant. You also listen in challenging situations, some that are emotionally charged; for example, a friend needs to vent or relieve stress. Most people who are blowing off steam

Have you ever noticed there's a play-by-play commentary going on inside your head, just like an NFL announcer during a big game: "On third down with no timeouts left. And here's the snap . . . rookie Davis Jones busts off tackle for an eight-yard gain! It's close to a first down. . . ." Compare that to your own play-by-play observations: "And here he comes . . . Matt's walking straight toward me. He's getting closer. Maybe this is my big chance."

It's normal to comment internally about what's going on around you, and it's perfectly human to think that your own internal dialogue is the most important thing on the planet. The question isn't whether or not you're engaged in constant conversation with yourself; it's whether that conversation is productive and useful, and if not, how to make it so.

Sometimes this incessant, internal chatter makes it hard to be fully present in class because of three P's: **p**ressure, **p**reoccupation, and **p**riorities. While you're sitting there, you feel a rush of stress about your assignments; you worry about a sick relative; and you obsess about whether you should tackle your calculus homework or start on your philosophy research paper tonight. You feel overwhelmed.

In his book *Quiet Your Mind,* author John Selby reports that we can learn better control over our thoughts, and that the psychological and physiological benefits are well worth it.[9] Here are some tips to coach yourself to quiet your mind:

- **Choose where to focus your attention.** Instead of allowing your mind to run you, make a conscious decision to run it.

- **Spend your free time; don't squander it.** Do you watch television, exercise, or surf the Net to *avoid* what you see as unpleasant but necessary tasks, rather than to *revitalize*? Consider whether your free time is about something or about nothing.

- **Worry less; do more.** Worry is counterproductive; it drains us of the energy we need to get things done and keeps us from enjoying the present. Write down what's worrying you most, identify the worst that could possibly happen, and ask yourself if your fear is realistic.

- **Forgive and forget.** Some people obsess over the past. They should have done X; if only Y had happened instead. Life is full of ups and downs, but it's important to keep moving.

- **Be present.** Remember grade school? Your teachers would call the roll every morning, and you'd answer "present" or "I'm here." Life coach Mark van Doren says, "There is one thing we can do, and the happiest people are those who can do it to the limit of their ability. We can be completely present. We can be all here. We can … give all our attention to the opportunity before us."

aren't looking for you to fix their problems. They just want to be heard and to hear something from you like "I understand." Listening to chit-chat and listening in emotionally charged situations require what are called soft listening skills. You must be accepting, sensitive, and nonjudgmental. You don't have to assess, analyze, or conclude. You just have to be there for someone else.

But these two types of listening situations don't describe all the kinds of listening you do. When you're listening to someone trying to persuade you of something, you have to pay close attention, think critically, and ultimately make decisions about what you're hearing. Is something true or false? How do you know? When you're listening to a person trying to inform or persuade you, you need hard listening skills instead of soft ones. In situations like these you must be discerning, analytical, and decisive.

One mistake many students make in class is listening the wrong way. They should be using their hard listening skills, rather than sitting back and letting information waft over them. Soft listening skills don't help you in class. You must listen intently, think critically, and analyze carefully what you're hearing.

It's important to note that neither listening mode is better than the other. They are each simply better suited to different situations. But soft listening won't get you the results you want in your classes. You don't need to be there for your instructor; you need to be there for yourself.[10]

Get Wired for Sound

Aural learners of the world unite! Increasingly professors are providing podcasts (and videocasts) of their lectures so that you can *preview* the lecture in advance or *review* it after class. Some textbooks (like this one) offer chapter summaries you can listen to on the subway, in the gym, or in bed while recovering from the flu via your computer or digital-audio player.

Regardless of your learning style, recorded lectures allow you to re-listen to difficult concepts as many times as needed. You can take part in the live action in class and take notes later while re-listening to the podcast. In one study, students who re-listened to a lecture one, two, or three times increased their lecture notes substantially each time and students who re-listen to a lecture and take notes can increase their test scores.[11] Of course, recorded lectures aren't meant to excuse you from attending class, and in order to take advantage of them, you actually have to find time to listen to them. They're supplemental tools to *reinforce* learning for busy students on the go, which is virtually *everyone* these days.[12]

Identify Lecture Styles So You Can Modify Listening Styles

Regardless of how challenging it is to listen with focus, being successful in college will require you to do just that—focus—no matter what class or which professor. Sometimes your instructors are *facilitators*, who help you discover information on your own in new ways. Other times they are *orators*, who lecture as their primary means of delivering information. If you're not an aural learner, listening with focus to lectures will be a challenge for you.

> *Great podcast available online on the CourseMate via www.cengagebrain.com/shop/ISBN/0495906425 for this chapter! I should check out podcasts for IS 102. Maybe listening to lectures more than once would help me understand my instructor's accent!*

©Larry Harwood Photography. Property of Cengage Learning.

" The most basic and powerful way to connect to another person is to listen. Just listen. Perhaps the most important thing we ever give each other is our attention."

**Rachel Naomi Remen,
physician and author**

Think about the courses you're taking this term. Use the following form to analyze your various professors' lecture styles. Be discrete as you listen and analyze their styles, of course, but after your chart is completed, decide what you can do as a listener to make adjustments in your toughest class. Filling out this chart for all your classes may give you some insights about why one particular class is your toughest and help you develop a plan to help you become more successful.

LECTURE STYLE ANALYSIS WORKSHEET					
COURSES	Information Systems 102				
EMPHASIS Content, students, or both?	Definitely on content. He doesn't seem to notice that students are in the room!				
ORGANIZATION Structured or unstructured?	Lectures seem unstructured with notes written all over the board.				
PACE Fast, slow, or medium?	Very fast. Instructor doesn't seem to notice when students are lost.				
VISUAL AIDS Used? Useful?	Board hard to see from the back of the room.				
EXAMPLES Used? Useful?	Few real examples are given that students can relate to.				
LANGUAGE Terms defined? Vocabulary understandable?	What is a logarithm, exactly? No, not defined.				
DELIVERY Animated via body language?	Although the teacher is trying to communicate, his delivery style isn't lively and interesting.				
QUESTIONS Encouraged?	He rarely pauses to take questions.				
Proposed adjustments in my toughest class:	Make special arrangements to meet with the instructor during his office hours. Must do right away!				

Chances are you won't be able to change your professors' lecturing styles. And even if you could, different students react differently to different lecture styles. But what you can do is expand your own skills as a listener—no matter what class or which instructor. Take a look at the lecture styles coming up and see if you recognize them.

> **The Rapid-Fire Lecturer:** You may have found yourself in a class with an instructor who lectures at breakneck speed. Listening and taking notes in a class isn't easy. By the end of class your hand aches from gripping your pen and writing furiously. Since there'll be no time to relax, you'll need to make certain you're ready for this class. Read ahead so that you recognize points the instructor makes. Also take advantage of whatever supplementary materials this teacher provides in the way of audio support, online lecture notes, or PowerPoint handouts.

> **The Slow-Go Lecturer:** Instead of rushing, some lecturers move very slowly. They contemplate, ruminate, and chew on every word before uttering it. This lecturer speaks so slowly that there are pauses—seconds long—between phrases, while he paces back and forth, pontificating. Your attention tends to drift because you become impatient. Discipline yourself to use the extra time to your advantage by predicting what's coming next or by clarifying what's just been said in your own mind.

> **The All-Over-the-Map Lecturer:** Organization is not this lecturer's strong suit. While the lecture may be organized in the lecturer's mind, what comes out is difficult to follow. In this case, it will be up to you to organize the lecture content yourself.

> **The Content-Intensive Lecturer:** This lecturer is hardly aware that anyone else is in the room, intent on covering a certain amount of material in a particular amount of time. This teacher may use extensive discipline-specific jargon that you will need to learn rapidly to keep abreast. Prepare yourself for a potentially rich learning environment, but be sure to ask questions right away if you find yourself confused.

This is him! Note to self: Ask questions in class.

> **The Review-the-Text Lecturer:** This lecturer will follow the textbook closely, summarizing and highlighting important points. You may assume it's not important to attend class, but watch out for this trap! Receiving the same information in more than one format can be a great way to learn.

> **The Go-Beyond-the-Text Lecturer:** This lecturer will use class time to provide examples, tell stories, and bring in outside materials. Keeping up with reading in the text will be important so that you understand the additional information that you receive in class.

> **The Active-Learning Lecturer:** This lecturer may choose not to lecture at all or to intersperse short lectures with activities and role plays. While you may find it easier to get engaged in class, and you'll most likely appreciate the teacher's creativity, remember that you are still responsible for connecting what happens in class to the course material itself. You will need to read, digest, and process the information on your own outside of class.

Taking Notes: Ask and You Shall Receive

? **challenge** **❝ reaction** **✳ insight** **❗ action**

Challenge: Are there different kinds of questions to ask during lectures and in-class discussions? If so, what are they?

Reaction: _____

_____

Even if you listen carefully to every word your instructor utters, it's likely you won't understand them all. After all, your instructor is an expert in the subject you're studying, and you're a novice. At some point or other, you'll need clarification or elaboration, and the best way to get it will be to ask. Even though that makes sense, not all students ask questions in class. Why? See if you've excused yourself from asking questions for any of these reasons:

> I don't want to look stupid. Everyone else seems to be understanding.

> I'm too shy.

> I'll get the answer later from the textbook.

> I don't think my question is important enough.

> I don't want to derail the lecture. The instructor's on a roll.

> I don't want to draw attention to myself.

 Yep!

> I'm just not into it.

If any of these reasons for not asking questions in class applies to you, the good news is . . . you're not alone. Unfortunately many students think this way. The bad news, of course, is that your question remains unasked, and therefore, unanswered.

The next time you find yourself in a situation where you don't understand something, consider these points.

1. **Become the class spokesperson.** If you do ask a question that's on your mind, not only will you be doing yourself a favor by asking, but you'll also be helping someone else who's too shy to speak up. When it comes to the discipline at hand—whether it's philosophy, psychology, or chemistry—remember that you and your classmates are novices and the instructor is an expert. Asking questions is a natural part of that equation.

2. **Ask academically relevant questions when the time is right.** As opposed to "Why do we need to know this?" or "Why did you make the test so hard?" ask questions to clarify information. Don't ask questions designed to take your instructor off on a tangent (to delay the impending quiz, for example). If you're really interested in something that's not directly related to the material being covered, bring it up during your instructor's office hours.

3. **Save *personally* relevant questions for later.** If your questions relate only to you (for example, you were ill and missed the last two classes), then don't ask in class. Set up an appointment with your instructor. You can also get answers by researching on your own, visiting or e-mailing your instructor, seeking out a teaching assistant or tutor, or working with a study group.

4. **Build on others' questions.** Listen to the questions other students ask. Use their questions to spark your own. Perhaps another student has a unique way of looking at the issue being discussed that will spark an idea for a follow-up question from you. Remember, to your instructor, good questions indicate *interest*, not *idiocy*.

5. **Consider that questions are a way to s-t-r-e-t-c-h your learning.** Of course, many of the questions you ask in class will be simple questions to clarify information. But be aware of this opportunity: You can ask questions that increasingly move you up the scale toward higher-order thinking. What does that mean? In 1956, learning expert Benjamin Bloom developed a classification system for ways of thinking—from simple to complex. His system, called "Bloom's Taxonomy," shows that thinking occurs on a progression of levels, from low (simple) to high (complex) as shown in Figure 6.2. Imagine listening to the lecture in Exercise 6.1, and think of questions you could ask to move yourself up this progressive ladder.[13]

> " He who is ashamed of asking is ashamed of learning."
>
> **Danish Proverb**

Level	Explanation	Example
Remembering	recall information and facts	*What are neurotransmitters?*
Understanding	explain ideas	*What do neurotransmitters do?*
Applying	use the information	*If a patient describes sleep disturbances and a general disinterest in life, which neurotransmitters may be involved?*
Analyzing	examine critically, separate into parts	*What role do neurotransmitters play in the overall functioning of the human brain?*
Evaluating	assess the relative value	*Is doing scientific research on neurotransmitters important?*
Creating	design or see from a new point of view	*What new drug therapies could be developed that affect neurotransmitters in diseased brains?*

FIGURE 6.2

Bloom's Taxonomy

Remember, your college education is an expensive investment. You've paid to learn, and asking questions is a natural part of that learning experience. Don't be shy—put that hand in the air!

One-Way versus Two-Way Listening

To demonstrate the value of asking questions, try this in-class exercise. A student volunteer, or class "lecturer," will briefly replace the instructor to describe to the rest of the class two different, simple figures that are provided. The rest of the class must then replicate the drawings as accurately as possible on their own paper as the class "lecturer" describes each figure during two rounds. The point of the exercise is to replicate the two figures as accurately as possible from the verbal description alone.

Round 1: The volunteer should turn her back to the group (to eliminate nonverbal cues), hiding her paper from view, and give the class instructions for drawing Figure 1. *No questions from the group are allowed.* Note the exact amount of time it takes for the rest of the class to listen to the instructions and complete the drawing.

Round 2: Next, the volunteer should now turn around and face the class, giving instructions for drawing Figure 2. *Students may ask questions of the "lecturer" to clarify and elaborate as much as is necessary to get the drawing right (without showing the figure).* Again, note the exact amount of time taken.

After both rounds of the exercise are done, the "lecturer" should ask class members whether they think their drawings closely resemble the two originals and count the number of students who think they drew Figure 1 correctly and the number of students who think they drew Figure 2 correctly. Then the "lecturer" should show the two original figures as drawn, and count the number of students who actually drew Figure 1 and Figure 2 correctly. Finally, as a group, discuss the two rounds and the value of asking questions in lecture classes. Even though questions take more time, the results are usually much better.

Elapsed Time	# Think Correct	# Actually Correct
Round 1		
Round 2		

How Well Do You Take Notes?

See which of the following statements apply to you. Check the box that most applies to what you usually do in the classroom to assess your current level of note-taking skills. Use this self-assessment to develop a plan for improvement.

	Always True of Me	Sometimes True of Me	Never True of Me
1. I have a system for taking notes that works well.	☐	☐	☐
2. I compare my notes with those of a classmate.	☐	☐	☐
3. I review my notes as soon after class as possible to make sure I understand what I wrote.	☐	☐	☐
4. I read my notes out loud.	☐	☐	☐
5. I try to summarize the information in my notes.	☐	☐	☐
6. I look for organizational patterns within my notes (*e.g.,* causes and effects, lists of items).	☐	☐	☐
7. I take notes while reading an assignment for class.	☐	☐	☐
8. I don't daydream during class and miss out on notes I should be taking.	☐	☐	☐

9.	I search for ways to reinforce the notes I take in class (podcasts, instructor's posted lecture notes, etc).	☐	☐	☐
10.	I take notes regularly in all my classes.	☐	☐	☐
11.	I use abbreviations to help me keep up with the lecturer.	☐	☐	☐
12.	I talk my notes through with someone else.	☐	☐	☐
13.	I revise my notes when I consult the textbook and find out that I've left out important material.	☐	☐	☐
14.	I organize my notes into a chart or graph, if appropriate.	☐	☐	☐
15.	I copy down items from the board or screen.	☐	☐	☐

Total check marks for each column: _____   _____   _____

Add up the check marks in each column to learn the results of your analysis. Pay particular attention to the total in the "Always True of Me" column.

13–15 "Always True of Me": You're probably an excellent note-taker. Keep up the good work.

10–12 "Always True of Me": You are a good note-taker, but you need to fine-tune a few of your note-taking skills.

7–9 "Always True of Me": You need to change some behaviors so that you get more out of your classes.

6 or less "Always True of Me" or 7 or more "Never True of Me": You need to learn better note-taking skills if you want to achieve academic success in college.

Taking Lecture Notes:
Different Strokes for Different Folks

? challenge **“** reaction **✳** insight **!** action

Challenge: Does taking notes help students learn? Why or why not?

Reaction: _____

Listening in class is one thing. Taking notes is quite another. You must be a good listener to take good notes, but being a good listener alone doesn't automatically make you a good note-taker. Note-taking is a crucial and complex skill, and doing well on tests isn't based on luck. It's based on combining preparation and opportunity, in other words, knowing how to take useful notes in class that work for you.

Marc Romanelli/Riser/Getty Images

Actually, one reason that note-taking is so important in the learning process is that it uses all four VARK categories: *visual* (you see your professor and the screen, if overheads or PowerPoint slides are being used), *aural* (you listen to the lecture), *read/write* (you write what you see and hear so that you can read it later to review), and *kinesthetic* (the physical act of writing opens up a pathway to the brain). As it turns out your transcription fluency—how quickly you can write clear, complete notes to review later—is a critical skill.[14]

According to one study, 99 percent of college students take notes during lectures, and 94 percent of students believe that note-taking is important.[15] These are good signs, but are these students taking notes correctly, as a result of focused listening? If 99 percent of college students are taking notes, why isn't nearly everyone getting straight A's? Here are some reasons:

> Students typically only record less than 40 percent of the lecture's main content ideas in their notes.[16]

> Only 47 percent of students actually review their notes later to see what they've written.

> Only 29 percent edit their notes later by adding, deleting, or reorganizing material.

> A full 12 percent do nothing other than recopy them verbatim.

> Some students never do anything with their notes once they leave class![17]

Does note-taking make a difference? Absolutely. During lectures, it serves two fundamental purposes: it helps you understand what you're learning at the time and it helps you preserve information to study later. In other words, both the *process* of note-taking (as you record information) and the *product* (your notes themselves) are important to learning. There is strong evidence that taking notes during a lecture leads to higher achievement than not taking notes, and working with your notes later increases your chances for academic achievement even more. Studies show that if you take notes, you have a 50 percent chance of recalling that information at test time versus a 15 percent chance of remembering the same information if you didn't take notes.[18]

But when it comes to note-taking, "different strokes for different folks" is literally true. Many different note-taking systems can work, and different systems work best for different learning styles.

Whichever strategy you choose to use, an important question to ask is: What constitutes *good* notes? The answer is: Writing down an *accurate, complete, organized* account of what you hear in class (or read in your textbook, which is discussed elsewhere in this book). How will you know if your notes are good? Show them to your instructor and get input, or assess your strategy after you see your results on the first exam. Your note-taking skills should steadily improve as you evolve as a student.[19]

Imagine that you are taking an Introduction to Psychology course, and the topic for today's class is neurotransmitters, a complicated subject with

Neurotransmitters	*Well over 60 different chemical compounds have been identified as neurotransmitters and researchers continue to investigate more substances that may affect neural signaling.*
ACh	*Acetylcholine was the first neurotransmitter discovered. In the early part of this century, ACh was found to inhibit the action of the heart and to excite skeletal muscles. Today, ACh is thought to play a role in our awareness or consciousness and to have a role in memory.*
Dopamine	*Dopamine appears to influence several processes, including movement, learning and attention. Dopamine may also play an important role in motivation by making some activities such as sex and eating very pleasurable or rewarding for us.*
Serotonin	*Serotonin is thought to play a role in many different behaviors, including sleep, arousal, mood, eating, and pain perception. Among the general public, serotonin is perhaps the most widely know neurotransmitter.*
Norepinephrine	*Norepinephrine is thought to play a role in regulating sleep, arousal, and mood.*
Gamma amino butyric acid	*Gamma amino butyric acid is thought to regular our general level of energy and alertness. It is estimated that one third of all synapses use GABA as their neurotransmitter.*
Glutamate	*Glutamate is used as a neurotransmitter by more than 50% of all synapses in the brain, and without it many brain processes would not take place. Ironically, glutamate can also be a deadly force in the brain.*
Endorphins	*Endorphins are neurotransmitters that are chemically very similar to the class of narcotic drugs called opiates. They are released in the central nervous system during times of stress, such as physical exertion or physical injury, to protect us from pain. In addition to their roles as painkillers, endorphins may also play a role in regulating eating behavior and cardiovascular functioning.*
Substance P	*Substance P may play a role in carrying signals of pain, physical and perhaps emotional.*

technical terminology. You need an effective way to write down important information as it flies by during your instructor's lecture. Here is one system you could use.

FIGURE 6.3

Neurotransmitters: Cornell System Example

The Cornell System

The Cornell format of note-taking, devised by educator Walter Pauk and illustrated in Figure 6.3, suggests this. On each page of your notebook, draw a line from top to bottom about one and a half inches from the left edge of your paper. Take notes on the right side of the line. Leave the left side blank to fill in later with key words or questions you'd like answered. After class as you review your notes, put your hand over the right side and use the words or questions you've written on the left side as prompts.[20] By doing this to recall the lecture, you can get a good idea of how much of the information you've understood.

Mind Maps

An alternative to the Cornell system, or a way to expand on it, is to create mind maps. Mind maps use both sides of your brain: the logical, orderly left side and

I think I could take notes like this, or at least turn my class notes into something like this to help me study! I love using different colored markers to help me remember!

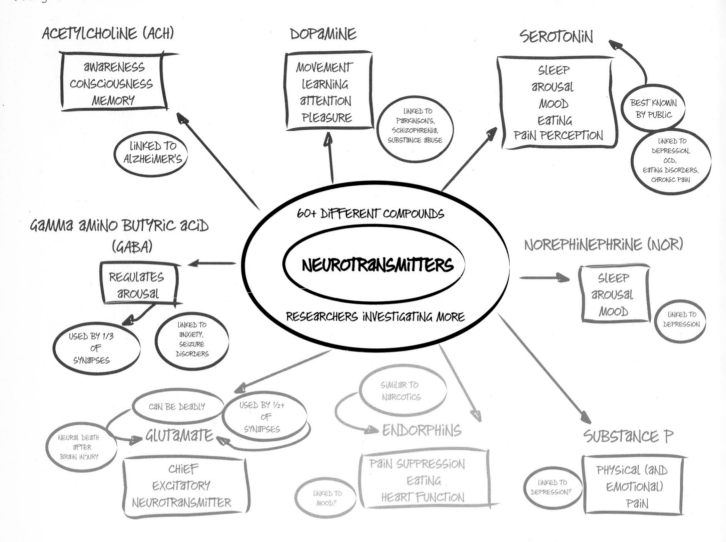

FIGURE 6.4

Neurotransmitters: Mind Map Example

the visual, creative right side. Or think of the left side of your brain as the heavy-duty, brick-and-mortar content side and the right side as the artistic, designer side. What they're particularly good for is showing the relationship between ideas. Mind maps are a good note-taking method for visual learners, and just drawing one may help you remember the information, particularly if you're a kinesthetic learner. To give mind mapping a try, here are some useful suggestions:

1. Use extra wide paper (11 × 17 or legal size, for example). You won't want to write vertically (which is hard to read) if you can help it.

2. Write the main concept of the lecture in the center of the page. Draw related concepts radiating out from the center.

3. Limit your labels to key words so that your mind map is visually clear.

4. Use colors, symbols, and images to make your mind map livelier and more memorable. Notice on the mind map in Figure 6.4 that the information about each neurotransmitter is grouped into a different color.

Psychology 100
NEUROTRANSMITTERS:
Chemical Messengers in the Brain

1. Acetylocholine (awareness, consciousness, memory)
2. Dopamine (movement, learning, attention, pleasure)
3. Serotonin (sleep, arousal, mood, eating, pain perception)
4. Norepinephrine (sleep, arousal, mood)
5. Gamma amino butyric acid (regulates arousal)
6. Glutamate (chief excitatory neurotransmitter)
7. Endorphins (pain suppression, eating, heart function)
8. Substance P (pain signals)

© Sebastian Kaulitzki, 2009/Used under license from Shutterstock.com

Neurotransmitters: PowerPoint Miniatures Example

I love it when teachers do this!

5. Use software such as MindManager, MindManuals, MindPlugs, Mindmapper, or MindGenius, which are all powerful brainstorming and organizing tools. As you type, these programs will intuit relationships and help you draw a mind map on screen.

PowerPoint Miniatures

Some instructors provide full-text lecture notes online or copies of their PowerPoint slides (three or six miniatures on a page), either as handouts in class or as e-mail attachments (see Figure 6.5). Tools such as these assure you that you have all the main lecture points on paper, and although it's helpful to have them available as a tool, you still need to take notes on your own to help you process the information you're listening to in class.

Parallel Note-Taking

Because many professors today provide e-support for lectures, either through web notes, hard copies of onscreen slides, lecture outlines, or a full transcript, new note-taking strategies may be particularly useful, if you go about them in the right way. One such strategy is called parallel note-taking.[21] Here's how it works, ideally.

If they're available, print out lecture notes *before* class and bring them with you, preferably in a ring binder. As your instructor lectures, use the back (blank) side of each page to record your own notes as the notes from the ongoing, real-time lecture face you. You can parallel what you're hearing from your instructor with your own on-the-spot, self-recorded notes, using a Cornell format on each blank page. It's the best of both worlds! You're reading, writing, and listening at the same time, fully immersing yourself in immediate and longer-lasting learning. Parallel note-taking can work after the lecture as well, or while you re-listen to a podcast version of the lecture. Figure 6.6 illustrates what parallel note-taking might look like.

FIGURE 6.6

Neurotransmitters: Parallel Note-Taking Example

(Fill in blank page during actual lecture.)
NEUROTRANSMITTERS
My In-Class Lecture Notes

60 different chemical compounds are known; there may be more.

Acetylcholine was the first neurotransmitter discovered. Early in this century, it was found to inhibit the action of the heart and to excite skeletal muscles. Today, it's thought to play a role in awareness, consciousness, and memory.

Dopamine influences movement, learning, and attention and makes sex and eating pleasurable.

(Print out instructor's notes and place in binder.)
NEUROTRANSMITTERS
Instructor's Lecture Notes

Well over 60 different chemical compounds have been identified as neurotransmitters, and researchers continue to investigate more substances that may affect neural signaling.

Acetylcholine was the first neurotransmitter discovered. In the early part of this century, ACh was found to inhibit the action of the heart and to excite skeletal muscles. Today, ACh is thought to play a role in our awareness or consciousness and to have a role in memory.

Dopamine appears to influence several processes, including movement, learning and attention. Dopamine may also play an important role in motivation by making some activities such as sex and eating very pleasurable or rewarding for us.

VARK It!

Complete the recommended activity for your preferred VARK learning modality. If you are multimodal, select more than one activity. Your instructor may ask you to (a) give an oral report on your results in class, (b) send your results to him or her via e-mail, (c) post them online, or (d) contribute to a class chat.

Visual: Color-code a set of notes you've taken as you read this chapter to mark important themes (blue highlighter for main points, yellow highlighter for examples, etc.).

Aural: Download a podcast for a class in which you have an upcoming exam this term. Re-listen to the lecture several times while filling in your notes from class, and notice whether your grade is higher than the one you earned on a previous exam in the same course.

Read/Write: Work with at least one other read/write student to create a survey to hand out to the rest of the class. Which of the four note-taking methods do they use? Have they developed another method that wasn't discussed? How well do their strategies work?

Kinesthetic: Conduct fake television news interviews in class with a classmate. Ask your classmates to be reporters and take down what they hear. Then have everyone "compare notes." Did they hear the same things? Did they emphasize different things? Did they get it all down?

Using Lecture Notes

Taking good notes is only part of the equation. To get the most value from your notes, you must actually *use* them. As soon as possible after class, take a few minutes to review your notes. If you find sections that are unclear, take time to fill in the gaps while things are still fresh in your mind. One professor found that students who filled in any missing points right after class were able to increase the amount of lecture points they recorded by as much as 50 percent. And students who worked with another student to reconstruct the lecture immediately after class were able to increase their number of noted lecture points even more![22]

This part of the note-taking process is often overlooked, yet it is one of the most helpful steps for learning and recall. If you don't review your notes within twenty-four hours, there's good evidence that you'll end up re*learning* rather than re*viewing*. Reviewing helps you go beyond just writing to actually making sure you understand what you wrote. These three techniques help you get the best use of your notes: manipulating, paraphrasing, and summarizing.

> **Manipulating** involves working with your notes by typing them out later, for example. Some research indicates that it's not writing down information that's most important. Manipulating information is what counts. Work with your notes. Fill in charts, draw diagrams, create a matrix, underline, highlight, organize. Cut a copy of the professor's lecture notes up into paragraphs, mix them up, and then put the lecture back together. Copy your notes onto flash cards. Manipulating information helps develop your reasoning skills, reduces your stress level, and can produce a more complete set of notes to study later.[23]

> **Paraphrasing** is a process of putting your notes into your own words. Recopy your notes or your professor's prepared lecture notes, translating them into words you understand and examples that are meaningful to you. Paraphrasing is also a good way to self-test or to study with a classmate. If you can't find words of your own, perhaps you don't really understand the original notes. Sometimes students think they understand course material until the test proves otherwise, and then it's too late! Practice paraphrasing key concepts with a friend to see how well you both understand the material. Or ask yourself, if I had to explain this to someone who missed class, what words would I use?

> **Summarizing** is a process of writing a brief overview of all of your notes from one lecture. Imagine trying to take all your lecture notes from one class session and putting them on an index card. If you can do that, you've just written a summary. Research shows that students who use the summarizing technique have far greater recall of the material than those who don't.

I never thought to look at my notes right after class, but that makes sense—when everything is still fresh in my mind...

> " I make progress by having people around me who are smarter than I am and listening to them. And I assume that everyone is smarter about something than I am."
>
> **Henry J. Kaiser, American industrialist (1882–1967)**

Some students think that simply going over their notes is the best way to practice. Research shows that simply reading over your notes is a weak form of practice that does not transfer information into long-term memory.[24] You must actually *work with* the material, rearrange or reword it, or condense it to get

Courtesy of Karen Springen.

CAREER OUTLOOK: *Karen Springen,* Newsweek *Journalist*

Q1: What do you do in your job? How important are listening and note-taking?

As a correspondent, I report stories for every section of the magazine. I often juggle many stories at once, reporting on a few pieces for the current week and several others for future weeks. Each of these stories requires talking to dozens of people. People often don't realize how many interviews we do because there isn't enough room in the finished article for quotes from most of the people we interview. I ask questions. Then I just listen and write—or type—furiously. Listening and taking notes are at the center of everything I do as a journalist.

Q2: What are the three most important skills you need for doing your job well?

First—being thorough. You simply need to reach everyone. People buy *Newsweek* because they expect us to be fair and complete, which you can't be if you've only talked to one person. Second—being fast. You simply can't ask for an "extension" when a story is this week's breaking news. You can't have a blank page in *Newsweek*! I often stay up most of the night finishing

my stories. It often feels like I'm still in college, finishing a term paper. And third—keeping an open mind. Every day on this job, I interview someone who changes my mind about something. You're a better reporter if you ask "open-ended" questions, which allow people to talk and talk rather than just say "yes" or "no."

Q3: What advice do you have for college students who are thinking about pursuing a journalism career?

Write for your college newspaper. Get summer internships at newspapers or magazines. You need to have published "clips" to get a journalism job. And college papers are a great place to get them, along with invaluable on-the-job experience. Summer internships are also a wonderful way to see how a news operation works, and for the news operation to see how you work, too. Get reporting and writing tips from the pros at the places you land internships. Journalists are usually quite generous and remember what it was like being in your shoes. One busy editor took me to lunch and showed me how

she carefully outlined her stories before she wrote them. Check your career counseling office and your college newspaper office for lists of alumni with jobs in journalism. Then you can e-mail those folks and ask them who you ought to contact about internships where they work. Just try to get your foot in the door, and once it's there, don't let it out!

HOW WOULD *YOU* LIKE IT?

Have you ever considered a career as a reporter?

Facts to Consider[25]

Academic preparation required: a college degree in mass communication or journalism, with experience writing for school newspapers or broadcasting stations, summer jobs, or internships

Future workforce demand: Jobs within large metropolitan areas will be highly competitive with only 2 percent growth projected between 2006 and 2016. Jobs working for smaller outlets, freelancing, or jobs requiring specialized skills in new technologies or specialized knowledge about scientific subject matter may be on the rise, however.

Work environment: Reporters (journalists) often have hectic work schedules. They

follow the news story, when it happens, where it happens. Travel may be required, and deadlines often dictate their schedules. Working hours vary, depending on their medium: newspaper, television or radio, or magazine.

Essential skills: writing, technology, interpretation, accuracy, flexibility, working quickly under pressure, and overall communication skills

Questions to Ponder

1. Do you have (or could you acquire) the skills this career requires?

2. Are you interested in a career like this? Why or why not?

For more career activities online, access the CourseMate via www.cengagebrain.com/shop/ISBN/0495906425 to do the Team Career exercises.

the most academic bang for your buck. Active strategies always work better than more passive ones.

Manipulating, paraphrasing, and summarizing are more effective learning techniques.

EXERCISE 6.3

Note-Taking 4-M

Practice your note-taking skills by doing this. Immediately after class, or during the lecture if your instructor allows, compare notes with a classmate by following these four steps:

1. **M**atching—look for content areas where your notes match those of your classmate's.

2. **M**issing—look for content areas where one of you has missed something important and fill in the gaps.

3. **M**eaning—talk about what this lecture means. Why was it included in the course? Do you both understand the lecture's main points?

4. **M**easuring—quiz each other. Measure how much you learned from the lecture. Give each other some sample test questions to see if you understand important concepts.

Note-Taking by the Book

So far this chapter has discussed taking notes in class. What about taking notes as you read from a textbook? Is that important, too? The answer: absolutely! It's easy to go on auto-pilot as you read and have no idea what you read afterwards! Instead, take notes in the margins, on sticky notes, or better yet, keep a spiral-bound notebook next to you, and fill it with your own words as you read. Jot down questions, summarize main points, or use the Cornell Method. Actually, the best thing to do is to read a section, close the book, and write down what you remember. You'll prove to yourself what you absorbed and what you didn't. Then you can dive back into the textbook again and clarify concepts that are still fuzzy.[26]

| ? challenge | " reaction | * insight | ! action |

Now What Do You Think?

1. At the beginning of this chapter, Lindsey Collier, a frustrated college student, faced a challenge. Now after reading this chapter, would you respond differently to any of the questions you answered about the "FOCUS Challenge Case"? Knowing what you know now, how would you advise her? Write a paragraph ending to the story, incorporating your best advice.

2. Look over the ten "Dare to Prepare" suggestions at the beginning of this chapter.

- Look ahead.
- Do the assigned reading.
- Show up physically.
- Show up mentally.
- Choose your seat strategically.
- Bring your tools.
- Don't sit by your best friend.
- Posture counts!
- Maintain your health.
- Focus.

Which of the suggestions do you find most difficult to do? For which of your classes? What can you do to help you prepare better for these classes?

3. Which behaviors will you target in order to become a better listener? Select three of the items you marked in Exercise 6.2 as "Never True of Me" to focus on. Practice doing that behavior in class for several days.

4. What are your strengths and weaknesses as a note-taker? Are you a good listener? Can you write quickly and legibly? Do you ask questions easily? Use this opportunity to critique yourself and identify some areas for improvement.

REALITY CHECK | What did you **Learn?**

On a scale of 1 to 10, answer the following questions now that you've completed this chapter.

1 = not very/not much/very little/low   10 = very/a lot/very much/high

In hindsight, how much did you already know about this subject before reading the chapter?

1 2 3 4 5 6 7 8 9 10

Can you answer these questions about engaging, listening, and note-taking in class more fully now that you've read the chapter?

1. **What does in mean to sit in the "T zone" in class and why is it important?**

2. **This chapter discusses "hard" and "soft" listening skills. What's the difference between the two and which one is the right one to use in class?**

3. **Identify three possible formats for taking notes in class.**

How useful might the information in this chapter be to you? How much do you think this information might affect your success in college?

1 2 3 4 5 6 7 8 9 10

How much do you think this information might affect your career success after college?

1 2 3 4 5 6 7 8 9 10

How long did it actually take you to complete this chapter (both the reading and writing tasks)? _____ Hour(s) _____ Minutes

Aced it!

 Challenge Yourself Online Quiz. To find out how much you've learned, access the CourseMate via www.cengagebrain.com/shop/ISBN/0495906425 to take the Challenge Yourself Online Quiz.

Take a minute to compare these answers to your answers from the "Readiness Check" at the beginning of this chapter. What gaps exist between the similar questions? How might these gaps between what you thought before starting the chapter and what you now think after completing the chapter affect how you approach the next chapter in this book?

chapter 7

Developing Your Memory

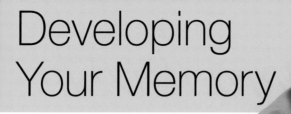

YOU'RE ABOUT TO DISCOVER...

✔ Why memory is a process, not a thing

✔ How your memory works like a digital camera

✔ How to improve your memory using twenty different techniques

✔ How your memory can fail you

©Larry Harwood Photography. Property of Cengage Learning.

READINESS CHECK | What do you **Know?**

Before beginning this chapter, take a moment to answer these questions. Your answers will help you assess how ready you are to focus.

1 = not very/not much/very little/low   10 = very/a lot/very much/high

How much do you *already* know?

Based on reading the "You're about to discover..." list and skimming this chapter, how much do you think you probably already know about this chapter's subject?

1 2 3 4 5 6 7 8 9 10

See if you can answer these questions about developing your memory *before* you read.

1. **What are the three "R's" of remembering?**

2. **This chapter discusses twenty ways to master your memory. Can you identify five?**

3. How can you deepen your memory?

How motivated are you to learn *more*?

In general, how motivated are you to learn more by reading this chapter?

1 2 3 4 5 6 7 8 9 10

How much do you think this information might affect your success in college?

1 2 3 4 5 6 7 8 9 10

How much do you think this information might affect your career success after college?

1 2 3 4 5 6 7 8 9 10

How ready are you to read *now*?

How ready are you to focus on this chapter—physically, intellectually, and emotionally? Circle a number for each aspect of your readiness to focus.

1 2 3 4 5 6 7 8 9 10

If any of your answers is below a 10, you might want to pay attention to whatever is distracting you before you start reading. For example, if you're feeling scattered, take a few moments to settle down and focus.

Finally, how long do you think it will take you to complete this chapter from start to finish?

_____ Hour(s) _____ Minutes

153

Darnell Williams

Quite honestly, Darnell Williams hadn't found high school all that challenging. Playing football his last two years had made it bearable. But at his school, if you showed up and had a pulse, you could count on passing your courses. There wasn't anything in particular he really wanted to do after high school, but he'd decided to go to the college in his hometown anyway. Maybe something there would appeal to him. So he increased his hours at the chain store where he worked to 40 hours per week and enrolled as a full-time student.

Fall Football Schedule

OPPONENT	TIME
Colorado State	7:00 PM ET
at Toledo	9:00 PM ET
Wyoming	3:30 PM ET
at West Virginia	7:30 PM ET
at Texas	7:00 PM ET
Kansas	9:00 PM ET
at Kansas State	3:30 PM ET
Missouri	9:00 PM ET
Texas A&M	3:30 PM ET
at Iowa State	9:00 PM ET
at Oklahoma State	7:30 PM ET
Nebraska	3:30 PM ET

Work Schedule
Darnell Williams

Mon - 29	Tue - 30	Wed - 1	Thu - 2	Fri - 3	Sat - 4

But after two weeks, Darnell admitted that he didn't find his classes all that engaging. Although he was strong physically from working out for football, he knew he was out of shape academically. In high school, he never cracked a book or did any homework, but just how well would that work here? Now he wished he'd buckled down more in high school instead of blowing it off.

What Darnell really liked to do could be summarized in three words: sports, movies, and photography. Armed with a couple of burgers, fries, and a shake, he spent most weekends watching movies half the night, cheering on his favorite football teams, or uploading his artsy shots to Flickr. He was a pretty good photographer, if he did say so, and increasingly, most of his friends were other online amateur photographers.

Since Darnell had no idea which college classes to take, he figured he'd just get some basic requirements out of the way during his first term: Introduction to Physics, Introduction to Psychology, Public Speaking, and English Composition. *Might as well start at square one*, he thought. But after his first few classes, Darnell had already decided that college might not be for him. His writing instructor assigned weekly papers, and his public speaking instructor required outlines for every speech.

By mid-semester, Darnell was really starting to get stressed out, especially about his two hardest classes. His psychology professor blasted through several chapters of the textbook every week, and his physics professor acted as if the entire class was made up of budding scientists. *Not quite*, Darnell privately objected. He didn't realize that college consisted of such challenging coursework, and he had no idea how to memorize all the information he needed to know for midterms. The psychology exam would cover the first twelve chapters of the book, and he knew his entire final grade in that class would be based on a midterm exam and a final exam, each worth 50 percent. Twelve chapters—at once? His Introduction to Psychology textbook had a 25-page glossary at the end of the book. Twenty-five pages of new terms to memorize! Impossible!

The physics midterm would require him to have memorized all kinds of mathematical formulas. The syllabus said: "The laws of nature can often be stated in words or written as a mathematical formula. In this course, you will learn to use mathematics and the rules of algebra to make predictions. . . . Students sometimes try to memorize the formula as just symbols and don't understand the meaning of the symbols."[1] *No kidding*, Darnell thought, cynically. He saw the words and symbols on the page

of his physics book, but what did they mean?

$$X = ½ at^2 + vt + x$$
X = distance traveled,
a = acceleration,
t = time,
v = starting velocity,
x = starting position
If X is what?

When it came time to study for his two midterm exams, Darnell stared at his open textbook for a while, trying to memorize complicated formulas or psych terms that made no sense to him. He'd think he had a handle on a term, and then the next thing he knew, it had flown out of his head. *How does anyone memorize all this stuff?* Darnell wondered. *Nobody takes a class to learn how to memorize even though that's what college is all about.* The only solution Darnell could think of was pulling a couple of all-nighters, which he did regularly when he got on a movie marathon jag, anyway. But he noticed that watching a movie when you're tired and studying physics when you're tired are two different things, so he just gave up and finished up the night on Flickr. Besides, posting his photos online was much more fun.

EAST HIGH SCHOOL
OFFICIAL TRANSCRIPT

STUDENT INFORMATION

FULL NAME: Darnell Williams
PARENTS/GUARDIAN: Michael and Joan Williams

ACADEMIC RECORD

SCHOOL YEAR: 2005–2006   GRADE LEVEL: 9th

Course Title	Credit Earned	Final Grade
English I	1.0	B
Mathematics I	1.0	C
Biology w/lab	1.0	C
Geography	1.0	B
World History	1.0	B
Spanish I	0.5	A
Phys Ed	0.5	B
Film Appreciation		

Total Credits: 7.0   GPA: 2.78   Cumulative GPA: 2.78

SCHOOL YEAR: 2007–2008   GRADE LEVEL: 11th

Course Title	Credit Earned	Final Grade
Literature II	1.0	B

SCHOOL YEAR: 2006–2

Course Title
English II
Mathematics II
Chemistry w/lab
Computer Lab
Ancient Civilizat
Spanish II
Phys Ed
Extra Curric. Act

Total Credits: 7.0   G

SCHOOL YEAR: 2008–

Course Title
Literature II
Trigonometry

Course Schedule
Main Campus
FALL SEMESTER
Williams, Darnell

e Title	Hrs	Days	Meeting Times	Bldg	Room	Meeting Dates	Status	Instructor
PSYCHOLOGY	3.0	T	0935AM-1215AM	SCI BLDG	331	8/17/10 - 12/18/10	ENROLLED	
COMPOSITION	3.0	M W F	0935AM-1040PM	UNIV HALL	215	8/17/10 - 12/18/10	ENROLLED	YOUNG, KARL
O PHYSICS	3.0	M W	1050AM-1215PM	SCI BLDG	412	8/17/10 - 12/18/10	ENROLLED	SCOTT, FRAN
CS LAB	1.0	W	122PM			8/17/10 - 12/18/10		

*Glossary and physics textbook excerpts (right margin):*

A

A-B-A design Experimental design in which participants rst e the experimental treatment (B), and then return to the baseline

Abnormal psychology The area of psychological investigat individual pathologies of mind, mood, and behavior.

Acquisition The stage in a classical conditioning experiment de by the conditioned stimulus.

Acute stress A transient state of arousal with typically clear onse

Addiction A condition in which the body requires a drug in or reactions to its absence; often the outcome of tolerance and dep

Aggression Behaviors that cause psychological or physical harm

Agoraphobia An extreme fear of being in public places or op embarrassing.

Altruism Prosocial behaviors a person carries out without conside

Alzheimer's disease A chronic organic brain syndrome charac intellectual ability, and deterioration of personality.

Ambiguity A perceptual object that may have more than "one inte

Amnesia A failure of memory caused by physical injury, disease, di

Amygdala The part of the limbic system that controls emotion, ag

Analytic psychology A branch of psychology that views the pe forces in a dynamic balance.

Anticipatory coping E orts made in advance of a potentially str imbalance between perceived demands and available resources.

Anxiety An intense emotional response caused by the preconscio emerge into consciousness.

Archetype A universal, inherited, primitive, and symbolic represent

Assimilation According to Piaget, the process whereby new cogn modi ed to t more easily; this process works in tandem with acco

Attachment Emotional relationship between a child and the "regul

Attention A state of focused awareness on a subset of the availabl

Attitude The learned, relatively stable tendency to respond to peop

Attribution theory A social-cognitive approach to describing the generate causal explanations.

Automatic processes Processes that do not require a without interference.

Axon The extended

Physics text excerpt:

for both observers. Although this assumption may seem obvious, it to be *incorrect* when treating situations in which v is comparab speed of light. In fact, this point represents one of the most differences between Newtonian concepts and the ideas con Einstein's theory of relativity.

Exercise 1 Show that although observers in S and S' measure differen for the ends of a stick at rest in S, they agree on the length of the stick. Ass has end coordinates $x = a$ and $x = a + l$ in S and use the Galilean transfor

An immediate and important consequence of the invariance of between two points under the Galilean transformation is the force. For example if $F = \dfrac{kqQ}{(x_2 - x_1)^2}$ gives the electric force charges q, Q located at x_1 and x_2 on the x-axis in frame S, F, th sured in S', is given by $F' = \dfrac{kqQ}{(x_2' - x_1')^2} = F$ since $x_2' - x_1' =$

any force would be invariant under the Galilean transformatio involved only the relative positions of interacting particles.

Now suppose two events are separated by a distance dx and dt as measured by an observer in S. It follows from Equatio corresponding displacement dt' measured by an observer in $dx' = dx - v \, dt$, where dx is the displacement measured by an Because $dt = dt'$, we find that

$$\frac{dx'}{dt'} = \frac{dx}{dt} - v$$

or

$$u_x' = u_x - v$$

where u_x and u_x' are the instantaneous velocities of the c and S', respectively. This result, which is called the **Galilean velocities** (or Galilean velocity transformation), is used in tions and is consistent with our intuitive notions of time an To obtain the relation between the accelerations meas S and S', we take a derivative of Equation 1.2 with respect results that $dt = dt'$ and v is constant:

$$\frac{du_x'}{dt'} = a_x' = a_x$$

Thus observers in different inertial frames measure the an accelerating object. The mathematical terminology

(handwritten notes in margin:) MEMORIZE; MEMORIZE formula →

What Do You Think?

1. Why is Darnell having problems remembering course content in his classes? List five reasons you identify from the case study.

2. Is Darnell overreacting? Is his situation common to first-year students? To you? Why or why not?

3. Identify three memory techniques that Darnell should use to help him memorize all the formulas and terms he needs to know.

4. If you were asked to explain how the memory process works and the scientific explanation behind his problems, what would you say?

Memory: The *Long* and *Short* of It

Challenge: List something you memorized as a child: perhaps a poem, a song, or lines from a school play. Why do you remember this passage verbatim after all these years?

Reaction: _____

Your grandparents used to dance to a popular song called "Memories Are Made of This." Of what, exactly? What are your earliest memories and how old were you? Most of us have "childhood amnesia," as Sigmund Freud called it, until we're three and a half or so. You may remember playing in the sand on the beach during a family vacation, dressing up to attend your cousin's wedding, or riding on an airplane for the first time. Before that age, you may not remember things because you weren't paying attention, because you didn't have the language skills to encode the memories, or because you hadn't yet formed the web of interconnections in your brain that you have now.[2]

Whenever it was that those first memories became available to you, and no matter what they are, think about how chock full your memory is now with both significant and seemingly insignificant memories, going all the way back to that poem your teacher asked you to memorize in fourth grade, the one you still remember ten or more years later, oddly enough. Through the years, your memories will continue to accumulate, and interestingly, you'll never run out of room! It's a good thing, too. Imagine what life without memory would be like. We'd have the same conversations with the same people over and over again, and we'd need to relearn how to drive each time we got behind the wheel of a car. Fortunately, our memories do an amazing job of streamlining life for us. But how much do we really understand about how our memories work—and why they sometimes don't?

Subjective Memory Test

How good is your memory? Fill out Parts A and B to begin applying the information in this chapter to your own memory.

How would you rate your memory overall?	Excellent		Good		Poor	
	1 2 3	4	5	6 7		

A. How would you rate your memory in terms of the following types of tasks? Remembering:

	Excellent	Good	Poor
1. Names	1 2 3	4 5	6 7
2. Where I've put things	1 2 3	4 5	6 7
3. Phone numbers I've just checked	1 2 3	4 5	6 7
4. Words	1 2 3	4 5	6 7
5. Knowing if I've already told someone something	1 2 3	4 5	6 7
6. Forgetting things people tell me	1 2 3	4 5	6 7
7. Faces	1 2 3	4 5	6 7
8. Directions	1 2 3	4 5	6 7
9. Forgetting what I started to do	1 2 3	4 5	6 7
10. Forgetting what I was saying	1 2 3	4 5	6 7
11. Remembering what I've done (lock the door, etc.)	1 2 3	4 5	6 7

B. How would you rate your memory when it comes to these academic tasks? Remembering:

	Excellent	Good	Poor
12. What I've just been reading	1 2 3	4 5	6 7
13. What I read an hour ago	1 2 3	4 5	6 7
14. What I read last week	1 2 3	4 5	6 7
15. Assignment/Exam due dates	1 2 3	4 5	6 7
16. Appointments with instructors	1 2 3	4 5	6 7
17. Assignment details	1 2 3	4 5	6 7
18. Factual information for exams	1 2 3	4 5	6 7
19. Theoretical information for exams	1 2 3	4 5	6 7
20. Information from readings for exams	1 2 3	4 5	6 7
21. Information from in-class lectures for exams	1 2 3	4 5	6 7
22. Including everything I should study for exams	1 2 3	4 5	6 7

Informal assessments, like this one, may help you understand your own perceptions of how well your memory works. The lower your score on each portion, the better you perceive your memory to be. Do your scores for Part A and Part B differ? The general tasks in Part A are presented in the order of concern reported by older adults cited in one study (with the top items perceived as most problematic).[3] Are your priorities similar? Did your numbers drop as you went down the list?

In one recent study in which college students were asked which aspects of memory they most wanted to improve among general and academic tasks, the top three items were improving schoolwork or study skills, remembering what was read, and remembering specific facts and details.[4] Understandably, the academic aspects of memory were those most personally valued. Is that true for you, too? Are the items in Part B generally higher priorities for you now as a college student?

My scores definitely higher in PART B— A kinesthetic learner. I wonder how that relates.

PART A #2 is a problem for me tho.

© Lester Lefkowitz/CORBIS

Most of us may not even realize just how important memory is. We talk about our memories as if they were something we own. We say we have good memories or bad memories, just like we have a crooked smile or nice one. But no one would ever say, "Hey, that's one nice-looking memory you've got there!" in the same way they'd say, "Wow, you have a really nice smile!" Memory isn't a thing; it's a process. You can't see it or touch it or hold it. Even one specific memory has many different features: You can remember something by what you saw, smelled, heard, or felt. And even within one of these categories, individuals may differ in what they recall. You may be able to hum the movie's theme song, but your friend may remember conversations between the main characters almost verbatim.

Don't believe it when someone claims to have a one-size-fits-all, magic formula to help you unlock the secrets of your memory. It isn't that easy. Still, there are techniques that, when applied to the way you read your assignments or study for exams, can help you do your best, academically. We can only begin to grasp the rich complexities of memory by understanding it as a process. However, it's important to recognize first that mastering memory depends on the answers to several questions like these:[5]

1. **Who is learning?** A calculus professor and a beginning calculus student would approach memorizing the main points of an article on math differently.

2. **What needs to be learned?** How you learn your lines for a play would differ from how you learn the Dutch masters' paintings for your art appreciation test.

3. **How will learning be tested?** Learning information to *recall* uses different memory techniques than learning information to *recognize*. Recognition requires that you select from several alternatives; recall requires that you come up with memorized information on your own.

4. **How long must the information be remembered?** Learning your multiplication tables as a child is something that must remain with you throughout your life. You use them on a daily basis. On the other hand, learning the date of the Battle of Hastings isn't quite as crucial to remember for the long haul.

> " The existence of forgetting has never been proved: We only know that some things don't come to mind when we want them."
>
> **Friedrich Nietzsche, German philosopher (1844–1900)**

EXERCISE 7.2

Test Your Memory

For a more objective assessment of your memory, try this test. Study the following list of words for up to one minute. Then cover them with your hand and see how many you can remember. List them in the right-hand column.

theory	_____
rehearsal	_____
student	_____
bone	_____
frostbite	_____
camera	_____
rose	_____
calculus	_____
lecture	_____

MAN! I only got 5 the first time!

How many words were you able to remember? Which words did you forget? Unfamiliar words? Words that had no relevance to your life? What memory techniques did you use to help you remember?

The Three R's of Remembering: Record, Retain, Retrieve

Challenge: Think of three ways in which using your memory is like taking pictures with a digital camera.

Reaction: _____

_____

_____

Improving your memory is easier if you understand how it works. Memory consists of three parts: your *sensory memory*, your *working memory* (called short-term memory by some psychologists), and your *long-term memory*. These three parts of the memorization process are connected to these three memory tasks: *recording*, *retaining*, and *retrieving* memories—the "Three R's of Remembering."[6]

We'll compare the three R's of remembering to the process involved when taking pictures with a digital camera: record, retain, retrieve.

Your Sensory Memory: Focus

Consolidating memories in your brain is similar to taking pictures with a digital camera. Before we discuss the first R of remembering—namely, *Record*—we have to talk first about focus. Most digital cameras today focus on things automatically, and unlike older cameras, you don't have to turn the focus knob until the image is clear. But you do need to decide what to focus *on*. What do you want to take a picture of? Where will you point the camera? When it comes to your college classes and the role your memory plays in your success, remember that focus doesn't come automatically. It requires consciously deciding where to direct your attention.

Imagine this: You're on your way to class. You walk through a student demonstration and get brushed by members of the crowd. Then you cross a busy intersection a little too slowly and get honked at by a speeding car. Finally, you see a billboard you've never noticed before: "I love you, Whitney. Will you marry me? Carl." *How romantic*, you think to yourself.

Three major sensations just passed through your *sensory memory* in a few seconds, in this case, your *haptic* memory (touch, the crowd), your *echoic* memory (sounds, the car horn), and your *iconic* memory (sight, the billboard), all parts of your sensory memory. You have a different channel for each of these three senses. Most experts believe that your sensory memory retains an exact copy of what you've seen or heard—pure and unanalyzed—for less than a second.[7] Some of these images, or icons, will be transferred to your working memory.

To help you with attention management, consider the following suggestions:

I totally get this! WHAT A cool COMPARISON!

> " I have a photographic memory but once in a while I forget to take off the lens cap."

Milton Berle, comedian (1908–2002)

1. **Slow down; you move too fast.** Imagine trying to take a photo of something on the way to class if you were running. Everything would be a blur; trying to take a picture would be futile. Focus requires your full attention aimed at one thing at a time. Turn down the music, turn off the television, shut down the six windows open on your browser, and focus.

2. **Deal with it.** If something is driving you to distraction, maybe you need to take care of it first so that you *can* focus.

3. **Notice where you go.** Wandering thoughts are normal. When *your* attention wanders off, where does it go? Knowing your mental tendencies helps you to recognize the pattern and work on changing it.

4. **Watch for signals.** As a college student, you'll probably take at least forty different courses from all sectors of your college and be exposed to literally thousands of facts. Not even a memory expert could master them all at once. You must be selective about focus. You're most likely to learn the material presented by your instructor and through your course readings. Your textbooks will guide you as you read by using bold fonts, different colors, charts, tables, and headings. Think of them as animated .jpegs on the page, calling out, "Hey, look at me!" In class, watch the instructor's body language; listen to her inflection; notice what gets written on the board or which PowerPoint slides stay on the screen longer than others.

5. **Get help if you need to.** If you have been diagnosed with ADHD, your brain is wired somewhat differently, affecting your memory and your ability to concentrate.[8] If you've not been diagnosed with a learning disability, but your attention appears to be extremely challenging to harness and you're not sure why, seek help from a counselor or learning specialist on campus.

Your Working Memory: Record

After you've focused your camera on your subject, you're ready to take a picture, right? But with a digital camera, you don't just click and walk away. You actually click and then review the picture on the small viewing screen to decide whether you want to save it or delete it.

Similarly, *recording* sensory impressions involves an evaluation process that takes place in your short-term or *working memory*. Your working memory is like a review screen, where you review recently acquired sensory impressions, enhancing them with related information that you retrieve from your long-term memory. In fact, your working memory is often involved in the focus process. You give selected, focused attention to some of what you see and hear because it has personal meaning for you or relates to something in your past experience. In our example of you walking to class, which of these three specific sensations you just experienced are you likely to remember: the crowd, the car, or the billboard? To stay true to the analogy, which one would you take a picture of? It depends, right? You may remember the billboard because you plan to show it to someone else later, or the demonstration because you disagree with its cause, or the car horn because it scared you.

The problem with working memory is that the length of time it can hold information is limited. You probably don't remember what you ate for dinner last Monday, do you? You'd have to reconstruct the memory based on other clues. Where was I? What was I doing? Who was I with?

The other problem with working memory is that it has limited capacity. It fills up quickly and then dumps what it doesn't need. If that weren't the case, our working memories would be cluttered with a chaotic array of useless information. If you look up a number in the campus directory, you can usually remember it long enough to walk over to the phone, right? A few minutes after you've dialed, however, the number is gone. Current estimates are that you can keep something in working memory for one to two minutes, giving your brain

I don't remember phone numbers at all anymore thanks to cell phones.

This is cool! I always wondered how actors learn lines.

Courtesy of DeLanna Studi.

CAREER OUTLOOK: *DeLanna Studi, Actress*

Q1: The most common question actors report getting is, "How do you learn all those lines?" What's the first thing you do when you look at a new script?

I look at the script's title. It's amazing how many clues are in the title! Then I read it through once and try to visualize it. I try not to guess what character I might be playing or pass any judgment on any of the characters. I usually read a script three times in a row, the last time aloud.

Q2: Most people assume that actors learn their lines by rote, repeating them over and over. Is that what you do?

First, I learn the story. If I know the story I'm telling, the lines and dialogue come to me. True, the language may not be what I use in my daily life, but I focus on that later. I find that if I can tell the story in my own words, I can act it. Then I start memorizing the lines, and yes, sometimes it is by rote. There is a reason why the writer has chosen the words that are on the page. My job is to make those words mine.

Q3: How do you go from memory to meaning? How do you make sure you mean what you're saying? How do actors make each performance unique so that their lines don't sound memorized and flat?

I understand the story, I try to make the language my own, and I lay the foundation for meaning while I am memorizing. I think the key element is visualizing the play or movie during the first read. This sets the first layer of meaning; however, the images I used in the first read-through may not be the ones in my head for the final performance. I will have discovered in rehearsal if those images (personalizations) work, and I will have either scrapped them or enhanced them. The key to making each performance unique is listening. It reminds me of playing catch. I know my partner is going to throw the ball to me, I just don't know what size ball or how he will throw it. If I pay attention, I can catch whatever he throws.

Q4: What advice do you have for first-year college students about acting as a career?

Acting is 85 percent work and 15 percent talent. I believe if you commit fully and practice, you will become a better actor. You have to love the craft because it's not as glamorous as the media might lead you to believe! If this is what you really want to do as a career, it is a tough journey, but well worth the adventure.

HOW WOULD *YOU* LIKE IT?

Have you ever considered a career as an actor?

Facts to Consider[9]

Academic preparation required: highly variable; actors come from many different academic backgrounds, including degrees in theatre and performing arts

Future workforce demand: Competition is fierce for prize roles, and actors may find themselves unemployed at times, supplementing their income in other ways.

Work environment: Actors work under pressure, typically for relatively short periods of time, ranging from one day to several months.

They work long, irregular hours on television or movie sets or on the stage live, so they must be devoted to their craft and enjoy entertaining others.

Essential skills: creativity, memory, ability to follow direction, stress management; singing or dancing skills may also be helpful

Questions to Ponder

1. Do you have (or could you acquire) the skills this career requires?

2. Are you interested in a career like this? Why or why not?

For more career activities online, access the CourseMate via www.cengagebrain.com/shop/ISBN/0495906425 to do the Team Career exercises.

a chance to do a quick review, selecting what to save and what to delete.[10] Just how much information can your working memory hold? Look at these letters in the first example, and then close your eyes and try to repeat them back in order.

SAJANISMOELIHHEGNR

Can't do it? This task is virtually impossible because the string contains eighteen letters. Researchers believe that working memory can recall only seven pieces of information, plus or minus two.[11] (There's a reason why telephone numbers are prechunked for us.) Chunking these eighteen letters into five units helps considerably. Now look at the letters again in this second example and try to recall all eighteen.

SAJA NISM OELI HHEG NR

If we rearrange the letters into recognizable units as in the third example, it becomes even easier, right?

AN IS MAJOR ENGLISH HE

And if the words are rearranged to make perfect sense as in example four, the task becomes simple.

HE IS AN ENGLISH MAJOR

The principle of chunking is also used to move information from your working memory to your long-term memory bank, and it's used in memorization techniques that we will describe later in this chapter.

Your Long-Term Memory: Retain and Retrieve

Let's go back to our camera analogy. Once your camera's memory card gets full, you probably transfer the photos to your computer, or you print them out, place them in picture frames, or upload them to Flickr or Facebook. However, before you do that, you generally review the photos, decide how to arrange them, where to put them, whether to print them, and so forth. In other words, you make the photos memorable by putting them into some kind of order or context.

Just as you must transfer photos from your camera's memory stick to a more permanent location with a larger capacity for storage, you must transfer information from short-term, or working, memory to long-term memory. You *retain* the information by transferring it, and this transfer is facilitated by

Totally! What a cool comparison!

FIGURE 7.1

Your Memory as a Digital Camera

Step 1:
Click, View, and Save or Delete

Step 2
Transfer and Store

Step 3
Locate and Use

The 3R's of Remembering: Record   Retain   Retrieve

www.morguefile.com

reviewing and using it in a way that makes it memorable. It is this review process that we use when we study for a test. You transfer information to long-term memory by putting the information into a context that has meaning for you, linking new information to old information, creating stories or particular memory techniques, or organizing material so that it makes sense. You can frame it by putting a mental border around it, just as you put pictures into frames. Sometimes you need to frame information to keep it distinct and separate from other information.

Your long-term memory is the computer in which you store new knowledge until you need to use it. However, while the memories that reside in long-term memory aren't easily disturbed, they can be challenging to retrieve.[12] Ideally, you'd like your memories to be readily available when you wish to retrieve them, just like the pictures or digital images that you have transferred to your computer or put in a photo album. You can click on them to view them again, arrange them into a slideshow and publish them on the web, send them to your friends as e-mail attachments, or just review them yourself to recapture the earlier experience. If you just dump your photos onto your hard drive, or print them out and then put them into a box, with no organization or labeling system, how easy will it be to find a specific photo? Difficult, right? Retrieving information from your long-term memory can be equally challenging if you haven't organized your information, or created mental labels that will trigger data retrieval. Good recall often depends upon good storage techniques. The remainder of this chapter will be about steps 2 and 3, specifically how to *retain* information by transferring it from working memory into long-term memory and how to *retrieve* information when you need to.

Twenty Ways to Master Your Memory

? challenge	66 reaction	* insight	! action

Challenge: If you were actually tasked with learning the random list of words presented in Exercise 7.2 to test your memory, how would you proceed? Identify the precise method you believe would work best for you.

Reaction: _____

What can you do to sharpen your memory for the reading and test-taking you'll do in college? Try the following twenty techniques, grouped into five major categories (to help you remember them). These techniques are specifically designed to help you with the *retain* and *retrieve* parts of the memory process. As you consider each one, think about what you know about your own learning style.

Make It Stick

How do you actually move material from your working memory to your long-term memory? What will work best for you? Some techniques are more effective than others, but the following suggestions are a good start.[13]

> 66 A memory is anything that happens and does not completely unhappen."
>
> **Edward de Bono, creative thinking expert and author of**
> *Lateral Thinking: Creativity Step by Step*

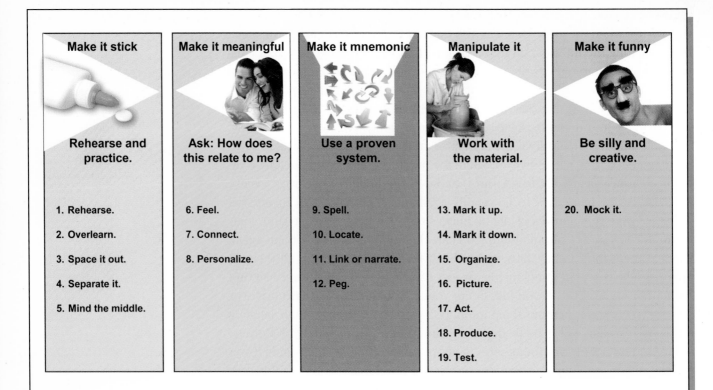

© Feng Yu, 2009. Used under license from Shutterstock.com; © Yuri Arcurs, 2009. Used under license from Shutterstock.com; Nishan Sothilingam/iStockphoto.com; © IKO, 2009. Used under license from Shutterstock.com; © Alex James Bramwell, 2009. Used under license from Shutterstock.com.

FIGURE 7.2

Twenty Ways to Master Your Memory

Maybe I should try REHEARSING my Physics formulas??

This is AN importANt point for me to REMEMBER!

1. **Rehearse.** Although it's not the most powerful memorization strategy available to you, especially by itself, repeating information helps. Nothing gets stored in your memory for long without practice. How did you learn those multiplication tables or that poem in fourth grade? Probably not by just reading it over once or twice.

   Memory experts distinguish between *maintenance* (or shallow) rehearsal and *elaborative* rehearsal. Maintenance rehearsal helps you keep something in working memory for a short time. Repeating a phone number twenty times while you look for your cell phone might help you keep it there for several minutes, but will you remember it tomorrow when you need to call again? Probably not. Shallow rehearsal, for example, just reading course material, doesn't work well. Elaborative rehearsal—actually working with the information—helps transfer information to long-term memory more effectively. Most of the techniques described in this chapter will focus on elaborative rehearsal techniques. Typically, we remember the elaborate over the simple.

2. **Overlearn.** Overlearning helps you truly hardwire information, so that you can practically work in autopilot. When you think you've learned something, don't automatically assume it's time to move on. Keep working at it. The more you continue to work at it, the greater your degree of mastery.[14]

3. **Space it out.** Many studies show that studying for several hours at a time, as opposed to one long stretch, is much more effective. Clearing your entire day so that you can study calculus for six hours isn't the best idea. Your anxiety level would mount over that time, and fatigue would set in, keeping you from maximizing your memory. Instead, study in shorter spurts for

Photolibrary

several days leading up to the exam. Cramming may work in the short run, but your working memory will most likely dump what you think you've mastered right after the exam.

4. **Separate it.** When you're tasked with learning similar, yet distinct, information, bleeding can occur. (No, it's not a health issue.) One body of knowledge can spill over into another. Imagine the confusion you'd experience if you tried to learn Spanish, French, Russian, and Chinese at the same time.

Let's say you're in a philosophy class, having trouble differentiating between Plato, Aristotle, and Socrates. You might benefit from deliberately working to separate the three philosophers you study by making your own compare-and-contrast chart.

Interference presents a particular problem for college students because the subject matter in different courses often overlaps; one social science course may contain information that's similar to another's. Knowledge is interconnected; that's not the issue. It's the challenge of keeping knowledge bases separate for exams. If your sociology test is on Wednesday and your psychology test is on Friday, study sociology on Tuesday and psychology on Thursday. But if both tests are on Friday, separating the two bodies of information will be a challenge. Differentiate your study sessions as much as possible by studying for each test in a specific location or at a particular time of day, for example.[15]

I must separate out hardcore study times for my hardest exams!

5. **Mind the middle.** Perhaps you've heard of the serial-position effect. Research shows that we tend to remember what comes first because of the impression it makes on us, and what comes last because it's most recent. But what's in the middle sometimes tends to get lost.[16] That's an important principle for you to know. If you need to memorize a list of items, or a timeline, for example, pay particular attention to the middle.

Make It Meaningful

Sometimes we make the mistake of creating artificial distinctions between thoughts and feelings, when in fact, emotions and personal connections play an important role in learning.

6. **Feel.** Emotions and memories can team up in powerful ways. A piece of new information that makes you feel happy, angry, or sad lights up your amygdala, a small area of your brain that serves as your emotional center

of operations. If a novel makes you cry or laugh or actually feel fear, you're likely to remember the story. If course content hooks into career goals you care about, you're likely to commit more of it to memory. Human beings care about other human beings and themselves, so the emotional side of new information (which you may have to create yourself) is a strong magnet for your memory.[17] All American adults remember where they were on September 11, 2001. Emotions enhance memory and recall.[18]

7. **Connect.** Create associations between what you're trying to commit to memory now and what you already know. That's why doing the reading assignment before class is so useful. During the lecture, you can think to yourself, *Oh, I remember that…and that…and that.* When you learn new information, it's almost as if you "file" it between other files already in place. If you know where to put it, instead of just stuffing it somewhere, that helps. Connecting it to previous knowledge also helps you retrieve the memory later.

CURIOSITY: *ACT ON YOUR MEMORY!*

Have you ever watched a movie, wondering how *do* actors learn all those lines? Do they have super-human memory powers? The average movie-goer assumes that actors simply repeat their lines over and over until they learn them. However, actors themselves say that's not all there is to it.[19]

Actually, what actors are most concerned with is convincing you that they're not playing a role. But actors' contracts require them to be absolutely precise in conforming to the script, so how do they do it? Four of the techniques used by actors may also be useful to you as you try to commit course material to memory. Maybe you've even tried some of these techniques.

Chunking: Actors chunk their material into beats. For example, an actor might divide a half page of dialogue into three beats: to flirt, to sweet-talk, and to convince. In other words, the character would first flirt with the other actor, then sweet-talk him to lower his guard, and then convince him to do something he might not want to do. The results? Three chunks to remember instead of twelve lines of double-spaced text.

Goal Setting: Notice that the chunks are based on goals, a strategy that also works well while you're studying. Actors ask themselves goal-oriented questions such as: "Should I be flirting with him here?" In the same way, you can ask yourself, "Am I trying to learn the underlying formula so that I can work other problem sets?" or "Should I be coming up with

AbleStock/Index Open/PhotostoGo

my own reasons for why the play is considered to be Shakespeare's best comedy?" When you ask yourself goal-oriented questions while you study, you steer your actions, as actors do, toward learning.

Moving: Going through the motions while rehearsing their lines helps actors memorize them. Imagine the hypothetical actor whose goals were to flirt, to sweet-talk, and to convince, glancing toward the other actor from across the room, moving closer and smiling, and then touching his arm while making the persuasive case. The actor must know the meanings behind the movements to give meaning to the lines. The meanings are tied to the movements, which are tied to the lines, and the lines become committed to memory. Likewise, when you study, moving around may help you learn. Even if you're not primarily a kinesthetic learner, pieces of information become tied to motions in ways that help you recall information.

Meaning: "Say what you mean" and "mean what you say" was Lewis Carroll's advice in *Alice's Adventures in Wonderland.* Researchers use the term *active experiencing* to refer to what actors do when they use all their physical, mental, and emotional channels to communicate the meaning of their lines to someone else, real or imagined. As you study course material, do the same thing. Imagine you need to communicate the information to someone you know who needs it.

8. **Personalize.** Find ways you can relate what you're memorizing to your own life. Okay, so you're thinking what do the plot and characters of *Pride and Prejudice*, a novel published by England's Jane Austen in 1813, possibly have to do with me now? Actually, there may be more similarities than you first think. Imagine the story taking place in your household. Do you have sisters? Does your mother worry about you marrying someone good enough for you? Do you have a close relationship with your father? Once you start actively searching for overlap, you may be surprised. This task is easier with some course content than others, but the very act of attempting to do this may be useful.

Make It Mnemonic

Some of the oldest ways to master your memory are through the use of mnemonic (pronounced *ne MON ik*) devices, verbal or visual memory aids, first used by Greek orators around 500 B.C. Imagine trying to remember a speech that goes on for hours; you'd need to devise specific ways to train your memory to keep working (without a teleprompter!). Although mnemonic devices can become complicated and aren't a solution to all memory challenges, for some students, these specialized elaborative rehearsal strategies can work well.

9. **Spell.** Acrostics and acronyms are the simplest type of mnemonic device, words you create by putting together the first letters of what you want to memorize. Let's say, for example, that you want to learn the first five items in the list of random words in Exercise 7.2: theory, rehearsal, student, bone, and frostbite. You could create a bizarre acrostic such as Ten rabbits' soup bowls fell. If you had vowels to work with, you may also be able to create an acronym you can pronounce, such as RAM for Random Access Memory.

10. **Locate.** The Loci (pronounced *LO si*) mnemonic system cues memory by using locations. Using the Loci system requires two steps. First, think of a familiar path, setting, or route. Perhaps you decide on the path from your residence hall room to the classroom where your exam will be given. On your way, you always pass distinct markers: the fountain in the quad, a tunnel that takes you beneath a busy street, the recreation center's pool, the Student Health Center, and the Humanities Building parking lot. Perhaps you want to use these five locations to cue your memory to produce the first five items on our random list: theory, rehearsal, student, bone, and frostbite. You might picture saying hello to your science professor, a foundation of knowledge who always espouses *theory* in class, in the quad. Then you might imagine conducting a *rehearsal* of the student philharmonic orchestra in the tunnel, which would be a ridiculous sight. Then you envision *students* on the swim team thrashing about in the pool during a competition. You know about a recent financial scandal involving the Student Health Center so you imagine skeletons (*bones*) in the closet. And finally, you think of how terrible it would be to lose your room key and get a case of *frostbite* from spending the night in your car in the parking lot. Now without looking back, try it and see if it works for you. Of course, the optimal way the Loci system works is if the locations are familiar to *you*. Its main benefits are that it uses cues, incorporates associations, and orders information into a sequence, all of which aid in memory transfer and storage.[20]

Psych, yes, but how do I PERSONALIZE physics?!

I'll try it for Psych: The Big Five Theory = Extraversion, Neuroticism, Openness, Agreeableness, and Conscientiousness = "Every Nerd Opens All Cabinets."

Hey! I remember people's names in class by where they sit!

11. **Link or narrate.** Instead of a Loci system, you can create a linking mnemonic to help you memorize a list. To do this, you must connect item A to item B, item B to item C, and so forth. Consider again the list of words you were challenged to remember and write down: theory, rehearsal, student, bone, frostbite, camera, rose, calculus, and lecture. Your visual links might go like this: (1) (theory + rehearsal) You imagine a *theoretician* at a *rehearsal* dinner. (2) (rehearsal + student) The rehearsal dinner is attended by student friends of the bride and groom. (3) (student + bone) One student is in a leg cast because of a broken bone, and so forth.

   Another way to use this method is to create a story that links each cue: A geeky theoretician went to a rehearsal dinner, where he sat next to a student from one of his classes who had a broken leg (bone). The student injured his leg in a hiking accident in which he suffered a fall and got frostbite from exposure, and so forth. Each item is linked to the item before, except for the first one. You must find a cue to remember it independently to get the chain started.

12. **Peg.** The Peg system uses rhyming syllables modified by England's John Sambrook in 1879.[21] Remember the old nursery rhyme, "One, two, buckle my shoe"? The Peg system uses these rhyming pairs:

one—bun	six—sticks
two—shoe	seven—heaven
three—tree	eight—gate
four—door	nine—wine
five—hive	ten—hen

   To use the Peg system, create *specific* images for yourself: a big, fat hamburger *bun*, a stiletto-heeled *shoe*, a weeping willow *tree*, and so forth, and hang the items you're trying to memorize on these mental "pegs" in order. To continue with our example, you'd picture a *theoretical* treatise stuffed between the hamburger *bun*, an image of a teenage girl's *rehearsal* of how to walk in her first pair of stiletto high-heeled *shoes*, a *student* sprawled out studying under a weeping willow *tree*, and so forth. Other types of Peg systems have been devised, but the rhyming system is the most common. But does it work with information other than lists, you might wonder? Try it for yourself to find out.

Manipulate It

Although some of us tend to favor other modalities than kinesthetic learning, all of us can benefit from memory techniques with a kinesthetic basis. Actively doing something with information is a better way to commit it to memory than remaining passively disengaged. If you had three hours to study a textbook chapter that takes one hour to read, what should you do: read the chapter three times, or work with the material after reading it once? The second option is generally more effective. So what kinds of things should you *do*?

13. **Mark it up.** Be an active reader; interact with the text. People who are used to reading complex material—your instructors, for example—read

chapter 8 Reading and Studying

You're about to discover . . .
- ✔ Why reading is important
- ✔ How to engage in focused reading
- ✔ How to tackle reading assignments as an ESL student
- ✔ What metacognition is and how it can help you
- ✔ How to become an intentional learner

READINESS CHECK — What do you **Know?**

Before beginning this chapter, take a moment to answer these questions. Your answers will help you assess how ready you are to focus.

1 = not very/not much/very little/low   10 = very/a lot/very much/high

How much do you *already* know?

Based on reading the "You're about to discover..." list and skimming this chapter, how much do you think you probably already know about this chapter's subject?

1 2 3 4 5 6 7 8 9 10

See if you can answer these questions about reading and studying *before* you read.

1. **How many words per minute does the average college student read?**

2. **What does SQ6R stand for?**

3. **What's the definition of the word "metacognition"?**

How motivated are you to learn *more*?

In general, how motivated are you to learn more by reading this chapter?

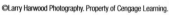

1 2 3 4 5 6 7 8 9 10

How much do you think this information might affect your success in college?

1 2 3 4 5 6 7 8 9 10

How much do you think this information might affect your career success after college?

1 2 3 4 5 6 7 8 9 10

How ready are you to read *now*?

How ready are you to focus on this chapter—physically, intellectually, and emotionally? Circle a number for each aspect of your readiness to focus.

1 2 3 4 5 6 7 8 9 10

If any of your answers is below a 10, you might want to pay attention to whatever is distracting you before you start reading. For example, if you're feeling scattered, take a few moments to settle down and focus.

Finally, how long do you think it will take you to complete this chapter from start to finish?

_____ Hour(s) _____ Minutes

Katie Alexander

College would be a lot more fun if it weren't for all the reading and studying required. That was Katie Alexander's take on things. She wasn't much of a reader; she much preferred playing softball or volleyball with her friends to sitting in one spot with a book propped open in front of her. Reading for fun wasn't something she'd ever even consider doing—at least not reading books. To Katie, reading 75 text messages a day was necessary; reading books was boring. *Anyway, why read the book when you can just watch the movie?* she always asked. Katie was an energetic, active, outgoing person, and "doing" and "socializing" were her things. Reading and studying definitely weren't.

Text Message:

Katie! are you still on campus? It's movie night tonight at 9... c u there!

Sept 6th, 8:10 pm

Actually, this was Katie's second attempt at college. She'd gone to a small liberal arts school right after high school, but the self-discipline required to read and study just wasn't there, so she dropped out. Working for two years at a big, local sports equipment store helped her earn enough money to go back to school. "This time, *you* foot the bills," her parents had insisted. So now she was attending the local university and determined to give it another go.

For Katie, reading and studying were hard work. She was smart enough to make it in college—she was sure of that—and this time around, she was more motivated. But reading was a labor-intensive activity that tried her patience, and after she'd read something, she was hard-pressed to summarize what it had been about. "In one eye and out the other" was the way she thought of her difficulties. Katie found it hard to focus, and things just didn't seem to stick. Before she knew it, she was off in some other world, thinking about her friends, or her schedule at work, or everything else she had to do.

Back in grade school, Katie had been labeled as a slow reader. She was never in the top reading group,

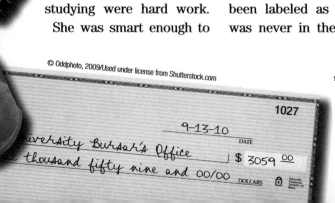

1027

9-13-10

University Bursar's Office

three thousand fifty nine and 00/00   DOLLARS $ 3059 00

ST# 34 OP#   TE#   TR#
005749801035   3.38
007065200750   2.97
007065200750   2.97
006025835603   14.96
068113176369   4.97
002340035457   0.93
005963148202   3.87
002340035458   0.93
005920000731   0.93
        SUBTOTAL 35.91
HST 15%   4.88
        TOTAL   40.79
DEBIT TEND   40.79
CHANGE DUE   0.00
RT
GST/HST

Metro Sports Equipment
PURCHASE TRANSACTION RECORD
40.79

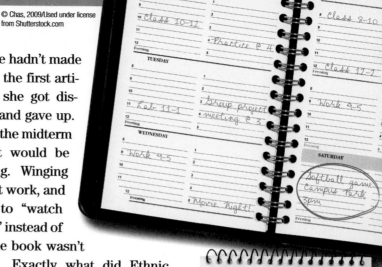

and although she resented the label, she didn't quite know what do to about it. The last time reading had actually been a subject in school was sixth grade. Now, eight years later, she wondered if one of those speed-reading courses advertised online might be the answer.

Katie's roommate, Amanda, was an English major who loved to read. In fact, that's all she ever seemed to do. Her best friend, Brittney, however, had a different strategy. "There's so much required reading in all my classes that I don't even know where to start," Brittney admitted, "so I just don't do it. I go to class, listen to the lectures, and write down what the instructor has said on the essay tests. Learn to play the game!"

But Brittney's strategy definitely wasn't going to work for Katie in Professor Harris-Black's Introduction to Ethnic Studies class. She'd assigned a shocking number of articles to read. The professor didn't even go over the readings in class, and her lectures were about all sorts of things, only some of which were related to the reading. Whenever she sat down to read an assignment, Katie found what to her were unfamiliar words and unnatural phrasing. The professor had suggested that students read with a dictionary at their sides, but who'd ever want to keep stopping to look up words? You'd never finish!

With a midterm exam coming up in her Ethnic Studies class next week, Katie was beginning to panic. She'd only read one of the nine articles assigned.

In fact, she hadn't made it through the first article when she got discouraged and gave up. She knew the midterm essay test would be challenging. Winging it wouldn't work, and choosing to "watch the movie" instead of reading the book wasn't an option. Exactly what did Ethnic Studies have to do with anything, she puzzled, and why had her advisor suggested the course in the first place?

The night before the test, Katie decided to get serious. She sat down at her desk, armed with her yellow highlighter. As she began reading, however, she realized she didn't know exactly what to highlight since she didn't really understand what she was reading. Looking back at the page she had just finished, she saw that she had basically highlighted everything. Exasperated, Katie told herself that she couldn't go to bed until she'd finished reading everything, no matter when that was. She started with the second article, since she'd read the first one, and by morning, she'd be as ready as possible. Anyway, it wasn't up to her—it was up to Professor Harris-Black; she was the one making up the test.

Getting an A on her Introduction to Ethnic Studies midterm exam was probably out of the question, but if she could just manage to pass, Katie knew she would have to settle for that. On the other hand, she secretly hoped that maybe she'd just luck out.

Ethnic Studies Reading List

Caste, Class and Race
            Cox, Oliver C.
Race: History of an Idea
            Gossett, Thomas F.
Ethnic Groups and Boundaries
            Barth, Frederick
The Predicament of Culture
            Clifford, James
Varieties of Ethnic Experience
            Di Leonardo, Micaela
In Search of Cultural History
            Gombrich, Ernst
Ethnic Enterprise in America
            Light, Ivan
Strangers From a Different Shore
            Takai, Ronald

Cross Cultural Dialogue:
A Participant Observer Study by an American Teacher in
Aaron Mohr

What Do You Think?

1. How would you characterize Katie as a student? Identify five specific problems described in this case study that could interfere with her college success.

2. Katie is probably an intelligent student, but she has decided that she dislikes reading and studying, so she avoids it. How important will these two skills be as she continues to pursue a college degree? Is she likely to succeed her second time around?

3. Is Katie like students you know? If so, in what ways, specifically?

4. Identify three specific things Katie should do to get her college career on track.

Who Needs to Read?

What's so important about reading? Teachers seem to think it's important, and parents consider it to be an admirable pastime, but times have changed, haven't they? Now you can just skim predigested information on websites, get a summary of the day's news from television, and watch movies for entertainment. Who needs to read? Look around the next time you're in a doctor or dentist's waiting room. You'll see some people staring at the TV screen mounted on the wall and others plugged into iPods. A few may be skimming through magazines, but does anyone ever pick up a book to actually read it cover to cover anymore? Does it matter?

The answer, according to many experts, is a resounding yes, it does![1] Reading helped create civilization as we know it and taught us particular ways of thinking.

One fairly predictable result of doing anything less is that eventually you may not do it as well. Practice keeps your skills sharp. Even an Olympic athlete who doesn't stick with training gets rusty after a while. As students read less, their reading skills deteriorate and they don't enjoy doing it. Conversely, the better you get at reading, the more you may enjoy it. Falling down every ten minutes the first time you get on skis isn't all that much fun, but once you can zip down the mountain like a pro, you begin to appreciate the sport.

Perhaps reading isn't your favorite pastime. You may feel about reading like many people do about eating cauliflower. You know it's good for you, but you'd prefer to avoid it. However, this chapter wouldn't be worth its weight in trees if it didn't try to convince you otherwise. One aspect of reading some people particularly dislike is that reading is not a social or physical activity. You can read with someone else in the room, of course, or talk about what you read afterward with friends, but basically, reading is something you do alone. It's a solitary activity that involves you, words on a page, an invisible author, and your brain. You need to do it with a minimum

cauliflower— yuck! That's right!

"" Perhaps the most valuable result of all education is the ability to make yourself do the thing you have to do, when it ought to be done, whether you like it or not."

**Thomas Henry Huxley,
British biologist (1825–1895)**

of physical movement. Reading while playing a game of volleyball would be tough to pull off.

If you enjoy reading, congratulations! When you settle in with an exciting novel, you can travel to the far corners of the Earth, turn back the clock to previous centuries, or fast-forward to a future that extends beyond your lifetime. Whether or not you enjoy reading, it will be one of the primary skills you need to cultivate in college. According to one study, 85 percent of the learning you'll do in college requires careful reading.[2] First-year students often need to read and comprehend 150–200 pages per week in order to complete their academic assignments.[3]

Tom McCarthy/PhotoEdit

What's more, reading skills go hand in hand with writing skills, which makes them even more important. The better you get at reading, the more you raise your probability of academic success. Many of your classes

will require intensive reading of complex material, including primary sources by original authors and scholarly research. If you complete reading assignments, and your classmates don't, think about how much ahead of the nonreaders *you* will be! But how do you become a better reader?

EXERCISE 8.1

What Is Your Reading Rate?

Before continuing, you'll need a stopwatch or a watch with a second hand. Keep track of how long it takes you to read the following article about getting a job. The object of the exercise isn't to race through; it's to read at your normal speed. After you read the article, you'll be asked to record your reading time and answer some questions to check your comprehension.

How Cool Is Your Job? Does It Even Matter?
By Adelle Waldman, Special to *The Wall Street Journal Online*

Dustin Goot has the kind of job that piques the interest of people he meets at parties, at least initially. The 27-year-old New Yorker is an associate editor of a glossy magazine aimed at young men, but his magazine—*Sync*—just launched last year, and many people haven't heard of it, which changes the dynamic.

"It seems like a cool job when you first say it," Mr. Goot says. But, "if you are at a magazine that not a lot of people have heard of, it's a bit of a letdown," he says. "People kind of shrug their shoulders." Mr. Goot may not be at a magazine with the name recognition of, say, *Sports Illustrated*, but in the complicated status hierarchy that emerges around the "coolness factor"—that is, how cool is your job?—Mr. Goot fares pretty well.

That's nothing to sneeze at. When we were in college, we all had the same job title—we were students. Sure, some schools are more prestigious than others, but at least among classmates at our own school, we were on pretty much equal ground. In a social setting, we might have bemoaned that we were judged on our appearances

(continued)

rather than our personalities, but it probably didn't occur to us that one day another basis for snap judgments would be added to the mix: the cachet of our jobs.

It's a biggie, and it's here to stay. For better or for worse, twentysomethings have to adjust to this new reality because for the rest of our lives, we can expect to be treated differently depending on the perceived prestige of our jobs.

So what happens if you love your job but it's not the kind of thing that commands instant respect at parties? Allison Predmore has been there. "When I tell people I am a social worker, they usually say something like, 'oh, that's nice, you must be a nice person,' and change the subject," says Ms. Predmore, who lives in Queens, N.Y., and turned 30 earlier this month.

Finding Your Own Niche

Her solution? She spends a lot of time with fellow social workers and others in the nonprofit sector—that is, people who tend to be on her same page, socially as well as financially. "I'm really not used to being with people who have a lot of disposable money to spend on a day to day basis," she says.

Besides, the fact that she really enjoys her work is more important to her than being treated like royalty at a party. That's something that many twentysomethings realize over the years, says Abby Wilner, co-author of "The Quarterlifer's Companion." We may be eternally judged by our jobs but that doesn't mean we'll always care quite so much if our title fails to bowl people over.

"When you are a senior in college or just a year or two out, a job is more conceptual or theoretical," Ms. Wilner says. That is, you don't have much else to gauge a job on other than how it sounds. But once the reality of working sets in—once you realize that work is not only a social signifier, but also the place where you'll spend about a third of your life—chances are, many other considerations, particularly how fulfilling the job is, tend to take precedence over the coolness factor, she says.

"After a couple years, you realize what's more important—the hours, who you are working with, what you are doing, possibilities for promotion," she says. "And you realize that while someone's job might sound cool, they might be miserable eight hours a day."

That doesn't mean that having a job that sounds glamorous isn't an added bonus, especially if it's an added bonus that comes on top of really liking the work, says Cathy Stocker, co-author with Ms. Wilner of "The Quarterlifer's Companion." "Glamour or coolness is just like another kind of compensation," Ms. Stocker says. Which is to say, it's one factor among many in evaluating a job, she says.

How Does Your Job Stack Up, Status-wise?

"In high school and college, there were set hoops to jump through," says Ms. Stocker. "You knew what the standards were and what being successful meant."

In the real world, it's not so clear. While investment bankers and management consultants rake in big bucks, money is far from the only factor in the complicated web of professional status. Some jobs are glamorous even if they're relatively low-paying—like, say, working in an entry-level position in fashion—while, to many people at least, doing things like the Peace Corps or Teach for America seem cool because they're considered exotic or admirable.

Hard to quantify as it is, you can measure your job status pretty easily. If you tell a stranger at a cocktail party what you do or where you work and, just like that, he or she seems to find you extremely smart and interesting and certainly worth talking to, then you have an impressive job. If that person instead reacts with a supercilious lack of interest and starts glancing around the room for other conversation partners, then your job is less glamorous (and the person you're talking to is unpardonably rude).

Some people seem to fare well in the brave new world of professional pecking orders, without ever breaking a sweat. It's just the nature of what they do.

Kevin Jasey didn't become an architect to impress people at parties, but he says it does the trick pretty well. Mr. Jasey, 29, is a project manager for a national architectural firm in Philadelphia. He has found that his chosen profession is creative and artsy enough to be interesting, but at the same time, it's seen as solid and professional. "It's pretty cool," he says. "It commands a certain type of respect."

And it counts even among people who make a lot more money, he says. Mr. Jasey's girlfriend is an investment banker, and he's often in crowds in which the majority of people are in a higher income bracket than he is.

But that doesn't mean they take him less seriously, he says. "They usually start asking my advice on their real estate holdings," he says. And more importantly, he really likes the work. "The profession is more important than the pay," he says.

Sometimes a particularly harrowing experience can also help us to put concerns with status in a better perspective. Huong Do had such an experience. The 28-year-old research assistant works in public health in New York City. Ms. Do, who has a master's degree in statistics, really enjoys her work, but knows that to really rise in her field, she should return to school for a Ph.D. But she's not in a hurry.

Nor is she worried that many of her friends are medical students and residents who, a few years down the line, will be full-fledged doctors, earning a lot more money than she does and treated with all the respect that our society affords physicians. "I used to be the overachiever who wanted to go off in a blaze of glory and discover the cure for cancer," she says. But when she was 23, she herself was diagnosed with cancer.

"That shifted my whole perspective," says Ms. Do, who is in remission. "I saw people who didn't make it, and I learned that it is important to do what makes you happy."

It's a key life lesson. After all, we spend a lot more time at our desks than we do making small talk at parties.

Now let's see how you did.

Reading Speed: Stop! Look at your watch. Mark down how long it took you to read the article: _____ Minutes _____ Seconds. If you read this article in four to six minutes, your reading rate is average for a college student. (Note: Article contains 1,262 words. College students read 200–300 words per minute, on average.) If you read faster or slower than that, what does that mean? If it took longer than six minutes, but you answer the three questions in the "Reading Comprehension" that follows correctly, reading slowly may not be as much of a problem for you as you may think it is. Right about now, however, you may be thinking, *Hey, I don't have time to spare! I'm juggling several different courses, a job, family responsibilities—a dozen things.* That's the point! Read with focus so that you can record, retain, and retrieve information. If you don't understand what you read, it's difficult, if not impossible, to learn it. Reading without comprehension is just going through the motions.

Reading Comprehension: Answer the following questions without going back and rereading the article.

1. What was this article's main point? _____

2. What is the social worker's strategy to cope with how her job is perceived by others? _____

3. What was the profession of the interviewee who believes that his job is seen as very prestigious even though he doesn't earn a high salary?

   _____

Now go back and check the accuracy of your answers. Are you "reading right"?

(handwritten margin note) Yikes! Took me 12 min. 30 sec. I'm slower than average :(

Read Right!

? **challenge** **❝❝ reaction** **✳ insight** **! action**

Challenge: Are there right ways to read? What have you learned about reading in college thus far? Provide as many suggestions about reading right as you can.

Reaction: _____

_____

What do we know about reading? How *should* you tackle your many reading assignments in college? Consider these twelve essential points:[4]   *???*

1. **Understand what being a good reader is all about.** Reading isn't a race. Remember the old children's story about the tortoise and the hare? The turtle actually won the race because he plodded along, slowly and steadily, while the rabbit zipped all over the place and lost focus. The moral of that story applies to reading, too. Reading is a process; understanding is the goal. The point isn't simply to make it through the reading assignment by turning pages every few minutes so that you can finish the chapter in a certain amount of time. When your instructors read difficult material, which they do regularly in their profession, they don't rush. They chew on the tough parts, reread sections, and make notes to themselves in the margins. Reading requires you to back up occasionally, just like when you back up a DVD to catch something you missed: "What did he say to her? I didn't get that."

   Students sometimes mistakenly think that good readers are speed-readers, when it's really about focus.[5] Science fiction writer Isaac Asimov once wrote, "I am not a speed reader. I am a speed understander."

2. **Take stock of your own reading challenges.** Which of the following are reading issues for you? Put a checkmark next to any that apply to you.[6]

boredom
amount
interest
speed
motivation

___ boredom	___ vision	___ speed	___ comprehension	___ time
___ amount	___ interest	___ motivation	___ surroundings	___ fear
___ fluency	___ fatigue	___ level	___ retention	___ laziness

   Many people find reading challenging. You may have worked with an impatient teacher as a youngster, or you may have been taught using a method that didn't work well for you—factors that still cause you problems today. Reading involves visually recognizing symbols, transferring those visual cues to your brain, translating them into meaningful signals—recording, retaining, and retrieving information (here's where your memory kicks in)—and finally using these meanings to think, write, or speak. Reading challenges can be caused by *physical factors* (your vision, for example) and *psychological factors* (your attitude). If you want to become a better reader in the future, it's a good idea to assess honestly what's most challenging about the process for you right now.[7]

3. **Adjust your reading style.** Reading requires versatility. Contrast these two situations: reading the menu on the wall at your local fast-food joint and poring over the menu at a fancy, high-end restaurant. You'd just scan the fast-food menu in a few seconds, wouldn't you? You wouldn't read word by word and ask: "Is the beef in that burger from grass-fed cattle?" "What, exactly, is in the 'special sauce'?" If you did, the exasperated attendant would probably blurt out, "Look, are you going to order something or not?" That kind of situation requires quick skimming. But you'd take some time to study the menu at a pricy restaurant you might go to with friends and family to celebrate your college graduation. It's an entirely different situation, and the information is more complicated. And if it's a fancy French restaurant, you might even need to ask the definitions of some terms like *canard* (duck) or *cassoulet* (a rich, hearty stew). That kind of situation requires slow, considered study, word by word. You're going to pay for what you choose, and you want the best results on your investment. That's true about college, too. You're investing in your college degree, so reading right is important!

You'll face an enormous amount of reading in your combined college classes. The question is, what's fast food (to carry through with the analogy) and what's fine dining? According to research on reading, good readers know the difference and adjust their reading styles.[8]

It's important to devote more time to reading and studying than you think you'll actually need. If you don't understand difficult material, go back and reread it, instead of assuming it will be explained by your instructor in class. Keep a dictionary at your side, and check unusual new terms. You'll be able to digest what you're reading much better.

4. **Converse with the author.** In every book you read, the author is trying to convince you of something. Take this book, for example. We have been engaged in a conversation all the way through. What do you know about me? What am I trying to persuade you to think about or do? Even though I'm not right in front of you in person on every page, you are forming impressions of me as you read, and I'm either convincing you to try the suggestions in this book or I'm not. As you read any book, argue with the author ("That's not how I see it!"), question her ("What makes you say that?"), agree with her ("Yes, right on!"), relate something she said earlier to something she's saying now ("But what about . . . ?"). Instead of just coloring with your yellow highlighter, scribble comments in the margins, or keep a running commentary in a notebook. Make small ticks in the margins to mark words you'll look up in your dictionary at a good breaking point. Reading is an active process, not a passive one in which the words just float by you. In fact, mark up this page right now! How do you decide what's really important? One thing you can do is ask your instructor in this course to show you his or her mark-ups in this book, and see if the two of you agree on what's important.

Huh...this is news to me—why didn't anyone teach me this??

> " Outside of a dog, a book is man's best friend. Inside of a dog, it's too dark to read."

Groucho Marx, American comedian, actor, and singer (1890–1977)

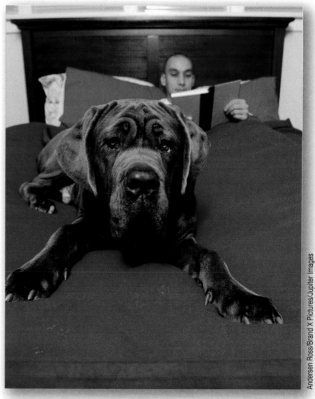

Andersen Ross/Brand X Pictures/Jupiter Images

CURIOSITY: *READING WHEN ENGLISH IS YOUR SECOND LANGUAGE*

Hints on Pronunciation for Foreigners

I take it you already know
Of laugh and bough and cough and dough?
Others may stumble but not you,
On hiccough, thorough, laugh and through.
Well done! And now you wish, perhaps,
To learn of less familiar traps?

Beware of heard, a dreadful word
That looks like beard and sounds like bird,
And dead: It's said like bed, not bead—
For goodness' sake don't call it "deed"!
Watch out for meat and great and threat
(They rhyme with suite and straight and debt.)

A moth is not a moth in mother
Nor both in bother, broth in brother
And here is not a match for there
Nor dear and fear for bear and pear,
And then there's dose and rose and lose—
Just look them up—and goose and choose,
And cork and work and card and ward,
And font and front and word and sword,

And do and go and thwart and cart—
Come, come, I've hardly made a start!
A dreadful language? Man alive.
I'd mastered it when I was five.

—T.S.W. (only initials of writer known) or possibly
written by George Bernard Shaw

Go ahead. Try reading the preceding poem aloud. Even if English is your first language, you probably had to pause and think about how to say a word occasionally. Most anyone would. English isn't exactly the easiest language in the world to learn, non-native English speakers say. It's filled with perplexing irregularities. Think about the raw courage it would take to pursue a college degree by reading and writing in a language other than your native tongue. If English is your first language, could *you* do it in German or Arabic or Hindi? That being acknowledged, what strategies can ESL (English as a Second Language) students use to help with challenging reading assignments?

1. Remember that spoken English differs from the written English you'll find in textbooks and academic articles. In casual conversation, you'll hear, "And she's … like, 'wow!' and I'm … like, 'really?'" If you read that in a book, you'd have no idea what the speakers were communicating about. But if you're standing next to the conversationalists in the hallway, you have a chance of figuring it out. Learning to speak informally in conversation is very different from learning to read scholarly discourse. Address these questions to your instructor or study-group mates instead.

2. Ask your English-speaking friends and instructors to coach you. For example, ESL speakers sometimes struggle with the hundreds of idioms found in English. Idioms are groups of words with a particular, nonliteral meaning. For example, "I have a frog in my throat" means your voice is hoarse, not that you literally have swallowed a green amphibian. Idioms must be learned as a set of words in order to communicate their intended meaning. If you change one word ("I have a *toad* in my throat"), the idiom doesn't work. Considering how many idioms English has and how freely English speakers use them without consciously thinking about it, non-native speakers may find learning them all to be a challenge. You'll more likely hear idioms spoken, rather than read them. If you're an international student, ask about unique phrases that don't make sense to you.

3. Use the Internet or an online course to improve your language skills. According to one study, international students in an online course made significant gains in their language skills, compared with a control group of students who sat through the same course in a classroom. Online courses provide good exposure and practice in your reading and writing skills via e-mail, web searching, threaded discussions, and online postings.[9]

4. Try explaining what you're reading to someone else. Talking something through while you're reading, especially with a native English speaker, can help you clarify meanings on the spot—and may help the other student achieve better comprehension, too.

5. Mark up the textbook so that you can pursue difficult passages in greater detail later. Insert question marks in the margin. Read with your English–native tongue dictionary in front of you. If you get completely stuck, find another book that may explain the concepts differently.

5. **Dissect the text.** Whether you did it virtually online or physically in a real lab, cutting up those little critters in your biology class helped you figure out what was what. The ability to dissect text is important in reading. As you read and make notes in the margins, write what and why statements. Try it: beside each paragraph on this page, write a one-sentence summary statement: a *what* statement. Put the author's words into your own words. Then write another sentence that focuses on *why* the paragraph is included. Does it contain *evidence* to make a point? Is it an *example* of something? If you can tackle this recommendation, you'll do wonders for yourself when exam time rolls around.

EXERCISE 8.2

Marginal Notes

Go back through the section of this chapter on reading that you just completed. If you used a highlighter, make notes to yourself in the margins (or on another sheet of paper) about *why* you underlined a word, phrase, or section. Why did you consider that part to be important? Knowing the answers to these questions is more important than the act of "coloring."[10]

6. **Make detailed notes.** You'll be more likely to master a challenging reading assignment if you keep a notebook beside you and take notes as you read. Go back and forth, detailing main points and supporting evidence, so that you have a set of notes by the time you've finished reading. If you're reading onscreen, open a new document and annotate there. The physical act of writing or typing can consolidate what you're reading and act as a form of rehearsal that helps you remember it later.

7. **Put things into context.** Reading requires a certain level of what's called cultural literacy, core knowledge that puts things into context and gives them meaning. Authors assume their readers have a common background. They refer to other books or current events, or historical milestones, and unless you know what they're referring to, what you're reading may not make sense to you. An example you might be familiar with is how the television show *Seinfeld* made real words that everyone now knows and uses out of fake ones: *yada yada yada*, for example. Those words are now part of our cultural literacy that have meaning for you and everyone you know, probably, but may not for people from another culture. They know the literacy of their own culture instead.

> " Force yourself to reflect on what you read, paragraph by paragraph."
>
> **Samuel Taylor Coleridge, British poet (1772–1834)**

8. **Don't avoid the tough stuff.** Much of the reading you'll do in college includes complicated sentences that are difficult to navigate. When you try reading complex passages aloud, you may stumble because you don't immediately recognize how the words are linked into phrases. But practicing reading aloud is one way you can become more familiar with difficult language. Many instructors teach their first-year students a common approach to reading and studying called SQ3R:

©Larry Harwood Photography. Property of Cengage Learning.

Survey—Skim to get the lay of the land quickly.

Question—Ask yourself what, why, and how questions. What is this article or chapter about? Why is it included? How might I use this information?

✓ **Read** (1)—Go ahead now and read the entire assignment. Make notes in the margins or even create a study guide for yourself.

✓ **Recite** (2)—Stop every now and then and talk to yourself. See if you can put what you're reading into your own words.

✓ **Review** (3)—When you've finished, go back and summarize what you've learned.

One expert suggests, however, that for scholarly articles, original published research, and complicated academic prose, you may need to add a few R's to make a new formula, SQ6R:

✓ **Reflect** (4)—You may need time to truly understand what you've read. Put it down and come back to it later—but definitely come back.

✓ **Rehash** (5)—Communicate your views to your study partners. They may be having trouble with the language, too, and multiple heads may be better than one. You may gain some insights from them, and vice versa.

✓ **Rethink** (6)—Evaluate whether or not you understood the article on your own. Do you understand it better after rehashing it with other students? And finally, how will you use put the information you read to good use?[11]

9. **Learn the language.** Every discipline has its own perspective and its own vocabulary. In many of the introductory classes you take, you'll spend a good deal of time and effort learning terms to be used in classes you'll take later. In order to study *advanced* biology, everyone has to learn the same language in *introductory* biology. You can't be calling things whatever you want to call them. You call it a respiratory system, but your classmate calls it a reproductive system. In college you will learn about the humanities (philosophy, for example), the natural sciences (astrophysics, for example), and the social sciences (psychology, for example) as you take what are often called general education or core courses. It's important to get to know a discipline. Pay attention to its perspective, priorities, and practices as you read, study, and learn.

10. **Bring your reading to class.** Some of your instructors will build the outside course readings into their lectures. They may justify the readings in their course syllabus, preview the readings in class, talk about their importance, or create reading worksheets for use in small groups. If they don't, however, it's up to you to integrate them. Bring up the reading in class, ask questions about it, and find out how it relates to particular points in the lecture. Doing so is an important part of being responsible for your own learning.

11. **Be inventive!** Students who are the best readers invent strategies that work for them. Perhaps you're an auditory learner. Reading assignments aloud might drive your roommate or another family member to distraction (so find a place where you can be alone), but it might be the perfect way for you to learn. If you're a kinesthetic learner, you might make copies of particular passages from your textbook, and build your own scrapbook

must try this out! I'll take any help!

" It matters, if individuals are to retain any capacity to form their own judgments and opinions, that they continue to read for themselves."

Harold Bloom, literary critic

for a course. Or cut up the professor's lecture notes into small chunks and reassemble them. Using what you know about yourself as a learner is a big part of college success, so don't just do what everyone else does or even follow your instructor's advice verbatim, if it doesn't work for you. Figure out what does, and then do it!

CAREER OUTLOOK: *Barbara Swaby, Literacy Expert*

Q1: You're a national expert on reading. What attracted you to the field?

Literacy has always been a value in my family. Both my parents were educators and were vitally involved in literacy efforts. More critical to my decision, however, is the fact that I am a native of Jamaica in the West Indies. The illiteracy rates in my country of origin are high as are the poverty rates. I have long realized that the major weapon against poverty is education and reading is certainly part of that.

Q2: What are some of the main challenges college readers face?

I believe that college students' literacy challenges begin with the sheer volume of reading they are expected to do (and rightly so) and the fact that they have not been exposed to these expectations in the past. Many students go about reading their required texts in unproductive ways. Many do not allocate sufficient time to study. Many confuse the acts of reading and studying. Many are not reading with enough personal engagement and not connecting themselves to what they're reading or connecting what they're reading to the world itself.

Q3: What's your best advice for first-year college students? How can they become better readers and therefore more successful in their college careers?

First, you should allocate enough time for reading texts and for study. Remember that all college texts are not equally difficult and that reading difficult texts successfully requires more than one reading. Second, separate the act of reading from that of studying. Although reading and studying have some things in common, purpose differentiates them. You can read with one of several purposes: to prepare for class discussion, for example, or simply to be entertained. When you study, however, you have a single, predetermined purpose. You will be accountable to someone else for what you read. Third, always stop often and think about what you have read. If you are unable to

remember the material, then reread it and try again. Taking notes on the text material may help, too. Finally, if you feel that you have a reading problem, get help from your advisor or from the learning center on your campus. They are available precisely for that purpose.

HOW WOULD *YOU* LIKE IT?

Have you ever considered a career as a teacher?

Facts to Consider[12]

Academic preparation required: Completion of a bachelor's degree, a teacher education program, and state licensure are required to teach in the U.S. public school system.

Future workforce demand: Because many current teachers are reaching retirement age, career opportunities are excellent although demand will vary somewhat by region, grade level, and subject matter.

Work environment: Many teachers work more than forty hours per week, including both classroom time and additional time required to prepare lesson plans and grade papers. They work ten months a year, typically, with two months off during the summer to travel, take college courses, or pursue outside

interests. Teachers find their work rewarding although unruly students, standardized testing, and enforced content for various subjects can increase stress levels. Facilities can range from new and state-of-the-art to run-down and out-of-date.

Essential skills: reading; writing; communicating with students individually and as a class, and with parents, administrators, and other teachers; planning and evaluating assignments; managing a classroom; using technology; working with committees or team teaching; sensitivity to diversity.

Questions to Ponder

1. Do you have (or could you acquire) the skills this career requires?

2. Are you interested in a career like this? Why or why not?

For more career activities online, access the CourseMate via www.cengagebrain.com/shop/ISBN/0495906425 to do the Team Career exercises.

12. **Make friends with your dictionary.** Okay, so it's annoying to stop every few minutes to look up a word. It's absolutely necessary, however. Yes, sometimes it's important to break your stride, stop, and look up a word or phrase because what follows in the reading is based on that particular definition. Other times, these strategies might be appropriate:

> Keep a stack of blank index cards next to you and write down the unknown word or phrase, the sentence it appears in, and the page number. Then when you have a stack, or when you have a chunk of time, look them all up.

> Try to guess the word's meaning from its context. Remember Lewis Carroll's "Jabberwocky" poem from *Through the Looking-Glass*? Even though the poem contains made-up words, when you read it, you infer that something was moving around sometime, somewhere, right?
>
> **'Twas brillig** ◄ ['twas usually indicates a time, as in 'twas daybreak],
>
> **and the slithy toves** ◄ [we don't know what *toves* are, but *slithy* sounds like a combination of slimy and slithering]

Often you can infer a word's meaning from how it's used or from other words around it, but not always. Many of your courses will require you to learn precise meanings for new terms. If you can't detect the meaning from the context, use your dictionary—and see it as a friend, rather than an enemy.

CONTROL: *YOUR TOUGHEST CLASS*

Look back over the section of this chapter on reading and honestly assess the extent to which reading is part of what you find challenging about your toughest class.

1. Do you understand what being a good reader in this discipline is all about?
2. Do you understand, accept, and work to improve your reading skills in this course?
3. Do you adjust your reading style? If the reading required in this course is challenging, do you read more carefully and with more focus?
4. Do you converse with the author of the textbook for this course as you read?
5. Do you dissect the text, writing what and why statements in the margins of the textbook?
6. Do you make detailed notes?
7. Do you put things you read for this course into context? Is cultural literacy a part of the challenge you face?
8. Do you tackle the reading with gusto, even if it's tough stuff?
9. Are you learning the language of this discipline?
10. Do you bring up questions about the reading in class?
11. Do you invent your own reading strategies to help you?
12. Do you make regular use of your dictionary to help you understand what you're reading for this class?

Honestly assess the extent to which you do or don't practice these suggestions in your most challenging class this term. Make an action plan, citing which recommendations you'll put into effect immediately and how you'll do it. If it's appropriate, e-mail your plan to your instructor in this class.

You Are What You Read!

To learn more about yourself and explore some new books, create your own reading profile. Open up your browser to the website of a major bookseller (amazon.com or barnesandnoble.com, for example). Search for six books whose titles communicate something about you: your likes and dislikes, hobbies and leisure-time activities, tastes and preferences, and so forth. Now, open up a PowerPoint or Word document, and copy and paste in the thumbnails of these six book covers. Line the pictures down the left side of the page, leaving yourself room beside each one to describe why you selected this book and something important the book's title communicates about you. Use these "You Are What You Read" sheets to learn more about your classmates—and commit to reading one of the books you've selected!

Meta-what? Metacognition, Reading, and Studying

Study Habit Self-Assessment

What are your study habits like? To what extent do these ten statements apply to you? Write the number for each statement on the line preceeding it.

Never			Sometimes			Always
1	2	3	4	5	6	7

_____ 1. I understand myself as a learner.

_____ 2. When I'm studying something difficult, I realize when I'm stuck and ask for help.

_____ 3. I make a study plan and stick to it in order to master class material.

_____ 4. I do whatever I need to do in order to learn something.

_____ 5. I talk to myself to help me understand things while I study.

_____ 6. After I study something I think about how well it went.

_____ 7. I know when I learn best: morning, afternoon, or evening, for example.

_____ 8. I know how I study best: alone, with one other person, in a group, etc.

_____ 9. I know where I study best: at home, in a library study carrel, at my computer, etc.

_____10. I believe I'm in control of my own learning.

Now tally your scores on this informal instrument. If you scored between 60 and 70 total points, you have excellent metacognitive skills. If you scored between 40 and 60 points, your skills are probably average. However, note any items you rated down in the 1 to 2 range, and then continue reading this section of the chapter carefully.

Talk about needing to use a dictionary! What does the word *metacognition* mean? *Meta* is an ancient Greek prefix that is often used to mean *about*. For example, metacommunication is communicating *about* the way you communicate. ("I feel humiliated when you tease me in front of other people. Can you *not* do that?") Since cognition means thinking and learning, metacognition is thinking about your thinking and learning about your learning. It's about identifying your learning goals, monitoring your progress, backing up or getting help when you're stuck, forging ahead when you're in the groove, and evaluating your results. Metacognition is about knowing yourself as a learner and about your

Andrew Ward/Life File/Photodisc/Getty Images

Being busy does not always mean real work. The object of all work is production or accomplishment and to either of these ends there must be forethought, system, planning, intelligence, and honest purpose, as well as perspiration. Seeming to do is not doing."

Thomas Edison, American inventor (1847–1931)

ability (and motivation) to control your own learning. Some things are easy for you to learn; others are hard. What do you know about yourself as a learner, and do you use that awareness *intentionally* to learn at your best?[13]

These questions may seem simple, but how do you know:

1. When you've finished a reading assignment?

2. When your paper is ready to turn in?

3. When you've finished studying for an exam?

?? When I've gotten to the end?

Whenever the due date is?

When it's late at night?

When you're eating a meal, you know when you're full, right? But when it comes to academic work, how do you know when you're done?

Metacognition is about having an "awareness of [your] own cognitive machinery and how the machinery works."[14] It's about knowing the limits of your own learning and memory capabilities, knowing how much you can accomplish within a certain amount of time, and knowing what learning strategies work for you.[15] Know your limits, but at the same time, stretch.

VARK It!

Complete the recommended activity for your preferred VARK learning modality. If you are multimodal, select more than one activity. Your instructor may ask you to (a) give an oral report on your results in class, (b) send your results to him or her via e-mail, (c) post them online, or (d) contribute to a class chat.

Visual: Make a chart comparing how much time you spend on three things this week: talking on your cell phone, watching TV, and studying. Which activity has the longest line?

Aural: Access the CourseMate via www.cengagebrain .com/shop/ISBN/ 0495906425 to listen to the iAudio summary for this chapter. Then repeat three main points you heard.

Read/Write: Make a stack of index cards with words you couldn't define in this chapter. Look them up in the dictionary and write out the definitions. Then compare your stack with the ones of other classmates.

Kinesthetic: Access the Course-Mate via www. cengagebrain .com/shop/ISBN/ 0495906425 to watch the Focus TV episode for this chapter.

Hill Street Studios/Blend Images/Corbis

Paul Burns/Corbis

Becoming an Intentional Learner:
Make a Master Study Plan

What's your favorite class this term? Or let's turn the question around: what's your least favorite class? Considering all you have to do, including your most and least favorite classes, what would making a master study plan look like? You've been there, done that all through your schooling, but do you *really* know how to study?

To begin, think about what you have to think about. What's your goal? Is it to finish your English essay by 10:00 P.M. so that you can start your algebra homework? Or is it to write the best essay you can possibly write? If you've allowed yourself one hour to read this chapter, but after an hour, you're still not finished, you have three choices: keep reading, finish later, or give up entirely. What's in your best interest, honestly? See if you find the following planning strategies helpful.

1. **Make sure you understand your assignments.** Understanding is critical to making a master plan. You can actually waste a great deal of time trying to read your instructor's mind after the fact: "Did she want us to *analyze* the play or *summarize* it?" "Were we supposed to do all the practice problems, or just the first set?" When you leave class, make sure you're clear on what's been assigned.

2. **Schedule yourself to be three places at once.** Making a master plan requires you to think simultaneously about three different time zones:

   The past: Ask yourself what you already know. Is this a subject you've studied before? Have your study habits worked well for you in the past? How have you done your best work—on papers, on exams, or projects?

   The present: Ask yourself what you need to learn now. How interested are you in this material? How motivated are you to learn it? How much time will you devote to it?

   The future: Ask yourself how you'll go about learning it. Will you learn it using the strategies that work best for you? What learning factors will you control? Will you do what you can to change what's not working?[16]

3. **Talk through your learning challenges.** There's good evidence that talking to yourself while you're studying is a good thing. Rather than worrying about the stereotype that only crazy people do that, researchers find it helps you figure things out: *Okay, I understand the difference between a neurosis and a*

*I'm aural—
maybe this
would help me...*

psychosis, but I'm not sure I can provide examples on the test. Once you've heard yourself admit that, you know where to focus your efforts next.[17]

4. **Be a stickler.** Have you ever thought about how important accuracy is? For example, an accuracy rate of 99 instead of 100 percent would mean 500 airplanes in U.S. skies each day wouldn't be directed by air traffic controllers.[18] Disastrous! As you read and study, remember this graphic example. Be thorough. Read the entire assignment. Pay attention to details. Accuracy counts!

5. **Take study breaks.** The human attention span is limited, and according to some researchers, it's shrinking, rather than expanding.[19] Plan to take brief scheduled breaks to stretch, walk around, or grab a light snack every half hour during study sessions. Of course, it's important to sit down and get back to work again. Don't let a quick study break to get a snack multiply into several hours of television viewing that wasn't in the plan.

6. **Mix it up.** Put a little variety into your study sessions by switching from one subject to another, or from one mode of studying—for example, reading, self-quizzing, writing—to another. Variety helps you fight boredom and stay fresh.

7. **Review, review, review!** Review your course material often enough that you can retain and retrieve information at the level expected by your instructor. If you have to start fresh each time you come to class, trying to work from your memory of what was discussed during the last class, you'll always feel behind.

> Good reason to talk to that cute guy in class!

8. **Find a study buddy.** Find a classmate who also values studying, and commit to keeping one another focused during study sessions. Create quizzes and hypothetical test questions for each other, and use your study partner to keep you on track.

9. **Estimate how long it will take.** Before starting an assignment, estimate the amount of time you will need to complete that assignment (just as you do at the start of each chapter of this book), and then compare that estimate to the actual amount of time the assignment took to complete. Getting into this habit helps you develop realistic schedules for future projects.

10. **Vary your study techniques by course content.** When you study math, it's important to do more than read. Working problem sets helps you actually develop the skills you need. When you study history, you study differently. You might draw a timeline of the events leading up to World War I, for example.

11. **Study earlier, rather than later.** Whenever possible, study during the daytime rather than waiting until evening. Research shows that each hour used for study during the day is equal to one and a half hours at night. Another major study showed that students who study between 6:00 P.M. and midnight are twice as likely to earn A's as students who put off their studying until after midnight.[20]

12. **Create artificial deadlines for yourself.** Even though your professors will have set deadlines for various assignments, create your own deadlines that come before the ones they set. Finish early, and you'll save yourself from any last-minute emergencies that may come up, like crashed hard drives or empty printer cartridges.

13. **Treat school as a job.** If you consider the amount of study time you need to budget for each hour of class time, and you're taking 12–15 credits, then essentially you're working a 36–45 hour/week job on campus. Arrive at "work" early and get your tasks done during "business hours" so you have more leisure time in the evenings.

14. **Show up.** Once you've decided to sit down to read or study, really commit yourself to showing up—being present emotionally and intellectually, not just physically. If you're committed to getting a college education, then give it all you've got! Get help if you need it. If you have a diagnosed learning disability, or believe you might, find out where help is available on your campus. One of the best ways to compensate for a learning disability is by relying on metacognition. In other words, consciously controlling what isn't happening automatically is vital to your success.[21]

> " The more I want to get something done, the less I call it work."
>
> **Richard Bach, American author**

Sprinting to the Finish Line: How to Study When the Heat Is On

Let's be realistic. Planning is important, but there will be times when you'll have to find some creative ways to survive the onslaught of all you have to study. You'll need to prioritize. When you do need to find a way to accomplish more than is humanly possible, keep these "emergency preparedness" suggestions in mind:

1. **Triage.** With little time to spare, you must be efficient. Consider this analogy: If you're the physician on duty in the ER, and three patients come in at once, who will you take care of first: the fellow with strep throat, the woman with a sprained wrist, or the heart attack victim who needs CPR? It's called triage. Of all the material you need to study, ask what is most important, less important, and omittable. If you have several assignments due the same week, evaluate where you stand in each course and then determine where to place your emphasis. For example, if you are earning an A– in art history, a B+ in world geography, and a C– in math, you know which course most needs your attention. Evaluate the material and ask yourself which topics have received the most attention in class and in the textbook. Then focus your study time on those topics, rather than trying to study everything.

2. **Use every spare moment to study.** If flashcards work for you, take your flashcards with you everywhere, for example. Organize your essay answer in your head while you're filling up at the pump. It's surprising: small amounts of focused time do add up.

3. **Give it the old one-two-three-four punch.** Immerse *all* your senses in the precious little amount of time you have to study: *read, write, listen,* and *speak* the material.

4. **Get a grip on your gaps.** Honesty is the best policy. Rather than glossing over what you don't know, assess your knowledge as accurately as possible, and fill in the gaps.

5. **Cram, but only as the very last resort.** If you're ultra short on time due to a real emergency, and you have studying to do for several classes, focus on one class at a time. Be aware, however, that interference can be an obstacle

to retrieving information. If you learn new information that is similar to something you already know, the old information can interfere. So if you're studying for a psychology test that contains some overlap with your sociology test, separate the study sessions by a day. Studies also show that cramming up to one hour before sleeping can help to minimize interference.[22] Nevertheless, continually remind yourself: What's my goal here? Is it to just get through twenty-five pages or is it to truly understand?

? challenge **" reaction** *** insight** **! action**

Now What Do You Think?

1. At the beginning of this chapter, Katie Alexander, a frustrated and disgruntled college student, faced a challenge. Now after reading this chapter, would you respond differently to any of the questions you answered about the "FOCUS Challenge Case"? Knowing what you know now, how would you advise her? Write a paragraph ending to the story, incorporating your best advice.

2. How would you characterize your reading skills, based on all your years of schooling and feedback you have received from teachers? Are you an above average, average, or below average reader? Why?

3. Considering how important reading will be to your college success, what can you do to improve? For example, would it be worthwhile to try reading for pleasure to see if you can become better at it? Can you set a timer to give yourself reading goals, or create practice quizzes to assess your comprehension?

REALITY CHECK | ## What did you Learn?

On a scale of 1 to 10, answer the following questions now that you've completed this chapter.
1 = not very/not much/very little/low   10 = very/a lot/very much/high

In hindsight, how much did you already know about this subject before reading the chapter?

1 2 3 4 5 6 7 8 9 10

Can you answer these questions about reading and studying more fully now that you've read the chapter?

1. **How many words per minute does the average college student read?**
2. **What does SQ6R stand for?**
3. **What's the definition of the word "metacognition"?**

How useful might the information in this chapter be to you? How much do you think this information might affect your success in college?

1 2 3 4 5 6 7 8 9 10

How much do you think this information might affect your career success after college?

1 2 3 4 5 6 7 8 9 10

How long did it actually take you to complete this chapter (both the reading and writing tasks)? _____ Hour(s) _____ Minutes

 Challenge Yourself Online Quiz. To find out just how much you've learned, access the CourseMate via www.cengagebrain.com/shop/ISBN/0495906425 to take the Challenge Yourself Online Quiz.

Take a minute to compare these answers to your answers from the "Readiness Check" at the beginning of this chapter. What gaps exist between the similar questions? How might these gaps between what you thought before starting the chapter and what you now think after completing the chapter affect how you approach the next chapter in this book?

chapter 9 Taking Tests

You're about to discover . . .
- ✔ Why you should change your thinking about tests
- ✔ What to do before, during, and after a test
- ✔ Why cramming doesn't always work
- ✔ What test anxiety is and what to do about it
- ✔ How to take different kinds of tests differently
- ✔ How cheating can hurt your chances for success

©Larry Harwood Photography. Property of Cengage Learning.

READINESS CHECK — What do you **Know?**

Before beginning this chapter, take a moment to answer these questions. Your answers will help you assess how ready you are to focus.

1 = not very/not much/very little/low   10 = very/a lot/very much/high

How much do you *already* know?

Based on reading the "You're about to discover. . ." list and skimming this chapter, how much do you think you probably already know about this chapter's subject?

1 2 3 4 5 6 7 8 9 10

See if you can answer these questions about taking tests *before* you read.

1. **What are the four components of test anxiety?**

2. **Identify three hints to managing your time during tests.**

3. **Why are subjective (essay) tests often perceived to be more challenging than objective (true-false, multiple-choice) tests?**

How motivated are you to learn *more*?

In general, how motivated are you to learn more by reading this chapter?

1 2 3 4 5 6 7 8 9 10

How much do you think this information might affect your success in college?

1 2 3 4 5 6 7 8 9 10

How much do you think this information might affect your career success after college?

1 2 3 4 5 6 7 8 9 10

How ready are you to read *now*?

How ready are you to focus on this chapter—physically, intellectually, and emotionally? Circle a number for each aspect of your readiness to focus.

1 2 3 4 5 6 7 8 9 10

If any of your answers is below a 10, you might want to pay attention to whatever is distracting you before you start reading. For example, if you're feeling scattered, take a few moments to settle down and focus.

Finally, how long do you think it will take you to complete this chapter from start to finish?

_____ Hour(s) _____ Minutes

195

Joe Cloud

"*Joe College," that's me,* Joe Cloud kept thinking to himself. His long-awaited opportunity to leave his small rural community on the reservation had finally arrived. He was at college in the big city, where life was vastly different. He would be different, too, he had convinced himself—somehow more outgoing, more athletic, more popular, more successful—more of everything.

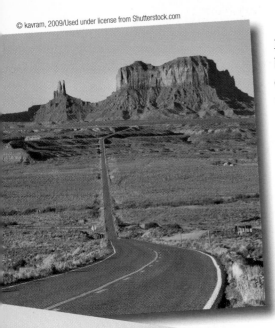

Growing up in his town of 1,000, he had been the basketball king, the after-school grocery store shelf stocker, and the smartest guy in his high school of thirty-five. He was leaving a trail of victories behind him, and everyone in town appeared to have a stake in his future success in college. As the end of the summer approached, whenever people saw him in the grocery store, they'd yell out, "Hey, Joe, when are you leaving for college?"

Much to his parents' delight, Joe had even won a scholarship that would pay for all of his expenses. The condition was that he would be successful, graduate, and return to the reservation to give back to the community in some capacity.

As midterms approached, Joe figured things were going well, except for his killer calculus course. There were 350 students in the lecture course, and Professor Buchanan was very businesslike and aloof. Joe was building up a great deal of anxiety over the course. Never before had he failed at anything, and if he didn't keep his grades up, he'd lose his scholarship.

The first week had been a review of what he had learned in his high school calculus class. But things became more challenging quickly. The pace quickened to the point that Joe found himself frantically trying to keep up. Math had never been his best subject.

However, as the midterm exam approached, Joe began experiencing a funny sensation when he entered class each week. As he approached the door, his breathing became shallow and rapid, his heart was pounding, and he felt lightheaded when he sat in his seat. He finally had to get up and leave before passing out. Unfortunately, it was exam review day, too.

That evening at dinner, he talked over his experience with his friend, Chris. "I've been telling you to eat breakfast!" Chris said. "You have to start rolling out of bed earlier, man!" But deep within himself, Joe knew his problem was more than just skipping breakfast.

Although he hated to admit it, calculus had become so distasteful that Joe hadn't cracked the textbook since the day he had to get up and leave. He knew cramming was a bad idea, but he also knew that he had given himself no choice. The night before the midterm, Joe started his studying by spending an hour looking up websites on how to cram for tests on the Internet; lots of coffee was the common theme. As the clock ticked into the wee hours of the morning, he was making trips to the coffee machine every forty-five minutes. He figured he had to pull an all-nighter if he wanted to pass at all. Dr. Buchanan had said the test would consist of calculus problems with the answers in multiple-choice format, so Joe got out his highlighter and started reading the textbook chapters.

The morning of the exam, Joe woke up suddenly and when he glanced at his alarm clock, he saw that he had overslept. The exam would start across campus in fifteen minutes. His palms were sweaty, and his heart was racing again. He leaped out of bed, threw on some clothes, and ran out the door. When he got to class, he noticed that he'd forgotten his watch and his book bag with his calculator in it. As he sat down in a random empty seat, a student next to him leaned over and whispered, "I am totally freaked out about this test, aren't you?" That didn't help.

Joe finally worked up the nerve to look at the first question and realized he couldn't answer it. Frantically, he paged through the rest of the exam. It all looked unfamiliar. He was so tired that he was having trouble focusing. His seat gave him a perfect view of another student's answer sheet one row down and over. He struggled with the temptation. It was the longest fifty minutes of his life, and when Dr. Buchanan called "time," Joe put down his pencil and slumped back into his chair.

The next week when the exams were handed back, Joe expected the worst—and he got it. What he stared at was the worst grade he'd ever gotten on any test in his entire life. Disgusted, he threw his exam in the trash can at the front of the lecture hall on his way out. *Why is there so much emphasis on exams in college, anyway? I'll never have to take a test again when I get out of here,* he muttered to himself. He was only halfway through his first term, and his scholarship was already on the line.

Calculus Midterm Exam

D−

Calculus I
Professor Buchanan

Name: Joe Cloud

1. Use integration by parts to evaluate $\int \chi \tan^{-1}(\chi)\, d\chi$.

(a) $\frac{1}{2}\chi^2 \tan^{-1}(\chi) - \tan^{-1}(\chi) + C$

(b) $\frac{1}{2}\chi^2 \tan^{-1}(\chi) + \frac{\chi}{2} + C$

(c) $\frac{1}{2}(\chi^2 + 1)\tan^{-1}(\chi) - \frac{\chi}{2} + C$

(d) $\frac{\chi}{1+\chi^2} - \tan^{-1}(\chi) + C$

(e) $\frac{1}{2}\chi^2 + \tan^{-1}(\chi) + C$

2. Find the slope of the tangent line to $y = \cosh^{-1}(\chi)$ at $\chi = 2$.

(c) $\frac{e^2 + e^{-2}}{2}$ (d) $\frac{e^2 - e^{-2}}{2}$ (e) $\frac{1}{2}$

What Do You Think?

1. What should Joe have done differently *before, during,* and *after* the exam?
2. Does Joe have test anxiety? Why or why not?
3. What's the *right* way to study for a multiple-choice exam in a calculus course?
4. Does cramming work? Why or why not?
5. If you were Joe, would you have cheated to save your scholarship? Why or why not?

Testing 1, 2, 3 . . . *Show What You Know*

L et's face it, life would be very different without grades in college, or time clocks on the job, or performance reviews throughout your career, wouldn't it? You wouldn't have to show up at work if you didn't feel like it, and you'd get a paycheck anyway. You wouldn't have to do a good job because no one would care. And you wouldn't have to write papers, or give presentations, or take tests in college. Not only would you benefit by having more free time, but your instructors wouldn't have to forge their way through stacks of papers assigning grades, either. What a wonderful world that would be—or would it? Realistically, it would probably bring total chaos.

Life's not like that. Results count. Accountability is the bottom line. Achievement is taken seriously. You may be thinking, "I'll never have to take another test once I get out of here," but exams are actually realistic representations of life's requirements. The experience of taking a test is similar to running a critical meeting or giving a high-stakes presentation on the job. You'll need to walk into the room, ready to show what you know, and answer unanticipated questions. The anxiety you feel before taking a test isn't much different from the anxiety you might feel in stressful situations in your career. Exams ask you to demonstrate your knowledge on the spot at a particular juncture in your learning. They help you compare your progress to that of other students and to your professor's set of expectations about what all students should know.[1] On the job, every day will be a test of your skills and abilities, and you'll get your "grade" when your supervisor gives you an accounting of your performance over the last six months or year. Tests are inevitable; so rather than bemoan them, perhaps we should change the way we think about them. According to experts, "Testing not only measures knowledge but changes it—and, happily, in the direction of more certainty, not less." Believe it or not, tests actually benefit you and your learning![2]

The first step of test-taking, of course, is to make sure you're prepared. All of the information in this chapter is worthless if you haven't gone to class or read the textbook or taken good notes during lectures. Miracles, by their very definition, are in very short supply. Nothing can substitute for being conscientious about your work. Think about preparing for an exam as you would for an athletic event. You'd have to work for months to develop the stamina you would need to

I watched the Focus TV episode on testing available on the CourseMate via www.cengagebrain.com/shop/ISBN/0495906425, and it says this!

finish successfully. You wouldn't want to just show up for kicks and wing it. If you did, at the very least, you'd probably pull a muscle. At the very worst, they'd carry you away on a stretcher.

The same principle holds true for exams in college. In order to have the stamina required and avoid the "injury" of not doing well, tests require this same kind of step-by-step, long-term preparation. Tests in your courses will usually ask you to do one or more of the following:

> *Remember* or *recognize* specific facts

> *Compare, contrast, synthesize,* or *interpret* information

> *Apply* theories and principles to recognizable or new problems

> *Predict* the outcomes to a set of variables

> *Evaluate* the usefulness of ideas, theories, or methods for a particular situation

Look at all those italicized verbs, and you begin to see the span of what will be required of you in all your courses.

Think about taking tests as a three-stage project with a beginning, middle, and end. What do you do *before* the test to get ready? What do you do *during* the test to do your best? What do you do *after* the test to ensure a productive learning experience you can use for future exams?

Before the Test: Prepare Carefully

? challenge	66 reaction	* insight	! action

Challenge: List your five best specific ideas about how to prepare for tests. What works for you? Assume you are giving advice to a brand new student.

Reaction: 1. _____

2. _____

3. _____

4. _____

5. _____

As you read the upcoming sections about *before, during,* and *after* a test, evaluate how many of these suggestions apply to you. Put a plus sign (+) in front of each item you already do regularly and a (✔) in front of items you could start doing more regularly to improve your test-taking skills.

1. _____ **Begin preparing for an exam on the first day of class.** Nothing can replace consistent, regular study before and after each class. If you work along the way, then when it comes time for the exam, you won't need to panic and begin sudden heroic efforts. Keep up with the reading, even if there are things you'd rather be doing.

2. _____ **Identify the days and times of all your exams for the whole term in your planner, cell phone, or online calendar.** At the beginning of the term, write in the days and times of all the exams in all your courses—even finals, which will seem very far off. You'll thank yourself many times over for completing this essential task.

3. _____ **Find out exactly what the test will cover.** There's nothing more terrifying than having a classmate next to you say something like this before the exam begins, "I can't believe this test covers the entire first six chapters," when you thought it only covered the first four chapters. Clarify anything you're not sure of. Phone or e-mail several other students, or better yet, ask your instructor questions like these: How long will the test be? What material will it cover? Which topics are most important? It's also a good idea to ask about criteria that will be used in grading. Do punctuation and grammar count? Will there be an in-class review? All these questions are usually fair game.

4. _____ **Understand that specific types of preparation are required for specific types of tests.** Objective and subjective tests should be approached differently, as described in later sections of this chapter. Online tests require that you know the answers to important questions up front. For example, will the test time out? Must you complete the exam once you start, or can you save your answers and come back to finish later? Should you compose essay answers elsewhere and paste them into the online exam so that you don't lose all your work in the case of a technology hiccup?

5. _____ **Make a study schedule.** How many days are left to study? What will you accomplish each day? Don't decide you'll use whatever time is left over to study for your test. Usually there isn't any time left over.

6. _____ **Begin serious reviewing several days before the test.** The best strategy is "tending" the class material, just as you take care of other things you care about on an ongoing basis, like your car or your dog. After each lecture, work with your notes, revising, organizing, or summarizing them. Then several days before the exam, step up your effort. Divide up the work by days or study blocks. Begin consolidating your lecture notes and reading notes. Make flashcards, outlines, charts, summaries, tables, diagrams, whatever works for your learning style and fits the material.

7. _____ **Maximize your memory.** Research indicates that specific techniques help transfer information from short-term to long-term memory. Remember to "Make It Stick" (rehearse, overlearn, space it out, separate it, and mind the middle), "Make It Meaningful" (feel, connect, and personalize), "Make It Mnemonic" (spell, locate, link or narrate, and peg), "Manipulate It" (mark it up, mark it down, organize, picture, act, produce, and test), and "Make It Funny" (mock it).

8. _____ **Get everything ready the night before.** To calm your nerves, lay out your clothes the night before the exam and pack your book bag with things you'll need: several pencils, erasers, scrap paper, your calculator, and a watch that works. Remove as much hassle as you can from test day.

" If you would hit the mark, you must aim a little above it."

Henry Wadsworth Longfellow, American poet (1807–1882)

Comstock/Jupiter Images

9. **_____ Manage your energy so that you're ready to focus and work quickly.** You've heard it before, but if you're exhausted or feverish, you're not as likely to "show what you know" as you will if you're healthy and rested. Don't resort to artificial stimulants, like drinking excessive amounts of coffee to stay awake. "All-nighters" are a college ritual, but they catch up with you, and they're a bad habit to get into. According to one expert, "for every hour of sleep we lose, we drop one IQ point."[3] A series of all-nighters during midterms or final exams can seriously impair your intellectual performance.

10. **_____ Don't give in to a nonproductive, negative attitude.** Emotions are contagious. Stay away from other students who are freaked out or pessimistic about the exam. Think—and feel—for yourself. Make sure your self-coaching is productive ("I've studied this section for an hour; if it's on the exam, I'll nail it."), rather than punishing ("I'm so stupid. Why didn't I keep up with the reading?").

I think I do this a lot.

11. **_____ Study with other students.** When you teach something to someone else, you must first learn it thoroughly yourself. Why not study with other students? You can take turns teaching one another, comparing class notes, and making practice exams for each other. Don't wait to be invited; take responsibility and start a study group yourself. And if you're concerned that a study group of several students may degenerate into a social club, study with just one other person—find a study partner and commit to doing the work.

12. **_____ Remind yourself of your long-term goals.** Why are you going to college? All this sweat and toil is worth something or you wouldn't be doing it. Keep your sights on the finish line! Enjoy the feeling of accomplishing something now that contributes to your goal-oriented success later. Ask people who finish the Boston Marathon how they feel. The answers you'll get won't focus exclusively on the ordeal; they will celebrate the accomplishment—guaranteed!

Christina Ripp wins the 2003 Boston Marathon Women's Wheelchair Division

13. **_____ Arrive at the classroom early, but not too early.** Get there early enough to get a seat where the lighting is good and you won't be distracted by other students, but don't arrive so early that you build up excessive anxiety during a long wait.

14. **_____ Don't pop pills to stay awake.** You may know students who use Ritalin, Adderall, Vicodin, and OxyContin as study aids. This is a bad idea. When these drugs are used for the wrong reasons, they can help you stay awake for hours and enter a dreamy state. The potential side effects include insomnia, nausea or vomiting, dizziness, palpitations, headaches, tremors and muscle twitching, even seizures. With such horrible potential health risks staring you in the face, not to mention possible legal sanctions if you obtain these drugs without a prescription, why not make things simple? Just study.[4]

15. _____ **Don't let open-book or take-home tests lull you into a false sense of security.** What could be easier than an open-book test? What could be better than taking a test in the comfort of your own home? Actually, these two types of tests require substantial preparation. Time is the issue here. If you're unfamiliar with the material, flipping through pages of notes or skipping around in the textbook won't help. Create a reference guide for yourself so that you can find various topics in your notes or textbook and use your time efficiently.

16. _____ **Don't mess with success.** If you're doing well and earning the grades you deserve, don't discard what is working for you. Honestly assess the efficiency and effectiveness of your current practices, and then decide what ideas from this chapter you should add to your test-taking preparation repertoire.

Cramming: Does "All or Nothing" Really Work?

? challenge ▌▌ reaction * insight ! action

Challenge: Why is cramming for tests a bad idea? List as many reasons as you can.

Reaction: _____

_____

Imagine yourself as the actor in the following scenarios. Compare these situations to cramming for tests.

> You haven't called your significant other since last year. Suddenly you appear at her door with candy, flowers, concert tickets, and dinner reservations at the most exclusive restaurant in town. You can't understand why she isn't happier to see you.

> You don't feed your dog for several months. When you finally bring him a plate loaded with ten T-bone steaks to make up for your neglect, you notice he's up and died on you. Oops!

Of course, these tongue-in-cheek, all-or-nothing situations are ridiculous, aren't they? How could anyone ever neglect such basic necessities of life? There's an important point to be made here. Many things in life require continuous tending: pets and people, for example. If you ignore them for a time, catching up is next to impossible. Your college courses should be added to the list.

Believe it or not, some students give themselves permission to follow this all-or-nothing principle in their academic work. They sail along without investing much time or energy in their studies, and then they try and make up for lost time right before an exam by cramming. The word *cram* provokes a distinct visual image, and rightly so. Picture yourself packing for spring break in a warm, sunny place and hardly being able to close your suitcase because it's crammed full. You can't decide what to bring so you bring everything you can think of.

The same holds for cramming for a test. You try to stuff your brain full of information, including things you won't need. Since you haven't taken the time to integrate the information and gather it into related chunks, you end up with random bits of unconnected data. Cramming is an attempt to overload information into your unreliable working memory. It's only available for a very short time. However, there are other reasons why cramming is a bad idea:

> Your anxiety level will surge.

> Your sleep will suffer.

> Your immune system may go haywire.

> You may oversleep and miss the exam altogether. ← —— *almost did that one!*

Despite the warnings here, most students cram at some time or other during their college careers, and doing so may even give them a temporary high and make them feel like they're suffering for a cause.[5] But generally, slow and steady wins the race.[6]

Test-Taking: High Anxiety?

EXERCISE 9.1

Do You Suffer from Test Anxiety?

What is test anxiety? What are the symptoms? Do you have it? Fill out the following informal survey to determine whether or not you may have test anxiety. For each of the twelve statements, rate your degree of agreement or disagreement.

1	2	3	4	5
Disagree Completely	Disagree Somewhat	Unsure	Agree Somewhat	Agree Completely

1. I cringe when I suddenly realize on the day of an exam that a test is coming up. _____

2. I obsess about the possibility of failing an upcoming exam. _____

3. I often experience disappointment, anger, embarrassment, or some other emotional reaction during an exam. _____

4. I think that instructors secretly get enjoyment from watching students squirm over exams. _____

5. I experience physical symptoms such as an upset stomach, faintness, hyperventilation, or nausea before an exam. _____

6. I tend to zone out during exams; my mind goes blank. _____

7. I feel extreme pressure to please others by doing well on exams. _____

8. If I'm honest, I'd have to admit that I really don't know how to study for tests. _____

9. I'd much rather write a paper or give a presentation than take an exam. _____

10. I usually fear that my exam grade will be lower than that of other students. _____

11. After taking an exam, I obsess on my performance, going over and over questions that I think I may have missed. _____

12. I convince myself that I'm not good at taking exams even though I often do fairly well on them. _____

If your score equals 49–60, you are a likely candidate for test anxiety. For suggestions on how to manage your anxiety, read on.

If you scored between 37 and 48, you have some signs of anxiety and may need help in managing your stress level.

If you scored 36 or below, you most likely experience a normal amount of anxiety and have already developed coping skills to help you.

Test anxiety—what is it? And, more importantly, does it affect you? While most people think of text anxiety as a negative, the truth is, it's natural to be anxious before, during, and even after an exam. Most everyone is. In fact, some anxiety is useful. The adrenaline rush that accompanies anxiety can keep you alert and focused.

But for some students test anxiety takes over and sabotages their efforts. They may say, "I knew it all before the test, but when I saw the questions, everything I knew vanished before my very eyes." These students experience fainting spells or even gastric distress that requires them to leave the testing room periodically. Some of them may be reacting to prior bad experiences with exams. Others may put intense pressure on themselves because they're perfectionists. Clearly, there's evidence from medical science that too much anxiety can work against you. Corticosterone, a hormone released during times of extreme stress, can actually impair your ability to retrieve information from long-term memory.[7] Regardless of the reason, the first part of the solution is understanding exactly what test anxiety is. It has four different, but related, components:[8]

> **cognitive aspects**—nonproductive thoughts that run through your head before, during, and after an exam ("I have to get an A on this test. If I don't, I'll flunk out of school.")

> **emotional aspects**—negative feelings you experience related to the exam (disappointment, frustration, sadness, and so on)

> **behavioral aspects**—observable indications of stress (fidgeting, drumming your fingers on the desk, walking quickly, and so on)

> **physiological aspects**—counterproductive physiological reactions (dry mouth, butterflies in your stomach, palpitations, a tension headache, lightheadedness, and so on)

Since you can't expect the tests you take in college to change for your sake—to alleviate your anxiety—the possibility for change must come from within *you*. Consider these suggestions as they relate to the four indicators of test anxiety.

Cognitive

> **Understand your testing strengths and challenges, based on your learning style.** Although research indicates that most students prefer multiple-choice tests over essay tests, you have your own strengths and preferences.[9]

> **Don't catastrophize!** Stop yourself from engaging in negative, unproductive self-talk. It's easy to imagine worst-case scenarios: "If I fail this exam, I'll lose my scholarship, and if I lose my scholarship, I won't be able to afford to go to college, and if I don't go to college, I'll probably end up as a homeless person, begging for change on the street." Negative thinking can easily spiral downward, and before you know it, you're thinking about major life catastrophes and the end of the world. Although some exams do have important outcomes, it's important to put things in perspective.

Emotional

> **Monitor your moods.** Your emotions fluctuate based on many factors; they vary by type, intensity, and timing.[10] If you eat well and get

[handwritten margin note:] If I flunk, I'll lose my scholarship!

[handwritten margin note:] These all sound like me!

[handwritten margin note:] catastrophize— good word!

enough sleep before an exam, your moods are more likely to be even-keeled than if you skip meals, ride the carbohydrate roller coaster, and pull all-nighters. An eight-hour sleep debt will cause your mood to take a nosedive.[11]

> **"Park" your problems if you can.** When you go into a store, you leave your car outside in the parking lot and come back to it when you're finished shopping. Think about how that analogy relates to taking a test. Focus on your work, and challenge yourself to do your best.

Behavioral

> **Relieve some stress with physical activity.** Expend some of that extra, pent-up energy before the exam. Sprint to class or take a walk to clear your head in the hour before the test begins.

> **"Step out of your life" by spending time outdoors.** Being in the outdoors is liberating. There's a big world out there; it's easy to forget that when you're spending large amounts of time in classrooms or at work.

Physiological

> **Teach yourself how to relax.** Relaxation training can be used to overcome test anxiety. As simple as it sounds, that may involve learning how to breathe. Watch a new baby sleep, and you'll see instinctive, deep, even breathing in which only the baby's stomach moves up and down. As adults, when we're anxious, we breathe rapidly and shallowly, which doesn't sufficiently oxygenate our brains.

> **Seek help from a professional.** An expert who works with anxiety-ridden college students can diagnose your problem and help you visualize success or take steps to overcome your fears.

> " Positive thinking will let you do everything better than negative thinking will."

Zig Ziglar, motivational speaker and author

I'll look up the campus number tonight.

During the Test: Focus and Work Hard

| ? challenge | " reaction | * insight | ! action |

Challenge: List five ways to focus and work hard during an exam. Choose methods that work well for you. List one other technique you've never tried that you suspect would help you.

Reaction: 1. _____

2. _____

3. _____

4. _____

5. _____

_____

Honestly, most people feel some twinge of anxiety about working a complex set of math problems on an exam. But if your level of anxiety interferes with your test success, you may suffer from math anxiety. One expert estimates that roughly 20 to 25 percent of college students are in that category.[12] Some estimates are that as many as 85 percent of college students in introductory math classes experience some degree of math anxiety.[13]

If you're one of them, admitting the problem is the first step. Next, it's important to understand how math anxiety can work against you during exams so that you can do something about it. The most effective strategies to cope are direct and uncomplicated.[14]

Think back; perhaps you can pinpoint where your fears began. It may have been a teacher or a class or a particular test. Experts believe math anxiety is learned, and that it's up to you to "unlearn" it.

Why and how does math anxiety affect people? Try this experiment: multiply 86 × 7. To arrive at the answer, you must first multiply 6 × 7, make note of the 2, and carry the 4. Then you must multiply 7 × 8 and add the 4 to arrive at 602. Notice the steps involved in this simple math problem. You have to keep certain numbers in your head while you continue to work through it, which is often the case with math. Your working memory allows you to pull it off.

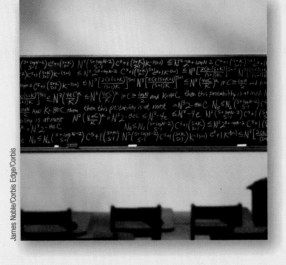

James Noble/Corbis Edge/Corbis

Working memory is your short-term, temporary-storage, limited-space memory. It's the memory you use to hold certain pieces of information—your brain's scratchpad— keeping them available for you to work with and update.[15] A task like multiplying 639 × 924 would be too much for most people's working memories, but some people have more capacity than others. Here's the kicker: Math anxiety actually eats up your working memory.

Why? Managing anxiety takes up working memory space that could be used to solve math problems. When you reduce your anxiety, you have more room to use your working memory productively. Math anxiety also causes people to take longer to do math and to make more mistakes.[16]

It's not the case that you use up your working memory because you think and think and think about how to work the problem and get the right answer. Instead, your working memory is hijacked by negative thoughts, causing you to choke.[17]

The solution? Practice for stressful exams under pressure. Set a timer, and tell yourself you must finish before it goes off. Make a game of it: for every question you miss on a practice exam, you must put a quarter in the kitty and pay off your friend, significant other, or mom. In other words, practicing in an equally stressful environment (or nearly so) can help during the actual test.[18] Since math anxiety is a learned fear, it can be unlearned.

During an exam, the heat is on! Do you use these strategies? If not, which ones can you incorporate to improve your performance? Put a plus sign (+) in front of each item you already do regularly and a (✔) in front of items you could start doing more regularly to improve your test-taking skills.

1. _____ **Jot down what you don't want to forget right away.** When you first receive your exam, turn it over and jot down everything you want to make sure you remember—mnemonic devices, charts you've created, acronyms—assuming, of course, that writing on the test is allowed. Some

students treat the exam itself as if it were a sacred document, but marking up your exam is usually allowed. Circle key words and strike through answers you eliminate.

2. _____ **Preview the exam.** Just going through all the questions may help you review terms you know. And you'll notice which questions are easier and which are harder right away. It's also likely that reading sample questions will trigger your memory and help you come up with information you need. After the first few minutes, you may relax a bit, and answers will come to you more easily.

3. _____ **Start with what you know.** Make sure you get credit for answers you know; don't waste time early on struggling with the more difficult questions. This strategy will also boost your confidence and help you relax. Studies show that running up against extremely difficult test questions at the beginning of a test can actually negatively impact accuracy on simpler questions later on.[19]

Just like my test! I always feel like this!

4. _____ **Manage your time.** Allocate your time based on the relative weight of the questions. Don't wrestle with one question for ten minutes when it's only worth one point. Go on to a more heavily weighted one.

5. _____ **Read directions thoroughly.** Misreading or skipping the directions altogether can be a lethal mistake. Remember that your instructor can't read your mind. ("But that's not what I meant!") Slow down and make sure you understand what you're being asked to do.

6. _____ **Read questions carefully.** Sometimes skipping over a word in the sentence (or filling one in where none exists) will cause you to jump to a false conclusion. Don't let your eyes (or your brain) play tricks on you!

7. _____ **If the test has a mixed format, complete the multiple-choice questions first.** Often instructors create exams using both *objective* (multiple-choice, true-false) questions and *subjective* questions (fill in the blank, essay). Generally, objective questions ask you to *recognize* answers from several alternatives, and subjective questions ask you to *recall* answers from memory. A multiple-choice question may remind you of something you want to include in an essay. Keep a pad of paper nearby during the exam. Jot down ideas as you answer multiple-choice questions. You'll feel more confident and do a better job if you keep a running list of ideas that occur to you as you go.

8. _____ **Explain your answer to an ambiguous question in the margin of your test.** You may point out a problem your instructor wasn't aware of or get partial credit.

9. _____ **Change your answers if you're convinced you're wrong.** Despite advice you've probably always received from teachers and classmates alike, changing answers when you're sure you've made a mistake is usually a good idea, not a bad one. In one study, less than 10 percent of students made changes that decreased their scores, while 74 percent made changes that increased their scores.[20]

Whoa!

10. _____ **Ask your instructor for clarification.** If the exam appears to have a typo or something seems wrong, ask your instructor or proctor to clarify for you. Of course, if you ask for the definition of a word that is a clue, you probably won't get an answer, but if you have a technical question or a question about the test-taking process, don't be afraid to ask.

11. _____ **Pay attention to "aha" moments.** Don't let your "aha" moments turn into "oh, no" moments. If you remember something you couldn't think of earlier, go back to that question and finish it right away.

12. _____ **Don't give in to peer pressure.** If, while you're working away, you look around and see that many students are leaving because they're already finished, don't panic. Take as much of the allotted time as you need. Everyone works at a different rate.

13. _____ **Save time for review.** When you're finished, go back over all your answers. Make sure you've circled the right letter or filled in the correct bubble. Be certain you've made all the points you intended to make in your essay. Look at your work critically, as if you were the instructor. Careless errors can be costly!

14. _____ **Be strategic about taking online tests.** Often tests posted online are timed. If you're taking a distance education course or a classroom course with an online test component, watch for e-mail announcements that tests have been posted, and note particular instructions. When will the test expire and disappear? Can you reenter the test site and redo answers before you hit the submit button? Can you take tests collaboratively with other students? With online tests, of course, the other recommendations in this chapter for true-false or multiple-choice tests apply as well.

> " We all have ability. The difference is how we use it."
>
> **Stevie Wonder, singer and composer**

Taking Objective Tests

? **challenge**   " **reaction**   * **insight**   ! **action**

Challenge: Are there specific ways to take objective tests? Identify five suggestions that apply to true-false and multiple-choice tests.

Reaction: 1. _____

2. _____

3. _____

4. _____

5. _____

Many of the exams you'll take in college will be objective, rather than subjective, tests. Let's examine the best strategies for taking objective tests.

True-False: Truly a 50–50 Chance of Getting It Right?

> Exam questions that test your recall are always more challenging than questions that test your recognition skills. T or F?
>
> *True?*

True-false tests may seem straightforward, but they can be tricky. You assume you have a 50–50 chance of answering correctly. But don't forget, you also have a 50–50 chance of answering incorrectly. Sometimes the wording of the statements makes the *process* of taking true-false tests more challenging than their *content*. Consider these helpful guidelines:

> **Watch for parts of statements that make the entire statement false.** The statement must be all true to be "true," and a few words may make an otherwise true statement "false." Here's an example:

> Derek Bok, who was president of Harvard University for thirty years, once said, "If you think education is expensive, try ignorance." T or F
>
> *Got me on this one!*

The main part of the statement is true; the quotation does belong to Derek Bok. Actually, however, Bok was president of Harvard from 1971 to 1991 (and returned to serve on an interim basis in 2006–2007), making the detail about him, buried in the middle of the sentence, false. The entire statement, then, must be marked "false."

> **Assume statements are true until you can prove them false.** Statistically, exams usually contain more true answers than false ones.

You have a better than 50 percent chance of being right if you guess "true." But teachers vary; yours may not follow the norm.

> **Watch for *absolutes*; they often make a statement false.** Words like always, never, and entirely often make otherwise true statements become false. "You can always get an A on an exam if you study for it." Unfortunately, no.

> **Look for *qualifiers*; they often make a statement true.** On the other hand, words like sometimes, often, and ordinarily often make statements true. "You can sometimes get an A on an exam if you study for it." Fortunately, yes.

> **Remember that negatives can be confusing.** Is this statement true or false? "Students who don't lack motivation are likely to excel." "Don't lack" really means "have," right?

Multiple *Choice* or Multiple *Guess*? Taking the Guess Work Out

Which of the following statements is (are) true?

    a. Richard Greener, who became Harvard's first African-American graduate in 1870, later became a lawyer, educator, and distinguished U.S. consul and diplomat.

    b. Elizabeth Blackwell, who graduated from Geneva Medical College in New York, was the first woman in the United States to earn a medical degree.

    c. Oberlin College was the first U.S. college to admit women and the last to admit African-American students on an equal footing with Caucasians.

    d. a and b

    e. a, b, and c

e?
Nope

Are multiple-choice tests difficult for you? Often what's difficult about multiple-choice tests has more to do with the structure of the test than the content. Studying for these tests requires a particular approach, and if you master the approach, you'll find taking multiple-choice tests to be much easier. You can actually think of them as variants of true-false tests. [The correct answer to the question, by the way, is (d).]

> **Think of answers on your own before reading your choices.** You may get hung up on the wording of an answer. Answer it on your own so that you can recognize it, no matter how it's worded. You may want to do this by covering up the alternatives initially, and then proceeding after you know what you're looking for. Sometimes the alternatives will differ by only one or two words. It's easy to become confused.

> **Line up your test and answer sheet.** This sounds like a simple suggestion, but getting off a line can be very disruptive when you have to erase like crazy and start over!

> **Determine the TPI (time per item).** Divide the number of questions by the allotted time. If there are seventy-five questions to answer in an hour, you know that you'll need to work faster than one question per minute. Remember to save some time for review and revision at the end.

This is a good strategy, if I can overcome my anxiety!

> **Don't decide answers based on the law of averages.** If you flip a coin three times, and it comes up "heads," most of us assume it's probably time for "tails" to come up next. Likewise, on exams, if you've answered (d) for three questions in a row, you may think it's time for an (a), (b), or (c). It may not be.

> **Using a process of elimination, guess if there's no penalty.** Some instructors subtract points for wrong answers, but if you do guess, guess wisely. And don't skip questions. Always mark something unless you're penalized for doing so. Take a look at this example:

Before you write an answer on an essay test, you should do all but the following:
 a. Read all the questions.
 b. Begin with the hardest question.
 c. Look at what the questions are asking you to do, specifically.
 d. Underline key words in the question.

You know that you should do (a). Reading all the questions before you start is a must. You know that option (d) makes sense, and so does (c). But you're not quite sure about option (b). You can eliminate (a), (c), and (d), so (b) must be the right answer based on a process of elimination. As you work, eliminate answers that you know are incorrect by marking through them ~~like this~~.

> **Look for highly similar pairs.** Sometimes two options will differ by a single word or the order of words. Often one of these is the right choice.

> **Look for contradictory answers.** If two statements are complete opposites, one of them is often the right choice.

> **Watch out for tricks intended to separate the prepared from the unprepared!** For example, avoid answers that are true in and of themselves, but not true when attached to the sentence stem or question being asked. For example, imagine this question option on a multiple-choice exam:

" I am easily satisfied with the very best."

Winston Churchill, Prime Minister of England (1874–1965)

Global warming is considered to be a serious issue among some scientists because:

    a. Former President Bill Clinton describes global warming as a greater threat to the world than terrorism.

While Clinton did espouse this view in a 2006 speech, it is not the reason for scientists' concern, so (a) isn't the correct answer.[21] Two other tips: generally, when numbers are in each alternative, choose numbers in the middle range. Choosing answers that are longer and more descriptive usually pays off, too.

> **Consider each answer as an individual true-false question.** Examine each option carefully, as if you had to decide if it were true or false, and use that analysis to make a decision about which option is correct.

> **Be wary of "all of the above" or "none of the above" options.** While instructors sometimes make these options the correct ones, it's also possible they resort to these options because making up enough plausible answers is challenging.

EXERCISE 9.2

Multiple Choice Test

Answer the following multiple-choice questions. Beneath each question, identify which of the principles of test-taking from this chapter you are using to identify the correct answer.

1. "I know of no more encouraging fact than the unquestionable ability of man to elevate his life by conscious endeavor." These words were said by:
   a. Bill Clinton
   b. Abraham Maslow
   c. Ronald Reagan
   d. Henry David Thoreau

   _____

2. Which of the following statements about the ACT test is not true?
   a. The ACT includes 215 multiple-choice questions.
   b. ACT results are accepted by virtually all U.S. colleges and universities.
   c. Students may take the ACT test as many times as they like.
   d. None of the above.

   _____

3. Which of the following suggestions about preparing for college is (are) true?
   a. Get involved in co-curricular activities in high school.
   b. Always take challenging courses that show your effort and ability.
   c. Involve your family in your decisions and preparation for college.
   d. Find a mentor, a teacher, or counselor who can give you good advice.
   e. All of the above.

   _____

[Answer key: (d), (d), (e)]

> **Watch for terminology that has been emphasized.** Look for key terms that appeared in your lecture notes and in chapters of the text. These words may provide links to the correct answer. Remember when taking multiple-choice tests that you are looking for the *best* answer, not simply the *right* one.[22]

CAREER OUTLOOK: *Beth Robinson, The College Board*

Used by permission of Beth Robinson

Q1: Since you're an executive with a national testing service, you're a good source of information on testing. According to media reports, the public appears concerned about how much today's college students are really learning. Are tests a good way to find out?

By some accounts, today's college students only skim the surface of what needs to be learned, rather than working to become truly educated. Tests can indeed be a good means to assess learning as long as they assess thinking and not just the recall of facts. If you've truly learned something, you should understand it fully enough to transfer the learning to new situations.

Q2: What constitutes a good test?

I consulted with other experts in the field, and here's what they say: A good test is one that fairly and consistently measures what it sets out to measure. A good test, therefore, always starts out with a clear sense of its intended purpose (to see if you know the rules of the road to obtain a driver's license, to see if you understand the main points covered in the chapter, and so forth). After the purpose

has been determined, a detailed set of specifications is agreed to. These specifications are the blueprint or recipe for the test. They say what material will be covered and in what detail, the kinds of questions, and how hard the questions will be. Every test—standardized or not—should be constructed based on focus, content, difficulty level, and most importantly the "goal" of the test: what it is supposed to measure.

Q3: In your view, why do some students choke on exams? Why do tests terrify them?

Sometimes students choke on exams because they simply aren't prepared. They hope they can fake it through whatever they don't understand well. Preparing well, of course, is the cure. Other students may be obsessed with getting good grades. They have high self-expectations and usually high expectations put on them from home. They need to calm down, put tests and life in perspective, and develop a healthy level of support. Other students do all the right things to prepare for tests, but they never really analyze what they're

studying, thus their depth of understanding may not hold up under the scrutiny of well-written tests. They have a history of poor test results that doesn't reflect their time investment, and that leads to fear at the mere mention of testing. These students could benefit by joining study groups and talking with teachers about what they've learned.

HOW WOULD *YOU* LIKE IT?

Have you ever considered a career in the nonprofit, as opposed to the for-profit, sector of the economy?

Facts to Consider[23]

Academic preparation required: Completion of a bachelor's degree is required and variable backgrounds are accepted, depending on the specific type of nonprofit organization and its mission.

Future workforce demand: Because of relatively low wages and high turnover, job prospects for the future are excellent.

Work environment: Those involved in advocacy, grant making, and civic organizations—nonprofits—affect many areas of our lives: politics, health, arts, religion, education, and social causes, for example. Typically,

nonprofits are run by a small core of paid staff, and whatever fees they charge for services (if any) must not exceed expenses. Most nonprofit employees work in a team environment (working with volunteers, for example) and have variable schedules. They believe in the causes for which their organizations stand, are challenged by the need to raise funds, and find their work rewarding.

Essential skills: communicating, fund-raising, being sensitive to social issues

Questions to Ponder

1. Do you have (or could you acquire) the skills this career requires?
2. Are you interested in a career like this? Why or why not?

For more career activities online, access the CourseMate via www.cengagebrain.com/shop/ISBN/0495906425 to do the Team Career exercises.

Short-Answer, Fill in the Blank, and Matching Tests

Short-answer tests are like essay tests, which we'll discuss shortly, in many ways. You're required to come up with an organized, well-thought-through answer on your own. But instead of a long essay, you only need to write a paragraph or two. Is that easier? It may be, but sometimes it's just as hard or harder to condense what you have to say about difficult concepts into fewer words. Generally, however, the suggestions for essay tests hold.

For fill in the blank tests, first think the statement through. What does it mean? Try inserting different words. Which one sounds best? Which one was used during lectures or appeared in the textbook? If one word looks awkward, try another one. Although it's not a completely reliable hint, look at the number of words, placement of spaces, and length of the space. If you don't know the exact terminology the question is looking for, insert descriptive words of your own. You may earn partial credit.

Matching tests require particular strategies, too. First of all, you must determine whether items should be used only once or if they can be reused. If it's not clear from the test directions, ask for clarification. Match the items you're certain about first and cross them out if once only is the rule. If you mismatch an item early on, the rest of your choices will be wrong, too.

Taking Subjective Essay Tests

> Essay Question: Please discuss the value of brain research in relation to our current knowledge of how learning takes place.

Essay questions are difficult for some students because details are required. Rather than being able to *recognize* the correct answer, you must be able to *recall* it totally from your own memory. Here are some recommendations you should consider:

> **Save enough time for essays.** If the test has a mixed format, it's important to save enough time to write well-thought-through essays. Often objective questions such as multiple choice or true-false only count a point or two, whereas essay questions often count into the double digits.

> **Read all the questions before you start.** To sharpen your focus and avoid overlap, give yourself an overview of all the questions before you start writing.

> **Make brief notes.** Somewhere on the exam or on scratch paper, write a brief plan for your responses to essay questions. A few minutes of planning may be time well spent. As you plan your answer, keep basic questions in mind—*who*, *what*, *when*, *where*, and *why*—as an organizing framework.

> **State your thesis up front.** How will you handle this question? What's your plan of attack? Your first paragraph should include your basic argument in a thesis statement.

> **Provide support for your thesis.** Writing an answer to an essay question requires you to make assertions. However, it's not enough that you assert things; you must try to prove that they are true. If your thesis asserts that college students cheat more today than they did when your parents went to college, you must present evidence—statistics, examples, or expert testimony—to demonstrate that what you're asserting is true.

> **Zero in on the verb.** The heart of an essay question is its verb. Take a look at this list and think about how each verb dictates what is required:

> **Analyze**—break into separate parts and examine or discuss each part

> **Compare**—examine two or more things, find the similarities and differences (usually you emphasize the similarities)

> **Contrast**—find the differences between two or more things

> **Critique, criticize, or evaluate**—make a judgment, describe the worth of something

> **Define**—provide the meaning (usually requires a short answer)

> **Describe**—give a detailed account, list characteristics or qualities

> **Discuss**—describe a cause/effect relationship, the significance of something, the pros and cons, or the role played by someone or something

> **Enumerate**—list qualities, characteristics, events, and so on

> **Explain**—similar to discuss

> **Illustrate**—give concrete examples

> **Interpret**—comment on, give examples, provide an explanation for, discuss

> **Outline**—describe the plot, main ideas, or organization of something

> **Prove**—support an argument with evidence from the text or class notes

> **Relate**—show the relationship or connection between two things

> **State**—explain in precise terms

> **Summarize**—give a condensed account of key points, reduce to the essential components

> **Trace**—describe a process or the development of something

> **Use terminology from the course.** Perhaps more than any other type of exam, an essay test allows you room to truly display your knowledge. Use the opportunity! Reflect new terms you have learned, and tie your answer directly to course content.

> **Rifle your answer, don't shotgun.** Here's an analogy: A shotgun fires many small metal pellets. A rifle fires a single bullet. When writing an essay answer, some students write down everything they know, hoping

"Knowing is not enough; we must apply. Willing is not enough; we must do."

Johann Wolfgang von Goethe, German writer and scholar (1749–1832)

This is something I've never even thought about. It's like a hint as to how to respond to the question!

Good analogy!

Think about your most challenging class this term. Identify one key challenge you face in this class that relates to this chapter. Now develop a step-by-step action plan to deal with this one challenge. For example, your action plan might look like this:

a. Reread the sections of the chapter on preparing for tests and test anxiety.
b. Meet with my professor to discuss my problems in her class.
c. Show her this action plan, and ask for her suggestions.
d. Keep a journal of my progress to note improvement and meet with her four more times this term.

This is what my list should be, I think.

Now do the same for your most challenging class.

1. _____
   _____

2. _____
   _____

3. _____
   _____

4. _____
   _____

that something will be correct. You may actually lose points by doing this. It's better to target your answer and be precise.

> **Generalize if you're unsure of small, exact details.** You can't quite remember, was it 1884 or 1894? The best idea is to write, "Toward the end of the nineteenth century" instead of choosing one of the two and being wrong.

> **Follow all the rules.** When answering an essay question, it's important to be as concise yet thorough as possible. Enumerate your ideas ("There are three major…"). Avoid slang ("Wordsworth elaborated…" not "Wordsworth jazzed up the poem."). Refer to researchers or authors or noteworthy people by their last names ("Jung wrote…" not "Dr. Carl Jung wrote…").

> **Watch your grammar.** The reason why its important, to do this, is because many student's dont and there answers are marked wrong. They wish they would of done better afterwards. You get the point.

> **Write an answer that corresponds to how much the question is worth.** It's important to be concise, but generally, if one essay answer is worth 10 points and another is worth 25 points, your instructor will expect you to write more for the question that's worth more. A more detailed, thorough response is what is called for.

> **Put down what you do know.** If you see a question you didn't predict, don't panic. If you've studied, you know something that might help give you partial credit even if you don't know the answer in full.

> **Proofread and make sure your handwriting is legible.** While most instructors will count the number of points you covered and use specific standards, grading essays is a slightly subjective process. That means instructors must use their own judgment. A good essay answer is taken less seriously if it's littered with mistakes or a real mess to read. This is

the real world; neatness counts. Anything you can do to create a positive impression may work in your favor.

> **If you run out of time, jot down any remaining points in the time that's left.** You may not get full credit, but partial credit is better than none.

> **Include a summary statement at the end.** Your essay answer should read like a real essay with an introduction, a body, and a conclusion. Don't just stop mid-sentence without wrapping things up.[24]

Don't Cheat Yourself!

What if you were in one of these situations? How would you respond?

> Many students in your communication major get through difficult exams by sharing answers via their cell phones. The professors never notice, and the courses aren't all that interesting anyway.

> A friend of yours sends herself an e-mail of all the names and dates she'll need to know for her history exams. With just one click on her smartphone she can call up whatever information she needs. "Try it," she says. "Everyone else does it, and you'll feel cheated if you don't cheat. If you don't do what other students do, you'll graduate with mediocre grades, and you'll never be able to compete for the jobs you've always wanted. Besides getting away with it here just helps prepare you for the business world where things are *really* cutthroat!"

> You hear about an online paper mill that will write your paper for you. For a set per-page price, they will even "doctor" each sentence so that the source can't be found on the Internet. You have four papers, a presentation, and an exam all due the same week, and one or two ghostwritten papers may cost you, but what choice do you have? That's not all that much considering the tips you make as a server. Hmm....

I've heard of people doing this kind of stuff for some of my classes.

How did you respond to these three scenarios? Are you aware of cheating schemes on your own campus? Could students you know be the ones these scenarios were written about? Notice that most of these students have practical-sounding reasons for what they are doing. If you want to cheat, it's not hard (in fact, technology makes it easy), and you can always blame someone else like your teachers or parents. What's the harm?[25] You get better grades, your parents are pleased, your teachers feel gratified, your school brags about the fine academic record of its students, and you pat yourself on your back for skillfully managing a very busy, demanding life. Everyone wins, right? Wrong.

According to some studies, fifty years ago, one in five college students admitted to cheating. Today's figures range from 75 to 90 percent. Here's some straight talk about cheating:[26]

1. **Remember that cheating snowballs.** What started as secretly pocketing some kid's CD or glancing at your neighbor's reading test in grade school turns into writing a math formula between your fingers or hiding the names of the constellations under your shirt cuff in middle school. Then these

juvenile violations turn into full-fledged, sophisticated infractions as students "download their workload" in high school and knowingly violate their school's Academic Integrity Policy in college. Where does it stop? With corporate scandal and newspaper headlines?

2. **Instead of saving time, cheating can take time.** Everyone is busy. Many students are working at jobs for pay in addition to taking classes. How can anyone get everything done that needs to get done? But instead of devising elaborate cheating schemes, which take time, why not just use that time to study?

3. **If you cheat now, you'll pay later.** Sooner or later, cheating will catch up with you. You may get past your history professor or your calculus instructor this time, and you may even get good grades on others' work you turn in as your own. But someday your boss will ask you to write something, or do some research, or use a skill a student is expected to have mastered in college, and you won't know where to start.

4. **If you do get caught, cheating may do you in.** Some students cheat because they know other students have gotten away with it. Cheating for them is a thrill, and not getting caught is like beating the system. Roll the dice and see what happens, they say. But you should know that professors are in the know these days. Academic hallways are abuzz with faculty talk about cheating. If you do get caught, your academic career may come to an abrupt halt.

5. **Cheating is just plain wrong.** You may or may not agree with this point, but it deserves some serious consideration. How would you like to be cheated out of money that's owed you or days off that are due you? The Golden Rule may sound old-fashioned, but the fact that it's been around for a long time with roots in a wide range of world cultures tells you something. "Intellectual Property" and "Academic Integrity" may not be as tangible as money you deserve or eight hours of free time, but they are increasingly protected by every college and university.

What are your personal ethical standards? Are you willing to cut corners? Would you cheat to achieve top grades in college? What kind of "devil's bargain" would you be willing to strike?

If you're tempted, remember this. Sooner or later, cheating costs you—big time! Don't cheat yourself out of learning what you need to learn in college. Learning is not all about *product*—the exams, papers, grades, and diplomas themselves—it's about *process*, too. The process involves gaining

> " For nothing can seem foul to those that win."

William Shakespeare, British poet and playwright (1564–1616)

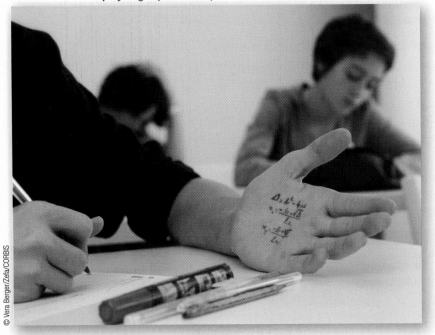

skills that will prepare you for life after college. That's a goal worth working toward.

You can't go through life devising elaborate schemes, or hiring someone else to do your work for you, or rationalizing about finding a way to beat the system because you're too busy to do your own work. Cheating in your college classes now just makes it that much easier to risk cheating your employer—and yourself—later on the job. Look through newspapers or watch the evening news to see who's been caught lately. It's a competitive world out there, but more and more companies find that having a good reputation, which comes from valuing integrity, is good business. Integrity starts now: *earn what you learn.*[27]

cheating is too easy— I'm a better pesron than that . . . and I have a lot of people looking up to me.

After the Test: Continue to Learn

| ? challenge | 66 reaction | * insight | ! action |

Challenge: What suggestions can you come up with for things to do after an exam—to help you remember the information, perhaps for a later exam or for another course, or do better next time?

Reaction: _____

After you finish an exam and get your results, you may be soaring or discouraged. Regardless, exams can be excellent learning experiences if you take these steps. Put a plus sign (+) in front of each item you already do regularly and a (✔) in front of items you could start doing more regularly to improve your test-taking skills.

discouraged! But I think I CAN DO THIS now.

1. _____ **Analyze your results.** Conduct a thorough analysis of your test results. For example, an analysis like this one might tell you what kinds of questions are most problematic for you.

Type of Question	Points Earned/Right	Points Deducted/Wrong	Total
Multiple Choice	32	3	35
Fill in the Blank	15	2	17
True-False	20	8	28
Essay	10	10	20
Total	77	23	100

Or analyze your results by examining lecture questions versus textbook questions to find out where to concentrate your efforts on future tests. Or do an analysis by chapter content to tell you where to focus your time when studying for the final exam.

Oops! I threw my test away immediately.

2. _____ **Read your instructor's comments and take them to heart.** After an exam, ask yourself: What was the instructor looking for? Was my writing ability critiqued? Does the test make more sense now than it did while I was taking it? Are there instructor's comments written on the test that I can learn from? What do the results of this exam teach me about preparing differently, perhaps, for the next test?

3. _____ **Explain your grade to yourself.** Where did you go wrong? Did you misread questions? Run out of time? Organize essay answers poorly? Does the grade reflect your effort? If not, why not? Did test anxiety get the better of you? On the other hand, if you studied hard and your grade reflects it, that's an explanation, too!

4. _____ **Be honest.** It's easy to get caught up in the blame game: "I would have gotten a better grade if the exam had been fairer, if the test had been shorter, if I'd had more time to study...." Your instructors have heard every excuse in the book. Of course, sometimes crises do overtake events. But rather than pointing fingers elsewhere if you're disappointed with your results, be objective and look at what *you* can do differently next time.

5. _____ **Make a specific plan for the next test.** Most courses contain more than one exam. You'll probably have an opportunity to apply what you've learned and do better next time.

6. _____ **Approach your instructor politely if you believe your exam has been mismarked.** Sometimes teachers make mistakes. Sometimes they're interrupted while grading and forget to finish reading an essay answer, or the answer key is wrong, or they miscalculate. Even if the scoring is correct, it may be a good idea to approach your instructor for help about how to improve your next test score.

7. _____ **Reward yourself for good (study) behavior.** After you've worked hard to prepare and the exam is over, reward yourself—take in a movie, go out with friends, do something to celebrate your hard work.[28]

©Larry Harwood Photography. Property of Cengage Learning.

" A man's errors are his portals of discovery."

James Joyce, Irish novelist (1882–1941)

VARK It!

Complete the recommended activity for your preferred VARK learning modality. If you are multimodal, select more than one activity. Your instructor may ask you to (a) give an oral report on your results in class, (b) send your results to him or her via e-mail, (c) post them online, or (d) contribute to a class chat.

Visual: Make a flow chart to show how you will proceed *before, during,* and *after* the next test in one of your more challenging classes. Personalize the chart to show exactly what you will actually do.

Aural: Talk to yourself as you study for an upcoming exam that will challenge your test-taking knowledge and skills. Ask yourself questions that you predict will appear on the exam and answer them aloud.

Read/Write: Write a press release describing your ideal performance on an upcoming exam. For example, "Midwestern first-year student aces exam by trying new study techniques" and then describe the new techniques used.

Kinesthetic: Construct a challenging practice test for an upcoming actual exam, and time yourself while taking it (to simulate the stress you'll face during the exam).

 challenge **reaction** ✳ **insight** ! **action**

Now What Do You Think?

1. At the beginning of this chapter, Joe Cloud, a frustrated and disgruntled college student, faced a challenge. Now after reading this chapter, would you respond differently to any of the questions you answered about the "FOCUS Challenge Case"? Knowing what you know now, how would you advise him? Write a paragraph ending to the story, incorporating your best advice.

2. Is test anxiety a problem for you? What are your reactions to taking tests in each of the four areas of test anxiety (Cognitive, Behavioral, Emotional, Physiological)?

3. Reflect on your own situation and answer the following questions. As you assessed your own test-taking strategies earlier in this chapter, how many checkmarks did you make for the suggestions on *before, during,* and *after* tests, indicating potential areas for improvement? Which of the suggestions from all three sections will you try to focus on in the future? What test-taking problems have you had in the past, and how will this information help you?

What did you **Learn?**

On a scale of 1 to 10, answer the following questions now that you've completed this chapter.

1 = not very/not much/very little/low   10 = very/a lot/very much/high

In hindsight, how much did you already know about this subject before reading the chapter?

    1 2 3 4 5 6 7 8 9 10

Can you answer these questions about taking tests more fully now that you've read the chapter?

1. **What are the four components of test anxiety?**

2. **Identify three hints to managing your time during tests.**

3. **Why are subjective (essay) tests often perceived to be more challenging than objective (true-false, multiple-choice) tests?**

How useful might the information in this chapter be to you? How much do you think this information might affect your success in college?

    1 2 3 4 5 6 7 8 9 10

How much do you think this information might affect your career success after college?

    1 2 3 4 5 6 7 8 9 10

How long did it actually take you to complete this chapter (both the reading and writing tasks)? _____ Hour(s) _____ Minutes

 Challenge Yourself Online Quiz. To find out just how much you've learned, access the CourseMate via www.cengagebrain.com/shop/ISBN/0495906425 to take the Challenge Yourself Online Quiz.

Take a minute to compare these answers to your answers from the "Readiness Check" at the beginning of this chapter. What gaps exist between the similar questions? How might these gaps between what you thought before starting the chapter and what you now think after completing the chapter affect how you approach the next chapter in this book?

You're about to discover . . .

✓ *What emotional intelligence is and how to improve it*

✓ *How EI relates to college success*

✓ *How to improve communication with people you care about*

✓ *How people manage conflict in five basic ways*

✓ *Why diversity makes a difference*

✓ *Why service-learning is valuable*

✓ *Why global learning is important*

©Larry Harwood Photography. Property of Cengage Learning.

READINESS CHECK | What do you **Know?**

Before beginning this chapter, take a moment to answer these questions. Your answers will help you assess how ready you are to focus.

1 = not very/not much/very little/low   10 = very/a lot/very much/high

How much do you *already* know?

Based on reading the "You're about to discover. . ." list and skimming this chapter, how much do you think you probably already know about this chapter's subject?

1 2 3 4 5 6 7 8 9 10

See if you can answer these questions about building relationships and valuing diversity *before* you read.

1. **What is emotional intelligence and how does it relate to college success?**

2. **Identify two characteristics of *productive* versus *destructive* conflict.**

3. **Describe three benefits of valuing diversity.**

How motivated are you to learn *more*?

In general, how motivated are you to learn more by reading this chapter?

1 2 3 4 5 6 7 8 9 10

How much do you think this information might affect your success in college?

1 2 3 4 5 6 7 8 9 10

How much do you think this information might affect your career success after college?

1 2 3 4 5 6 7 8 9 10

How ready are you to read *now*?

How ready are you to focus on this chapter—physically, intellectually, and emotionally? Circle a number for each aspect of your readiness to focus.

1 2 3 4 5 6 7 8 9 10

If any of your answers is below a 10, you might want to pay attention to whatever is distracting you before you start reading. For example, if you're feeling scattered, take a few moments to settle down and focus.

Finally, how long do you think it will take you to complete this chapter from start to finish?

_____ Hour(s) _____ Minutes

Kia Washington

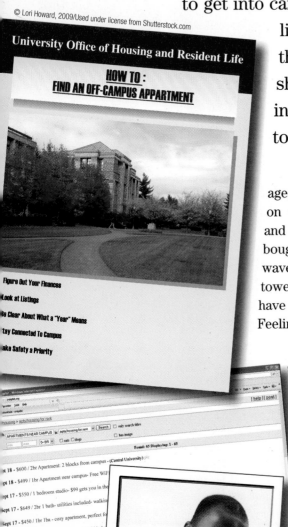

University Office of Housing and Resident Life

HOW TO :
FIND AN OFF-CAMPUS APPARTMENT

Figure Out Your Finances

Look at Listings

Be Clear About What a "Year" Means

Stay Connected To Campus

Make Safety a Priority

An emotional wreck. That's what Kia Washington was. Since she first arrived on campus, it seemed that everything had gone wrong. Her best friend, Alicia, had decided to go to a different school at the last minute, she was closed out of what probably would have been her favorite class—Introduction to Literature—and she hadn't been able to get into campus housing because of a computer mix-up. If she lived off campus now, the Housing Office told her, they'd guarantee her a room next term. To top it off, she was questioning her choice of classes and wondering why she couldn't decide on a major that would lead to a good job.

The apartment she'd managed to find close to campus on Craigslist was run down and barely affordable. She bought an inexpensive microwave, a mattress, and some towels, but she really didn't have the money to fix it up. Feeling completely alone and isolated, she found herself in tears more than once those first few weeks. Home, for all its faults, was looking better than it had when she lived there.

For most of her teenage years, Kia had lived with her Mom, who worked two jobs to support her and her brother, William. Although they got along well, her Mom was always too tired to do anything, it seemed, so they rarely spent much time together. And she never saw her father anymore. He'd remarried after the divorce and moved to another state. All through school, her family life had been rocky. Kia's parents, who probably cared for each other deep down, just couldn't get along. As a child, Kia sometimes retreated to her bedroom to wait out the arguments. Their decision to divorce five years ago had actually come as a relief.

Despite trouble at home, Kia had been a very good student in high school. Perhaps because home was a difficult place, she threw herself into her studies. She liked to read anything she could get her hands on, and doing homework had been a good escape. In fact, Kia kept to herself a good deal of the time. Meeting new people was one aspect of college she'd never really looked forward to. She preferred to just do her own thing, like listen to music by herself with her earplugs in between classes. Visiting the University Center to meet people and get connected wasn't something that interested her at all.

There really was only one other person that Kia cared about—Quentin. Throughout all of her high school years, Kia and Quentin had been inseparable. He was older than she was, and that was definitely part of the appeal. Quentin also happened to be smart, and he was the funniest person Kia knew. They spent most evenings on their cell phones, sometimes into the early morning hours. No wonder every member of the female species was after him or so it seemed to Kia. Luckily, he always told her that he wasn't in the market. But now that she'd gone off to college, she worried that it would become harder to keep him. Holding onto Quentin was her most important goal right now.

Most of the time, they got along really well, and fights were over quickly. Whenever a conflict came up, Kia exploded and Quentin just took it. He was the proverbial nice guy and she was—as her mother put it—moody. She often felt as

Q, where are you? I haven't heard from you...K

© Tiplyashin Anatoly, 2009/Used under license from Shutterstock.com

if she was on an emotional roller coaster, and her temper got the best of her. Trying to communicate her way through a disagreement never seemed worth it to Kia. She'd spit out a few rude comments and then walk away or hang up. Fortunately, Quentin never seemed to hold a grudge.

But last Thursday, they'd had the worst fight ever on the phone over something silly; she couldn't even remember what. Suddenly she heard herself yelling into the phone, saying things she knew she'd regret. Quentin managed to get the words "control freak" out, and then this time *he* hung up. She hadn't heard from him since. He didn't return voicemails or e-mails, and his text messages abruptly stopped. She found herself obsessing about him, not able to sleep well or eat much over the weekend, and she couldn't face going to her classes on Monday or Tuesday. By Wednesday, she was so sick with worry that she couldn't drag herself out of bed.

Why does this have to be so hard? Kia kept asking herself. She'd decided to go to college to make a better *future* for herself. But right now the most important thing she had to do was get through the *present. My life is a soap opera*, she thought. And to anyone watching right now, she was right.

Hi Kia!
1 message

Remember to call Mom tonight!

Michelle Washington <MWashington@googlemail.com>
To: kwashington@gmail.com

Sun, Aug 30 at 10:51 A

Hi Kia!

How is school going? It has been too long since we've heard from you.

William misses you and wants to know when you're coming to visit. How are things with you an Quentin?

Give us a call once in a while!

Love,

Mom

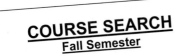

COURSE SEARCH
Fall Semester

Course / Description / Information	Call #	Status	Days	Time	Instructor
	47395	CLOSED	TR	8:00 AM - 9:15 AM	REED, PATRICIA
5 English Lecture		Max: 24			
o Literature		Enrolled: 24			
3:0		Waitlist: 0			
of Letters, Arts & Sciences					
5. Introduction to Literature. Fundamental literary of poetry, drama and fiction. This course is a site to all other literature courses.					

University Hall 115

What Do You Think?

1. How would you characterize Kia's adjustment to college? Identify five specific problems described in this case study that could interfere with her college success.

2. To have done so well in school, Kia must be an intelligent person. But is her emotional quotient (EQ) different from her intelligence quotient (IQ)? Why or why not?

3. Kia's relationship with Quentin is the most important one in her life. What is she doing to contribute to the problems in the relationship? Will the relationship survive? If so, what would it take?

4. Identify three things Kia should do to get her college success and her life on track.

The Heart of College Success

College is a time of transition; it can be an emotionally turbulent time that will require you to make some major adjustments in your life.

Here's a fundamental truth you may not have thought about: College isn't just about your head. Yes, academics are the reason you're in college, but your heart plays a critical role in your success, too. From friends to romantic partners, how you handle relationships can make or break you academically.

Could this be me?? Emotional reactions to troubling circumstances have the raw potential to stop you dead in your tracks. Some students, for example, have the *academic* skills required for success, but *nonacademic* issues can interfere. There's no doubt about it: How you manage your emotions and respond to stressful situations will impact your college success.

In college and in life, your EQ (emotional quotient), or *emotional intelligence*, can be just as important as your IQ (intelligence quotient). Studies show that first-year students often feel overwhelmed and lonely. Begin now to refine the emotional skills you'll need to face whatever challenges come your way.

EXERCISE 10.1

How Would You Respond?

Read these five scenarios and identify your most likely reactions.[1]

Hmm, let me try this . . .
1. a

1. You peer over a classmate's shoulder and notice she has copied your online response from a class chat and submitted it as her paper in the course, hoping the professor won't notice. What do you do?
   a. Tell the student off to set the record straight, right then and there.
   b. Tell the professor that someone has cheated.
   c. Ask the student where the research for the paper came from.
   d. Forget it. It's not worth the trouble. Cheaters lose in the end.

2. You're riding on a plane that hits a patch of extreme turbulence. What do you do?
   a. Grab hold of the person in the next seat and hold on for dear life.
   b. Close your eyes and wait it out.
   c. Read something or watch the movie to calm yourself until things improve.
   d. Panic and lose your composure.

2. b

3. You receive a paper back in your toughest course and decide that your grade is unacceptable. What do you do?
   a. Challenge the professor immediately after class to argue for a better grade.
   b. Question whether or not you're really college material.
   c. Reread the paper to honestly assess its quality and make a plan for improvement.
   d. Deemphasize this course and focus on others in which you are more successful.

3. d

4. While kidding around with your friends, you hear one of them tell an offensive, blatantly racial joke. What do you do?
   a. Decide to ignore the problem and thereby avoid being perceived as overly touchy.
   b. Report the behavior to your residence hall advisor or an instructor.
   c. Stop the group's conversation. Make the point that racial jokes can hurt and that it's important to be sensitive to others' reactions.
   d. Tell your joke-telling friend later that racial jokes offend you.

4. d

5. You and your romantic partner are in the middle of a heated argument, and tempers are flaring. What do you do?
   a. Stop, think about what you're trying to communicate, and say it as clearly and neutrally as possible.
   b. Keep at it because if the issue generated that much emotion, it must be important to get to the bottom of it.
   c. Take a twenty-minute time out and then continue your discussion.
   d. Suggest that both of you apologize immediately and move on.

5. b.

Perhaps you've found yourself in settings such as those described in Exercise 10.1. You might need more actual details to make the best choice in these five scenarios, but according to some experts, choice (c) is the most emotionally intelligent one in each case. Do you agree? How do *you* make decisions such as these? What constitutes an emotionally intelligent response?

What Is Emotional Intelligence?

? **challenge** **❝ reaction** **✱ insight** **❗ action**

Challenge: Have you ever heard the term emotional intelligence? How would you define it?

Reaction: _____

©Larry Harwood Photography. Property of Cengage Learning.

Many experts believe that intelligence is multifaceted. Rather than a narrow definition of intelligence, they believe in Multiple Intelligences: Linguistic, Logical-Mathematical, Spatial, Kinesthetic, Musical, Interpersonal, Intrapersonal, and Naturalistic.[2] Emotional intelligence may well be a combination, at least in part, of *intrapersonal* and *interpersonal* intelligences.

Emotional intelligence is a set of skills that determines how well you cope with the demands and pressures you face every day. How well do you understand yourself, empathize with others, draw on your inner resources, and encourage the same qualities in people you care about? Emotional intelligence involves having people skills, a positive outlook, and the capacity to adapt to change. Emotional intelligence can propel you through difficult situations. The bottom line? New research links emotional intelligence to college success, and learning about the impact of EI in the first year of college helps students stay in school.[3]

As you read about the five scales of emotional intelligence, begin assessing your own competence in these areas. As each scale is introduced, ask yourself whether you agree or disagree with the sample statement presented as it pertains to you.[4]

Intrapersonal Skills (Self-Awareness)

Hemera Technologies/Jupiter Images

"It's hard for me to understand the way I feel." Agree or disagree?

To what extent are you in tune with your emotions? Do you fully realize when you're anxious, depressed, or elated? Or do you just generally feel up or down? Are you aware of layers of emotions? Sometimes we show *anger*, for instance, when what we really feel is *fear*. (For example, you might scream at your brother in anger when you're actually really afraid he'll embarrass you in front of your friends.) Are you emotionally self-reliant, rather than emotionally dependent on others? Do you realize that no one else can truly make you happy, that you are responsible for creating your own emotional states? Do you set goals that relate to things *you* value and work toward achieving them? How well do you understand yourself and what makes you tick?

Interpersonal Skills (Relating to Others)

Hemera Technologies/Jupiter Images

"I'm sensitive to the feelings of others." Agree or disagree?

Are you aware of others' emotions and needs? Do you communicate with sensitivity and work to build positive relationships? Are you a good listener? Are you comfortable with others, and do you have confidence in your relationships with them?

Stress Management Skills

Hemera Technologies/Jupiter Images

"I feel that it's hard for me to control my anxiety." Agree or disagree?

Can you productively manage your emotions so that they work *for* you and not *against* you? Can you control destructive

> **"** Our emotions are the driving powers of our lives."
>
> **Earl Riney, American clergyman (1885–1955)**

emotions? Can you work well under pressure? Are you in control, even when things get tense and difficult?

Adaptability Skills

"When trying to solve a problem, I look at each possibility and then decide on the best way." Agree or disagree?

Are you flexible? Do you cope well when things *don't* go according to plan? Can you switch to a new plan when you need to? Do you manage change effectively? Can you anticipate problems and solve them as they come up? Do you rely on yourself and adapt well?

General Mood

"I generally expect things will turn out all right, despite setbacks from time to time." Agree or disagree?

Are you optimistic and positive most of the time? Do you feel happy and content with yourself, others, and your life in general? Are you energetic and self-motivated? Do people tell you you're pleasant to be around?

From EQ-i: Post Secondary version. Reprinted by permission.

Emotional intelligence and its effects reverberate throughout our lives. For example, researchers study related concepts: "hardiness," "resilience," and "learned optimism."[5] Some people are more resistant to stress and illness. Hardy, resilient, optimistic people are confident, committed to what they're doing, feel greater control over their lives, and see hurdles as challenges. Emotional intelligence is part of the reason why.

Look up these words!

Emotional intelligence and its five scales are important in all aspects of life, including your future career.[6] When *Harvard Business Review* first published an article on the topic in 1998, it attracted more readers than any article in the journal's previous forty years. When the CEO of Johnson & Johnson read it, he ordered copies for the company's 400 top executives worldwide.[7]

Why? Emotional intelligence is a characteristic of true leaders. Immediately after the first shock of the September 11, 2001, tragedy, the world tuned in to a press conference with New York's Mayor Rudy Giuliani. He was asked to estimate the number of people who had lost their lives in the World Trade Center collapse that day, and his reply was this: "We don't know the exact number yet, but whatever the number, it will be more than we can bear." In that one sentence, Giuliani demonstrated one of the most important principles of true leadership. Leaders inspire by touching the feelings of others.[8]

Can Emotional Intelligence Be Improved?

Everyone wants well-developed emotional intelligence, but how do you get it? Can EI be learned? While researchers admit that genes definitely play a role, most experts believe that emotional intelligence can be increased. One of the most convincing pieces of evidence is from a study that followed a cohort of

Robert Recker/Crush/Corbis

Call next week???

students over seven years. Students assessed their emotional intelligence, selected particular competencies to strengthen, and then each created an individual plan to develop them. Seven years later, their competencies remained high.[9]

If you believe what this chapter says about the importance of emotional intelligence and college success, you're probably asking yourself what you can do about it. Are the skills related to emotional intelligence something *you* can work to improve?[10] And if so, how?

Seek honest input from others. It's hard to be objective about yourself. But it is possible to tap some of that necessary objectivity from those who interact with you regularly. How do they see you? Use other people as coaches to help you see which aspects of your emotional intelligence need strengthening.

Find an EI mentor. A mentor on the job is someone who's older and more experienced than you are and can help you navigate your way through tough problems and manage your career. Mentors help, and an EI mentor—someone with finely honed EI skills you admire—can provide you with invaluable advice about handling challenging emotional situations.

Complete an assessment tool. Other than just feeling up or down, or reflecting on how you handled problems when they came up, is there a way to know more about your own level of emotional intelligence? The oldest and most widely used instrument to measure emotional intelligence is the Emotional Quotient Inventory, the EQ-i, from which the sample statements for the five scales we have been discussing come. It was the first instrument of its kind to be published and the first to be validated by psychologists in the well-respected *Mental Measurement Yearbook* (1999).[11] The instrument asks you to respond to various statements by indicating that they are "very seldom true of me" to "very often true of me," and the results provide you with a self-assessment of your emotional intelligence on each of the five major scales and further subscales.

As a part of the course for which you're using this textbook, you may have an opportunity to complete the EQ-i or an equivalent instrument. Check your campus's Counseling Center, too, to see if it offers EI assessment tools for students. You can also locate plenty of informal instruments online. They may not be valid, however, so be cautious about fully trusting their results.

Work with a counselor to learn more. Some areas of emotional intelligence may be too challenging to develop on your own. You may need some in-depth, one-on-one counseling to work on areas that need enrichment. Recognize that doing so isn't a stigma. Instead, you are taking advantage of the resources available on your campus and maximizing the potential for growth that can come during your college years.

Be patient with yourself. Learning to become more empathetic or more attuned to a friend or romantic partner's emotions in a close relationship aren't skills you can enhance overnight using cookbook techniques. Building emotional skills is a gradual process that involves awakening insights, acting on them, and noting the results over time.

After the Korean War, the U.S. Army's chief psychiatrist studied the psychological warfare used against 1,000 American prisoners of war who had been kept at a North Korean camp. He made a startling discovery: negativity kills.[12]

The prisoners had not been treated cruelly. They were given food, water, and shelter. They hadn't been tortured, yet many American soldiers died in the camp. They weren't surrounded by barbed wire and armed guards, yet no one ever tried to escape. Instead, many of them turned against each other or formed relationships with their North Korean guards, and when they were finally freed, many didn't even bother to call home when given the opportunity to let their loved ones know they were alive.

Many of these men died of extreme hopelessness caused by a total removal of emotional support. Soldiers were rewarded for informing on one another and required to stand up in groups of their peers and tell all the bad things they had ever done, as well as the good things they should have done. All positive letters from home were withheld, but negative ones telling of relatives passing away or wives divorcing their husbands were delivered right away. Even notices of overdue bills from collection agencies were passed along. Eventually, many of these American prisoners simply gave up. They died of "give up-itis," as they called it, raising the overall death rate in the camp to 38 percent—the highest American POW death rate in U.S. history.

The record of what happened raised this fundamental question, described in the *New York Times* and *Wall Street Journal* bestseller *How Full Is Your Bucket?* If negativity can have such a devastating impact, what can positivity do? That's where the analogy of buckets and dippers begins. Most of us will never endure the kind of psychological warfare these soldiers did, but all of us can examine the negativity we inflict on others, and by contrast, the positivity we can bring to others' lives.

How Full Is Your Bucket? by Tom Rath and Donald Clifton claims that each of us has an invisible bucket; we function at our best when our buckets are full. We each also have an invisible dipper. In every interaction, we use our dipper to fill others' buckets *or* to dip from them. The principle of the book is simple; following its advice, however, is challenging. *How Full Is Your Bucket?* makes these five recommendations:

1. **Dip less.** Get in the habit of listening to yourself. Are your words cynical, insensitive, or critical? If so, push the pause button and rephrase what you're trying to communicate. Keep track by scoring your interactions as positive or negative, and set a goal of five positive exchanges for every negative one.

2. **Bring out the best.** By filling others' buckets, we set off a chain reaction that comes back to us. Imagine a scenario in which something really annoys you about your romantic partner, and you find yourself being critical much more often than you should be. If you make a conscious decision to focus instead on all the good things instead of the one bad thing, you'll have a positive impact on the relationship, and your partner will begin responding more positively to you. Watch and see!

3. **Make more than one best friend.** Who ever said people are only allowed one best friend? High-quality relationships improve the quality of your life. Bucket filling from the start is the way to begin a new best friendship, and regular bucket filling is how to keep it.

4. **Fill a drop at a time.** Giving a small unexpected gift is a great way to fill someone else's bucket. It needn't be much: a token, a trinket, a compliment, or a thank you. Put your positive comments in an e-mail or a note to make them last. Make a habit of giving "drops."

5. **Apply the Golden Rule backwards.** Rather than "Do unto others as you would have them do unto you," try this: "Do unto others as *they would have you do unto them.*"

How full is your bucket? In your interactions, are you filling or dipping? Building a relationship is a process that occurs one drop at a time.

Keep at it: It's safe to say that EI is something all of us can strengthen, if we're willing to work at it. Relationships that are important to us require the best of our emotional intelligence skills. In fact, studies show that the way in which we provide emotional support is strongly related to relationship satisfaction.[13]

This is making me think . . .

BOX 10.1 # What Is This Thing Called Love?

Ah, romance....Relationships—they're what make the world go 'round. Relationships count, and for many of us, romantic ones count as much or more than others.

Most of us have strong ideas about what we want in someone else: good looks, intelligence, or honesty, for example. But if your parents, a friend, or a previous partner were to put your profile on a matchmaking website, what would they say about you? What qualities do you bring to a relationship—loyalty, humor, caring?

Anthropologist Helen Fisher defines love in ways you may not have thought about before: the psychological and physiological characteristics of love. Interestingly, Fisher found that neither age, gender, sexual orientation, religion, nor ethnic group made a difference. Love is love, she found. Participants in the study shared characteristics such as these five.[14]

1. *Extreme energy.* When you're in love, your heart pounds, you are breathless, you feel as if you could "leap over tall buildings with a single bound." Your brain is "hopped up" on chemicals, and you have energy to spare.

2. *Imagined betterment.* Although most people in love can easily point out faults in their romantic partners, they tend to persuade themselves that these characteristics are unimportant, or even charming.

3. *Interfering thoughts.* People in love spend huge amounts of time thinking about their partners. No matter how hard they try to think about other things, their thoughts return to him or her. In some studies, participants report that they spend more than 85 percent of their waking hours thinking about their romantic partners.[15]

4. *Mood swings.* Lovers soar with ecstasy and sink to the depths of despair, based on their romantic partners' responses. "She loves me; she loves me not" is a realistic obsession.

5. *Hypersensitivity.* People in love continuously watch and wait for clues about how their romantic partners feel about them. They hover by the phone or computer, and search endlessly for a meaningful sign, reinterpret a facial expression, or translate a word or phrase into relational terms.

When you're newly infatuated with someone, your brain has elevated levels of dopamine and norepinephrine, chemicals that result in the characteristics just explained. Scientists also believe that lovers have lower levels of serotonin in their brains. These three chemicals appear to be the physiological basis for passionate, exhilarating, romantic love. However, later in life, after years of marriage, perhaps, these chemicals are overtaken by others. None of us could tolerate a continuous rush of stimulating chemicals and their intense effects forever! Unbridled passion and wild ecstasy are replaced by feelings of contentment and security. However, many couples remain "in love" for twenty, thirty, fifty, or more years. They may even describe themselves as more in love than when they first met. In one remarkable study, couples married more than twenty years rated themselves higher on romantic love than couples married only five years. Researchers noted that some long-term couples' results looked like those of high school seniors![16]

The chemistry of love points to a truth worth noting: Love is not just an emotion. Chemicals wax and wane; emotions come and go. Commitment goes beyond attraction, beyond emotion. It's a *decision* to invest—and continually *reinvest*—in a relationship. As Fisher writes, "Don't assume the relationship will last forever; build it one day at a time. And never give up."

"Eighty percent of life's satisfaction comes from meaningful relationships."

Brian Tracy, personal and career success author

©Larry Harwood Photography. Property of Cengage Learning.

How Do You Relate?

Are you are involved in an intimate relationship right now? If so, which of these ten statements describe it? Put a checkmark in the "yes" or "no" column for each one.

	Yes	No
1. My partner is a very good listener.	_____	_____
2. My partner does not understand how I feel.	_____	_____
3. We have a good balance of leisure time spent together and separately.	_____	_____
4. We find it easy to think of things to do together.	_____	_____
5. I am very satisfied with how we talk to each other.	_____	_____
6. We are creative in how we handle our differences.	_____	_____
7. Making financial decisions is not difficult.	_____	_____
8. Our sexual relationship is satisfying and fulfilling.	_____	_____
9. We are both equally willing to make adjustments in the relationship.	_____	_____
10. I can share feelings and ideas with my partner during disagreements.	_____	_____

Now continue reading to find out how other couples responded in a national study.

Communicating in Important Relationships

Think of all the kinds of communicating you do—and with whom. Classmates and instructors deserve your best communication, even when you disagree with the perspective they're voicing in class. You may see your instructors as intimidating or helpful, but you'll need to make the first move to get to know them, rather than the other way around. Take the initiative to meet them during their office hours and bring up points from class that you'd like to know more about. You have many classmates, and your instructor may not be able to pay attention to each individual student. It'll be your job to go to your professor to get the clarification you need. You'll want to get to know your classmates, too, to make your classes more engaging. You're likely to work with them on class projects. Do some of your best communicating here. Chances are your group-mates—and the group's grade—will depend on it. Participate, do your part, and keep your word. No one will appreciate it if you promise to come to every planning meeting outside of class and turn out to be a no-show every week. Group work in your college classes is a great place to practice

Walt Disney/courtesy Everett Collection

> Piglet sidled up to Pooh from behind. "Pooh!" he whispered." "Yes, Piglet?" "Nothing," said Piglet, taking Pooh's paw. "I just wanted to be sure of you."
>
> **A. A. Milne, British author (1882–1956)**

Over the course of your college career, you'll take classes from excellent teachers, mediocre ones, and less preferable ones. What role does the relationship you have (or don't have) with your instructor play in your toughest class? Relationships with teachers have different power dynamics than other relationships in your life. Unlike your friends or romantic partners, instructors give grades (although students *earn* them) that can have long-term, high-stakes impact. Is the relationship you have with the instructor in your most challenging class as productive as it could be? Perhaps it is, but if not, try doing something about it.

Relationships of any kind have two participants. The only person you can control is yourself; however, your choices can affect the other person's actions. What can you do to make the relationship as productive as possible? Ask yourself these questions:

1. What behaviors or habits do I exhibit in this class that might be adversely affecting my relationship with my instructor?
2. What could I do instead to draw a more positive reaction?
3. If I were an instructor, what kinds of behaviors would I expect from students?
4. Can students help instructors become better teachers?
5. Can I make changes in my behavior that might improve my own learning?

Try a new set of behaviors in this class for a month, and then come back to this exercise and note the results you have observed.[17]

the exact skills that will be required of you in the workplace. Whatever the type of important relationship—friends, family, classmates, or instructors—how you communicate is vital. Some would go so far as to make this broad generalization: the quality of your communication directly affects the quality of your life.

Beyond friends, family, classmates, and instructors, think about how very important communication is in romantic relationships. If you're in a romantic relationship right now, you may have wondered from time to time if it's truly a good one. What does it take? A study of 21,501 couples across the country compared the answers of the happiest couples to those of the unhappiest.[18] The areas of maximum difference between the two groups were found on responses like the following.

I'm sensitive to the feelings of others sometimes, but I'm not always sensitive enough with Quentin . . .

	Happy Couples	Unhappy Couples
1. My partner is a very good listener.	83%	18%
2. My partner does not understand how I feel.	13%	79%
3. We have a good balance of leisure time spent together and separately.	71%	17%
4. We find it easy to think of things to do together.	86%	28%
5. I am very satisfied with how we talk to each other.	90%	15%
6. We are creative in how we handle our differences.	78%	15%
7. Making financial decisions is not difficult.	80%	32%
8. Our sexual relationship is satisfying and fulfilling.	85%	29%
9. We are both equally willing to make adjustments in the relationship.	87%	46%
10. I can share feelings and ideas with my partner during disagreements.	85%	22%

[Note: numbers do not total 100 percent because of the study's design.]

Look at the highest percentages in the "Happy Couples" column. These results point to an all-important truth: Communication is at the heart of every quality relationship.

In relationships we sometimes communicate in ways that aren't productive. The work of communication specialist Deborah Tannen focuses on miscommunication between men and women. Remember the *Seinfeld* episode in which George's date asks him if he'd like to come up to her apartment for coffee when he takes her home? George completely misses the point and replies that he never drinks coffee late at night. She meant, "Would you like to continue our date?" but he took the question at face value. Later he kicked himself for being so slow-witted. Trying to "listen between the lines" in romantic relationships is a challenge. We say one thing and mean another, or we hope a partner can read our minds and then resent it when they do.

The classic work of psychiatrist Dr. George Bach and others can help relational partners communicate more openly and honestly and meet conflict head on. He described types of "crazymaking" that cause communication breakdowns and, at their worst, relationship failures. See if you recognize people you know—romantic partners or even friends—in these six types of crazymakers.[19]

> The TRAPPER: *Trappers* play an especially dirty trick by requesting a desired behavior from the other person and then attacking when the request is met.

> The BLAMER: *Blamers* are more interested in whose fault the problem is than they are in solving it.

> The MINDREADER: *Mindreaders* try to solve the problem by telling their partners what they're really thinking.

> The GUNNYSACKER: *Gunnysackers* save grudges. They fill up proverbial gunnysacks, and then dump all the contents on their partners at some "opportune" moment.

> The HIT AND RUN FIGHTER: *Hit and run fighters* attack and then leave the scene quickly without giving their partners a chance to explain or defend themselves.

> The "BENEDICT ARNOLD": *Benedict Arnolds* like to stir up trouble behind the scenes by playing "let's you and someone else fight."

I've definitely been all these things with Quentin . . .

If you think you're a victim of crazymaking communication, what should you do about it? Try these five suggestions:

1. **Step back and try to figure out the situation.** Is the crazymaker making a request of you (to be more open, trustworthy, or responsible, for example)? If so, is the request reasonable, and are you willing?

2. **Become aware of the feelings behind the crazymaking.** Is your partner feeling powerless or vulnerable, for example?

3. **Try not to respond with anger, even though it's difficult.** Piling more wood on the fire certainly won't help to put it out.

4. **Check out your assumptions with the other person.** Ask, "Are you feeling frustrated? Is that what this is about? What would you like me to do?"

5. **Try and reach a mutually agreeable solution by changing communication patterns that aren't productive.**

Once you've identified any unproductive communication habits, you can work on improving your skills as well as your relationships. The following five suggestions are a place to start. These recommendations work for any type of close relationship—friends or romantic partners.

Choose wisely. When it comes to selecting someone you may want to build a future with, as a friend or romantic partner, don't settle. Seek someone who shares your values, whose background is compatible, but who is different enough to make life interesting. Choose someone who values productive communication as much as you do.

Let go of unrealistic expectations. Remember that although people live happily ever after in movies, in truth, all relationships have ups and downs. We're human; we make mistakes as communicators. Metaphorically speaking, one blip on the screen doesn't necessarily indicate that the whole program should be scrapped. Conversely, working on problems together strengthens your relationship.

Engage in preventative maintenance. You take your car in for a checkup every so many thousand miles to prevent major breakdowns; it's a good idea to do the same with relationships you care about. Keep the channels of communication open, and talk about small issues before they escalate into colossal ones. Make deposits into a positive "memory bank." Experts say that doing interesting new things together—going on a vacation, for example—can trigger renewed romantic love.[20]

Monitor your own communication. You can't change someone else, but you can change your own communication: "Although it takes two to have a relationship; it takes only one to change its quality."[21] Eliminate an annoying behavior or modify your conflict style. Be more tolerant of someone else's communication faults, too. Communicate your needs; relationships aren't guessing games. Check, don't assume. Remember that listening is one of the highest compliments you can pay someone.

Take the high road. Don't give in to momentary temptations that may lead to regret and possibly the end of a relationship with great potential. Without trust as the bedrock of your communication, little else matters. If you've promised yourself to someone, keep your promise.[22]

I wish I'd known more about this sooner . . .

Managing Conflict: Life Is Not a Sitcom

Interesting . . . I usually only think about conflict in terms of who wins and who loses.

> I'm very loyal in relationships. Even when I go out with my mom I don't look at other moms."

Garry Shandling, comedian

Research documents the far-reaching effects of bad relationships. They can hurt your job performance, your finances, your physical and mental health—even your life span.[23] Conflict with romantic partners, or with anyone you're in close proximity to—roommates, for example—can bring on major stress that affects your academic performance, not to mention your overall happiness.[24]

Unfortunately, movies and television often communicate—subtly or not so subtly—that conflict can be resolved by the end of the show. Just lighten up or settle down and you can resolve almost any problem. And if you can't, just swallow, take a deep breath, and move on. But life isn't like that, nor should it be. Managing the conflict in your life takes time, energy, and persistence. It requires understanding your natural tendencies, considering why you communicate as you do, and making productive choices as a communicator.

If you've ever monitored yourself during a particularly heated conflict, you may remember doing something like this: yelling in anger at someone at the top of your lungs, being interrupted by a phone call and suddenly communicating calmly and quietly to the caller, and then returning to the original shouting match after you hang up.

Why? We make *choices* as communicators. Sometimes our choices are productive ones, and sometimes they aren't. It's important to remember that we *do* choose what we say and how we behave. Our choices affect both the *process*—how things go during the conflict—and the *product*—how it turns out in the end. Negative choices produce destructive conflict that includes personal attacks, name calling, an unwillingness to listen, or the crazy-making strategies described earlier in this chapter. Positive choices are much more likely to bring productive conflict that helps us learn more about ourselves, our partners, and our relationships.

Ron Nickel/Design Pics/Corbis

Just like healthy relationships, unhealthy ones have identifying characteristics, too. While every relationship can teach us something important about future ones, some red flags are worth our attention. Here are three to think about.[25] If you see these danger signals, it may be time to end the relationship, or, if you and your partner both agree, to devote more time and energy toward improving it.

Danger signal 1: "All we ever do is fight!" This point seems obvious, but sometimes it's so obvious it's overlooked. All some couples talk about is how much they disagree or how wrong things are between them. As a general rule, if 50 percent or more of what you talk about is devoted to managing conflict, sit up and take notice. Fifty percent isn't a hard and fast number, of course. But when so much of your time is spent walking on eggshells to avoid conflict, airing your differences during conflict, or smoothing things over afterward, there's little time or energy left for other topics.

Danger signal 2: "Let's dig in deeper!" Can you imagine anyone saying something like this: "We've been going out for two years now, but we're just not getting along. I think if we got engaged, we'd both be more committed." Or consider a couple who is unhappily married, who say, "Maybe we should have a baby. That would bring us closer together." Whoa!

Statements such as these are danger signals. Relationships should escalate (or reach the next level of commitment) when we're satisfied with them, when we find them fulfilling, and when we are ready to take the next step together. Trying to force intimacy doesn't work. While this point makes sense intuitively, it's surprising how many couples fall into this trap.

Danger signal 3: "This relationship just isn't worth it!" From two unique individuals, a third entity—a unique relationship—is born. The relationship you create with one person is unlike the one you'll create with anyone else. In a sense, you're a different person with Jack than you are with John or Mary. Not only are *you* different in many ways, but *your relationship* with each of these individuals is unique, too. Relationships, like individuals, have their own attitudes, values, and sensitivities.

At some point, you may decide that a relationship just isn't worth it anymore. The costs outweigh the rewards. The relationship is suffocating or lifeless, and you find yourself thinking about having a relationship with someone else, or you're actually on the lookout for a new one. It may be best to face this realization squarely and end the dissatisfying relationship honestly, rather than allowing another one to develop in secret. When relationships end, the quality

Was Quentin thinking this??

and quantity of communication between the two participants change. But as the golden oldie goes, "Breaking Up Is Hard to Do," and applying all the emotional intelligence you can muster will help you through it.

Diversity Makes a Difference

EXERCISE 10.3

What Are Your Views on Diversity?

Look at the following ten statements and indicate the extent to which you agree or disagree.

	Strongly Agree 1	Agree 2	Not sure 3	Disagree 4	Strongly Disagree 5

1. Race is still a factor in hiring decisions today.
2. Multiculturalism implies that all cultures have equally valid viewpoints.
3. Workforce diversity improves the quality of work.
4. The number of male versus female corporate CEOs is nearing the halfway mark in the United States.
5. In some situations, sexual orientation is a justifiable basis for discrimination.
6. All cultures tend to see the rest of the world through their own cultural lens.
7. Feminism is a set of beliefs held by females.
8. A global perspective ensures objectivity.
9. Religious persecution is a thing of the past.
10. There is less racism in the United States today than there was ten years ago.

As you continue reading this section of the chapter, search for points relating to these topics. Also, your instructor may wish to use these ten items to begin a discussion in class.

These ten statements are intentionally provocative to stimulate your thinking. They relate to diversity: the differences between human beings based on gender, race, ethnicity, age, culture, physical features and abilities, mental capability, socioeconomic status, religion, politics, sexuality, gender identity, and points of view. Throughout your life, you've had relationships with all types of people and you always will. It's important to think about the richness diversity adds to your life by providing for potential relationships with people who are unlike you.

Although some of you may have grown up in a fairly homogeneous community with less racial, ethnic, or cultural diversity than others, no doubt you have experienced the multicultural nature of our society in many different ways, even in terms of food, music, and clothing, for example. The media have introduced you to aspects of diversity vicariously, and perhaps you've even traveled to other parts of the United States or the world yourself.

But here's the challenge: Have your experiences with diversity and your learning about it in school truly made a difference in the way you think and act? Do you choose to diversify your awareness, your relationships, and yourself as a person? Do you think that the fact that we live in a multicultural society in which we've all been taught to respect and appreciate diversity means that discrimination no longer exists?

If you conducted a survey on your campus to find out if discrimination exists, you might be surprised at the results. Research continues to show that minority students experience discrimination at higher rates than majority students. Many of us downplay the prejudice all human beings harbor to one extent or another. Our brains are "programmed" to group like entities and standardize our views about these groups, resulting in stereotypes.

But refraining from stereotyping groups of people and appreciating individuals for what they are could drastically alter the way we think and act. Perhaps you've always assumed that all nerds are A, all athletes are B, and all sorority women are C. What if you switched the labels around? Are the results ludicrous? When labels come to us easily, they are probably negative, and it's likely they apply to groups *other than* the ones *we* belong to. However, when you liberate yourself to think differently, you're not bogged down by tired, old labels. If you open up your thinking to new possibilities, all kinds of new options present themselves.

Appreciate the American Mosaic

? challenge	66 reaction	* insight	! action

Challenge: Identify three advantages diversity brings to any society.

Reaction: _____

_____

_____

This November 18, 1993, *Time Magazine* cover featured a multiracial, computer-generated woman's face. The blended features were intended to show that increasingly Americans are a composite: the "New Face of America," the magazine called it. It's becoming more and more impossible to draw clear lines between what separates us physically. Actress Jessica Alba has a Mexican American father and a mother who is of Danish and French Canadian descent. Keanu Reeves is Hawaiian, Chinese, and Caucasian; Mariah Carey is Black,

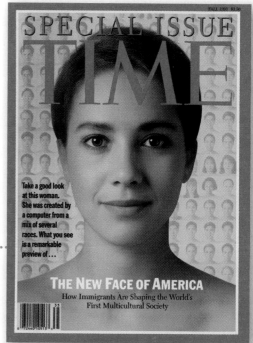

" We have become not a melting pot, but a beautiful mosaic. Different people, different beliefs, different yearnings, different hopes, different dreams."

Jimmy Carter, thirty-ninth president of the United States

Venezuelan, and Caucasian; and Johnny Depp is Cherokee and Caucasian.[26] Most of us are a blend, but diversity is about more than physical appearance. Each of us is a unique human being.

Actually, college is a perfect time to immerse yourself in diversity—in the classroom and beyond it. Classrooms are becoming more diversely populated; it's true. By the standard definition, only 27 percent of today's college students are "traditional" (meaning a high school graduate who immediately goes on to college, depends on parents fully for financial support, and doesn't work or works only part-time). Most traditional students today don't fit the traditional definition of "traditional."[27] Adult nontraditional learners have varied backgrounds, interests, and approaches to getting an education. Often they try to work their way through systems that are designed around the needs of younger students.[28] Today, twice as many minority students are enrolled in college than were enrolled twenty years ago, and the number of Hispanic college students has tripled since 1980.[29] Diversity in higher education gives you an opportunity to expand your world view and develop empathy for others who have vastly different experiences.

Aside from meeting students of other races and ethnicities in college, taking advantage of diversity can help you become a more sophisticated thinker, one who can see problems from multiple perspectives, and a better-prepared employee, ready to hit the ground running in today's highly diverse workplace. Appreciating diversity also helps us become better citizens and develop sensitivities to other cultures.

EXERCISE 10.4

Circles of Awareness

Write your name in the center of the drawing, then label each of the surrounding circles with a word that represents a group with whom you identify. You may use categories such as age, gender, ethnicity, social, political, and so forth. After your drawing is labeled, your instructor will ask you to circulate around the room and find three classmates who have listed at least three of the same subgroups. Following that, you will be asked to find three students who listed at least three categories that you did not. In the second group you formed, based on differences, use the activity to discuss diversity, differences between individuals and groups, and how awareness can change behavior. Look over everyone's list, and to diversify your thinking, select one group on someone else's list, but not on yours. Find out more about that group, or decide to attend a group meeting to raise your awareness of differences between yourself and the group or between your preconceptions of what the group would be like, and what it's actually like.[30]

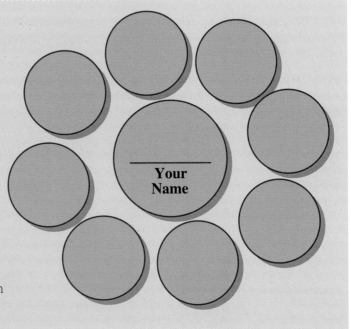

BOX 10.2 Service-Learning: Learning by Serving

One of the best ways to learn about diversity in college is by serving others. Instead of spending all your time in a classroom, imagine a class on aging in which you team up with an elder in your community and work together on a term project. You might help a senior write her memoirs, for example, or help an elderly man create a family tree for the next generation. You might be wondering, *How would that work? What could we possibly have in common—an 18-year-old teamed up with an 88-year-old?* You might be surprised.

Campus Compact, a national organization with 1198 member colleges, estimates that college student volunteering was worth $7.4 billion to the communities they served in 2008–2009. They report that nearly one-third of students in member colleges regularly do community service for approximately 3.8 hours per week.[31]

Beyond the dollars calculated, college students' community service provides invaluable support. Literally thousands of college students volunteered to help with Hurricane Katrina and Rita relief efforts in 2005, for example, to help displaced victims of one of the country's worst natural disasters ever.

However, here's an important point: *community service* and *service-learning* aren't quite the same thing.[32] Service-learning is specifically about the learning. It's a learning experience in which you connect what you're learning for credit in the classroom with what you're learning in the community. You're applying what you're learning, which in turn solidifies—and modifies—your perspective. "Service, combined with learning, adds value to each and transforms both."[33] While you're engaged in a service-learning experience, you'll also be engaged in critical reflection. Critical reflection is like critical thinking, recalling or looking back at the service experience and writing about what you're learning in a continuous, connected, challenging, and contextualized way.[34] That's not the same thing as donating your time for a good cause, as important as that is, in terms of you and your own personal development and the lives of the people you help.

The average number of college professors who include service-learning in their courses nearly tripled between 2000 and 2005. Search out these opportunities to enhance your own learning and your appreciation for diversity by serving other people.[35]

Sounds interesting—maybe I'll look for a service learning course for next semester . . .

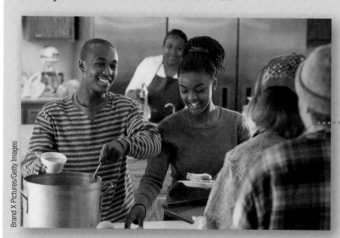

Brand X Pictures/Getty Images

" We make a living by what we get, but we make a life by what we give."

Winston Churchill, Prime Minister of England (1874–1965)

Great quote!

Diversity makes a difference, and as educator Adela A. Allen once wrote, "We should acknowledge differences, we should greet differences, until difference makes no difference anymore." What can we do about it? Some campuses have launched programs in Sustained Dialogue, used in the past to deal with international tensions. This structured approach brings together students with different backgrounds for a year of deep conversation in small groups. Other colleges have developed similar programs to allow students to dialogue about deeply rooted prejudices—sometimes buried to an extent that they are not even realized—to discuss commonalities, and to recognize the potential for conflict—and change.[36] Raising awareness is a first step on the road to recognizing the reality and the richness of diversity.

Use by permission of Dena Samuels

Q1: You're a trainer. Are you an internal trainer, working within the Human Resources department of an organization, or are you an external trainer who works with a variety of companies as a consultant?

I'm an external consultant. I teach at a university and lead workshops both on my own campus and for universities, non-profit organizations, and K-12 schools across the country. For my campus, I have co-developed and facilitated diversity and inclusiveness training for the administration, faculty, staff, and student leaders.

Q2: How did you become interested in diversity training? What prepared you to do what you do?

As a sociologist, I always think about inequalities that exist in society, like racism, sexism, and heterosexism. As a college instructor, I am always looking for ways to facilitate my students' awareness and social action around these issues. My focus is on personal transformation because I believe that unless learners (myself included) think about

how we perpetuate these inequalities, even without realizing it, we will not be successful in dismantling them. So diversity training was a natural extension of my basic interests.

Q3: Describe a typical diversity training session. What types of skills do you teach participants? Does it work?

My diversity workshops are interactive and include three key objectives: raising awareness about social inequalities; reflecting on personal

attitudes and behaviors; and making a commitment to creating change. The workshops are rooted in research and actual data from the fields of sociology, psychology, women's studies, ethnic studies, and education. Typically, they provide an academic framework for understanding social inequalities; engage participants in activities, discussion, and small group work; and offer the opportunity for participants to set personal goals. Two things make these workshops work. First, they cut across all

kinds of discrimination, for example, age, socio-economic status, sexual orientation, and religion/spirituality. Second, they include everyone, not just those who have been traditionally discriminated against in society. Since I'm asking people to make a commitment to take action, I can go back later to ask if they have followed through. Generally, what I find is that they have.

HOW WOULD *YOU* LIKE IT?

Have you ever considered a career in Human Resources?

Facts to Consider[37]

Academic preparation required: a college degree in human resources, liberal arts, and often a business background, certification, or internship

Future workforce demand: Competition for entry-level jobs will be high.

Work environment: Human Resources departments, particularly in large organizations, fulfill many employee-oriented functions: training and development; recruiting, interviewing, and hiring; employee relations; and compensation and benefits (health insurance

and pension plans). Increasingly, employers realize the value of training employees to improve their skills, build company loyalty, and increase business results through on-the-job training, classroom training, and e-learning.

Essential skills: speaking, writing, teamwork, and problem solving

Questions to Ponder

1. Do you have (or could you acquire) the skills this career requires?

2. Are you interested in a career like this? Why or why not?

For more career activities online, access the CourseMate via www.cengagebrain.com/shop/ISBN/0495906425 to do the Team Career exercises.

VARK It!

Complete the recommended activity for your preferred VARK learning modality. If you are multimodal, select more than one activity. Your instructor may ask you to (a) give an oral report on your results in class, (b) send your results to him or her via e-mail, (c) post them online, or (d) contribute to a class chat.

Visual: Make a chart of the five scales of emotional intelligence and select representative artwork or graphics for each scale to help you remember its meaning and importance.

Aural: Ask a friend or classmate to describe a real, model relationship they know or have been a part of. Following their description, discuss the specific qualities that make this relationship work.

Read/Write: Write a case study about a real relationship using fictitious names that demonstrates some of the principles of conflict management described in this chapter.

Maybe I'll write about myself . . .

Kinesthetic: Access the CourseMate via www.cengagebrain.com/shop/ISBN/0495906425 to watch the Focus TV episode for this chapter. Or interview an international student on your campus about how college life differs between what he or she experiences on your campus and what would be different at colleges in their home country.

I watched this episode—really funny!

(from left to right) Marcela Barsse/MarsBars/iStockphoto.com; Johanna Goodyear/Dreamstime.com; Nadezda Firsova/iStockphoto.com; Pascal Genest/iStockphoto.com

? challenge | **" reaction** | ***** insight** | **! action**

Now What Do You Think?

1. At the beginning of this chapter, Kia Washington faced a series of challenges as a new college student. Now after reading this chapter, would you respond differently to any of the questions you answered about the "FOCUS Challenge Case"? Knowing what you know now, how would you advise her? Write a paragraph ending to the story, incorporating your best advice.

2. Of the five EI scales, which do you experience as most challenging? Why? What can you do to improve your emotional intelligence in this area?

3. Do you agree with the suggestions for effective communication in this chapter? Which one do you think is most important? Why? Give an example of its importance from your own experience.

4. Do you think most college students value diversity? Why or why not?

5. Are there particular groups on campus you'd like to learn more about to develop and diversify your awareness? What might you learn by doing so?

6. Have you traveled outside the United States? If so, have those experiences broadened your worldview? How? If not, how might you do so even without the opportunity to travel and see differences firsthand?

On a scale of 1 to 10, answer the following questions now that you've completed this chapter.

1 = not very/not much/very little/low   10 = very/a lot/very much/high

In hindsight, how much did you already know about this subject before reading the chapter?

1   2   3   4   5   6   7   8   9   10

Can you answer these questions about building relationships and valuing diversity more fully now that you've read the chapter?

1. **What is emotional intelligence and how does it relate to college success?**

2. **Identify two characteristics of *productive* versus *destructive* conflict..**

3. **Describe three benefits of valuing diversity.**

How useful might the information in this chapter be to you? How much do you think this information might affect your success in college?

1   2   3   4   5   6   7   8   9   10

How much do you think this information might affect your career success after college?

1   2   3   4   5   6   7   8   9   10

How long did it actually take you to complete this chapter (both the reading and writing tasks)? _____ Hour(s) _____ Minutes

 Challenge Yourself Online Quiz. To find out just how much you've learned, access the CourseMate via www.cengagebrain.com/shop/ ISBN/0495906425 to take the Challenge Yourself Online Quiz.

Take a minute to compare these answers to your answers from the "Readiness Check" at the beginning of this chapter. What gaps exist between the similar questions? How might these gaps between what you thought before starting the chapter and what you now think after completing the chapter affect how you approach the next chapter in this book?

chapter 11

Choosing a College Major and Career

You're About to Discover . . .

- ✔ Why "College in a Box" isn't an accurate view of coursework
- ✔ How the disciplines connect in the Circle of Learning
- ✔ How to choose a major and a career
- ✔ What a SWOT analysis is
- ✔ Why majors and careers aren't the same thing
- ✔ How to launch a career
- ✔ How internships, co-ops, and service-learning can give you experience

READINESS CHECK | What do you Know?

Before beginning this chapter, take a moment to answer these questions. Your answers will help you assess how ready you are to focus.

1 = not very/not much/very little/low   10 = very/a lot/very much/high

How much do you *already* know?

Based on reading the "You're about to discover. . ." list and skimming this chapter, how much do you think you probably already know about this chapter's subject?

1 2 3 4 5 6 7 8 9 10

See if you can answer these questions about choosing a major and career *before* you read.

1. **What is a SWOT analysis and how might it help you choose a major and career?**

2. **Which comes first—major or career?**

3. **What is your academic anatomy?**

How motivated are you to learn *more?*

In general, how motivated are you to learn more by reading this chapter?

1 2 3 4 5 6 7 8 9 10

How much do you think this information might affect your success in college?

1 2 3 4 5 6 7 8 9 10

How much do you think this information might affect your career success after college?

1 2 3 4 5 6 7 8 9 10

How ready are you to read *now?*

How ready are you to focus on this chapter—physically, intellectually, and emotionally? Circle a number for each aspect of your readiness to focus.

1 2 3 4 5 6 7 8 9 10

If any of your answers is below a 10, you might want to pay attention to whatever is distracting you before you start reading. For example, if you're feeling scattered, take a few moments to settle down and focus.

Finally, how long do you think it will take you to complete this chapter from start to finish?

_____ Hour(s) _____ Minutes

Ethan Cole

One thing was certain: Ethan Cole was unsure. Unsure of his abilities, unsure of which major to choose, unsure of what he wanted to do with his life, unsure of himself. Unsure of almost everything.

Ethan came from a good family, and his parents were actually his best friends. They had been very successful, and they wanted to share the wealth—literally—with their three children. They supported Ethan, no matter what. When he ended up in the principal's office time after time in grade school, they defended him. When he totaled his car in high school, they bought him another one. When he wanted to take a term off to travel and "find himself," they said yes without raising one, single eyebrow. And now that he was thinking of dropping out of college, they said he could move back home, so long as he agreed to a few ground rules and promised to take back his old chores, like mowing the yard. That seemed only fair to him.

The only thing Ethan was sure of was that skateboarding was his life right now. It's all he wanted to do and all he ever thought about. He'd look at a curve on a window frame or an arc in a picture and imagine what skating on it would feel like. All his friends were skateboarders, too, and he read skateboarder magazines and dreamed of the day he might even go pro. He realized not many people make a living at it, but a few really talented athletes did, and maybe—just maybe—he'd be one of them. Recently, he'd found out about the largest concrete skatepark on the globe, Black Pearl in the Grand Cayman Islands—62,000 square feet! He'd made a promise to himself to skate there someday. *Life couldn't get much better than that*, he thought.

But school . . . that was a different story. Schoolwork had never captured his attention. In primary school, his physician had diagnosed Attention Deficit Disorder (ADD), and in middle school,

Facts about Learning Disabilities

Quick Facts

in 7 Americans has a learning
sability

% of students with learning
abilities have reading
blems

ning disabilities can be
atic

ple learning disabilities can
at the same time

Types of LDs

- Dyslexia- trouble understanding written words

- Dyscalculia- trouble grasping mathematical concepts

- Dysgraphia- trouble writing letters or words

- Aural and Visual Processing Disorders

BLACK PEARL SKATEPARK
GRAND CAYMAN
WORLD'S LARGEST CONCRETE SKATEPARK

a learning specialist had discovered that Ethan was dyslexic. *No wonder I don't like school*, he remembered thinking then. But finally knowing why he couldn't focus didn't change his attitude. He still hated sitting in a classroom.

Despite these challenges, his parents had always told him he was smart. "You can do anything you want to do," they'd said. "Look at you: you're a good-looking kid with plenty of talents. The world is your oyster!" *What a funny phrase*, he'd always thought when they said that. By the time he finally learned what it meant, he totally believed it. His life would become whatever he chose to make of it.

The problem was there were too many choices. How could anyone decide what he wanted to be when he was only nineteen? Ethan remembered liking geometry, he was good at creative writing, he played the drums like a real jazz musician, and he was an incredible artist. *But what do you do with that combination of skills?* he'd asked himself more than once. What possible college major and career would really fit him? He'd spent plenty of time on career websites to try and figure it out.

He'd managed to pull decent grades his first term—a B average—at the arts college close to home. He'd taken Freshman Composition, Introduction to Communication, Drawing 101, and Study Skills, and while he'd done well, none of the course material really sparked a genuine interest. His professors didn't take much of an interest in him, either. His Study Skills instructor was friendly and tried to get him interested in class, and he knew the material could really help him. But frankly, Ethan just wasn't motivated when it came to school. Instead, he skateboarded every minute he could.

The more he thought about it, the more he thought it was a good idea to take a year off from college. He could get a job delivering pizzas, think about his life, and try to figure it all out. He'd have nobody to tell him what to do, nobody to hold him accountable, nobody to pressure him to study, nobody to force him into making decisions—and plenty of free time to skateboard.

Study Skills (ID 102)
Course Syllabus

INSTRUCTOR: Anna Morgan
OFFICE: 342 University Hall
HOURS: 9 a.m.-12 p.m. Mon-Thurs

TEXT: *FOCUS on College Success* by Constance Staley

COURSE OBJECTIVES: This course is designed to give you the tools more productive, and a more successful learning experience. The make you a better student by building your study skills and enhar strategies.

EXPECTATIONS: Students are expected to be respectful of instructor Assignments should be turned in on time unless you have a valid due date. Please see me if you have any questions. Water bottle but no food or sugary drinks are permitted. Please turn off your come to class.

GRADING: 100 Possible Points
-Participation: 10 Points.
-Final Presentation: 20 Points.
-Final Exam: 20 Points.
-Assignments (3) and Quizzes (2): 50 Points (10 each)

GRADES: 100-90 = A   89-80 = B   79-70 = C   69-60 = D

Course Schedule

WEEK 1:   Overview and Pre-Test

WEEK 2:   Managing Time and Stress

WEEK 3:   Reading Skills

WEEK 4:   Test Taking

WEEK 5:   Listening and Memory

WEEK 6:   Diversity

WEEK 7:   Effective Writing

What Do You Think?

1. In your view, what will become of Ethan? What are his prospects for the future? Do you think he'll decide on a major and finish college? Why or why not?

2. Why is Ethan experiencing problems? Are these problems serious? Should they hold him back? List all the problems you can identify.

3. Which majors and careers might Ethan be well suited for? If you were an academic advisor, what advice would you give him?

4. Who would you send Ethan to on your campus for help? What are his options? What do you think he should do at this point?

What's the Connection?

challenge   reaction   insight   action

Challenge: Is there a connection between what you study in art, psychology, engineering, and chemistry? If so, how would you try to explain the relationships?

Reaction: _____

College is about becoming an educated person, learning how to think, solving problems, and making decisions. College is much more than the "sum of its tests." It's about developing yourself as a person and becoming well-educated. What does it mean to be well-educated? Simply put: Being well-educated is about the pursuit of human excellence.[1]

Colleges and universities help societies *preserve the past* and *create the future*. Studying the history of the U.S. Constitution in a political science course (past) as opposed to studying potential cures for cancer in a cell biology course (future) are concrete examples. Colleges and universities help us look back (preserve the past) and look ahead (create the future).

College in a Box?

Have you ever thought about the fact that college courses appear to exist in discrete "boxes"? Schools tend to place courses in academic departments, and your class schedule reflects these divisions. For example, your schedule this term might look something like the one in Figure 11.1.

This organizing system helps you keep things straight in your head, and it also helps your school organize a complex institution. Professors normally work in one department or another. And classes are categorized into particular academic disciplines.

But something first-year students often wonder about is how to connect the dots. What's the big picture? Knowledge isn't quite as neat as departments and boxes; it's messy. It overlaps and converges. Despite the convenient institutional compartmentalization of knowledge on a college campus, you might be able to take a somewhat similar course in visual art from the art department, the computer science department, or the communication department. You've probably noticed that you sometimes hear something discussed in one of your classes that's also being discussed in another one. Knowledge is interconnected. College in a Box isn't an accurate way of looking at things.

Even though each discipline has its own history and identity and way of asking questions and finding answers, the disciplines aren't as distinct as your class schedule might lead you to believe.

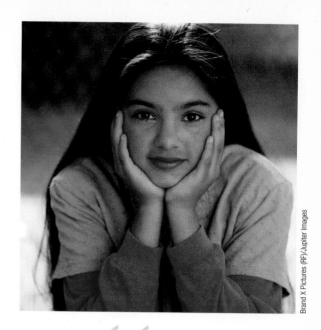

Brand X Pictures (RF)/Jupiter Images

How Do the Disciplines Connect?

The Circle of Learning (see Figure 11.2) illustrates the interconnectedness of knowledge. Although this circle could be drawn in many different ways, using many different traditional academic disciplines, here is an example to get you thinking.[2]

It works like this. Let's start at the top of the circle with *math*, which is a basic "language" with rules and conventions, just like spoken language. You manipulate numbers and operations and functions, just as you manipulate sounds and words and sentences. Now, move clockwise around the circle.

Math is the fundamental language of *physics*, one branch of which studies atomic and subatomic particles. When atoms combine into molecules, such as carbon dioxide, the academic discipline involved is called *chemistry*. Chemicals combine to create living organisms studied in *biology* courses. Living organisms don't just exist, they think and behave, leading to the study of *psychology*. They also interact in groups, families, and organizations, which you study in *sociology*. You can also study units of living beings throughout time and across

> " It takes courage to grow up and become who you really are."
>
> **e. e. cummings, American poet (1894–1962)**

	M	T	W	Th	F
9–10	ENG			SOC	
10–11		PHY			
11–12			PSCI		PSCI

Figure 11.1

Most Schools Compartmentalize Learning

huh . . . never thought of it like that!

Figure 11.2

The Circle of Learning

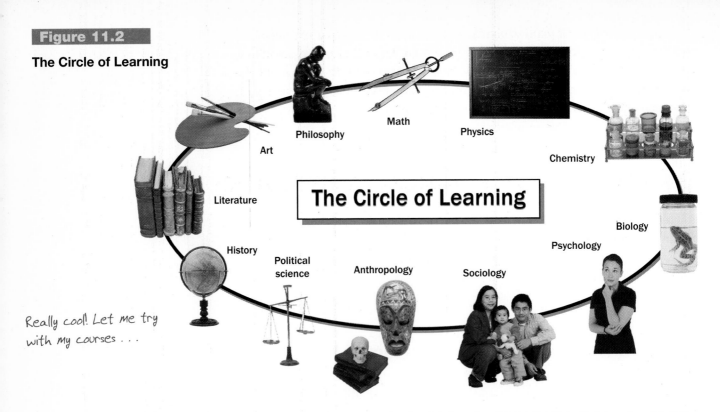

The Circle of Learning

Really cool! Let me try with my courses . . .

(clockwise from top center): © Travis Klein, 2009/Used under license from Shutterstock.com; Image Source/Jupiter Images; Hemera Technologies/PhotoObjects.net/Jupiter Images; Hemera Technologies/PhotoObjects.net/Jupiter Images; Hemera Technologies/PhotoObjects.net/Jupiter Images; PhotoObjects.net/Jupiter Images; © OlegD, 2009/Used under license from Shutterstock.com; Photos.com; © Sebastian Kaulitzki, 2009/Used under license from Shutterstock.com; photos.com; Photos.com; © originalpunkt, 2009/Used under license from Shutterstock.com; © aquatic creature, 2010/Used under license from Shutterstock.com

cultures in the discipline of *anthropology*. These units—people—who live and work together are typically governed or govern themselves, leading to *political science*. Let's keep going.

When an account of peoples and countries and their rulers is recorded, you study *history*. These written accounts, sometimes factual or sometimes fictional (for pleasure or intrigue) comprise the study of *literature*. Literature is one way to record impressions and provoke reactions—poetry is a good example—through the use of words. But images and symbols can do the same things—enter *art*. A particular question artists ask is "What is beauty?" otherwise known as *aesthetics*, which is also a particular topic of study in *philosophy*. Philosophy also includes another subspecialty called *number theory*, one of the earliest branches of pure mathematics. And now we're all the way around the Circle of Learning, arriving right back at *math*.

That's a quick rundown. Of course, many academic disciplines don't appear on this chart, but they could and should. A philosophy major might see her discipline at the center of the circle, or a geography major might say, "Hey, where's geography on this chart?" The circle, as it appears here, is representative. The point isn't which disciplines are represented. Instead, the Circle of Learning demonstrates that academic disciplines are interconnected because knowledge itself is interconnected. *Anthropology* (understanding people throughout time and across cultures) can provide an important foundation for *political science* (how people are governed or govern themselves), and *history* (a record of peoples and countries and rulers) can easily be the basis for *literature*. Capitalizing on what you're learning in one discipline can lead to deeper understanding in another.

In your career, you'll need to use knowledge without necessarily remembering in which course you learned it. You'll be thinking critically and creatively, solving problems, and calling upon all the skills you're cultivating in all the courses you're studying in college. The bottom line is that connections count. Recognize them, use them, and strengthen them to reinforce your learning.

How to Choose a Major and a Career

Like many students, you probably put value in how well college prepares you for a profession.[3] Choosing a college major and directing yourself toward a prospective career can be stressful. Many students feel pressure to make the right decision—and make it right now! You might hear conflicting advice from family members that put a high priority on financial success above other important factors, and feel overwhelmed by the number of possibilities from which to choose.[4] You may know what you want to do with the rest of your life right now, but many of your classmates don't, and even if they *say* they do, they may well change their minds several times. Yes, these decisions are important. But where do you start? The decision-making process should involve these critical steps. If you're still deciding, or even if you think you already have, consider how they apply to you.

Pay attention here since I'm clueless!

Step 1: Follow Your Bliss

In an ideal world, which major and career would you choose? Don't think about anything except the actual content you'd be studying. Don't consider career opportunities, requirements, difficulty, or anything else that might keep you from making these choices in an ideal world. What are you passionate about? If it's skateboarding, think about which majors might apply. Majoring in physics would help you understand skateboard ascent versus decent, trajectories, spin, and angles. Majoring in landscape architecture would allow you to design skateparks. Majoring in journalism would put you in a good position to write for a skateboarding magazine.

Hey! Cool! This is what I would love to do!

Like many students, you may be wondering what to do with your life. Perhaps the *idealist* in you has one potential career in mind and the *realist* in you has another. The $300,000 salary you'd earn as a surgeon may look very

CONTROL: YOUR TOUGHEST CLASS

Think about your most challenging class this semester. Is it a general education course or one required for your major? If it's a general education course, make a list of all the ways this course can help you either to further your career or to become a well-educated person. If this course is one in your major, ask yourself why the challenge is so great. Do you understand the course content? Do you keep up with readings and assignments? Can you follow your professor's teaching style? If appropriate, send your instructor in this class an e-mail indicating your specific efforts to do your best and detailing your progress.

compelling until you consider the years of medical school required after college, the time invested in an internship and residency, and the still further years of necessary specialization. It takes long-term diligence, commitment, dedication, and resources—yours or borrowed ones—to make that dream come true. Do these factors lessen the appeal?

I love this guy!

Perhaps there's conflict between your *idealism* and your family's *pragmatism*. Comedian Robin Williams once said, "When I told my father I was going to be an actor, he said, 'Fine, but study welding just in case.'"

Or perhaps you just don't know yet. If that's the case, don't panic. Despite the increased pressure these days to choose the right major because of rising tuition and a changeable economy, it's hard to have it all figured out from the start.[5]

One thing is certain: you'll be a happier, more productive person if you do what *you* want to do *and* pursue it vigorously. When it comes to success, ability (*Can* you do it?) and effort (Are you *willing* to invest what it takes?) go hand in hand. Whatever your motivation, remember this. It's unusual for people to become truly successful halfheartedly. There are undeniable emotional and psychological components involved in success. Wayne Gretzky, called the greatest player in the history of hockey, once said, "God gave me a special talent to play the game . . . maybe he didn't give me a talent, he gave me a *passion*."

Having said that, what if your "bliss" just isn't feasible? You'd give anything to play for the NBA, but you're five foot two and female. You dream of being a rock star, but you can't carry a tune. Then it may be time to set aside the idealism and resurrect the realism in you. Maybe then it's time to translate—or shift—your dreams into goals.

Can you translate your dream into a goal and become a pro? How many professional athletes are there—especially compared to other professionals such as teachers, architects, and physicians? When the statistics are against you, achieving success isn't impossible, but it might take more than expert skill. It might also take some luck, very specific planning, and perseverance.

Step 2: Conduct Preliminary Research

Has it ever occurred to you that you may not have all the facts—accurate ones—about your ideal major? Do you know what it *really* takes? Have you gotten your information from qualified sources—or are you basing your opinion on your roommate's reaction to one course he took in the major or on the campus grapevine?

Try an experiment. Choose three majors you're considering, one of which is your ideal major, and send yourself on a fact-finding mission. To find out if you're on target, get the answers to the following ten questions for each of the three possibilities. Go to the physical location (department) where each major is housed, and interview a professor. The experiment requires legwork; don't just let your fingers do the clicking.

1. What is the major?

2. Who is the interviewee?

3. What is the name of the academic department where this major is housed? Where are the department offices physically located on campus?

The huge printing presses of a major Chicago newspaper began malfunctioning on the Saturday before Christmas, putting all the revenue for advertising that was to appear in the Sunday paper in jeopardy. None of the technicians could track down the problem. Finally, a frantic call was made to the retired printer who had worked with these presses for over forty years. "We'll pay anything; just come in and fix them," he was told.

When he arrived, he walked around for a few minutes, surveying the presses; then he approached one of the control panels and opened it. He removed a dime from his pocket, turned a screw ¼ of a turn, and said, "The presses will now work correctly." After being profusely thanked, he was told to submit a bill for his work.

The bill arrived a few days later, for $10,000.00! Not wanting to pay such a huge amount for so little work, the printer was told to please itemize his charges, with the hope that he would reduce the amount once he had to identify his services. The revised bill arrived: $1.00 for turning the screw; $9,999.00 for knowing which screw to turn. (Anonymous)

So what does it take? After forty years on the job, the retired printer knew many things, including one elusive but critical piece of knowledge—which screw to turn. But perhaps you're just starting out, and experience is something you don't have yet. Or perhaps you're an adult returning to school to boost your career and shift to a new one. No matter where you are on your journey, how will you achieve life and career success?

Mel Levine, author of *Ready or Not, Here Life Comes,* says, "We are in the midst of an epidemic of work-life unreadiness because an alarming number of young adults are unable to find a good fit between their minds and their career directions. . . . Because they are not finding their way, they may feel as if they are going nowhere and have nowhere to go."[6]

How can anyone have nowhere to go with more than 12,000 different occupations or careers to choose from with 8,000 alternative job titles—for a total of over 20,000 options?[7] Some students start college and become overwhelmed. Sometime during the first year, or possibly later, they take a step back and announce in so many words, "There are too many choices. I refuse to choose at all."[8]

Here's another tough issue many college graduates face when entering the world of work. Many of them have already decided that work is boring because their part-time jobs in high school and college were boring. They don't want to climb the ladder of success. They'd like to skip the bottom and start somewhere closer to the top rung. But every job involves some element of grunt work, even those at the top. No job is round-the-clock fun, and in every new job, eventually the honeymoon is over, and the tough challenges begin. The simple truth is this: building a career takes time, persistence, dedication, and focus. Seemingly overnight successes like J. K. Rowling of *Harry Potter* fame are rare; steady progress toward a goal is the norm.[9]

So what does it take to launch your career successfully? You'll need to focus your I's on four things: Inner direction, Interpretation, Instrumentation, and Interaction—the four I's of career-life readiness. Here's what they mean.[10]

Inner direction. You've lived with yourself for some time now, but how well do you know yourself? How accurate is your view of yourself? Are you honest about your potential? You must first understand the inner you before you can direct it toward a career that fits.

Interpretation. Memorization isn't the most important skill you'll need in most careers. On the job there's more required than repeating back what the boss has told you. You must interpret the information and apply it in your own way, which demonstrates whether you do (or don't) understand what you're doing.

Instrumentation. In your career, you'll need a toolkit filled with different kinds of abilities—engaging in high-level thinking, brainstorming, problem solving, making decisions, tapping your creativity, and cultivating both hard (technical) and soft (interpersonal) skills. And not only must you know how to use each of these tools, but you'll need to know when and why.

Interaction. Business (or any profession) isn't just about facts and figures. It's about people, values, and relationships. People will be what help you build your career. Without people to buy, sell, trade, consume, or produce, there is no business.

These four I's are keys to your future. The more you focus your I's, the better prepared you'll be for the challenges ahead.

My I's are NOT focused yet, especially Inner Direction.

4. Which introductory courses in this major would inform you about your interests and abilities?

5. Which upper-level courses in this major interest you? (List three.)

6. What are the department's entry requirements to become a major?

7. How many students major in this discipline on your campus?

8. Which required course in the major do students usually find most challenging? Which is most engaging? Which is most valued? Why?

9. How would the interviewee describe the reputation of this department on campus? What is it known for?

10. From the interviewee's perspective, why should a student major in this discipline?

After you complete your interviews, review the facts. Did you change any of your opinions, based on what you learned?[11]

Step 3: Take a Good Look at Yourself

How Do You Look?

Take a good look at yourself and answer the following questions about how you prefer to work. Rank each item 1 or 2 based on your general preference. While many careers, if not most, require both, your task is to decide which of the two you prefer.

I prefer to work at a job:

				My answer
1. Alone	_____	With other people	_____	alone
2. Indoors	_____	Outdoors	_____	outdoors!
3. With people	_____	With equipment or materials	_____	equipment
4. Directing/leading others	_____	Being directed/led by others	_____	??
5. Producing information	_____	Managing information	_____	??
6. In an organized, step-by-step way	_____	In a big-idea, holistic way	_____	big idea w
7. Starting things	_____	Completing things	_____	starting
8. Involving a product	_____	Involving a service	_____	product
9. Solving challenging problems	_____	Generating creative ideas	_____	creative
10. Finding information	_____	Applying information	_____	applying
11. Teaching/training others in groups	_____	Advising/coaching others one-on-one	_____	one-on-on

Now look at your eleven first choices. Identify several career fields that come to mind that would allow you to achieve as many of them as possible.

Here's a bottom-line question: What do you want to do with the rest of your life? Many first-year college students don't know. They don't have enough experience under their belts to plan for a lifetime. They're in college to *discover*. It all comes down to questions this book has been asking you all along: Who are you? And what do you want? If you're unsure of how to proceed in your decision making, follow these recommendations to see if they help you bring your future into focus.

Send in the SWOT Team!

A SWOT analysis is an excellent way to begin taking a good look at yourself in relation to your future. SWOT stands for Strengths, Weaknesses, Opportunities, and Threats. SWOT analyses are typically used in business, but creating one for yourself may be useful when it comes to deciding on a college major and a career. Make a matrix with four quadrants, label each one, and fill them in as objectively as you can.

> **Strengths** are traits that give you a leg up. These are talents you can capitalize on and qualities you can develop.

> **Weaknesses** are traits that currently work against you. You can, however, work to reduce or eliminate them.

> **Opportunities** are conditions or circumstances that work in your favor, like a strong forecast for your prospective career's future.

> **Threats** are conditions that could have adverse effects. Some of these factors are beyond your control; however, sometimes you can successfully lessen their potential effects.

As you create the matrix, begin with two basic questions:

What kinds of forces will impact your potential career?

Internal—forces inside you, such as motivation and skill

External—forces outside you that may affect your success: the job market or economy, for example

What kind of influence can these forces exert?

Positive—some forces will give you a boost toward your goals

Negative—other forces will work against you[12]

Let's complete a SWOT analysis for the earlier example of becoming a professional skateboarder. Of course, you might say that, technically, you don't need an academic degree for that particular career. But if you want to pursue related, more traditional careers—design a new skatepark or write for a skateboard magazine, for example—you would need an array of knowledge and enhanced skills from writing and design to finance and marketing. Besides, college isn't just about jobs, it's about living a fuller life as a well-educated person. Look at this SWOT analysis for a college student who dreams of becoming a professional skateboarder in Figure 11.3. What do you think? Is professional

Figure 11.3

SWOT Analysis

Ah-ha! This helps!

skateboarding a good career option for him? In your view, do the opportunities outweigh the threats? For example, does the potential earning power of a professional skateboarder outweigh the risks associated with possible incapacitating injuries? Do his well-cultivated athletic skills compensate for his lack of focus in other areas? If not, might he gravitate toward other potential careers, perhaps those that also involve skateboarding, like a degree in business to run a sports facility, for example, or a degree in journalism to write for a sports magazine?

Step 4: Consider Your Major versus Your Career

challenge **reaction** **insight** **action**

Challenge: What is the relationship between choosing a major and choosing a career?

Reaction: _____

Which comes first, the chicken or the egg? The major or the career? Silly question? The obvious answer, of course, is that you must first major in something in college before you can build a career on it. But the question isn't as straightforward as it seems.

Should you choose a major based on an intended career? Perhaps you know you want to be a science teacher, first and foremost. You don't know whether to major in one of the sciences or in education. You like all sciences,

BOX 11.1

Five Ways to Open the Door (or Close It) during an Interview

By the time you graduate from college, you will have been interviewed many times to get a new job or to be admitted to graduate school. And after you graduate, you'll go through a series of interviews on your career path.

Often interviewers aren't particularly skilled at asking questions. They haven't been trained on how to interview prospective employees, so they just ask whatever questions come to them. And often, interviewees don't quite know what they're doing either.

Of course, you should always be honest, but there are various ways to communicate the same information. Telling an interviewer you "like to work alone" sounds antisocial. But if you say you "like to really focus on what you're doing without distractions," you've shown dedication to your work ethic. You also need to be aware of real pitfalls to avoid.

1. **"You've got to ac-centuate the positive; e-liminate the negative."** A trap question interviewers sometimes ask is, "What's your worst fault?" While you may be tempted to say the first thing that comes to mind, that could be a big mistake. "Umm . . . sleeping too much! I really like to sleep in." Not good. But some faults you could identify might actually be construed as strengths: "I have a little too much nervous energy. I'm always on the go. I like to stay busy."

2. **Stay focused.** "Tell me about yourself" is a common question interviewers ask. How much time do you have? Most of us like to talk about ourselves, but it's important to stay on track. Think possible questions through in advance, and construct some hypothetical answers. Keep your answers job-focused: what you liked about your last job, why you liked those aspects of it, what your long-term career goals are, and how this job can help you prepare. You don't need to go into your family background or your personal problems. And it's always a bad idea to bash a previous job or former boss. The interviewer may worry that you'll bring whatever didn't work there with you to this new job.

3. **Don't just give answers, get some.** A job interview is like a first date. Find out what you need to know. If the job is one you're interested in long-term, ask questions such as these three key ones:

   • **What does this company value?** Listen to the answer. Doing things by the book? The answer will tell you about the personality of the company.

   • **What's a typical day like for you?** An answer like "I get up at 5:00 a.m., get here at 6:30 a.m., and go home around 7:00 p.m.—and then I do paperwork all evening" tells you something. This may—or may not—be the job or the company for you.

   • **What happened to the last person in this job?** If you find out he was promoted, that's one thing. But if you learn he was fired or quit, see if you can find out why. Maybe he had job performance problems, or maybe this is an impossible job that no one could do well.

   Remember, too, that interviews are conversations with give and take, not just one person doing all the giving and the other doing all the taking. Listen to the interviewer. She may be looking for an opportunity to tell you things she thinks are important, too.

4. **Watch for questions out of left field.** Some companies like to get creative with their interviewing. Microsoft, for example, is known for asking problem-solving questions, such as "If you could remove any of the fifty states, which would it be? Be prepared to give specific reasons why you chose the state you did." There is no right or wrong answer, although some answers are better than others. ("We should just nuke state X. I had a bad experience there once" would probably furrow some brows, and naming Washington state, where Microsoft is located, might be a bad choice.) The interviewer just wants to hear how you think. Talk through your underlying reasoning.[13] Remember: Today's interviewers are looking for more than technical skills; they're looking for critical thinking skills, problem-solving skills, and creativity.[14]

5. **Don't start off with salary questions.** Make sure the first question out of your mouth isn't, "So tell me about the salary, again? Any way to notch that up a bit?" The last thing you want to do is give the interviewer the idea you're just in it for the money. Of course, you are, but not just for that. More importantly, in every job you have, you'll gain experience and knowledge that will always better prepare you for the next job to come.

I should practice for this!

but teaching is your real interest. If you major in science, which one should it be (see Figure 11.4)?

Or instead, should you choose a major first, and then decide on a career? Say you made a firm decision to major in chemistry when your favorite science teacher did "mad scientist" experiments for the class in eighth grade. But at this point, you're not certain of the professional direction you'd like to pursue. Chemistry is your passion, but should you apply your chemistry degree as a forensic scientist, a physician, a researcher, or a teacher (see Figure 11.5)?

A few schools don't actually use the word *major*, preferring the term *concentration*, and some schools encourage *interdisciplinary studies*, a tailor-made system in which you create your own major with guidance from advisors and faculty. Other schools may even encourage double majors, which can make sense, particularly some combinations (international business and Chinese

Used by permission of Tanya Sexton

Career Outlook: Tanya Sexton, Recruiter

Q1: You're a recruiter. What's the job like, and how did you become one?

I was an accounting major in college, and now I am a recruiter with a specialty in the accounting and finance fields, so it's a perfect fit. As a former accountant, I have credibility when it comes to bringing job candidates to prospective employers. I understand the responsibilities of the positions, structure of departments, and complexities of the profession.

Q2: What do you and your colleagues do on a day-to-day basis?

Honestly, every day is different. We continually recruit talent and market the talent to hiring authorities. We spend lots of time on the telephone, screening candidates, matching them to the right jobs, presenting them to clients, briefing and debriefing them for interviews, and negotiating job offers.

Q3: What are employers looking for in the best college graduates today?

Employers look for many things. Internships add marketability to a college degree. Employers look at grade point averages overall and in graduates' majors. They look for strong verbal, written, and interpersonal communication skills. More and more, we hear that you can teach responsibilities of the job on the job, but the "soft skills," the "people skills," are not easily taught.

Q4: If employers were asked to identify which skills are in need of further development in today's college graduates, which skills would those be?

Work ethic. Employers say more recent graduates sometimes expect to automatically progress through the ranks without necessarily putting in the time to "earn their stripes."

HOW WOULD *YOU* LIKE IT?

Have you ever considered a career as a recruiter, placement, or employment specialist?

Facts to Consider[15]

Academic preparation required: A college degree in business, human resources, management, or communication would be good preparation.

Future workforce demand: Competition may be stiff because of plentiful numbers of qualified college graduates.

Work environment: Recruiters can either work inside a specific company's human resources department in its personnel office, or as a third-party agent, possibly within a consulting firm, that helps individual organizations find the best candidates for particular types of positions.

Essential skills: interviewing, speaking, writing, decision-making, and technology skills (using the Internet for job searches, etc.)

Questions to Ponder

1. Do you have (or could you acquire) the skills this career requires?

2. Are you interested in a career like this? Why or why not?

For more career activities online, access the CourseMate via www.cengagebrain.com/shop/ISBN/0495906425 to do the Team Career exercises.

Figure 11.4

Which Science Should a Science Teacher Major In?

egg or chicken for me?

Figure 11.5

Which Career Should a Chemistry Major Choose?

language, for example). But by and large, the concept of having a major (and sometimes a minor) in college is the norm.

So which comes first—major or career? It depends.[16] The answer sounds ambivalent, and it's meant to. Although some professional degree programs put you into a particular track right away (nursing or engineering, for example), generally either direction can work well. Doors will open and close for you, and as you gain more knowledge and experience, you'll narrow your focus. As you learn more about your chosen major, you'll also learn about its specific career tracks. But it's important to remember that a major doesn't have to lock you into one specific career. And you can always narrow or refocus your area of emphasis in graduate school after you earn your undergraduate degree.[17]

Figure 11.6

What's Your Academic Anatomy?

Definitely these:
1. whole body
2. hands
3. heart
4. head

Another way of analyzing your preferences is by considering your "Academic Anatomy." What do you find most satisfying? Working with your

Head?
Heart?
Hands? or
Whole Body?

Hemera Technologies/Jupiter Images

What's Your Academic Anatomy?

Thinking about your academic anatomy is a simple way to begin to get a handle on what you find fulfilling. If you had to rank order the four parts of you listed in Figure 11.6, what would you put in first place? Second, third, and last? To get yourself thinking, ask these questions:

1. Do you find fulfillment by using your *head*? Do you enjoy solving complex problems or thinking through difficult situations? Do you like to reason things out, weigh evidence, and think critically? A philosophy major who continues on to a career in law might be what students with this preference choose, for example.

2. Do you find it satisfying to work with matters of the *heart*? Are you the kind of person others come to with problems because you listen and care? Does trying to make others happy make you happy? A psychology major who pursues a counseling career might be what students with this preference choose, for example.

3. Do you like to create things with your *hands*? Do you enjoy making art? Doing hands-on projects? Building things out of other things? An architecture major who designs and builds models might be what students with this preference choose, for example.

4. Do you excel at physical activities that involve your *whole body*? Are you athletic? Do you like to stay active, no matter what you're doing? A physical therapy major who goes on to work in a rehabilitation facility helping stroke victims relearn to walk might be what students with this preference choose, for example.

Now look at your academic anatomy rankings. Of course, the truth is that "all of you" is involved in everything you do. And achieving balance is important. But what are your priorities? This type of simple analysis can be one way of informing you about who you are and where you should be headed.

However, no system for choosing a major is perfect. In fact, most are imperfect at best. Here are four things to consider.

1. Sometimes students who don't select a likely major based on their "anatomical preferences" can still be successful. A whole-body person may decide to major in art (using his hands). But he'll have to find other ways to meet his whole-body needs unless he becomes a sculptor involved in creating large constructed projects.

2. You may intentionally choose an unlikely major. Perhaps art (using your hands) comes so naturally to you that you decide to major in astrophysics (using your head). You need the challenge to stay fully involved in getting your education. While it may sound unlikely, it's been known to happen.

3. You may choose an unlikely major because one particular course turns you on. You had no idea majoring in this subject was even possible, and you didn't know what it entailed. But you find studying it fascinating—so you shift gears to focus all your attention on it.

4. You may be equally engaged, no matter what. You love subjects that require using your head, hands, heart, and whole body. The anatomy of learning is less important to you than other factors—a teacher whose enthusiasm is contagious, for example.[18]

Think about your rankings. And if "head" is in last place for you, don't assume you're doomed in college. A career as a financial analyst sitting behind a desk might not be your cup of tea, for example. But it may well be someone else's. Whatever major and career you're thinking about, you may want to consider whether it's "anatomically correct."

How to Launch a Career

EXERCISE 11.2

Career Auction

Assume you have $100,000 to spend on the following items. In a few minutes, your instructor will begin a real-live auction, putting one item at a time up for auction. Before the auction begins, budget your money in the first column. You may select as many items as you wish to bid on, but you may not place all your money on any single item. As the group auction proceeds, fill in the appropriate amounts that are actually spent by members of the class for each item.

	BUDGETED AMOUNT	WINNING BID
1. Becoming the CEO of a leading Fortune 500 company	_____	_____
2. Being a top earner in your career field	_____	_____
3. Being the number one expert in your profession	_____	_____
4. Having good friends on the job	_____	_____
5. Being your own boss	_____	_____
6. Creating a good balance between productive work and a happy family life	_____	_____
7. Having opportunities for travel and adventure in your job	_____	_____
8. Doing work you find fully satisfying	_____	_____
9. Working in a beautiful setting	_____	_____
10. Being a lifelong learner so that your career can develop and change over time	_____	_____

I'd put most of my money on these.

After you graduate from college, it'll be time to launch your career, right? What do you really want from a career? What's important to you? Even though your views may change over time, it's important to start thinking about them now. Item 7, "Having opportunities for travel and adventure in your job," may be a top priority now, but item 6, "Creating a good balance between productive work and a happy family life," may be more appealing a few years down the road if you have several young children to parent.

Interestingly, according to research, the most important factor in job satisfaction isn't any of these ten items. The number one contributor to job satisfaction, statistically speaking, is the quality of your relationship with your boss.[19]

If all your jobs thus far have been just that—*jobs*—to help you pay the bills, how do you know what you want in a *career*? Your career is something you haven't launched yet. Exactly how do you do that? You have to start somewhere, so perhaps you'd go online or open the want ads. You'd be likely to read this: *"Opening in... (anything). Experience required."* Isn't that the way it always goes? You have to *have* experience in order to get a job that will *give* you experience. So how do you launch a career?

This problem is one many college graduates face. Sure, they have experience. It's just not the right kind. They've bagged fries, mowed yards, bussed tables, and chauffeured pizzas to help pay for college expenses. If that's not the kind of experience the posted opening is looking for, how do you get the right kind? Try a job on for size.

	Description: What is a ...?	What kind of experience do I get?	Why would I want to do it?	How do I get involved?
Internships	An internship is an opportunity for you to work alongside a professional in a career field of interest to you.	Your supervisor will mentor you, and you'll get a clearer picture of what the career field is like.	Some majors will require you to complete an internship as a part of your program, for licensure or certification, for example.	Internships may be offered through your academic major department, or through a central office on campus, or you can pursue one on your own.
Co-op Program	Co-op programs allow you to take classes and then apply what you've learned on the job, either after or while you take classes.	You may take classes for a term and then work full-time for a term. You can test a career field.	A potential employer can get a sense of your potential, and you can gain practical experience to put on your résumé.	Your advisor will be able to tell you if your program has co-op opportunities.
Service-Learning	Some classes contain service-learning experiences in which you volunteer your time.	A service-learning component built right into the syllabus can give you valuable, practical experience.	The emphasis is on hands-on learning and connecting what you're learning in class with what you're experiencing out of class.	If you're particularly interested in hands-on learning, ask your advisor to recommend classes with service-learning components that will benefit you.

These experiences help you in two ways. First, they allow you to test a potential career field. The actual day-to-day work may be exactly what you

BOX 11.2

A Model Résumé

In today's competitive world, when literally hundreds of people may be applying for one choice position, how should a résumé be written? Can a résumé be appealing, but not flashy? Solid, but not stuffy? Professional, but still personal? Thorough, but brief? Take a look at Jennifer's and see what you think.

> This résumé uses a skills approach, rather than a chronological approach. A chronological approach works best if you have a career underway and can list various relevant positions that prepared you for this one.

JENNIFER DANIELS

> Center your name, and use a standard résumé format. Many companies now scan résumés so that they can be read conveniently from one source. Skip the neon pink paper. Go for a highly professional look.

Current Address:

Evelyn Edwin Living-Learning Center
Rocky Mountain State University
Great Bluffs, CO 89898
(100) 555–6543 or jdaniels@rmsu.edu

Permanent Address:

1234 Aspen Way
Vail, CO 81657
(101) 555–9128

> Provide both your temporary address, if you're attending college away from home, and your actual home address. The employer may save your résumé and call you later, over the summer, for example, if the current opening is filled by someone else.

CAREER OBJECTIVE

> Build your career objective according to the position's advertised needs. "One size fits all" doesn't work when it comes to résumés.

To obtain a position as a communications specialist in a large company, designing web pages, creating internal e-newsletters, and planning corporate events.

EDUCATION

> Provide numbers whenever you can. Text can be glossed over, but numbers stand out and make your accomplishments more quantifiable.

Dog ear this page for when I need to write my résumé!

Rocky Mountain State University, Great Bluffs, CO
Bachelor of Arts, Communication Major, 2010 (Minor: Spanish)
GPA 3.6/4.0
Personally financed 80% of college tuition through employment and athletic scholarship

HONORS

Secretary, RMSU Freshman Honor Society
Vail "Invest in the Future" League Soccer Scholarship (4 years, chosen from 150 applicants)

SUMMARY OF BEST ACADEMIC COURSEWORK

> Select coursework that applies directly to the advertised position.

Organizational Communication
Business and Professional Communication
Principles of Web Design

Advanced Composition
Emerging Technologies
Event Planning

SKILLS

Technology

> Technology is important in today's workplace. Don't underrate your competence. Many senior employees don't know as much as you do!

Part-time work, web page design
Proficient in Word, PowerPoint, Excel, Access, Macromedia Flash, Adobe Acrobat, and Photoshop
Event Planning
RMSU Freshman Honor Society, planned campus ceremonies for 1,000 guests (2 years)
Student Government, Campus Life Committee Chair (1 year)
Soccer Fundraising Events, Planning Committee Chair (3 years)
Writing
1st place winner, campus creative writing competition, 2009

EMPLOYMENT HISTORY

> If you're able, show that you have worked all throughout college to demonstrate your commitment to your goal.

Intern, Peak Industries, Human Resources Department, fall 2009
Student Assistant, Office of the Dean, Arts and Sciences, spring 2008
Residence Life, Floor Supervisor (2 years)
Hostess, Pancake Heaven, summers, 2006–2009

REFERENCES (available on request)

> Always obtain preapproval from your references, even if you don't list their names. You may be asked to provide them on a moment's notice.

Jose Luis Pelaez, Inc./Corbis Edge/CORBIS

expected, or not. They show you whether or not that particular career field is one you'd really be interested in. *I had no idea this field was so cutthroat, hectic, dull . . . exciting, stimulating, invigorating. . . .* A thumbs-down can be just as informative as a thumbs-up. At least you can eliminate one option from your list. Second, internships, co-ops, and service-learning opportunities give you experience to list on your résumé. That's invaluable!

Sometimes internships are offered through your academic major department, or through a central office on campus, or sometimes you can pursue one on your own through the Internet or personal connections. If you want to major in journalism, for example, you might try contacting your local newspaper, a business magazine that focuses on your city, or some other published outlet to find out if they're willing to sponsor you. *I'm a journalism major at X university, and I'm looking for an internship opportunity. I'm particularly interested in working at the* Daily Planet, *especially on the Education Beat, because I'm trying to learn more about this city and its school system.* If you receive pay, it may be a modest amount. You're in a learning mode, and you don't have experience, after all. If you land the internship through your school, you may receive course credit instead of pay.

The key to successful "trial" experiences such as internships is the relationship between you and your sponsor in the host organization. If you're not being given enough to do, or not allowed to test your competence in a particular area, speak up. The answer may be put in terms of "company policy," your "not quite ready for prime time" skills, or your supervisor's unwillingness to experiment in high-stakes areas. Nevertheless, the two of you must communicate about these kinds of important issues. No one can read your mind!

As you work your way toward launching your career, keep up with the latest information. Read up on interviewing (see Box 11.1), résumé writing (see Box 11.2), networking, hot career fields, and the latest employment trends. As you continue studying in your college courses, apply what you're learning—in your major and in your general education courses—to your future career. You'll be the winner!

Managing Money for Success

So how do you make all these dreams come true—while you're in college and afterwards as you launch your career? College is an investment. It takes your time, energy, attention, focus—and yes, your money. College is about self-responsibility. You're in charge of your education; you call the shots. If you manage your time and money, you can focus as you should on your courses. If you "spend" unwisely—in either area—you lose your focus and your performance slips. In your career, the same will be true. Your ability to manage money will affect your personal and professional future.

So what does financial management in college have to do with financial success in life? Studies show that working too many hours for pay increases your chances of dropping out of college.[20] Many students find themselves working more so that they can spend more, which in turn takes time away from their studies, or taking a semester off from college to make a pile of money and never coming back. While there's evidence that working a moderate amount can help you polish your time and energy management skills, the real secret to financial success in college can be reduced to one word: budget. You have to earn your money through hard work and spend and save it wisely.

Creating a budget may sound like hard work, but it is important. A budget is simply an itemized estimate of income and expenses that helps you develop a personal spending plan. When you break down your money in versus money out, you see reality in black and white, and you may be surprised by comparing the two totals. You may also realize that you need stop any unplanned spending.

BOX 11.3 The Perils of Plastic

The "newly minted" Credit Card Act of 2009 has changed some things about how credit cards work. In 2008 before the law went into effect, college students carried a balance of $3,173 (a ten-year high), and a full 82 percent kept paying on a balance every month.[21] Under the new law, credit cards cannot be issued to people under the age of 21 unless they have an adult co-signer or can show proof that they have enough income. College students will need permission from parents/guardians to increase their credit limits. And those under 21 will be protected from "sneaky" credit card offers unless they opt to get them. Read up on credible Internet sites about the new law and the protections and restrictions it provides. If you already have a credit card or plan to get one, however, keep this general advice in mind.

1. **Think about the difference between needs and wants.** You may think you need particular things so that your friends will like you ("Hey, let's stop for a burger"), so that you have a new item (like a new car you can't afford), or so that you look fabulous (like pricey manicures). Here's a rule of thumb: If buying something simply helps you move from acceptable to amazing, it's not an emergency. Do you really need a mocha latté every day? A regular old cup of coffee a day sets you back $500 per year!

2. **Leave home without it.** Don't routinely take your credit card with you. Use cash and save your credit card for true emergencies or essentials, like gas and groceries. Do you really want to risk paying interest on today's ice cream cone years from now?

3. **Don't spend money you don't have.** Only charge what you can pay for each month. Just because your credit card limit is $2,000 doesn't mean you need to spend that much each month. A vacation that costs $1,000 will take 12 years of minimal payments

to pay off at an 18 percent interest rate. And that $1,000 trip will eventually cost you $2,115!

4. **Understand how credit works.** It's important to know the basics. In one study, 71 percent of new college students had no idea how much interest they were paying on their credit card bills.[22] Here are some terms you need to know:

   • **Credit reports.** Your credit history is based on (1) how many credit cards you owe money on, (2) how much money you owe, and (3) how many late payments you make. Bad grades on your credit report can make your life difficult later.

   • **Fees.** Credit card companies charge you in three ways: (1) annual fees (a fee you must pay every year to use the card); (2) finance charges (a charge for loaning you the money you can't pay back when your bill is due); and (3) late fees (for missing a monthly payment deadline). Think about what's most important to you—no annual fee, frequent flyer miles, lower interest rate—shop around!

   • **The fine print.** How can you learn more? Read your credit card contract carefully. Credit card companies must give you certain important information, which is often on their website. Go to the Federal Reserve website for vital, bottomline information, and search online to find out more about ways the new law could affect you.[23]

5. **Track your expenses.** All kinds of tools—technology-based and otherwise—can help you discover where your money actually goes. To control your spending, use a credit card with caution or use a debit card.

6. **If you're already in financial trouble, ask for help.** Talk to an expert who can help you figure out what to do.[24]

Your Monthly Budget

Part A: Monthly Income

How much income do you expect to make per month? Make sure you figure in everything.

Loans, grants, scholarships	$_____
Support from parents, other family members, spouse, etc.	$_____
Paycheck	$_____
Cash on hand	$_____
Other	$_____
Total	$_____

Next, begin recording your monthly expenditures. Start with fixed costs that remain the same from month to month, such as rent or a car payment. Do you pay tuition in installments, or is all your tuition due by a certain date? It may help to collect actual receipts or bills and have them in front of you as you work. Once you begin recording, you may be surprised to find out exactly where your money goes.

Part B: Monthly Expenses

Tuition	$_____
Room or rent/mortgage	$_____
Board or food (groceries)	$_____
Books, supplies for school	$_____
Transportation, car payment, etc.	$_____
Computer/electronics (printer cartridges, high-speed Internet hookup, etc.)	$_____
Travel (trips home, vacations, etc.)	$_____
Entertainment (movies, music, DVDs, eating out)	$_____
Utilities (phone, electricity, heat, water, garbage removal, etc.)	$_____
Personal items (haircut/color, cosmetics, gym membership, etc.)	$_____
Credit card payments	$_____
Cash withdrawals	$_____
Other (child care, vet visits, etc.)	$_____
Total	$_____
Money IN from Part A	$_____
(Minus) Money OUT from Part B	$_____
Amount remaining to save or invest	$_____

Look over your expenses. Obviously, if your expenditure total is larger than your income, it's time to reevaluate and come up with a budget you can actually live with. But, how much money do you spend on an average day?

Create a Spending Log

Take a look at this student's spending log, then complete one for yourself. Money has a way of slipping through our fingers. Choose one entire day that is representative of your spending, and use this chart to keep track of how you spend money. Write down everything from seemingly small, insignificant items to major purchases, and explain why you made that purchase. Your log may look something like this student's:

TIME	ITEM	LOCATION	AMOUNT	REASON
8–9 a.m.	coffee and bagel	convenience store	$3.50	overslept!
9–10 a.m.	computer paper	office supply store	$2.50	English paper due
10–11 a.m.	gas fill-up	gas station	$65.00	running on fumes!
11 a.m.–12 p.m.	burger and fries	fast-food restaurant	$6.00	lunch on the run
12–1 p.m.	toiletries, etc.	drugstore	$18.00	out of stock
1–2 p.m.	bottled water	convenience store	$2.50	forgot to bring
2–3 p.m.	supplies	bookstore	$12.00	forgot to get earlier
3–4 p.m.	STUDY TIME			
4–5 p.m.	STUDY TIME			
5–6 p.m.	pizza	pizza place	$12.00	meet friends
6-7 p.m.	soft drink	bookstore	$1.50	Bring to library
8-9 p.m.	candy bar	vending machine	$1.50	munchies!
9–10 p.m.	laundry	laundromat	$5.00	out of clean clothes
10–11 p.m.	STUDY TIME			
11 p.m.–12 a.m.	weekend movie, online tickets, DVDs, cell phone upgrade	Internet retail websites, phone service	$129.00 $20.00	friend's recommendations, need more minutes

This student has spent $249 today without doing anything special! When you analyze his expenditures, you can find patterns. He seems to (1) spend money at the campus bookstore throughout the day, (2) spend relatively large amounts of money online, (3) be particularly vulnerable late at night, and (4) spend money grabbing food on the run. These are patterns he should be aware of if he wants to control his spending. He could pack food from home to save a significant amount of money, for example. Now create your own chart.

TIME	ITEM	LOCATION	AMOUNT	REASON
8–9 a.m.				
9–10 a.m.				
10–11 a.m.				
11 a.m.–12 p.m.				
12–1 p.m.				
1–2 p.m.				
2–3 p.m.				
3–4 p.m.				
4–5 p.m.				

(continued)

5–6 p.m.				
6-7 p.m.				
8-9 p.m.				
9–10 p.m.				
10–11 p.m.				
11 p.m.–12 a.m.				

What patterns do you notice about your spending? What kinds of changes will you try to make to curb any unnecessary spending?

Finanical Aid: Top Ten FAQs

Tuition, books, housing, transportation—it all adds up. Most students need financial help of some kind to earn a college degree. Here is some information to help you navigate your way financially to ensure that you can keep on working towards your career goals.[25]

1. **Who qualifies for financial aid?** You may not think you qualify for financial aid, but it's a good idea to apply anyway. You won't know until you try, and some types of aid are based on criteria other than need.

2. **What does FAFSA stand for? And where do I get a copy?** FAFSA stands for Free Application for Federal Student Aid, and you can get a copy from your campus Financial Aid office, a public library, by calling 1-800-4-FED-AID, or go to www.fafsa.ed.gov and fill out the FAFSA online.

3. **What types of financial aid exist?** You can receive financial aid in the form of scholarships, fellowships, loans, grants, or work-study awards. Generally, scholarships and fellowships are for students with special academic, artistic, or athletic abilities; students with interests in specialized fields; students from particular parts of the country; or students from underrepresented populations. Typically, you don't repay them. Loans and grants come in a variety of forms and from several possible sources, either government or private. Typically, loans must be repaid. In addition, if you qualify for a need-based work-study job on or off campus, you can earn an hourly wage to help pay for school.

4. **When should I apply?** You can apply for financial aid any time after January 1 of the year you intend to go to college (because tax information from the previous year is required), but you must be accepted and enrolled to receive funds.

5. **Do I have to reapply every year?** Yes. Your financial situation can change over time. Your brothers or sisters may start college while you're in school, for example, which can change your family's status.

6. **How can I keep my financial aid over my college years?** Assuming your financial situation remains fairly similar from year to year, you must demonstrate that you're making progress toward a degree in terms of credits and a minimum GPA.

7. **Who's responsible for paying back my loans?** You are. Others can help you, but ultimately the responsibility is yours and yours alone. If your parents forget to make a payment or don't pay a bill on time, you will be held responsible.

8. **If I leave school for a time, do I have to start repaying my loans right away?** Most loans have a grace period of six or nine months before you must begin repayment. You can request an extension if you "stop out," but you must do so before the grace period ends.

9. **If I get an outside scholarship, should I report it to the Financial Aid office on campus?** Yes. They'll adjust your financial aid package accordingly, but those are the rules.

10. **Where can I find out more?** Your best source of information is in the Office of Financial Aid right on your own campus. Or call the Federal Student Aid Information Center at 1-800-433-3243 and ask for a free copy of The Student Guide: Financial Aid from the U.S. Department of Education.

My, How You've Grown! Goodbye and Good Luck!

Remember Aunt Ruth (or whatever her name was)? Every time she visited when you were a kid, she remarked about how much you'd grown. She loved watching you grow, and the fact that she noticed made you feel special. In this first term of college, you have grown. You have gained new perspectives, new insights, and new ways of thinking about things. If those close to you are threatened by these changes, reassure them that your newfound knowledge hasn't made you think less of them. Remember: "You should have education enough so that you won't have to look up to people; and then more education so that you will be wise enough not to look down on people." If they are proud of you and your accomplishments, and have supported you along the way, thank them!

The important thing is to keep learning and never stop. Continuing to learn—whether in college or in life—is what will determine who you are and what you will become. This book, and the course for which you're reading it, have begun that process. Now the rest is up to you!

> " The self is not something that one finds. It's something one creates."

Thomas Szasz, Professor Emeritus in Psychiatry, State University of New York Health Science Center, Syracuse

Complete the recommended activity for your preferred VARK learning modality. If you are multimodal, select more than one activity. Your instructor may ask you to (a) give an oral report on your results in class, (b) send your results to him or her via e-mail, (c) post them online, or (d) contribute to a class chat.

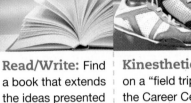

Visual: Select a quotation from this chapter that was particularly memorable to you. Create a poster of the quote, using large font and graphics, to hang on a wall in your room.

Aural: Talk through the Circle of Learning aloud to help you remember the connections between academic disciplines.

Read/Write: Find a book that extends the ideas presented in this chapter. Select a passage that impresses you from the book to share with your classmates.

Kinesthetic: Go on a "field trip" to the Career Center on your campus. Collect resources you find there and bring them to class.

(from left to right) Marcela Barsse/MarsBars/iStockphoto.com; Johanna Goodyear/Dreamstime.com; Nadezda Firsova/iStockphoto.com; Pascal Genest/iStockphoto.com

Very funny video episode available on the CourseMate via www.cengagebrain.com/shop/ISBN/0495906425 :)

? challenge " reaction * insight ! action

Now What Do You Think?

1. At the beginning of this chapter, Ethan Cole, a frustrated and discouraged college student, faced a challenge. Now after reading this chapter, would you respond differently to any of the questions you answered about the "FOCUS Challenge Case"? Knowing what you know now, how would you advise him? Write a paragraph ending to the story, incorporating your best advice.

2. Do a SWOT analysis on yourself. Describe your strengths, weaknesses, opportunities, and threats as they relate to a particular major you may be interested in. Describe the insights you gain from the process.

3. Describe your academic anatomy. Is this something you've thought about before? What majors and careers might be "anatomically correct" for you?

On a scale of 1 to 10, answer the following questions now that you've completed this chapter.

1 = not very/not much/very little/low   10 = very/a lot/very much/high

In hindsight, how much did you already know about this subject before reading the chapter?

1 2 3 4 5 6 7 8 9 10

Can you answer these questions about choosing a major and a career more fully now that you've read the chapter?

1. **What is a SWOT analysis and how might it help you choose a major and career?**

2. **Which comes first—major or career?**

3. **What is your academic anatomy?**

How useful might the information in this chapter be to you? How much do you think this information might affect your success in college?

1 2 3 4 5 6 7 8 9 10

How much do you think this information might affect your career success after college?

1 2 3 4 5 6 7 8 9 10

How long did it actually take you to complete this chapter (both the reading and writing tasks)? _____ Hour(s) _____ Minutes

 Challenge Yourself Online Quiz. To find out just how much you've learned, access the CourseMate via www.cengagebrain.com/shop/ISBN/0495906425 to take the Challenge Yourself Online Quiz.

Take a minute to compare these answers to your answers from the "Readiness Check" at the beginning of this chapter. What gaps exist between the similar questions? How might these gaps between what you thought before starting the chapter and what you now think after completing the chapter affect how you approach your next term of college?

FOCUS Exit Interview

Although you have not quite completed your first term as a college student, we're interested in your reactions to college so far: how you have spent your time, what challenges you've experienced, and your general views about what college has been like. Please answer thoughtfully.

INFORMATION ABOUT YOU

Name _____

Student Number _____ Course/Section _____

Instructor _____

Gender _____ Age _____

INFORMATION ABOUT YOUR COLLEGE EXPERIENCE

1. **How did you find you learned best in college? (Check all that apply.)**

   ____ by looking at charts, maps, graphs   ____ by reading books
   ____ by looking at color-coded information   ____ by writing papers
   ____ by looking at symbols and graphics   ____ by taking notes
   ____ by listening to instructors' lectures   ____ by going on field trips
   ____ by listening to other students during in-class discussions   ____ by engaging in activities
   ____ by talking about course content with friends or roommates   ____ by actually doing things

2. **For each of the following pairs of descriptors, which set sounds most like you based on what you've learned about yourself this term? (Please choose between the two options on each line and place a checkmark by your choice.)**

   ____ Extraverted and outgoing   or   ____ Introverted and quiet
   ____ Detail-oriented and practical   or   ____ Big-picture and future-oriented
   ____ Rational and truthful   or   ____ People-oriented and tactful
   ____ Organized and self-disciplined   or   ____ Spontaneous and flexible

3. *FOCUS* **is about different aspects of college life. Which did you find most interesting personally? Which contained information that you found to be most challenging to apply in your own life? (Check all that apply.)**

Most interested in	Most challenging to apply to myself		Most interested in	Most challenging to apply to myself	
____	____	Building dreams, setting goals	____	____	Developing your memory
____	____	Learning to learn	____	____	Reading and studying
____	____	Managing time and energy	____	____	Taking tests
____	____	Thinking critically and creatively	____	____	Building relationships, valuing diversity
____	____	Developing information literacy, writing, and speaking skills	____	____	Choosing a major and career
____	____	Engaging, listening, and note-taking in class			

4. **Which one of your classes was most challenging this term and why?**

   Which class? (course title *or* department and course number) _____
   Why? _____
   Did you succeed in this class? ____ yes ____ no
   Somewhat (please explain): _____
   _____

5. **How many total hours per week did you spend outside of class studying for your college courses this term?**

___ 0–5	___ 16–20	___ 31–35
___ 6–10	___ 21–25	___ 36–40
___ 11–15	___ 26–30	___ 40+

6. **Which of the following on-campus resources did you use once or more this term? (Please check all that apply.)**

___ library

___ campus learning centers (whatever is available on your campus, such as a Writing Center, Math Learning Center, etc.)

___ computer labs

___ the Student Success Center or New Student Center, if one is available

___ the Counseling Center, if one is available

___ professors' office hours for individual meetings/conferences/help

___ student clubs or organizations

___ none

7. **For the following sets of opposite descriptive phrases, please put a checkmark on the line between the two that best represents your response.**

My first term of college:

challenged me academically	___ ___ ___ ___ ___	was easy
was very different from high school	___ ___ ___ ___ ___	was a lot like high school
was exciting	___ ___ ___ ___ ___	was dull
was interesting	___ ___ ___ ___ ___	was uninteresting
motivated me to continue	___ ___ ___ ___ ___	discouraged me
was fun	___ ___ ___ ___ ___	was boring
helped me feel a part of this campus	___ ___ ___ ___ ___	made me feel alienated

8. **Please mark your _top three areas of concern_ relating to your first term of college by placing 1, 2, and 3 next to the items you choose.**

___ I did not fit in.

___ I did have difficulty making friends.

___ I was not academically successful.

___ My performance disappointed my family.

___ My personal life interfered with my studies.

___ My studies interfered with my personal life.

___ I had financial difficulties.

___ My job(s) interfered with my studies.

___ My studies interfered with my job.

___ My social life interfered with my studies.

___ My studies interfered with my social life.

___ My professors did not care about me as an individual.

___ I may not finish my degree.

___ I missed the company of my friends.

___ I missed the company of my family.

___ I did not manage my time well.

___ I was bored in my classes.

___ I felt intimidated by my professors.

___ I was overwhelmed by all I had to do.

___ other (please explain) _____

9. **Have you changed your thinking about selecting a major since entering college? Broadly speaking, now which area do you expect to major in?**

___ Arts & Sciences	___ Nursing/Health Sciences
___ Education	___ Business
___ Engineering	___ other (please explain) _____

10. **How certain are you now of a chosen major (1 = totally sure, 5 = totally unsure) _____**

11. **How certain are you now that you will complete your degree? (1 = totally sure, 5 = totally unsure) _____**

12. **How certain are you now that you will complete your degree at this school? (1 = totally sure, 5 = totally unsure) _____**

13. **How certain are you now of your intended career choice? (1 = totally sure, 5 = totally unsure) _____**

14. **How certain are you now about whether you'll obtain an advanced degree after you finish college?**
   (1 = totally sure, 5 = totally unsure) _____

15. **What will your grade point average to be at the end of your first term of college?**

____ A+ ____ B+ ____ C+ ____ D or lower

____ A ____ B ____ C

____ A− ____ B− ____ C−

16. **Which of the following sources of information about college turned out to be most accurate? (Mark your top three information sources with 1, 2, and 3.)**

____ TV and movies

____ friends/siblings who have already gone to college

____ discussions with teachers/counselors in high school

____ information I received from colleges in the mail

____ talks with my parents

____ talks with my friends who are also now freshmen

____ the Internet

____ other (please explain) _____

17. **How confident are you in yourself in each of the following areas now? (1 = very confident, 5 = not at all confident)**

____ overall academic ability

____ mathematical skills

____ leadership ability

____ reading skills

____ public speaking skills

____ study skills

____ technology skills

____ physical well being

____ writing skills

____ social skills

____ emotional well being

____ teamwork skills

18. **Why did you decide to go to college? Now that you've experienced your first term of college, how would you respond? (Check all that apply)**

____ because I want to build a better life for myself.

____ because I want to build a better life for my family.

____ because I want to be very well off financially in the future.

____ because I need a college education to achieve my dreams.

____ because my friends were going to college.

____ because my family encouraged me to go.

____ because it was expected of me.

____ because I was recruited for athletics.

____ because I want to continue learning.

____ because the career I am pursuing requires a degree.

____ because I was unsure of what I might do instead.

____ other (please explain) _____

19. **Looking ahead, how satisfied do you expect to be with your decision to attend this school?**

____ very satisfied ____ somewhat dissatisfied

____ satisfied ____ very dissatisfied

____ not sure

20. **Which of the following statements best reflects your educational intention?**

____ I plan to stay at this school until I complete my degree.

____ I plan to transfer to another institution (please identify which one _____)

____ I plan to stop out of college for awhile (to work, for example) and then return to this school.

____ I plan to drop out of college.

21. **If you are thinking about transferring to another institution, why are you thinking of doing so?**

____ This school does not offer my intended major (which is _____).

____ This school is too small.

____ This school is too large.

____ This school is too expensive.

____ I don't feel I fit in.

____ I want to go to a school closer to home.

_____ I want to go to a school further from home.

_____ I want to be closer to my boy/girlfriend.

_____ I want to be closer to my friends.

_____ I will change job locations.

_____ I want to transfer from a two-year to a four-year institution.

_____ I want to transfer from a four-year to a two-year institution.

_____ other (please explain) _____

22. **Did you achieve the outcomes you were hoping to achieve at the beginning of this term? Why or why not?** _____

_____

23. **What was the biggest difference between what you thought college would be like and what it was actually like for you?** _____

_____

Notes

CHAPTER 1

1. Multi-tasking adversely affects brain's learning, UCLA psychologists report. (2006, July 26). *ScienceDaily.* Available at http://www.sciencedaily.com/releases/2006/07/060726083302.htm.

2. Spielberg finally to graduate. (2002, May 15). *BBC News.* Available at http://news.bbc.co.uk/2/hi/entertainment/1988770.stm.

3. Cranton, P. (1994). *Understanding and promoting transformative learning: A guide for educators of adults.* San Francisco: Jossey-Bass.

4. Davis, J. R. (1993). *Better teaching, more learning.* Phoenix, AZ: Oryx Press.

5. French, B. F., & Oakes, W. (2003). Measuring academic intrinsic motivation in the first year of college: Reliability and validity evidence for a new instrument. *Journal of the First-Year Experience, 15*(1), 83–102; French, B. F. Executive summary of instruments utilized with systemwide first-year seminars. Policy Center on the First Year of College.; French, B. F., Immerkus, J. C., & Oakes, W. C. (2005). An examination of indicators of engineering students' success and persistence. *Journal of Engineering Education, 94*(4), 419–425.

6. For more information, see U.S. Department of Labor, Bureau of Labor Statistics, *Occupational Outlook Handbook, 2010–2011 Edition.* Also available at http://www.bls.gov/oco/ocos056.htm.

7. Based on Harrell, K. (2003). *Attitude is everything: 10 life-changing steps to turning attitude into action.* New York: HarperBusiness.

8. Dweck, C. S. (2000). *Self-theories: Their role in motivation, personality, and development.* New York: Psychology Press, p. 1.

9. Brooks, D. (2009, April 30). Genius: The modern view. *The New York Times.* Available at http://www.nytimes.com/2009/05/01/opinion/01brooks.html.

10. Dweck, C. S. (2000). *Self-theories: Their role in motivation, personality, and development.* New York: Psychology Press; Dweck, Mindset.

11. Robins, R. W., & Pals, J. (1998). *Implicit self-theories of ability in the academic domain: A test of Dweck's model. Self and Identity, 1,* 313–356.

12. Mangels, J. A., Butterfield, B., Lamb, J., Good, C. D., & Dweck, C. S. (2006). Why do beliefs about intelligence influence learning success? A social cognitive neuroscience model. *Social Cognitive and Affective Neuroscience, 1*(2), 75–86.

13. Bauer, A. R., Grant, H., & Dweck, C. S. (2006). *Personal goals predict the level and impact of dysphoria.* Unpublished manuscript.

14. Anderson, S. (2009, May 17). In defense of distraction. *New York* (nymag.com). Available at http://nymag.com/news/features/56793/; Gallagher, W. (2009). *Rapt: Attention and the focused life.* New York: Penguin Press; Hamilton, J. (2009, May 13). Think you're multitasking? Think again. *NPR.* Available at http://www.npr.org/templates/story/story.php?storyId=95256794; Tierney, J. (2009, May 4). Ear plugs to lasers: The science of concentration. *The New York Times.* Available at http://www.nytimes.com/2009/05/05/science/05tier.html.

15. Hoover, E. (2006, February 24). Study finds school-college "disconnect" in curricula. *The Chronicle of Higher Education, 52*(25), A1.

16. Omara-Otunnu, E. (2006, July 24). Conference examines transition from high school to college. University of Connecticut *Advance.* Available at http://advance.uconn.edu/2006/060724/06072407.htm.

17. Data show value of college degree. (2005, April 8). *The Chronicle of Higher Education, 51*(31), A22.

18. Pascarella, E. T., & Terenzini, P. T. (2005). *How college affects students: A third decade of research.* San Francisco: Jossey-Bass, p. 403.

CHAPTER 2

1. Leamnson, R. (1999). *Thinking about teaching and learning: Developing habits of learning with first year college and university students.* Sterling, VA: Stylus.

2. Livermore, B. (1992, September–October). Build a better brain. *Psychology Today.* Available at www.psychologytoday.com/articles/pto-19920901-000024.html.

3. Jozefowicz, C. (2004, May–June). Sweating makes you smart. *Psychology Today.* Available at http://psychologytoday.com/articles/pto-20040514-000004.html; Wu, A., Ying, Z., & Gomez-Pinilla, F. (2004). Dietary omega-3 fatty acids normalize BDNF levels, reduce oxidative damage, and counteract learning disability after traumatic brain injury in rats. *Journal of Neurotrauma, 21,* 1457–1467; PT Staff. (1998, March–April). Brain Boosters. *Psychology Today;* Alzheimer's Association. (2004). Think about your future. Maintain your brain today. Available at http://www.alz.org/we_can_help_brain_health_maintain_your_brain.asp.

4. Neergaard, L. (2005, June 20). Brain exercise is key to healthy mind. Available at http://www.online-ambulance.com/articles/doc/13/grp/Senior/art/Brain.htm.

5. Springer, M. V., McIntosh, A. R., Winocur, G., & Grady, C. L. (2005). The relation between brain activity during memory tasks and years of education in young and older adults. *Neuropsychology, 19* (2), 181–192.

6. Csikszentmihalyi, M. (2006). *Flow: The psychology of optimal experience.* New York: Academic Internet Publishers; Csikszentmihalyi, M. (1997). *Creativity: Flow and the psychology of discovery and invention.* New York: Harper Perennial; Gross, R. (1999). *Peak learning.* New York: Tarcher.

7. Caine & Caine, *Making connections;* Jensen, E. (2000). *Different brains, different learners.* San Diego: The Brain Store.

8. Brandt, R. (1998). *Powerful learning.* Alexandria, VA: Association for Supervision and Curriculum Development, p. 29.

9. Campbell, B. (1992). Multiple intelligences in action. *Childhood Education, 68*(4), 197–201; Gardner, H., & Hatch, T. (1989). Multiple intelligences go to school: Educational implications of the theory of multiple intelligences. *Educational Researcher, 18*(8), 4–9; Gardner, H. (1983). *Frames of Mind: The Theory of Multiple Intelligences.* New York: Basic Books. Gardner, H. (2008). *5 minds for the future.* Boston: Harvard Business Press.

10. Armstrong, T. (2000). *MI and cognitive skills.* Available at http://www.ascd.org/publications/books/100041/chapters/MI_and_Cognitive_Skills.aspx.

11. Law of Supply and Demand. *Wikipedia.* Available at http://en.wikipedia.org/wiki/Supply_and_demand.

12. Davis, B. (2009). *Tools for teaching,* second edition. San Francisco: Jossey-Bass, p. 273.

13. Fleming, N. D. (1995). I'm different; not dumb: Modes of presentation (VARK) in the tertiary classroom. In A. Zeimer (Ed.), *Research and Development in Higher Education, Proceedings of the 1995 Annual Conference of the Higher Education and Research Development Society of Austral-asia (HERDSA), HERDSA, 18,* 308–313; Fleming, N. D., & Mills, C. (1992). Not another inventory, rather a catalyst for reflection. *To Improve the Academy, 11,* 137–149. Available at http://www.ntlf.com/html/lib/suppmat/74fleming.htm.

14. Fleming, I'm different; not dumb.

15. Macdaid, G. P., McCaulley, M. H., & Kainz, R. I. (1986). *Atlas of type tables.* Gainesville, FL: Center for Applications of Psychological Type. For more information, see U.S. Department of Labor, Bureau of Labor Statistics, *Occupational Outlook*

Handbook, 2010–2011 Edition. Also available at http://www.bls.gov/oco/ocos066.htm.

16. Fleming, N. D. (2005). *Teaching and learning styles: VARK strategies.* Christchurch, NZ: Microfilm Limited.

CHAPTER 3

1. Eade, D. M. (1998). Energy and success: Time management. *Clinician News,* July/August. Available at http://www.adv-leadership-grp.com/articles/energy.htm.

2. Loehr, J., & Schwartz, T. (2003). *The power of full engagement: Managing energy, not time, is the key to high performance and personal renewal.* New York: Free Press

3. Bittel, L. R. (1991). *Right on time! The complete guide for time-pressured managers.* New York: McGraw-Hill, p. 16.

4. Bittel, *Right on time!* p. 16.

5. Loehr, The power of full engagement.

6. Nathan, R. (2005). *My freshman year: What a professor learned by becoming a student.* Ithaca, NY: Cornell University Press.

7. Schaubhet, N. A., & Thompson, R. C. (2008). MBTI type tables for occupations. Mountain View, CA: CPP, Inc. For more information, see U.S. Department of Labor Statistics, *Occupational Outlook Handbook, 2010–2011 Edition.* Also available at http://www.bls.gov/oco/ocos086.htm.

8. Based on Covey, S. R., Merrill, A. R., & Merrill, R. R. (1996). *First things first: To live, to love, to learn, to leave a legacy.* New York: Free Press, 37.

9. Fortino, M. (2001). *E-mergency.* Groveland, CA: Omni Publishing. Also see The American Time Use Survey results at http://www.bls.gov/news.release/atus.nr0.htm.

10. Hobbs, C. R. (1987). *Time power.* New York: Harper & Row, pp. 9–10.

11. Solomon, L. J., & Rothblum, E. D. (1984). Academic procrastination: Frequency and cognitive-behavioral correlates. *Journal of Counseling Psychology, 31,* 503–509.

12. Hoover, E. (2005, December 9). Tomorrow I love ya! *The Chronicle of Higher Education, 52*(16), A30–32. Available at http://chronicle.com/free/v52/i16/16a03001.htm.

13. Ferrari, J. R., McCown, W. G., & Johnson, J. (2002). *Procrastination and task avoidance: Theory, research, and treatment.* New York: Springer Publishing.

14. Schouwenburg, H. C., Lay, C. H., Pychyl, T. A., & Ferrari, J. R. (Eds.). (2004). *Counseling the procrastinator in academic settings.* Washington DC: American Psychological Association.

15. Steel, P. (2007). The nature of procrastination. *Psychological Bulletin, 133*(1), 65–94.

16. Hoover, Tomorrow I love ya!.

17. Sandholtz, K., Derr, B., Buckner, K., & Carlson, D. (2002). *Beyond juggling: Rebalancing your busy life.* San Francisco: Berrett-Koehler Publishers.

18. Adapted from Sandholtz et al., *Beyond juggling.*

19. Ibid.

CHAPTER 4

1. Halx, M. D., & Reybold, E. (2005). A pedagogy of force: Faculty perspective of critical thinking capacity in undergraduate students. *The Journal of General Education, 54*(4), 293–315.

2. Diestler, S. (2001). *Becoming a critical thinker: A user friendly manual.* Upper Saddle River, NJ: Prentice Hall.

3. Falcione, P. A. (1998). *Critical thinking: What it is and why it counts.* Millbrae, CA: California Academic Press.

4. Twale, D., & Sanders, C. S. (1999). Impact of non-classroom experiences on critical thinking ability. *NASPA Journal, 36*(2), 133–146.

5. Thomas, C., & Smoot, G. (1994, February/March). Critical thinking: A vital work skill. *Trust for Educational Leadership, 23,* 34–38.

6. Kaplan-Leiserson, E. (2004). Workforce of tomorrow: How can we prepare *all* youth for future work success? *Training & Development, 58*(4), 12–14.

7. Van den Brink-Budgen, R. (2000). *Critical thinking for students.* (3rd ed.). Oxford: How to Books; Ruggiero, V. R. (2001). *Becoming a critical thinker.* (4th ed.). Boston: Houghton Mifflin.

8. Buddy, T. (2003, November 20). *About.com: alcoholism.* Crime and alcohol. Available at http://alcoholism.about.com/cs/costs/a/aa980415.htm.

9. Blakey, E., & Spence, S. (1990). Developing metacognition. ERIC Clearinghouse on Information Resources, Syracuse NY. Available at http://www.vtaide.com/png/ERIC/Metacognition.htm.

10. Schaubhut, N. A., & Thompson, R. C. (2008). *MBTI type tables for occupations.* Mountain View: CA: CPP, Inc. For more information, see U.S. Department of Labor Statistics, *Occupational Outlook Handbook, 2010–2011 Edition.* Also available at http://www.bls.gov/oco/ocos053.htm.

11. Florida, R. (2002). The rise of the creative class: And how it's transforming work, leisure, community and everyday life. New York: Basic Books, xii.

12. Ibid.

13. Vance, E. (2007, February 2). College graduates lack key skills, report says. *The Chronicle of Higher Education, 53*(22), A30.

14. Kurtz, J. R. (1998). It's all in your mind! Creative thinking essential in times of change. *Outlook, 66*(3), 5.

15. Rowe, A. J. (2004). *Creative intelligences: discovering the innovative potential in ourselves and others.* Upper Saddle, NJ: Pearson Education, pp. 3–6, 34.

16. Ibid.

17. Adapted from Adler, R., & Proctor, R. F. II. (2011). *Looking out/Looking in.* (13th ed.). New York: Holt, Rinehart, and Winston, pp. 110-116.

18. Douglas, J. H. (1977). The genius of everyman (2): Learning creativity. *Science News, 111*(8), 284–288.

19. Harris, R. (1998). Introduction to creative thinking. *VirtualSalt.* Available at http://www.virtualsalt.com/crebook1.htm.

20. Eby, D. Creativity and flow psychology. Available at http://talentdevelop.com/articles/Page8.html.

CHAPTER 5

1. Guess, A. (2007, September 17). Students' "evolving" use of technology. *Inside Higher Ed.* Available at http://www.insidehighered.com/news/2007/09/17/it; Caruso, J. B., & Salaway, G. (2007, September). Key findings: The ECAR study of undergraduate students and information technology, 2007. *Educause.* Available at http://net.educause.edu/ir/library/pdf/ERS0706/EKF0706.pdf.

2. Caruso, J. B., & Salaway, G. (2007, September). Key findings: The ECAR study of undergraduate students and information technology, 2007. *Educause.* Available at http://net.educause.edu/ir/library/pdf/ERS0706/EKF0706.pdf.

3. Ibid.

4. Hendry, E. (2009, July 20). Students may not be as software-savvy as they think, study says. *The Wired Campus: The Chronicle of Higher Education.* Available at http://chronicle.com/blogPost/Students-May-Not-Be-as/7276; Grant, D. M., Malloy, A. D., & Murphy, M C. (2009). A comparison of student perceptions of their computer skills to their actual abilities. *Journal of Information Technology Education, 8.* Available at http://jite.org/documents/Vol8/JITEv8p141-160Grant428.pdf.

5. *Internet World Stats.* Available at http://www.internetworldstats.com/stats.htm.

6. Greene, L. (2006, March 8). You might be a Facebook stalker if. . . . *Winonan;* Hollister, L. (2005, October 4). Facebook addiction is needless, yet compelling. *The Volante Online.* Available at http://www.volanteonline.com/2.7412/facebook-addiction-is-needless-yet-compelling-1.787418.

7. Greenfield, D. N. (1999). *Virtual addiction.* Oakland, CA: New Harbinger Publications; Yair, E., & Hamburger, A. (2005). *The social net.* Oxford: Oxford University Press; Young, K. S. (1998). Caught in the net. New York: John Wiley.

8. What is research? In Leedy, P. (1997). *Practical Research: Planning and Design*, Sixth Edition, Upper Saddle River, NJ: Merrill Prentice Hall.

9. Fitzgerald, M. A. (2004). Making the leap from high school to college. *Knowledge Quest*, *32*(4), 19–24; Ehrmann, S. (2004). Beyond computer literacy: Implications of technology for the content of a college education. *Liberal Education*. http://www.eric.ed.gov/PDFS/EJ682582.pdf.; Thacker, P. (2006, November 15). Are college students techno idiots? *Inside Higher Ed.* Available at http://www.insidehighered.com/news/2006/11/15/infolit.

10. Ableson, H. Ledeen, K., & Lewis, H. (2008). *Blown to bits: your life, liberty, and happiness after the digital explosion.* Boston, MA: Pearson Education, Inc.

11. McCarroll, C. (2001). To learn to think in college, write—a lot. *Christian Science Monitor*, *93*(177), 20.

12. Portions of this section are based on Staley, C., & Staley, R. (1992). *Communicating in business and the professions: The inside word.* Belmont, CA: Wadsworth.

13. Portions based on Staley & Staley, *Communicating in business and the professions.*

14. Engleberg, I. N. (1994). *The principles of public presentation.* New York: HarperCollins; Daley, K., & Daley-Caravella, L. (2004). *Talk your way to the top.* New York: McGraw-Hill.

15. Schaubhut, N. A., & Thompson, R C. (2008). *MBTI type tables for occupations.* Mountain View, CA: CPP, Inc.; For more information, see U.S. Department of Labor, Bureau of Labor Statistics, *Occupational Outlook Handbook, 2010–2011 Edition.* Also available at http://www.bls.gov/oco/ocos020.htm.

CHAPTER 6

1. Based on http://www-sop.inria.fr/acacia/personnel/Fabien.Gandon/lecture/uk1999/history/.

2. Burchfield, C. M., & Sappington, J. (2000). Compliance with required reading assignments. *Teaching of Psychology*, *27*(1), 58–60; Hobson, E. H. (2004). *Getting students to read: Fourteen tips.* IDEA Paper No. 40, Manhattan, KS: Kansas State University, Center for Faculty Evaluation and Development; Maleki, R. B., & Heerman, C. E. (1992). *Improving student reading.* IDEA Paper No. 26, Manhattan, KS: Kansas State University, *Center for Faculty Evaluation and Development.* Most Idea Center papers available at http://www.idea.ksu.edu/.

3. Gump, S. E. (2005). The cost of cutting class: Attendance as a predictor of student success. *College Teaching*, *53*(1), 21–25.

4. Marburger, D. R. (2001). Absenteeism and undergraduate exam performance. *Journal of Economic Education*, *32*, 99–109.

5. Perkins, K. K., & Wieman, C. E. (2005). The surprising impact of seat location on student performance. *The Physics Teacher*, *43*(1), 30–33. Available at http://scitation.aip.org/journals/doc/PHTEAH-ft/vol_43/iss_1/30_1.html.

6. Armbruster, B. B. (2000). Taking notes from lectures. In R. F. Flippo & D. C. Caverly (Eds.), *Handbook of college reading and study strategy research* (pp. 175–199). Mahwah, NJ: Erlbaum.

7. Staley, C. C., & Staley, R. S. (1992). *Communicating in business and the professions: The inside word.* Belmont, CA: Wadsworth, p. 223.

8. Hughes, C. A., & Suritsky, S. K. (1993). Notetaking skills and strategies for students with learning disabilities. *Preventing School Failure*, *38*(1).

9. Selby, J. (2004). *Quiet your mind.* Makawao, Maui, HI: Inner Ocean Publishing.

10. Staley & Staley, *Communicating in business and the professions*, pp. 229–236.

11. Kiewra, K. A., Mayer, R. E., Christensen, M., Kim, S., & Risch, N. (1991). Effects of repetition on recall and note-taking: Strategies for learning from lectures. *Journal of Educational Psychology*, *83*, 120–123. Cheng, J. (2009, February 25). Study: Class podcasts can lead to better grades. *ars technica.* Available at http://arstechnica.com/web/news/2009/02/study-listening-to-podcasts-better-than-going-to-lectures.ars.

12. Brock, R. (2005, October 28). Lectures on the go. *The Chronicle of Higher Education*, *52*(10), A39–42; French, D. P. (2006). iPods: Informative or invasive? *Journal of College Science Teaching*, *36*(1), 58–59; Hallett, V. (2005, October 17). Teaching with tech. *U.S. News & World Report*, *139*(14), 54–58; *The Horizon Report.* (2006). Stanford, CA: The New Media Consortium.

13. 13. Bloom, B. S. (Ed.). (1956). *A taxonomy of educational objectives (cognitive domain).* New York: Longman.

14. Peverly, S. T., Ramaswamy, V., Brown, C., Sumowski, J., Alidoost, M., & Garner, J. (2007). What predicts skill in lecture note taking? *Journal of Educational Psychology*, *99*(1), 167–180.

15. Palmatier, R. A., & Bennett, J. M. (1974). Note-taking habits of college students. *Journal of Reading*, *18*, 215–218; Dunkel, P., & Davy, S. (1989). The heuristic of lecture notetaking: Perceptions of American and international students regarding the value and practices of notetaking. *English for Specific Purposes*, *8*, 33–50.

16. Armbruster, *Handbook of college reading and study strategy research.*

17. Van Meter, P., Yokoi, L., & Pressley, M. (1994). College students' theory of note-taking derived from their perceptions of note-taking. *Journal of Educational Psychology*, *86*, 323–338.

18. Davis, M., & Hult, R. (1997). Effects of writing summaries as a generative learning activity during note taking. *Teaching of Psychology 24*(1), 47–49; Boyle, J. R., & Weishaar, M. (2001). The effects of strategic notetaking on the recall and comprehension of lecture information for high school students with learning disabilities. *Learning Disabilities Research & Practice 16*(3); Kiewra, K. A. (2002). How classroom teachers can help students learn and teach them how to learn. *Theory into Practice 41*(2), 71–81; Aiken, E. G., Thomas, G. S., & Shennum, W. A. (1975). Memory for a lecture: Effects of notes, lecture rate and informational density. *Journal of Educational Psychology*, *67*, 439–444; Hughes, C. A., & Suritsky, S. K. (1994). Note-taking skills of university students with and without learning disabilities. *Journal of Learning Disabilities*, *27*, 20–24.

19. Bonner, J. M., & Holliday, W. G. (2006). How college science students engage in note-taking strategies. *Journal of Research in Science Teaching*, *43*(8), 786–818.

20. Pauk, W. (2000). *How to study in college.* Boston: Houghton Mifflin.

21. Pardini, E. A., Domizi, D. P., Forbes, D. A., & Pettis, G. V. (2005). Parallel note-taking: A strategy for effective use of Webnotes. *Journal of College Reading and Learning*, *35*(2), 38–55. Available at http://www.biology.wustl.edu/pardini/TeachingMaterials/JCRL_spring2005_pardini.pdf.

22. Kiewra, How classroom teachers can help students learn and teach them how to learn.

23. Porte, L. K. (2001). Cut and paste 101. *Teaching Exceptional Children*, *34*(2), 14–20.

24. Craik, F. I. M., & Watkins, M. J. (1973). The role of rehearsal in short-term memory. *Journal of Verbal Learning and Verbal Behavior*, *12*, 599–607.

25. For more information, see U.S. Department of Labor, Bureau of Labor Statistics, *Occupational Outlook Handbook, 2010–2011 Edition.* Available at http://www.bls.gov/oco/ocos088.htm.

26. Glenn, D. (2009, May 1). Close the book. Recall. Write it down. *The Chronicle of Higher Education.* Available at http://chronicle.com/article/Close-the-Book-Recall-Write/31819.

CHAPTER 7

1. http://sci.gallaudet.edu/Physics12/Syllabus04.html

2. Gordon, B. (1995). *Memory: Remembering and forgetting in everyday life.* New York: Mastermedia Limited.

3. Bolla, K. I., Lindgren, K. N., Bonaccorsy, C., & Bleecker, M. L. (1991). Memory complaints in older adults: Fact or fiction? *Archives of Neurology*, *48*, 61–64.

4. Higbee, K. L. (2004). What aspects of their memories do college students most want to improve? *College Student Journal, 38*(4), 552–556.

5. Higbee, K. L. (1988). *Your memory: How it works and how to improve it* (2nd ed.). New York: Prentice Hall.

6. Ibid.

7. Nairine, J. S. (2006). *Psychology: The adaptive mind.* Belmont, CA: Wadsworth/Thomson Learning.

8. Klingberg, T., Fernell, E., Olesen, P. J., Johnson, M., Gustafsson, P., Dahlström, K., Gillberg, C. G., Forssberg, H., Westerberg, H. (2005). Computerized training of working memory in children with ADHD—a randomized, controlled trial. *Journal of the American Academy of Child and Adolescent Psychiatry, 44*(2), 177–186.

9. Macdaid, G. P., McCaulley, M. H., & Kainz, R. I. (1986). *Atlas of type tables.* Gainesville, FL: Center for Applications of Psychological Type. For more information, see U.S. Department of Labor, Bureau of Labor Statistics, *Occupational Outlook Handbook, 2010–2011 Edition.*

10. Nairine, *Psychology.*

11. Miller, G. A. (1956). The magical number seven plus or minus two: Some limits on our capacity for processing information. *Psychological Review, 63*, 81–97.

12. Narayanan, K. (2004, July 7). The neurological scratchpad: What is working memory? *Brain Connection.com.* Available at http://brainconnection.positscience.com/topics/?main=fa/working-memory2; Kotbagi, H. (1997). Human memory. Available at http://www.cc.gatech.edu/classes/cs6751_97_winter/Topics/human-cap/memory.html; Clark, D. Memory: Learning and memory. Available at http://www.nwlink.com/~donclark/hrd/learning/memory.html; Kerry, S. (1999–2002). Memory and retention time. *EducationReform.net.* Available at http://www.education-reform.net/memory.htm; Goodhead, J. (1999). The difference between short-term and long-term memory [On-line].

13. Rozakis, L. (2003). *Test-taking strategies and study skills for the utterly confused.* New York: McGraw Hill; Meyers, J. N. (2000). *The secrets of taking any test.* New York: Learning Express; Ehren, B. J. Mnemonic devices. *Back to College.* Available at http://itc.gsu.edu/academymodules/a304/support/xpages/a304b0_20600.html; Lloyd, G. (1998–2004). Study skills: Memorize with mnemonics. Available at http://www.back2college.com/memorize.htm.

14. Willingham, D. T. (2004). Practice makes perfect—but only if you practice beyond the point of perfection. *American Educator.* Available at http://www.aft.org/newspubs/periodicals/ae/spring2004/willingham.cfm.

15. Tigner, R. B. (1999). Putting memory research to good use: Hints from cognitive psychology. *College Teaching, 47*(4), 149–152.

16. Murdock, B. B., Jr. (1960). The distinctiveness of stimuli. *Psychological Reports, 67*, 16–31; Neath, I. (1993). Distinctiveness and serial position effects in recognition. *Memory & Cognition, 21*, 689–698.

17. Cahill, L. (2003). Similar neural mechanisms for emotion-induced memory impairment and enhancement. *Proceedings of the National Academy of Sciences, 100*(23), 13123–13124. Available at http://www.pnas.org/cgi/content/full/100/23/13123.

18. Dingfelder, S. F. (2005, September). Feelings' sway over memory. *Monitor on Psychology, 26*(8). Available at APA Online at http://www.apa.org/monitor/sep05/feelings.html.

19. Noice, H., & Noice, T. (2006). What studies of actors and acting can tell us about memory and cognitive functioning. *Current Directions in Psychological Science, 15*(1), 14–18.

20. Higbee, *Your memory.*

21. Ibid.

22. Bean, J. (1996). *Engaging ideas.* San Francisco: Jossey-Bass.

23. Tigner, Putting memory research to good use.

24. Higbee, *Your memory.*

25. Caine, R. N., & Caine, G. (1997). *Education on the edge of possibility.* Alexandria, VA: Association for Supervision and Curriculum Development.

26. Berk, R. A. (2002). *Humor as an instructional defibrillator.* Sterling, VA: Stylus; Berk, R. A. (2003). *Professors are from Mars®, students are from Snickers®.* Sterling, VA: Stylus.

27. Tagg, J. (2004, March–April). Why learn? What we may really be teaching students. *About Campus,* 2–10; Marton, F., & Säljö, R. On qualitative differences in learning: I-Outcome and process. (1976). *British Journal of Educational Psychology, 46*, 4–11.

CHAPTER 8

1. Rogers, M. (2007, March–April). Is reading obsolete? *The Futurist,* 26–27; Waters, L. (2007, February 9). Time for reading. *The Chronicle of Higher Education, 53*(23), 1B6.

2. Caverly, D. C., Nicholson, S. A., & Radcliffe, R. (2004). The effectiveness of strategic reading instruction for college developmental readers. *Journal of College Reading and Learning, 35*(1), 25–49; Simpson, M. L., & Nist, S. L. (1997). Perspectives on learning history: A case study. *Journal of Literacy Research, 29*(3), 363–395.

3. Caverly, Nicholson, & Radcliffe, The effectiveness of strategic reading instruction for college developmental readers; Burrell, K. I., Tao, L., Simpson, M. L., & Mendez-Berrueta, H. (1997). How do we know what we are preparing students for? A reality check of one university's academic literacy demands. *Research & Teaching in Developmental Education, 13*, 15–70.

4. Bean, J. C. (1996). *Engaging ideas: The professor's guide to integrating writing, critical thinking, and active learning in the classroom.* San Francisco: Jossey-Bass; Wood, N. V. (1997). College reading instruction as reflected by current reading textbooks. *Journal of College Reading and Learning, 27*(3). 79–95.

5. Saumell, L., Hughes, M. T., & Lopate, K. (1999). Under-prepared college students' perceptions of reading: Are their perceptions different than other students? *Journal of College Reading and Learning, 29*(2), 123–125.

6. Buzan, T. (1983). *Use both sides of your brain.* New York: E. P. Dutton.

7. Ibid.

8. Sternberg, R. J. (1987). Teaching intelligence: The application of cognitive psychology to the improvement of intellectual skills. In J. B. Baron & R. J. Sternberg (Eds.), *Teaching thinking skills: Theory and practice.* New York: Freeman. pp. 182–218

9. Al-Jarf, R. S. (2002). Effect of online learning on struggling ESL college writers. San Antonio, TX: National Educational Computing Conference. Available at http://faculty.ksu.edu.sa/aljarf/My%20Press%20Room/al-jarf%20-%20NECC%20paper.pdf.

10. Based on Bean, *Engaging ideas.*

11. Based partly on Williams, S. (2005). Guiding students through the jungle of research-based literature. *College Teaching, 53*(4), 137–139.

12. Schaubhut, N. A., & Thompson, R. C. (2008). *MBTI type tables for occupations.* Mountain View, CA: CPP, Inc. For more information, see U.S. Department of Labor, Bureau of Labor Statistics, *Occupational Outlook Handbook, 2010–2011 Edition.* Also available at http://www.bls.gov/oco/ocos069.htm.

13. Soldner, L. B. (1997). Self-assessment and the reflective reader. *Journal of College Reading and Learning, 28*(1), 5–11.

14. Melchenbaum, D., Burland, S., Gruson, L., & Cameron, R. (1985). Metacognitive assessment. In S. Yussen (Ed.), *The growth of reflection in children.* Orlando, FL: Academic Press. p. 5

15. Hall, C. W. (2001). A measure of executive processing skills in college students. *College Student Journal, 35*(3), 442–450; Taylor, S. (1999). Better learning through better thinking: Developing students' metacognitive abilities. *Journal of College Reading and Learning, 30*(1), 34–45.

16. Learning to learn. *Study Guides and Strategies*. Available at http://www.studygs.net/metacognition.htm.

17. Simpson, M. L. (1994/1995). Talk throughs: A strategy for encouraging active learning across the content areas. *Journal of Reading, 38*(4), 296–304.

18. How Air Traffic Control Works. Available at http://travel.howstuffworks.com/air-traffic-control.htm.

19. Elias, M. (2004, April 5). Frequent TV watching shortens kids' attention spans. *USA Today*. Available at http://www.usatoday.com/news/health/2004-04-05-tv-kids-attention-usat_x.htm.

20. When students study makes a difference too. (2005, November). *Recruitment & Retention*.

21. Trainin, G., & Swanson, H. L. (2005). Cognition, metacognition, and achievement of college students with learning disabilities. *Learning Disability Quarterly, 28*, 261–272.

22. Meyers, D. (2001). *Psychology* (6th ed.). New York: Worth Publishers.

CHAPTER 9

1. Petress, K. (2004). What do college examinations accomplish? *College Student Journal, 38*(4), 521–522.

2. Carey, B. (2010, September 6). Forget what you know about good study habits. *The New York Times*. Available at http://www.nytimes.com/2010/09/07/health/views/07mind.html?_r=1&ref=science.

3. Coren, S. (1996). *Sleep thieves*. New York: Free Press; Cox, K. (2004, October 14). The lights are on, but nobody's home. *The Oxford Student*.

4. Grant, K. B. (2003, September 4). Popping pills and taking tests. *The Ithacan Online*. Available at http://www.ithaca.edu/ithacan/articles/0309/04/news/2popping_pill.htm.

5. Brinthaupt, T. M., & Shin, C. M. (2001). The relationship of academic cramming to flow experience. *College Student Journal, 35*(3), 457–472.

6. Tigner, R. B. (1999). Putting memory research to good use: Hints from cognitive psychology. *Journal of College Teaching, 47*(4), 149–152.

7. Small, G. (2002). *The memory bible*. New York: Hyperion.

8. (2010). Test anxiety. *University of Oregon Counseling and Testing Center*. Available at http://counseling.uoregon.edu/dnn/SelfhelpResources/StressandAnxiety/TestAnxiety/tabid/337/Default.aspx.

9. Tozoglu, D., Tozoglu, M. D., Gurses, A., & Dogar, C. (2004). The students' perceptions: Essay versus multiple-choice type exams. *Journal of Baltic Science Education, 2*(6), 52–59.

10. Schutz, P. A., & Davis, H. A. (2000). Emotions and self-regulation during test taking. *Educational Psychologist, 35*(4), 243–256.

11. Coren, *Sleep thieves*.

12. Perina, K. (2002). Sum of all fears. *Psychology Today*. Available at http://www.psychologytoday.com/articles/pto-20021108-000001.html.

13. Perry, A. B. (2004). Decreasing math anxiety in college students. *College Student Journal, 38*(2), 321–324.

14. Perry, Decreasing math anxiety in college students.

15. Jonides, J., Lacey, S. C., & Nee, D. E. (2005). Processes of working memory in mind and brain. *Current Directions in Psychological Science, 14*(1), 2–5.

16. Ashcraft, M. H., & Kirk, E. P. (2001). The relationships among working memory, math anxiety, and performance. *Journal of Experimental Psychology: General. 130*(2), 224–237.

17. Beilock, S. L., Kulp, C. A., Holt, L. E., & Carr, T. H. (2004). More on the fragility of performance: Choking under pressure in mathematical problem solving. *Journal of Experimental Psychology: General, 133*(4), 584–600.

18. Mundell, E. J. (2005, March 9). Test pressure toughest on smartest. *Healingwell.com*. Available at http://news.healingwell.com/index.php?p=news1&id=524405.

19. Firmin, M., Hwang, C., Copella, M., & Clark, S. (2004). Learned helplessness: The effect of failure on test-taking. *Education, 124*(4), 688–693.

20. Heidenberg, A. J., & Layne, B. H. (2000). Answer changing: A conditional argument. *College Student Journal, 34*(3), 440–451.

21. See http://news.bbc.co.uk/2/hi/uk_news/scotland/glasgow_and_west/4755297.stm.

22. Preparing for tests and exams. (2006). York University. Available at http://www.yorku.ca/cdc/lsp/skillbuilding/exams.html#Multiple.

23. Hammer, A. L. (1993). *Introduction to type and careers*. Palo Alto, CA: Consulting Psychologists Press; Henderson-Loney, J. (1996). Steps and types: How the MBTI helped a treatment non-profit develop an effective volunteer program. *Journal of Volunteer Administration, 15*(1), 29–34. For more information, see U.S. Department of Labor, Bureau of Labor Statistics, *Occupational Outlook Handbook, 2010–2011 Edition*. Also available at http://www.bls.gov/oco/cg/cgs054.htm.

24. Taking exams. Brockport High School. Available at http://www.frontiernet.net/~jlkeefer/takgexm.html. Adapted from Penn State University; On taking exams. University of New Mexico. Available at http://www.unm.edu/~quadl/college_learning/taking_exams.html; Lawrence, J. (2006). Tips for taking examinations. Lawrence Lab Homepage. Available at http://cobamide2.bio.pitt.edu/testtips.htm; The multiple choice exam. (2003). Counselling Services, University of Victoria. Available at http://www.coun.uvic.ca/learning/exams/multiple-choice.html; General strategies for taking essay tests. *GWired*. Available at http://gwired.gwu.edu/counsel/asc/index.gw/Site_ID/46/Page_ID/14565/; Test taking tips: Guidelines for answering multiple-choice questions. *Arizona State University*. Available at http://neuer101.asu.edu/additionaltestingtips.htm; Landsberger, J. (2007). True/false tests. *Study Guides and Strategies*. Available at http://www.studygs.net/tsttak2.htm; Landsberger, J. (2007). Multiple choice tests. *Study Guides and Strategies*. Available at http://www.studygs.net/tsttak3.htm; Landsberger, J. (2007). The essay exam. *Study Guides and Strategies*. Available at http://www.studygs.net/tsttak4.htm; Landsberger, J. (2007). Short answer tests. *Study Guides and Strategies*. Available at http://www.studygs.net/tsttak5.htm; Landsberger, J. (2007). Open book tests. *Study Guides and Strategies*. Available at http://www.studygs.net/tsttak7.htm; Rogers, T., & Kline, D. Test-taking advice: Especially for the multiple-choice challenged. *University of Calgary*. Available at http://psych.ucalgary.ca/undergraduate/student-support; Rozakis, L. (2003). *Test-taking strategies and study skills for the utterly confused*. New York: McGraw-Hill; Meyers, J. N. (2000). *The secrets of taking any test*. New York: Learning Express; Robinson, A. (1993). *What smart students know*. New York: Crown Trade Paperbacks.

25. Snyder, T. (2009, January 21). Cheating goes digital. *Edutopia*. Available at http://www.edutopia.org/technology-student-cheating-prevention.

26. *Plagiarism.org*. Available at http://www.plagiarism.org/facts.html; A cheating crisis in America's schools. (2007, 17 April). ABC News. Available at http://abcnews.go.com/Primetime/print?id=132376.

27. Caught cheating. (2004, April 29). *Primetime Live*, ABC News Transcript. Interview of college students by Charles Gibson; Zernike, K. (2002, November 2). With student cheating on the rise, more colleges are turning to honor codes. *The New York Times*, p. Q10, column 1, National Desk; Warren, R. (2003, October 20). Cheating: An easy way to cheat yourself. Available at http://uwf.edu/voyager/archives/102903/page02.pdf; Thomson, S. C. (2004, February 13). Amid wave of cheating, universities push "academic integrity." Knight Ridder/Tribune News Service. Available at http://www.highbeam.com/doc/1G1-113209265.html; Heyboer, K. (2003, August 23). Nearly half of college students say Internet plagiarism isn't cheating. *The Star-Ledger Newark, New Jersey*; Kleiner, C., & Lord, M. (1999). The cheating game. *U.S. News & World*

Report. Available at http://www.usnews.com/usnews/culture/articles/991122/archive_002427.htm.

28. Grant, K. B. (2003). Popping pills and taking tests. *The Ithacan Online*. Available at http://www.ithaca.edu/ithacan/articles/0309/04/news/2popping_pill.htm; Cummins, C. (2004, May 14); Rogers & Kline, Test-taking advice; Rozakis, *Test-taking strategies and study skills for the utterly confused*; Meyers, *The secrets of taking any test*.

CHAPTER 10

1. Some situation topics suggested Hay Group Transforming Learning EI Quiz. *Haygroup.com*. Available at http://www.haygroup.com/leadershipandtalentondemand/Demos/EI_Quiz.aspx.

2. Gardner, H. (1993). *Multiple intelligences: The theory in practice*. New York: Basic Books; Checkley, K. (1997). The first seven . . . and the eighth: A conversation with Howard Gardner. Expanded Academic ASAP (online database). Original Publication: *Education*, 116.

3. Parker, J. D. A., Duffy, J. M., Wood, L. M., Bond, B. J., & Hogan, M. J. (2005). Academic achievement and emotional intelligence: Predicting the successful transition from high school to university. *Journal of the First Year Experience & Students in Transition 17*(1), 67–78; Schutte, N. S., & Malouff, J. (2002). Incorporating emotional skills content in a college transition course enhances student retention. *Journal of the First Year Experience & Students in Transition 14*(1), 7–21; Di Fabio, A., & Palazzeschi, L. (2009). An in-depth look at scholastic success: Fluid intelligence, personality traits or emotional intelligence? *Personality and Individual Differences 46*, 581–585.

4. EQ-i:S™ Post Secondary, Multi-Health Systems, Inc. North Tonawanda, NY. Available at http://www.mhs.com. Used with permission.

5. Turning lemons into lemonade: Hardiness helps people turn stressful circumstances into opportunities. (2003, December 22). *Psychology Matters*. Available at *APA Online* at http://www.apa.org/research/action/lemon.aspx; Marano, H. E. (2003). The art of resilience. *Psychology Today*. Available at http://www.psychologytoday.com/articles/200305/the-art-resilience; Fischman, J. (1987). Getting tough: Can people learn to have disease-resistant personalities? *Psychology Today*, 21, 26–28; Friborg, O., Barlaug, D., Martinussen, M., Rosenvinge, J. H., & Hjemdal, O. (2005). Resilience in relation to personality and intelligence. *International Journal of Methods in Psychiatric Research*, *14*(1), 29–42; Schulman, P. (1995). Explanatory style and achievement in school and work. In G. M. Buchanan & M. E. P. Seligman (Eds.), *Explanatory style* (pp. 159–171). Hillsdale, NJ: Lawrence Erlbaum; American Psychological Association. (1997). Learned optimism yields health benefits. *Discovery Health*. Available at http://health.discovery.com/centers/mental/articles/optimism/optimism.html.

6. Maher, K. (2004) Emotional intelligence is a factor in promotions. *CollegeJournal from the Wall Street Journal*.

7. Cherniss, C. (2000). *Emotional Intelligence: What it is and why it matters*. Paper presented at the Annual Meeting of the Society for Industrial and Organizational Psychology, New Orleans, LA. Available at http://www.eiconsortium.org/research/what_is_emotional_intelligence.html.

8. Goleman, D. (2002, June 16). Could you be a leader? *Parade Magazine*, pp. 4–6.

9. Boyatzis, R. E., Cowan, S. S., & Kolb, D. A. (1995). *Innovations in professional education: Steps on a journey from teaching to learning*. San Francisco: Jossey-Bass.

10. Saxbe, D. (2004, November/December). The socially savvy. *Psychology Today*. Available at http://www.psychologytoday.com/articles/200501/the-socially-savvy.

11. Bar-On, R. (2006). The Bar-On model of emotional-social intelligence (ESI). *Psicothema*, *18* (Suppl.), 13–25. The Consortium for Research on Emotional Intelligence in Organizations. Available at http://www.ressourcesetmanagement.com/Article%20prof%20%20Baron%20.pdf

12. Rath, T., & Clifton, D. O. (2004). *How full is your bucket?* New York: Gallup Press.

13. Cramer, D. (2004). Satisfaction with a romantic relationship, depression, support and conflict. *Psychology and Psychotherapy: Theory, Research and Practice*, 77(4), 449–461.

14. Fisher, H. (2004). *Why we love*. New York: Henry Holt.

15. Beach, S. R. H., & Tesser, A. (1988). Love in marriage; a cognitive account. In R. J. Sternberg & M. L. Barnes (Eds.), *The Psychology of Love*. 330–355 New Haven, CT: Yale University Press; Hatfield, E., & Walster, G. W. (1978). *A new look at love*. Lanham, MD: University Press of America.

16. Knox, D. H. (1970). Conceptions of love at three developmental levels. *The Family Coordinator*, *19*(2), 151–157; Fisher, *Why we love*.

17. Based on Walter, T. L. (2003). Turn a negative student-to-instructor relationship into a positive relationship. In C. Staley, *50 Ways to leave your lectern* (pp. 146–149). Belmont, CA: Wadsworth.

18. Schwartz, P. (2003, May–June). Love is not all you need. *Psychology Today*. Available at http://www.psychologytoday.com/articles/200302/love-is-not-all-you-need.

19. Bach, G. R., & Goldberg, H. (1974). *Creative aggression: The art of assertive living*. Garden City, NJ: Doubleday; Bach, G. R., & Wyden, P. (1972). *The intimate enemy: How to fight fair in love and marriage*. New York: Avon; Bach, G. R., Deutsch, R. M., (1985). *Stop! You're driving me crazy*. New York: Berkley Publishing Group; Tucker-Ladd, C. E. (1996–2006); *Driving each other crazy*. Psychological self-help. Available at http://psychologicalselfhelp.org/Chapter9/chap9_90.html.

20. Fisher, *Why we love*.

21. Fisher, R., & Brown, S. (1988). *Getting together: Building a relationship that gets to yes*. Boston: Houghton Mifflin, p. xi.

22. Based in part on Marano, H. (2002). Relationship rules. *Psychology Today*. Available at http://www.psychologytoday.com/articles/200410/relationship-rules.

23. Dakss, B. (2006, March 3). Study: Bad relationships bad for heart. *CBS News*. Available at http://www.cbsnews.com/stories/2006/03/03/earlyshow/contributors/emilysenay/main1364889.shtml; (2005, December 5) Unhappy marriage: bad for your health. *WebMD*. Available at http://www.webmd.com/sex-relationships/news/20051205/unhappy-marriage-bad-for-your-health. Based on Keicolt-Glaser, J. (2005). *Archives of general psychiatry*, 62, 1377–1384.

24. Dusselier, L., Dunn, B., Wang, Y., Shelley, M. C., & Whalen, D. F. (2005). Personal, health, academic, and environmental predictors of stress for residence hall students. *Journal of American College Health*, *54*(1), 15–24; Hardigg, V., & Nobile, C. (1995). Living with a stranger. *U.S. News & World Report*, *119*(12), 90–91. Nankin, J. (2005). Rules for roomies. *Careers & Colleges*, *25*(4), 29.

25. Miller, G. R., & Steinberg, M. (1975). *Between people: A new analysis of interpersonal communication*. Chicago: Science Research Associates.

26. Bucher, R. D. (2004). *Diversity consciousness: Opening our minds to people, cultures, and opportunities* (2nd ed.). Upper Saddle River, NJ: Pearson Education.

27. Moore, D. G. (2003, November 14). Toward a single definition of college. *The Chronicle of Higher Education*, *50*(12), B7; Diversity defines new generation of college students. (2009, June 18). *The Chronicle of Higher Education*. Available at http://www.phoenix.edu/colleges_divisions/office-of-the-president/articles/diversity-defines-new-generation-college-students.html.

28. Pusser, B., Breneman, D. W., Gansneder, B. M., Kohl, K. J., Levin, J. S., Milam, J. H., & Turner, S. E. (2007). *Returning to learning: Adults' success in college is key to America's future*. Lumina Foundation. Available at http://www.luminafoundation.org/publications/ReturntolearningApril2007.pdf.

29. Gomstyn, A. (2003, October 17). Minority enrollment in colleges more than doubled in past 20 years, study finds. *The Chronicle of Higher Education*, *50*(8), A25; Schmidt, P. (2003,

28 November). Academe's Hispanic future. *The Chronicle of Higher Education, 50*(14), A8.

30. Based on Nilsen, L. B. (1998). The circles of _____. *Teaching at Its Best.* Bolton, MA: Anker Publishing.

31. Farrell, E. F. (2005, August 5). Student volunteers are worth billions. *The Chronicle of Higher Education, 51*(48), A33.

32. Zlotkowski, E. (1999). Pedagogy and engagement. In R. G. Bringle, R. Games, & E. A. Malloy (Eds.). (1999). *Colleges and Universities as Citizens* (pp. 96–120). Needham Heights, MA: Allyn & Bacon.

33. Honnet, E. P., & Poulsen, S. J. (1989). *Principles of good practice for combining service and learning: A Wingspread special report.* Racine, WI: The Johnson Foundation.

34. Eyler, J., Giles, Jr., D. E., & Schmiede, A. (1996). *A practitioner's guide to reflection in service-learning: Student voices and reflections.* Nashville, TN: Vanderbilt University Press.

35. Farrell, Student volunteers are worth billions.

36. Parker, P. N. (2006, March–April). Sustained dialogue: How students are changing their own racial climate. *About Campus,* 17–34.

37. Schaubhut, N. A., & Thompson, R. C. (2008). *MBTI type tables for occupations.* Mountain View, CA: CPP, Inc. For more information, see U.S. Department of Labor, Bureau of Labor Statistics, *Occupational Outlook Handbook, 2010–2011 Edition.* Also available at http://www.bls.gov/oco/ocos021.htm.

Chapter 11

1. Gregory, M. (2003, September 12). A liberal education is not a luxury. *The Chronicle of Higher Education, 50*(3), B16.

2. Staley, R. S., II. (2003). In C. Staley, *50 ways to leave your lectern* (pp. 70–74). Belmont, CA: Wadsworth.

3. Farrell, E. F. (2006, December 12). Freshmen put high value on how well college prepares them for a profession, survey finds. *The Chronicle of Higher Education.* Farrell, E. F. (2007, January 5). Report says freshmen put career prep first. *The Chronicle of Higher Education, 53*(18), A32. Available at http://chronicle.com/article/Report-Says-Freshmen-Put-Ca/19260/.

4. AP. (2007, January 22). Polls say wealth important to youth. Available at http://cbs11tv.com/national/wealth.youth.money.2.277926.html; Schwartz, B. (2004, January 23). The tyranny of choice. *The Chronicle of Higher Education, 50*(20), B6.

5. Koeppel, D. (2004, December 5). Choosing a college major: For love or for the money? *The New York Times,* section 10, p. 1, column 4. Dunham, K. J. (2004, March 2). No ivory tower: College students focus on career. *Wall Street Journal* (Eastern Edition), pp. B1, B8.

6. Levine, M. (2005). *Ready or not, here life comes.* New York: Simon & Schuster, p. 4; Levine, M. (2005, February 18). College graduates aren't ready for the real world. *The Chronicle of Higher Education, 51*(24), B11.

7. *Dictionary of occupational titles.* (1991). Washington, DC: Bureau of Labor Statistics. Or see O*Net Online (Occupational Information Network) at http://online.onetcenter.org/find/.

8. Based on Schwartz, The tyranny of choice.

9. See J. K. Rowling Biography at http://www.biography.com/ http://www.biography.com/articles/J.-K.-Rowling-194904.

10. Levine, *Ready or not, here life comes.*

11. Based in part on Gordon, V. N., & Sears, S. J. (2004). *Selecting a college major: Exploration and decision making, 5th edition.* Upper Saddle River, NJ: Pearson Education.

12. Based on Hansen, R. S., & Hansen, K. *Using a SWOT analysis in your career planning.* Quintessential Careers. Available at http://www.quintcareers.com/SWOT_Analysis.html.

13. *Job interviews get creative.* (2003, August 22). NPR. Available at http://www.npr.org/templates/story/story.php?storyId=1405340.

14. Vance, E. (2007, February 2). College graduates lack key skills, report says. *The Chronicle of Higher Education, 53*(22), A30.

15. Schaubhut, N. A., Thompson, R. C. (2008). MBTI type tables for occupations. Mountain View, CA: CPP, Inc. For more information, see U.S. Department of Labor, Bureau of Labor Statistics, *Occupational Outlook Handbook, 2010–2011 Edition.* Also available at http://www.bls.gov/oco/ocos021.htm; Recruiter. *Wikipedia.* Available at http://en.wikipedia.org/wiki/Recruiter.

16. Rowh, M. (2003, February–March). Choosing a major. *Career World, 31*(5), 21–23.

17. Ezarik, M. M. (2007, April–May). A major decision. *Career World, 35*(6), 20–22.

18. Rask & Bailey, Are faculty role models?

19. Goldhaber, G. M. (1986). *Organizational communication* (4th ed.). Dubuque, IA: Wm. C. Brown, p. 236. In Staley, R. S., II, & Staley, C. C. (1992). *Communicating in business and the professions: The inside word.* Belmont, CA: Wadsworth.

20. Farrell, E. F. (2005, February 4). More students plan to work to help pay for college. *The Chronicle of Higher Education, 51*(22), A1. Available online at http://chronicle.com/article/More-Students-Plan-to-Work-to/16019/.

21. See http://www.bankrate.com/finance/credit-cards/8-major-benefits-of-new-credit-card-law-1.aspx.

22. Norvilitis, J. M., & Santa Maria, P. (2002). Credit card debt on college campuses: Causes, consequences, and solutions. *College Student Journal, 36*(3), 356–364.

23. Choosing a credit card. The Federal Reserve Board. Available at http://www.federalreserve.gov/pubs/shop/default.htm.

24. Source: Muller, K. New credit card laws (2009) and students. ezine@articles.com. Available at http://ezinearticles.com/?New-Credit-Card-Laws-(2009)-And-Students&id=2410035; Miranda. (2009, May 21). Credit CARD Act of 2009: How it affects you. *Personaldividends.com.* Available at http://personaldividends.com/money/miranda/credit-card-actof-2009-how-it-affects-you.

25. Kantrowitz, M. (2007). FAQs about financial aid. *FinAid: The Smart Student Guide to Financial Aid.* Available at http://www.finaid.org/questions/faq.phtml.

Index

C